INDUSTRIAL RESEARCH UNIT - MAJOR STUDY NO. 54

OPEN SHOP CONSTRUCTION

by

HERBERT R. NORTHRUP
Professor of Industry
Director, Industrial Research Unit

and

HOWARD G. FOSTER
Associate Professor of Industrial Relations
State University of New York at Buffalo

Published by

INDUSTRIAL RESEARCH UNIT
The Wharton School
University of Pennsylvania

Distributed by

University of Pennsylvania Press
Philadelphia, Pennsylvania 19174

Library of Congress Catalog Card Number 75-13130
MANUFACTURED IN THE UNITED STATES OF AMERICA
ISBN: 0-8122-9089-5

Foreword

For some years it has been apparent that the open shop sector of construction has been expanding at the expense of the unionized one. This has been indicated by the growth of open shop contractor associations, the comments of union and contractor association officials, and in some cases, the violent reactions of unionists to the activities of nonunion builders. Moreover, it has also been clear from casual observation that open shop construction firms recruit, train, utilize, and compensate labor quite differently than do their unionized counterparts.

Despite the fact that open shop construction firms undoubtedly perform a majority of the construction work in this country, no study exists which deals extensively with this sector. The major exception is the earlier work by my coauthor, Dr. Howard G. Foster, *Manpower in Homebuilding: A Preliminary Analysis*, which the Industrial Research Unit published in 1974. For the most part, books dealing with manpower or labor relations in construction have dealt with the unionized sector and ignored the rest of the industry. The major reason for this preoccupation with the unionized sector is perhaps that the unions and the collective bargaining systems provide a source and body of centralized data that are reasonably easy to obtain and unionism induces uniformity of conduct that can be studied and modeled with comparative dispatch.

The open shop group presents a different pattern even though the growth of open shop associations and the formalization of some hiring and training programs have provided the beginnings of centralized information. For the most part, however, almost each open shop contractor performs somewhat differently and utilizes labor according to his own needs. To learn about open shop contractor practices one must do extensive field work, interview numerous persons throughout the country and collect information bit by bit wherever it exists. To attempt to determine how the highly individualized open shop contractors operate and man their jobs is a costly, time consuming process, but a fascinating one.

The genesis of this work occurred in 1971 at a U.S. Department of Labor conference on apprenticeship at which Dr. Foster discussed his research among open shop homebuilders. At that time I was attempting to learn the extent to which the open and unionized sector of construction differed in their treatment of minorities and in so doing was also learning a bit about the open shop sector. Dr. Foster's initial research encouraged me to propose to the Manpower Administration of the U.S. Department of Labor that it fund a study of manpower training and development in the open shop sector. This request was not granted, but in discussing it in industry circles, I found tremendous interest in the subject.

At this point, two most helpful individuals took a hand: Dr. John M. Baitsell, Corporate Labor Relations Manager, Mobil Oil Corporation, and Mr. Paul Bell, Jr., head of the Houston construction firm that bears his name—a firm incidentally that operates union shop. Dr. Baitsell secured a small grant from Mobil and was helpful, along with many other persons, in obtaining an additional larger one from the Business Roundtable, Inc. Mr. Bell's interest sparked grants from the Associated General Contractors, Houston and Texas Highway Chapters, and helped to open the doors to numerous contractors and associations for instructive interviews. Mr. N. C. Monroe of the firm which bears his name was helpful in yet another grant from the Carolinas AGC. The H. B. Zachry Company and E. I. du Pont de Nemours & Company also made small contributions to the Industrial Research Unit specifically for this study.

These specific grants paid for approximately one-half of the cost of research and publication. The balance of the cost was met by the unrestricted contributions which the Unit receives annually from numerous companies and foundations to carry on various facets of its "relevant research." It is gratifying to note that all specific and unrestricted grants were given with the clear understanding that all research of the Industrial Research Unit, including this study, must at all times be under the direction and control of the authors, who take full responsibility for its conduct, results, opinions, and conclusions. It is axiomatic that no opinions nor conclusions should in any way be attributed to the University of Pennsylvania, the State University of New York at Buffalo, nor to any subdivision nor part of either. We hope that the results of our study will shed light on hitherto neglected areas of the labor market and employee relations and will spark further inquiries of their value.

Many persons were extremely helpful in our research including above all, numerous contractors, association executives, and government officials who submitted to tiresome interviews, answered bothersome telephone calls, and supplied information. The staffs of the Associated Builders and Contractors, particularly John P. Trimmer, Executive Vice-President, and the Associated General Contractors, especially Arthur Hintze, were extremely helpful, as were their respective chapter executives throughout the country. Three former students in the Graduate Division of the Wharton School, Robert G. Liney, David B. Oguss, and Robert A. Walk, all now MBA recipients working in industry, aided the study immeasurably, the first by handling the computerization of the Industrial Research Unit and Associated General Contractor surveys utilized in the study, the latter two by doing extensive field work in the East, Southeast, and Southwest. The Unit's Office Manager, Mrs. Margaret E. Doyle, handled the numerous administrative details and its editor, Michael J. McGrath edited the manuscript and prepared the index.

Professor Foster would like to dedicate his portion of the work to his late father and I to my family.

HERBERT R. NORTHRUP, *Director*
Industrial Research Unit
The Wharton School
University of Pennsylvania

Philadelphia
June 1975

TABLE OF CONTENTS

CHAPTER PAGE

PART THREE

LABOR MARKETS IN OPEN SHOP CONSTRUCTION

LIST OF TABLES

CHAPTER VII

CHAPTER IX

CHAPTER X

TABLE PAGE

APPENDIX A

LIST OF FIGURES

PART ONE

Introduction and Overview

CHAPTER I

The Industry And Its Organizations

During the past decade, there has developed a significant and still growing public concern with various features of the construction industry, and especially with problems involving construction labor. This concern has been reflected not only in the popular media, but also in a burgeoning professional literature and in public debate over appropriate directions for governmental policy. Although racial discrimination in employment and the inflationary impact of wage settlements have undoubtedly spurred the most conspicuous controversy, these issues themselves are intricately linked to a host of other, more prosaic elements of union relations and of labor market behavior.

At the center of much of the controversy are the building trades unions, few of whose activities have escaped criticism. Their wages are attacked as excessive and inflationary; their work rules and jurisdictional barriers as inefficient and wasteful; their hiring halls as rigid and discriminatory; their apprenticeship programs as numerically inadequate and too lengthy; and their overall control of the labor force as insensitive to the legitimate aspirations of minority groups. Whether these charges are true in whole or part, they have served to perpetuate a conspicuous imbalance both in the popular and the scholarly literature, and to encourage the continued disregard, by professional researchers, of a major and growing segment of the construction industry.

The reference here, of course, is to that portion of the construction industry which operates nonunion, or more accurately "open shop." (We use the term open shop as synonymous with nonunion because it is truly descriptive of much of nonunion construction. Often the general contractor is nonunion but some subcontractors operate union, or occasionally vice versa.) This sector has long been the neglected stepchild of the industry; not only are the unions frequently seen as coincident with the industry, but even when union behavior is itself the subject of analysis, it is seldom explicitly approached in terms of response to nonunion competition. The situation is especially anomalous when, as now, union members do not appear to constitute even a majority of the industry's work force, and also appear to have lost significant ground since the mid-1960's. This book, then, addresses what is a virtual void in the area.

In this introductory chapter, we shall briefly describe the construction industry and the organizations which operate within its boundaries and affect its destiny; the following chapter will outline the major questions which are addressed, summarize the factors which have propelled open shop construction to the forefront, and conclude with an account of the information sources and research methodology on which our study is based.

THE CONSTRUCTION INDUSTRY[1]

Construction in the aggregate constitutes over 10 percent of the nation's economic activity. In 1974, new construction was valued at $135.4 billion, over 71 percent of which was privately owned.[2] In most recent years, the private component of new building has grown at a much faster rate than public work, so that the public share declined from 32.9 percent in 1967 to 24.0 percent in 1973. A major factor in this development was the extraordinary expansion of residential construction, which more than doubled in that six year period and increased by over two-thirds since 1970 alone. In 1974, however, these trends were abruptly reversed, largely because of soaring interest rates, public construction rose to 28.5 percent of the total, and residential building was off nearly 20 percent from the year before.

Contract construction activity currently generates about 3.5 million full-time equivalent jobs. Because of the nature of its labor market, however, a much larger number of individual workers find employment in the industry in any given year. In 1972, for example, 5.3 million workers had their longest job in construction, and the number with any such work is obviously a

---

[1] For the reader's convenience, we note here only the most salient features of the construction industry. A more comprehensive discussion of the industry's characteristics may be found in Appendix A.

[2] All data in this paragraph are from the *Economic Report of The President* (Washington, D.C.: Government Printing Office, 1975), Table C-38.

good deal higher.[3] Thus, every full-time job is filled, on average, by nearly two workers, a ratio which reflects a turnover rate much higher than that in most other industries.

The labor force in construction is growing, having nearly doubled since 1947, and has maintained about the same proportion of total employment over the period. Its major component is the skilled, blue collar worker (defined in government statistics as craftsmen, foremen, and kindred workers), who comprise about one-half of the employed. Unskilled and semiskilled manual workers account for some 30 percent of the total with the remainder various salaried groups. Over the years the latter group's proportion has grown and the unskilled declined. There have also been significant shifts among the various crafts; the major relative gains have been registered by the electro-mechanical trades and the machine operators, with relative losses by carpenters, painters, and trowel tradesmen (bricklayers, masons, and plasterers).

As in most industries, the salient characteristics of the construction industry and its labor market are reflections of the nature of the construction product. Although there is great variation in the kinds of facilities produced by the industry, all construction products exhibit a number of common properties from which devolve the structure and organization of the industry and, derivatively, the problems associated with labor force adjustment. The matter is put succinctly by Colean and Newcomb:

> The products of construction, despite the wide diversity already revealed, share certain common characteristics: they are immobile, complex, durable, costly, and speculative in value. The degree to which these characteristics are shared differs among the various kinds of structures and facilities; but in some degree they are universally present and affect all the other considerations with which we must deal.[4]

In one sense, there is no "market" for most kinds of construction products. With the significant exception of single unit residences, virtually all construction is "made to order." Work is started at the behest of the buyer, not the producer, and the specifications are tailor-made to the individual project. "In other words, the decisions as to what will be produced and when it

---

[3] *Manpower Report of the President* (Washington, D.C.: Government Printing Office, 1974), p. 308, Table B-16.

[4] Miles L. Colean and Robinson Newcomb, *Stabilizing Construction: The Record and Potential* (New York: McGraw-Hill, 1952), p. 22.

will be produced come mainly from sources external to the industry." [5] The result is an extreme heterogeneity of demand, a condition necessitating a kind of industry organization which is capable of adjusting rapidly to sharp fluctuations in organizational and manpower requirements.

The need for flexibility, together with the vast heterogeneity and complexity of construction products, has led to a system of functional specialization. In the typical case, a buyer engages a general contractor who has overall responsibility for the project. The general contractor, in turn, may engage any number of specialized contractors who perform certain specific operations such as wiring, plumbing, or painting.[6] Such an arrangement is indispensable in light of the nature of the product. To draw again from Colean and Newcomb's perceptive analysis:

> Without the large and almost infinitely diverse aggregation of special trade contractors, the construction industry could not function under its existing requirements. This group provides the specialization within flexibility that permits the industry to accommodate itself to any assignment. The subcontractors, moreover, make possible the rapid mobilization and dismissal of job organizations necessitated by the changes both in the kind and volume of demand.[7]

The construction product is also distinguished by its immobility. Most structures obviously cannot be erected in one place and transported to another; hence the mass production technique found in other goods-producing industries are largely absent.[8] The resulting market structure is predominantly a local one.[9] To be sure, there are nationwide construction firms whose gross receipts run into the billions of dollars, but these typically undertake only the most extensive and costly projects, leaving the small and medium-sized jobs, the bulk of all construction work, to local contractors. And, with respect to labor market problems, even the large national contractors will often recruit much of

---

[5] *Ibid.*, p. 81.

[6] Of course, the general contractor may perform some of these functions with his own work force, although he will seldom, if ever, perform them all.

[7] Colean and Newcomb, *op. cit.*, p. 97.

[8] This characteristic has been tempered by the growing use of prefabricated materials which allow certain portions of buildings to be produced on what approaches an "assembly-line" basis. In addition, large-scale housing tracts utilizing one basic plan may permit a kind of "factory" approach.

[9] See Daniel Quinn Mills, *Industrial Relations and Manpower in Construction* (Cambridge: MIT Press, 1972), p. 8.

their work force from the area where the projects are located. In sum, the factors which control the construction labor supply are preponderately local in character, a condition which stems to a large degree from the immobility of construction, and which creates a diversity of labor supply determinants somewhat impervious to central influences.

Moreover, the durability and costliness of construction products renders the demand for them highly unstable. The replacement or renovation of most existing structures can be deferred to a time when the economic horizons appear brightest. As a result, the demand for construction tends to fluctuate much more dramatically than for other products. This imposes on the industry a need for flexibility much greater than that required for other industries. Moreover, it creates an element of uncertainty which magnifies the problems otherwise inherent in developing and maintaining a skilled labor force.

The composition of the work force on different projects will vary widely. A brick building and a frame building will obviously require different mixes of carpenters and bricklayers. It is also common for the crew of an individual project to change markedly in composition and size over a relatively short time. In some cases the necessary work force adjustments are very abrupt. In the union sector of the industry, these adjustments are effected by the use of a labor "pool" situated, in part, in the union hall. In open shop construction, the "pool" is more amorphous, the mechanics of the adjustment process are less structured, and the adjustments themselves are smaller because the open shop contractor has, as we shall see, very practical reasons to go to greater lengths to keep his employment patterns steady.

Types of Construction

Construction embraces a wide variety of building activity. The product may range from a small, single-family home erected in a few months by a three man work crew and some specialty subcontractors, to a gigantic dam or oil refinery, worth hundreds of millions of dollars and requiring the labor of thousands over several years. The industry, unfortunately, has no consistently defined breakdown of its constituent parts. Most employment statistics, for example, use only the categories: general building contractors, highway and heavy contractors, and special trades contractors.[10] It is thus impossible to discern the number of workers employed in residential construction at a point in time.

Since we shall have occasion to distinguish among various types of construction throughout this report, it will be useful to delineate and to describe briefly those industrial subdivisions to which reference may be made. *Residential* construction includes predominantly the building of single-family homes and apartments. (Government statistics include also such structures as dormitories and hotels.) For many purposes, including the extent of unionization, the residential portion of the industry may be divided into homes, town houses and low rise apartment complexes (under four stories) on the one hand, and high rise apartment buildings on the other. *Commercial* construction includes such projects as stores, office buildings, warehouses, smaller factories, hospitals, nursing homes, and service stations. *Industrial* construction refers primarily to major factories, power plants, refineries, and other large structures built for establishments engaged in secondary economic activity. *Heavy and highway* construction includes streets, roads, bridges, dams, pipelines, airports, subways and the like. Government data do differentiate between private and public construction, but public projects may be in any of the aforementioned classes: residential (low-income housing), commercial (schools, office buildings), industrial (power plants), and heavy and highway in obvious ways.

Firms operating in the various industrial subdivisions tend to differ in a number of ways. Most firms throughout the industry are small;[11] residential and (to a lesser extent) commercial construction are especially characterized by an atomistic structure, with most work performed by local firms. Industrial, heavy, and major highway work, largely because of the size of the projects involved, is more likely to be concentrated in the hands of large nationwide contractors whose yearly volume is well into the eight or nine figure range. Furthermore, there tends to be more specialization in residential construction among both gen-

---

[10] In addition, however, there are firms engaged principally in land development and construction which are officially classified as "subdividers and developers" and "operative builders" under the general umbrella of "real estate."

[11] According to the *1967 Census of Construction Industries*, the average firm employed nine workers. This figure, moreover, refers only to "firms" with at least one employee, thus excluding the self-employed, a significant group, especially in residential construction.

eral contractors and subcontractors. A firm that builds homes and small apartments is likely to build only homes and small apartments. Commercial and industrial contractors, on the other hand, are usually more diversified. Heavy and highway construction is more seasonal than the other divisions, and also utilizes larger proportions of unskilled labor. Finally, there are differences in the amount of work under the direct control of the general contractor. Although this characteristic is to a great extent a feature of the specific contractor involved, the amount of subcontracting is generally greatest in residential construction (many home builders subcontract *all* their building work) and least in heavy and highway work.

In short, we are dealing with an industry of prodigious variety and generalizations are often hazardous. For that reason we shall examine the extent of open shop activity in Part Two, separately by industry sector, before bringing our findings together in state and regional summaries.

ORGANIZATIONAL STRUCTURE

Basic to an understanding of the extent of open shop construction is an explanation of the complex organizational structure of the industry. There are literally hundreds of thousands of contracting firms with payroll, and a like number of others doing business as individuals. Many contractors are organized into an intricate and sometimes overlapping network of trade associations, of which there are currently about sixty operating nationally and an unknown number of unaffiliated local groups.[12] An undetermined but apparently substantial number of firms, especially among the smaller ones, do not belong to any association. Contractors' associations may be classified into three broad categories: those comprising general contractors; those comprising contractors who specialize in a particular type of project; and those comprising contractors who specialize in a particular phase of construction work.

We estimate, on the basis of evidence presented throughout this study, that 40 to 50 percent of all construction workers are unionized. Although there are a few local labor organizations which function on an industrial basis, most unionized workers

---

[12] A directory of National Trade Associations, professional societies, and labor unions involved in the construction and building material industries is found in *Construction Review*, XXI (Jan./Feb., 1975), pp. 7-8.

belong to one of the craft unions which are together commonly referred to as the "building trades." The union structure is thus highly fragmented, with eighteen national organizations and thousands of locals across the country. Seventeen of these unions are affiliated with the Building and Construction Trades Department of the AFL-CIO. The eighteenth, the Teamsters Union, is not now a member of the AFL-CIO, but in many areas Teamsters locals representing construction truck drivers still work closely with the other trades.

The multiplicity of employer and employee organizations naturally makes for a highly complex collective bargaining structure in the industry. Thousands of separate labor agreements are negotiated annually; the number will reach some 3,500 in 1975 alone. Most of these agreements are executed at the local level, in many cases covering only a single metropolitan area and sometimes only a portion of a given labor market. Although there has been some tendency in recent years toward a more centralized structure with contracts covering wider areas and several local unions, the trend has not been headlong. There is, moreover, some bargaining at the national level, particularly on certain very specialized projects (e.g., elevator or pipeline construction) or on large, remote projects (e.g., some dams where no local agreement adequately covers the work).

General contractors associations usually negotiate directly with each of the "basic trades": carpenters, bricklayers, ironworkers, cement masons, laborers, and teamsters. Some of the basic trades, however, may also have contracts with associations of specialty contractors, such as the Mason Contractors Association (bricklayers) or the Drywall Contractors Association (carpenters). Specialty contractors, who characteristically perform work that is subcontracted by general contractors, deal primarily with a single union representing the craft they predominantly employ. Examples are the Mechanical Contractors Association (plumbers and steamfitters), the National Electrical Contractors Association (electricians), and the Painting and Decorating Contractors (painters and paperhangers).

Contractors associations often expend much of their energies dealing with labor relations matters. In the unionized sector, they assume such key functions as negotiating contracts and assisting contractor members in the grievance process. They also invariably become involved in such issues as jurisdictional disputes and the administration of apprenticeship programs.

Associations representing open shop contractors have different kinds of labor relations problems: they are principally concerned with assisting members who are objects of union organizing campaigns. In both cases, therefore, the building trades constitute major preoccupations for staff members of these associations.

It should not be inferred, however, that labor issues comprise the entire *raison d'etre* for contractor groups. The broad range of their activities has been well summarized by Mills:

> The local associations perform a wide variety of functions for their members, including public relations, lobbying, legal advice, labor relations activities, and members' benefits (such as group life insurance for contractors or types of liability insurance) and they deal with architects, owners, suppliers, and others. The national office of the association also conducts lobbying and public relations and provides legal and industrial relations advice. It often publishes periodicals carrying trade news, innovations, legislative reports, and analyses of the national scene as it affects members' concerns. Each national association normally holds a national convention and may sponsor trade shows as well.[13]

The following sections are devoted to a more detailed examination of the various organizations which are important components of the construction industry. We begin with the building trades unions, since an understanding of the history, role, and function of contractors' associations—both union and open shop—depends in large measure on an appreciation of the character of the labor organizations with which they deal. We turn then to the associations themselves, with special focus on those which have had significant roles in the growth of open shop activity.

The Building Trades Unions

The building trades represent about 2.5 million workers in a variety of crafts and subcrafts. Table I-1 summarizes certain pertinent data about the seventeen organizations which comprise the Building and Construction Trades Department (BCTD). As the table indicates, some of these unions have a substantial proportion of their memberships outside the contract construction industry. The Carpenters, Ironworkers, and Sheet Metal Workers, for example, also represent workers in various manufacturing industries, while the Electrical Workers have a large number of members both in manufacturing and electric utility companies.

---

[13] Mills, *op. cit.*, p. 11.

TABLE I-1
AFL-CIO Building Trades Unions 1971

Union	Total Membership[a]	Percent in Construction	Number of Locals
Asbestos Workers	18	99	121
Boilermakers	138	n.a.	425
Bricklayers	143	100	862
Carpenters	820	75[b]	2,435
Electrical Workers (IBEW)	922	19	1,677
Elevator Contractors	17	100	109
Granite Cutters	3	n.a.	23
Ironworkers	178	61	320
Laborers	580	79	900
Lathers	15	100[b]	289
Marble Polishers	8	83[b]	123
Operating Engineers	393	75[b]	279
Painters	210	77	1,000
Plasterers	68	99	500
Plumbers	312	85[b]	680
Roofers	24	100	209
Sheet Metal Workers	120	n.a.	n.a.

Source: U.S. Bureau of Labor Statistics, *Directory of National Unions and Employee Associations, 1971,* Bulletin 1750 (Washington, D.C.: Government Printing Office, 1972), *passim.*
[a] Numbers in thousands.
[b] Figure from earlier BLS Directory; not given in Bulletin 1750.
n.a.: not available.

The BCTD itself, like the AFL-CIO in which it is housed, is a federation of national unions whose primary function is to advance the interests of unionized construction labor generally. There are also state and local branches of the Department (sometimes called "Councils"). In many instances, these interunion bodies have no collective bargaining responsibilities, but rather perform various political, public relations, and research activities designed to benefit all the member unions.

The issue of union jurisdiction has long been endemic to the labor relations scene in construction. The preservation of job opportunities is a vital responsibility of the union leadership, especially in an industry marked by intermittent and uncertain employment. A loss of jobs to the members of a sister union is only slightly less distasteful than losses to technology, recession, or nonunion firms. The craft unions guard their jurisdictional terrain with great vigor, often striking to protest job assignments to a different craft despite the illegality of such strikes under section 8(b) (4) (D) of the National Labor Relations (Taft-Hartley) Act. The building trades have sought, with varying degrees of success over the years, to develop and maintain private adjudication mechanisms for the resolution of jurisdictional disputes.[14] Nevertheless, the problem remains, with "interunion or intraunion matters" constituting the basis for approximately 38 percent of the 701 construction strikes that occurred in 1972.[15] It is significant that many of the contractors and association executives we interviewed—both union and nonunion—cited jurisdictional strikes as a major factor in the recent growth of the open shop sector.

Jurisdictional rivalries may pose serious problems for contractors in several ways. First and most obvious, of course, are the delays caused by stoppages which grow out of conflicting jurisdictional claims. Although jurisdictional strikes tend to be shorter than those for other causes, the loss of a few days can wreak havoc with a construction schedule. Second, even if the dispute is settled without a stoppage, the resolution may not be the one preferred by the contractor. Employers are not always indifferent with respect to who wins a job assignment, especially if there is an appreciable wage differential between the competing crafts, or if the settlement requires additional costly labor and/or man-hours. Finally, jurisdictional stipulations may require that assignments be given to a craft whose union is less able to provide the number or quality of workers needed to man the job, again adding to expenses.

The locus of authority within the building trades is generally centered at the local level. Local officials have the major responsibility for executing and policing collective bargaining agreements, administering apprenticeship programs, and operating hiring halls or job referral services. The national organizations

---

[14] See Kenneth T. Strand, *Jurisdictional Dispute in Construction: the Causes, the Joint Board, and the NLRB* (Pullman, Washington: Washington State University Press, 1961).

[15] U.S. Bureau of Labor Statistics, *Analysis of Work Stoppages, 1972*, Bulletin 1813 (Washington, D.C.: Government Printing Office, 1974), Table A-12.

promulgate general guidelines and provide technical staff assistance to the locals through international representatives, but their actual power over the affairs of the locals is severely limited. Since local autonomy is a principle of long historical tradition in the building trades, national officers who attempt to exert authority (sometimes even authority given to them by the union constitution) over important locals, may do so only at considerable political risk.

The key personage in a building trades local is the business agent, an elected, salaried official who in larger locals may appoint several full-time representatives to help him run the union.[16] The business agent is often the union's chief spokesman at the bargaining table, and between contracts his major responsibility is policing the trade. Through a network of union stewards and other officials, he ensures that the provisions of the agreement are followed, that the union's jurisdiction is not violated, and that individual grievances at the site are addressed. Because of his various functions, he is highly visible to the membership; and thus his job tenure depends largely upon his ability to respond to the needs of his constituency. The other officers of the local—president, treasurer, and so forth—deal principally with the internal affairs of the organization, and have relatively little influence over the relationship between the union and employers.

Partly because of their decentralized political structure, most locals in the building trades tend to be workably democratic organizations. But the relative weakness of the national officers, and the need for local officials to respond aggressively to the demands of the membership, make it difficult to correct some of the policies for which the unions have been roundly criticized. National leaders and a few brave local officers may speak passionately about the dangers of excessive wage increases, and about the contributions which restrictive union practices have made to the growth of open shop competition, but the political realities of their positions usually preclude them from going significantly beyond speechmaking. There is some evidence, moreover, that the higher the official in the union hierarchy, the more likely he is to be sensitive to the claims of minority groups that they have been systematically and invidiously excluded

---

[16] For an insightful account of the role of the business agent, see George Strauss, "Business Agents in the Building Trades," *Industrial and Labor Relations Review,* X (January, 1957), pp. 237-251.

from job opportunities.[17] In short, since construction workers like most people tend to define their interests narrowly, the challenges which the building trades now face are attributable more to policies dictated by their own organizational structures, than to any particular human failing of their leadership. Their failure to meet these challenges have resulted, to a major extent, in the increasing popularity of open shop construction.

Contractors Associations

As noted above, there are about sixty national associations of construction contractors in the United States. Some contractors hold membership in two or more of these associations, while others belong to none of them. Some associations are comprised predominantly or exclusively of unionized contractors; others have a substantial number of open shops among their membership. In this section we shall introduce some of the larger and more important associations, with special emphasis on those with a significant open shop component.

The principal association of general contractors is the Associated General Contractors (AGC), described in more detail below, whose membership is currently 35 to 40 percent open shop. Many of the very largest general contractors in the nation who specialize in expansive industrial and heavy construction projects belong to the National Constructors Association (NCA). The NCA negotiates national agreements with some of the international unions, which either may specify certain terms and conditions of employment or merely guarantee strike-free operations in exchange for the employer's promise to meet locally determined standards. The NCA is comprised exclusively of unionized firms. Recently NCA merged with Contractors Mutual Association (CMA), whose members are also the large unionized national contractors. CMA is devoted to improving the industry's bargaining position with unions and has particularly worked to enlarge the area of bargaining. Its objective is to reduce whipsawing, whereby one local group of contractors is played off against another by local unions, and thus make it more difficult for construction unionists on strike in one city to obtain work in another for the duration of a strike.

---

[17] Derek C. Bok and John T. Dunlop, *Labor and the American Community* (New York: Simon and Schuster, 1970), pp. 134-135; Herbert R. Northrup, *Organized Labor and the Negro* (New York: Kraus Reprint Company, 1971), pp. 232, 236-238.

Unionized specialty contractors have their own associations. Such organizations as the Mechanical Contractors Association, the Painting and Decorating Contractors Association, and the Sheet Metal and Air Conditioning National Association include only unionized contractors. The great majority, but not all, of the members of the National Electrical Contractors Association (NECA) are also unionized. There are no truly national associations of nonunion contractors which parallel these organizations, although there are local and regional groups throughout the country which could grow in that direction. In the electrical contracting industry, for example, the Associated Independent Electrical Contractors Association (AIECA) has about 500 members concentrated in the South and Southwest, organized into 28 local chapters, but it has recently chartered chapters in the Middle Atlantic states as well. In both the Philadelphia and Buffalo areas, there are local electrical contractor associations which could some day affiliate with AIECA, or another national body that, unlike NECA, is not dominated by union contractors. Other nonunion specialty contractors belong to the Associated Builders and Contractors (ABC), a fast growing organization which is described more thoroughly below.

Some contractors belong to associations which bring together firms specializing in a particular branch of construction. Such groups may include both union and open shop firms and both general and specialty contractors. One such organization is the American Road Builders Association (ARBA). ARBA actually competes with the ABC for members, although some highway contractors belong to both. ARBA membership is divided between union and open shop contractors, as is the highway component of ABC (See Chapter VI).

The National Association of Home Builders (NAHB) is the largest contractor organization in terms of members, and is also devoted to one branch of construction. It too is examined in more detail below.

Associated General Contractors.[18] The AGC is an organization of almost 10,000 general contractors in about 120 state and local chapters. In many states, there are separate chapters for building contractors and heavy and highway contractors, with a few affiliates comprised of municipal utility contractors. Heavy and highway chapters are often organized on a state-wide basis,

---

[18] The more or less "official" history of the AGC is recounted in Booth Mooney, *Builders for Progress* (New York: McGraw-Hill Book Co., 1965).

while in building construction there are usually separate chapters in several metropolitan areas within a state. In smaller states both building and highway contractors are included in a single chapter. The Carolinas Chapter is unique in that it covers two states and all branches of construction within AGC's jurisdiction. It has long been a powerful open shop force in the industry.

Although open shop contractors constitute more than one-third of the AGC's membership, their numbers vary greatly from chapter to chapter. Virtually all of the highway chapters have open shop representation, with open shops comprising a majority in some southern and plains states. Building chapters are less likely to serve both union and nonunion firms. The bylaws of some building chapters require the contractor to give power of attorney to the association, which in practical terms means that the contractor is bound by any labor agreements that are negotiated by the chapter. The effect, of course, is to preclude open shop membership. In other chapters this power of attorney is optional, which therefore permits open shops to take advantage of the other services offered by the association. In recent years, some building chapters have amended their bylaws to allow nonunion contractors to join; the Massachusetts and New York State chapters are cases in point.

Although labor relations matters occupy a substantial portion of the energies of association staff members at the local level, there are other valuable services which make membership attractive to the nonunion contractor. Where AGC chapters have effectively barred open shops from membership, other associations, most notably the ABC, have stepped into the vacuum. The recent receptiveness displayed by some AGC chapters toward the interests of nonunion contractors has doubtless, in large measure, been occasioned by the growing organizational challenge mounted by the ABC.

At the national level, the AGC participates in a wide range of activities, most of which hold no relevance to the union status of the contractor. There are, for example, some forty national committees dealing with such varied topics as environment, fuel and material supply, metric conversion, tax and fiscal affairs. Most of the committees have full-time AGC staff members serving with them. On labor related matters, there are committees on equal employment opportunity, labor, manpower and training, and open shop. The very existence of a national open shop committee, which among other things sponsors conferences across the country dealing with the distinct problems of open shop contractors, attests to the growing interest in open shop operations within the AGC. Open shop contractors are also beginning to exert greater influence in the councils of the national AGC, with an open shop contractor recently serving as the Association's President.

Associated Builders and Contractors. The ABC, currently with about 8,000 members in 48 chapters, including some material supplier members, is probably the fastest growing association in the construction industry. The organization was founded in the early 1950's in Maryland, and has expanded to include members from almost every state in the nation. Active chapters in such union strongholds as Pittsburgh, Detroit, and the Philadelphia area, and newly formed chapters in Kansas City and Southern California, attest to the increased willingness of open shops to meet the unions on their home turf. Most of the ABC's membership is open shop, although in some areas (Pittsburgh, for example), some members hold contracts with industrial unions like District 50. In a few other cases, formerly all-union contractors have joined the ABC through open shop branches which are operated on a "double-breasted" basis, a term designating common ownership by one party or company of two firms, one operating union, the other open shop. A number of firms are members both of AGC and ABC.

The ABC is an association both of general and specialty contractors. As noted earlier, many open shop specialty contractors do not have an organizational home elsewhere in the construction industry. As a result, specialty contractors comprise a majority of the membership in certain chapters, although most ABC members are general contractors in commercial construction, for whom the ABC offers more effective representation than their local AGC chapter. There are relatively few highway builders in the Association, and in some chapters there is a substantial component of residential builders, especially those specializing in apartment construction. On the whole, it is fair to characterize the bulk of the ABC membership as relatively small firms, compared to the membership of AGC, NECA, and other predominantly union associations.

The most dramatic feature of the ABC has been its recent growth, as detailed in Chapter IV. Its membership has nearly tripled in the past five years. Furthermore, and perhaps as significant, much ABC activity has been concentrated in areas where open shops have not traditionally been conspicuous. There are nine active chapters in the Northeast and six more in the Midwest. ABC is not strong in the South except in Florida and New Orleans. In other southern areas, open shop contractors are more likely to be members of the AGC. Thus the ABC has not generally been duplicating the open shop AGC, but rather supplementing it in areas where AGC chapters are union oriented.

The ABC maintains a growing central staff specializing in law, public relations, training, benefits and other relevant matters. It has led the fight against illegal picketing, construction violence, and has been playing an increasing role in congressional and state legislative relations. Its staff operates and advises on benefit and apprentice programs and its home office in Glen Burnie, Maryland, is considered by friend and foe alike as the central headquarters of open shop interests.

National Association of Home Builders.[19] NAHB has about 16,000 builder members engaged predominantly in residential construction. Homebuilders comprise the vast majority of the membership, with a relatively small number of specialty contractors who service the builders. Most NAHB members do little work outside the residential sector of the industry, although a fair number engage in such related activities as land development, remodeling, and real estate brokering. Much of the homebuilders' work tends to be contracted out to specialty firms. In an earlier study one of the authors found that two-thirds of the homebuilders in Erie County, New York, performed no building work with their own labor. This condition was found to be largely true elsewhere as well.[20]

As we shall see in Chapter III, residential construction is the most unorganized sector of the industry. Only a few NAHB chapters currently have labor agreements with some or all of the building trades unions, and even in these jurisdictions, an increasing number of builders are conducting open shop operations outside the geographic coverage of the contracts. There are

---

[19] The NAHB conducts a comprehensive survey of its membership at five year intervals. The most recent one is reported in Michael Sumichrast and Sara A. Frankel, *Profile of the Builder and his Industry* (Washington, D.C.: National Association of Home Builders, 1970).

[20] Howard G. Foster, *Manpower in Homebuilding: A Preliminary Analysis*, Manpower and Human Resources Studies No. 3 (Philadelphia: Industrial Research Unit, The Wharton School, University of Pennsylvania, 1974), pp. 31-36.

also a few cases of individual builders with union contracts, but these instances are infrequent and dwindling. On the whole, the NAHB is an organization comprised predominantly of open shop employers, a direction in which the Association has steadily moved for the past quarter century.

NAHB chapters are found in most labor market areas of any appreciable size. In some localities where the ABC has not yet established itself, the NAHB constitutes the principal organizational home for residential contractors. On the whole, however, the Association has not filled the need of accommodating the large numbers of subcontractors who specialize in residential work, a constituency to which the ABC has had a special appeal. Since the ABC has also made significant inroads among contractors specializing in apartment building, we can expect to find a growing overlap in the kinds of firms served by the two organizations.

The NAHB has a sizable national staff headquartered in Washington, D.C., which deals with a wide range of issues of general concern to the homebuilding industry. Its Department of Labor Relations is principally a staff advisory and research service; it engages in no collective bargaining activities directly. Although some building trades unions have recently begun new efforts to organize the residential sector, our interviews with NAHB personnel suggest that these efforts are not likely to result in any dramatic breakthrough. Since residential builders tend to perform relatively little work outside that sector, NAHB does not occupy a prominent position on the unions' enemies list, a status largely reserved for the ABC. The Association has historically neither promoted nor fought open shop construction, and as a consequence has not had a conspicuous role in open *vs.* union shop controversies.

User Organizations

A new factor on the horizon is the Business Roundtable. Organized in the late 1960's as the "Construction Roundtable", it merged with a sister group which also was composed of major American manufacturing, service and public utility concerns which have a keen interest in labor relations and are also major purchasers, or "users", of construction. Its frank purpose is to give support to contractors in order to decrease the upward spiral of construction costs. It has succeeded, for example, in obtaining user agreement to limit scheduled overtime; to shut down construction under national agreements when local strikes occur, thus avoiding giving work to unionists who are on strike; and it has lent talent to local groups engaged in bargaining. To effectuate its work, the Roundtable has also established chapters in various parts of the country.

The Roundtable does not campaign for open shop construction as such. It does, however, encourage alternatives to the union shop where it is feasible, and this, of course, involves opening up bid opportunities to open shop contractors. Moreover, by furthering an exchange of information among users, problems of union construction are aired and opportunities to overcome them by special arrangements are discussed, such as: "project agreements," as explained in Chapter VIII; wider area agreements; and turning to open shop contractors who are not strong (with few exceptions) in industrial construction, as we shall see in Chapter V. The construction branch of the Business Roundtable maintains offices and staff in New York City.

CONCLUSION

The construction industry thus has a diverse organizational structure of many components each created because of a particular need. The interplay of these organizations in an industry which is itself highly complicated, both affects and is affected by the extent of union organization. In the following chapter, we give an overview of the extent of organization; examine the economics which has pushed the industry toward a larger open shop component; and the methodology upon which the detailed information in the chapters of Parts Two and Three are based.

CHAPTER II

Overview

The wide scope and atomistic structure of the construction industry makes estimates of any kind difficult, and particularly so for such an emotion-packed subject as the extent of union organization for which there is no systematic collection of data. In later chapters we piece together the spotty data available by industry, sector, and region, adding where appropriate those data which we have been able to generate ourselves. Here we state our findings largely in order to put our study in perspective for the reader.

EXTENT OF UNIONIZATION

In his recent book, Professor Daniel Quinn Mills well summarizes the evidence on the extent of construction unionization for the period prior to 1970:

> There are no continuous data reporting degree of organization for the industry as a whole or for its branches. There have been, however, several one-time surveys of parts of the industry that offer some insight into organization. Perhaps most useful is the Census Bureau's special Survey of Economic Opportunity in 1967, taken from a sample of 30,000 households. The survey reported union membership or nonmembership, (and annual earnings in 1966), based on occupation of longest job. It showed that 53.7 percent of construction craftsmen (private wage and salary workers) were union members and 30.4 percent of construction laborers. However, on an annual average, only some 70 percent of construction craftsmen are employed in the construction industry. Because craftsmen employed in construction are almost certainly more fully organized than those in other industries, these estimates of organization are probably lower limits. Estimates prepared from membership data provided by the international unions suggest that in 1967 an average of 63 percent of carpenters employed in construction itself were organized. For all crafts combined, census estimates based on a 1967 survey show 44 percent of those employed in construction (as major source of earnings) in 1966 were union members. Another

> special survey that dealt only with general building contractors for 1965 reported that 45 percent of workers (without regard to craft) were working in firms with collective bargaining contracts covering a majority of the firm's workers.[1]

A U.S. Bureau of Labor Statistics report based on the March 1971 *Current Population Survey* provides the most recent data on union membership.[2] In 1970, 54.7 percent of all craftsmen and 29.9 percent of all laborers in the industry were union members. Not suprisingly, the figure for whites was greater than that for nonwhites (42.2 percent versus 33.7 percent), although the opposite was true in manufacturing industry. Regionally the percentages ranged from 51.0 in the West to 22.2 in the South. In sum, the findings of the study, even though it was based on a rather small sample, suggest strongly that the open shop sector of construction was numerically dominant in 1970. Our information indicates that the open shop sector has since expanded.

Locus of Open Shop Construction

Although in recent years open shop contractors have made gains throughout the industry, the level of nonunion construction varies along a number of dimensions. Moreover, the general configurations of these variations follow generally those detected in much earlier studies. These patterns may be examined in terms of geography, industry sector, and type of specialty. Here we summarize our findings which will be analyzed in much greater detail in later chapters.

Industry Sector

It is clear that a major center of nonunion construction activity is in the residential sector. A figure of 80-90 percent is often used (although never documented) to represent the proportion of housing units now built on an open shop basis. Even in such highly industralized and generally unionized cities as Buffalo and Pittsburgh, low rise residential construction is almost entirely open shop. In many places, moreover, even high rise apart-

---

[1] Daniel Quinn Mills, *Industrial Relations and Manpower in Construction* (Cambridge: MIT Press, 1972), pp. 16-17 (footnotes omitted).

[2] U. S. Bureau of Labor Statistics, *Selected Earnings and Demographic Characteristics of Union Members, 1970,* Report No. 417 (Washington, D.C.: Government Printing Office, 1972), Table 1, p. 6; Table 8, p. 21.

ment buildings are going up nonunion. Often, however, the open shop residential contractor does not have the resources or the expertise to undertake such a large project.

The residential sector has remained nonunion primarily because of the small size and geographical dispersion of its jobs. Indeed, the erosion of union strength may be directly coupled with the exhaustion of residential land in the central cities and the centrifugal movement of building away from their core. The result has been a much broader territory for the unions to police, and when this burden is coupled with the meager fruits of this type of organization in terms of members gained or maintained, many unions have simply abandoned the residential market.

The size of projects is also an important variable in other sectors of the industry. In any given area, small commercial jobs (under, e.g., a million dollars) such as stores, professional buildings, service stations, and moderately sized shopping plazas may be predominantly open shop; large projects, like major shopping centers, high rise office buildings, and university complexes are likely to be built by union labor. Since much new commercial building (especially smaller structures) has tended to follow residential movement, it seems probable that the smaller commercial work is as much open shop as residential building.

Large commercial and industrial construction is still strongly unionized, although nonunion contractors are making inroads here as well. With the exception of a few giant firms, open shop contractors tend to lack the resources to undertake huge projects, and furthermore, they have historically been reluctant to provoke the unions by intruding upon their domain. As these contractors have become more experienced and better organized, however, they have moved more and more into direct competition with unionized firms. The unions are faced with still another threat in the industrial sector: as the cost of contracted construction mounts, manufacturers are finding it advantageous to perform much of their building work with their own crews. In the aggregate, however, the open shop movement appears to have had less penetration in major commercial and industrial construction than in the residential and commercial sectors.

Highway and heavy sector unionization is less than commercial and industrial, but more than residential. It is insulated in part from open shop competition by the existence and administration of prevailing wage laws, especially the Davis-Bacon Act,[3] as we shall point out in Chapters VI and XI. Large segments of these sectors are nonetheless dominated by open shop contractors.

Public construction generally follows much the same patterns as the private sector: discernibly greater nonunion work in smaller, less complex projects. As populations move to the suburbs, there is a great deal of public building work that follows them: schools, sewer lines, streets, sidewalks, municipal buildings, and the like. Much of this small work is going nonunion, despite the operation of prevailing wage laws which effectively remove the advantage of lower wage rates enjoyed by open shop contractors. The larger projects, however, many of which tend to be located either in the central cities or in remote areas with virtually no local labor supply, are still union built in the main.

One additional factor which can account for the varying levels of unionization by industry division is relative skill requirements. Large scale commercial and industrial projects tend to employ a larger component of craftsmen and a smaller component of laborers than either highway or residential building work. Unions have historically been stronger among skilled occupations, since these workers are more difficult to recruit or replace. Thus it is perhaps no accident that the growth of open shop construction recently appears to have coincided with the increased development of formal, multi-employer training programs in the open shop sector. Chapters III through VI explore the extent of open shop penetrations in the various sectors of the industry.

Geographic Area

Geography influences the extent of open shop construction activity in several ways. Within a market, union strength wanes as work moves farther from the core city. Exurban and rural areas tend to find considerably higher proportions of their building performed open shop compared with the building in the central city and its immediate suburbs. The size and nature of the project, of course, is still a factor. A power plant, even in a rural area, may be built with union labor simply because of historical relationships between the utility and a union contractor; or because there are no nonunion contractors (large enough)

[3] For a complete analysis of this subject, see Armand J. Thieblot, Jr., *The Davis-Bacon Act,* Labor Relations and Public Policy Series, Report No. 10 (Philadelphia: Industrial Research Unit, The Wharton School, University of Pennsylvania, 1975).

who desire to bid on the job. Small residential and commercial jobs within a central city are often open shop. Other things equal, however, in most market areas there is a direct relationship between unionization and distance from the metropolitan center.

There are also discernible variations in unionization among different parts of the country. In the South, most notably, open shop contractors predominate and in some southern states the union project is a rarity. In part, the situation in the South is related to a relative lack of population concentration. Rural areas generally are not congenial for the unions; northern New England, for example, has little union building. But that is not the whole story, and in Chapter VII we shall examine those factors which distinguish one part of the nation from another.

Finally, the size of a metropolitan area probably has a substantial relationship with the extent of unionization. Open shop penetration in such giant population centers as New York, Chicago, Detroit, and San Francisco, has been substantially less marked than in cities like Columbus, Denver, and Rochester. The reasons behind this observation relate in part to factors discussed before—size of projects and centralization of building activity. Another factor, however, may be the extent of unionization in other industries in an area, since the work forces of larger cities often tend to be heavily unionized generally. This, in turn, will affect such influences as the attitudes of purchasers and the impact of local politics. The relationship between unionization of a community as a whole, and that of its construction industry will also be discussed in Chapter VII, and noted in other chapters as well.

Other Trades

As we noted in Chapter I, the union work force is organized along jealously guarded craft lines, and a metropolitan area of any size will usually headquarter locals from ten to fifteen different national unions. Major population centers may have building trades locals numbering in the scores. Until recently—and for the most part even now—the locals go about their organizing and bargaining activities largely independently of each other. Consequently, for a variety of possible reasons, some trades in a given locality may be more strongly unionized than others.

Although the skeletal features of the open shop construction sector have occasionally been noted in the past, their complexity has never been thoroughly examined. There is much to suggest, moreover, that important changes are taking place within the broad parameters depicted above. The growing phenomenon of contractors operating both union and nonunion subdivisions—the so-called "double-breasted" company discussed in Chapter VIII—is one case in point. Another is the mobilization of open shop contractors in something approaching a movement with the growth of the Associated Builders and Contractors (ABC) and the increasing influence of open shop firms in associations of predominantly union firms like the Associated General Contractors (AGC). Thus, although there are historical antecedents for much of what now constitutes open shop construction, other, later developments need systematic inquiry. This volume represents the first major effort to explore in some depth both the recent structural and institutional configurations, as well as the never well delineated historical dimensions of the nonunion sector.

Union Response to Open Shop Competition

Perhaps the best evidence of the increasing penetration of nonunion construction into the previously unchallenged domain of the building trades is found in the rhetorical and substantive reaction of the unions. This reaction has taken various forms, ranging from impassioned speeches by national leaders urging their members to improve their productivity, to major outbursts of violence against nonunion contractors. In-between, many parts of the country have seen the unions on the defensive in their negotiations over new contract terms, and making significant concessions both within and without the confines of their labor agreements, sometimes with special project agreements. The union reaction to open shop expansion is the subject of Chapter VIII.

THE LABOR MARKET IN NONUNION CONSTRUCTION

Construction unions play a central role in the labor market processes of their industry, much more so than most other labor organizations. Wages and other forms of compensation are set through negotiations in which, as commonly recognized, unions enjoy a preponderance of bargaining power. A significant amount of worker training (although by no means all of it as popularly imagined), is carried on through apprenticeship programs in which the major decisions, such as the number of new applicants to be admitted, are effectively controlled by the unions. Many unemployed workers, and employers seeking help, rely on union administered hiring halls to find each other. Perhaps most important, the allocation of the work force within the employing unit is constrained by various contractual rules, inserted at the insistence of the unions, relating to work assignments, crew sizes, utilization of nonworking foremen, manning requirements, and job classifications. Foremen and lower supervision must belong to the appropriate craft union, thus effectively restraining management direction at this level.

This union role, and the widespread but increasingly inaccurate notion that unionized construction comprises almost the entire industry, have served to direct scholarly attention away from labor markets in the nonunion sector.[4]

This study represents the first comprehensive effort to describe and evaluate the allocation, development, and compensation of manpower resources in open shop construction. The chapters in Part Three of this volume deal with the various aspects of labor market practice: recruitment and deployment, training, wage setting and minority employment. Emphasis, as throughout this book, will be on the differences between the union and open shop sector.

Hiring

Turnover is an important feature of the construction labor market. Some of it is occasioned by influences endemic to the industry: demand tends to be exceptionally volatile both cyclically and seasonally. Additionally, employment patterns in the individual firm will fluctuate according to the size and number of contracts which it is able to obtain. When work falls off, employees are released, and they are not always available when activity resumes. This condition, of course, characterizes all industries to some extent, but the large and often abrupt swings in demand, along with an atomistic and competitive structure, exacerbate it in construction. Furthermore, the relatively large component of skilled labor imposes a still greater burden on the recruitment process.

Union hiring halls, whatever their abuses and restrictions, do provide a central pool of labor to which employers can readily

[4] For example, Mills, *op. cit.*, which contains the most comprehensive treatment of manpower in construction, gives open shop labor markets only the most fleeting reference.

turn. The open shop contractor and the nonunion worker must use other avenues of communication. Much recruitment and job seeking is informal, consisting either of random solicitations or a "grapevine" of workers, employers, and suppliers. On a more formal level, newspaper ads, the public employment service, and (rarely) the placement service of vocational schools may be utilized. Recently, open shop associations have begun to develop their own hiring halls or systems. Very little is known, however, about any of these open shop employment mechanisms or how effective they are, or potentially may be. Chapter IX analyzes what we have been able to discern on this subject.

Manpower Allocation and Utilization

Open shop contractors and their spokesmen contend that their major advantage over union builders is the greater flexibility which they enjoy in utilizing their work force, and the point is frequently echoed by representatives of the union firms themselves. In broadest terms, this flexibility has three components: (1) the contractor's use of unskilled and semiskilled workers to perform work of which they are capable, rather than his being required to assign it to a higher paid craftmen; (2) the ability to use a skilled worker for a variety of tasks, some of which may be part of the commonly defined "job description" of a different skilled occupation; and (3) the ability to dispense with unnecessary and/or unproductive labor.

Occupational distinctions in the open shop sector are often blurred. For example, cement is poured and finished with crews consisting of laborers, carpenters, ironworkers, and cement masons, with the group including workers who perform most or all of these jobs at different times. Similarly the helper, a worker who labors alongside a craftsman and may perform the more routine aspects of the trade, is an integral part of the nonunion work force although he may not be called by that name, but the classification is all but extinct in the union sector.

Another element of manpower utilization is the setting of manning requirements: the stipulation of crew sizes for a particular job; the required use of nonworking foremen; and limitations on what jobs a worker can perform or the number of times he may be shifted during the day. The open shop contractor, of course, is free of these restrictions found in many union contracts. Nor is he necessarily burdened with having to pay workers for time not on the job, showup pay, travel pay, and a guaranteed 40 hour workweek regardless of hours actually worked.

To what extent is flexible manpower utilization a practice rather than merely a right in the open shop sector? What impact does it have on relative costs and competitiveness? These questions, of obvious importance to an analysis of construction labor economics, are also addressed in Chapter IX.

Seasonality

Seasonal fluctuations impose an uncommonly heavy burden on the labor market in construction. In a typical year, summer employment in the industry will exceed the levels of the previous winter by 30-35 percent. In part, these swings are accomplished by simply releasing workers during the off season and recalling them when activity resumes. But since seasonal changes in employment are almost invariably greater than changes in unemployment, it is clear that other forms of labor force adjustment are at play.

Although seasonality is a problem endemic to the industry, spokesmen for the nonunion sector usually assert that employment patterns in the open shop are steadier than those among union employers. The proposition, moreover, is a plausible one. Since the nonunion contractor's sources of new skilled workers may well be less reliable than those of their unionized counterparts, they have a greater incentive to make special efforts to retain their regular employees. If this is correct, what does the open shop builder do to avoid layoffs in the off season?

The peak season, of course, presents a very different problem: how are manpower needs to be met? How are the industry's regular work force supplemented by the influx of temporary workers and by overtime schedules? Such adjustments in the open shop sector are likewise examined in Chapter IX.

Manpower Development and Training

More than 50 percent of those employed in the construction industry are officially classified as "craftsmen, foremen and kindred workers." The industry depends heavily upon processes of skill development both internal and external to it. Yet virtually no research has been done on the ways in which these methods operate in the open shop sector. Apprenticeship programs in the open shop sector, unlike those in the unionized one, are relatively new, in part because of the difficulty that open shop associations have had in obtaining government approval. But some programs are now fully registered, most notably those sponsored through the Associated Builders and Contractors, and the National Association of Home Builders. Chapter X reports in detail on the history and current status of these programs, which in many localities are either nascent or only a few years old. The same chapter also analyzes less formal approaches to training, the needs of open shop contractors for training, and the innovative approaches to training of three of the largest open shop contractors.

Wages and Benefits

Wages in construction are commonly identified with the rates negotiated by the building trades unions. Thus, while the explosive settlements of the late 1960's and early 1970's (discussed below) served to focus popular concern on those wages and their contribution to overall inflationary pressures, little attention was directed toward pay scales in the nonunion sector. But as it becomes increasingly clear that the wages of large numbers of construction workers are not set through collective bargaining, this omission comes to present an ever more consequential gap in our knowledge of the industry.

It will not be seriously disputed that, on average, hourly rates of nonunion workers are lower than those fixed in union agreements. But beyond such gross generalizations, very little has heretofore been understood about wage relationships both within the open shop sector and those between union and nonunion construction. In Chapter XI, we shall examine and evaluate a number of salient questions regarding relative compensation practices. A large part of our task, however, will be simply to relate what has been learned about wage levels and structures in open shop construction.

There are five subject areas which shall be given scrutiny. The first is the factors which influence the setting of nonunion wages; the second is the extent to which union-nonunion differentials in hourly wages are reflected in relative annual earnings, or whether more steady employment in the open shop sector offsets lower rates; the third pertains to relative wages within the open shop sector—whether rates vary with individuals as compared with single job rates in the union sector; the fourth area of concern is the extent to which fringe benefits are paid in open shop construction. It can rather easily be shown that union agreements, although still devoting a smaller proportion of compensation to wages than the economy-wide average, have placed ever increasing emphasis on such benefits as health insurance, pensions, vacations, and supplemental unemployment benefits. The extent to which this practice may have been followed in the open shop sector has up till now, been totally ignored.

Finally, we shall discuss briefly the impact of public policy, and particularly prevailing wage laws, on wage rates. (The discussion will be brief because the subject of prevailing wage laws, particularly the Davis-Bacon Act is explored in depth in a separate study already published by the Industrial Research Unit.) [5] As noted earlier, nonunion contractors are winning an increasing number of public jobs. The question is therefore raised as to how these contractors accommodate prevailing (often union) wages, when the wages which they pay on private projects may be substantially lower. Chapter XI will deal with these issues and also analyze daily and weekly hours, overtime and related issues in the open shop sector.

Minorities

Members of minority groups, and especially blacks, have long been underrepresented in the skilled occupations of the construction industry, which is often regarded as a center of discrimination and racial restriction, with the building trades unions as the prime offenders. Again, however, much of the scrutiny given to the industry has been based on the assumption that the union sector is much the whole story. Not only have past research efforts mostly ignored the open shop, but government programs designed to increase and upgrade minority employment have conspicuously failed to include nonunion contractors in their plans to bring more minorities into the industry. Chapter XII examines the relative positions of minorities in the union and open shop sector.

THE COMPETITIVE FACTORS

The picture that emerges from the chapters that follow is one of a growing open shop challenge to the status and influence

[5] Thieblot, *loc. cit.*

of the building trades unions. That the challenge has gone largely unacknowledged in the scholarly and popular literature attests to the tenacity with which conventional assumptions survive. That it is real enough will, we believe, be apparent to the reader, as we explore the factors which have contributed heavily to the competition now faced by unionized construction labor. Here we pause briefly to summarize these factors.

In our interviews with scores of union and nonunion contractors and with spokesmen for their associations, we repeatedly sought their perceptions on the reasons for the broad-based increase in open shop activity which most agreed had recently taken place. In their responses we encountered three refrains: wages, productivity, and strikes, although not necessarily in that order. The unions' success in winning prodigious wage increases, instituting inefficient and restrictive work rules and practices, and interrupting production has given concern not only to contractors but also to their customers. The formation of the Construction Users Roundtable in the early 1970's attests to the latter point.

Figure II-1 shows the annual percent change in hourly wage and benefit rates for union construction workers, 1969-1974. Figure II-2 compares construction collective bargaining settlements with those in manufacturing for the same period. The precipitous construction settlements in the 1969-1971 period are clearly indicated by the data in these charts. The evidence presented in Part Two clearly points to this period as the time when the open shop construction sector made some of its quoted advances.

There is little question that open shops enjoy a substantial wage advantage over their unionized competitors. As we shall see, even where open shop employers pay their top mechanics the equivalent of the union scale, their freedom to pay a range of rates to individuals with diverse capabilities results in a significantly lower average wage. But wages are far from the whole story, for even in public construction, where prevailing wage laws often require the universal payment of union scales, open shops have also had some success in chipping away at traditional union domains. The cost impact of these wage differentials, moveover, is not unambiguous. It cannot easily be determined, for example, whether higher wages allow union contractors to choose among the best qualified and most productive workers, assuming union rules permit such selection.

FIGURE II-1
Annual Percent Change in Hourly Wage And Benefit Rates, Union Construction Workers Percent Change From Year Ago

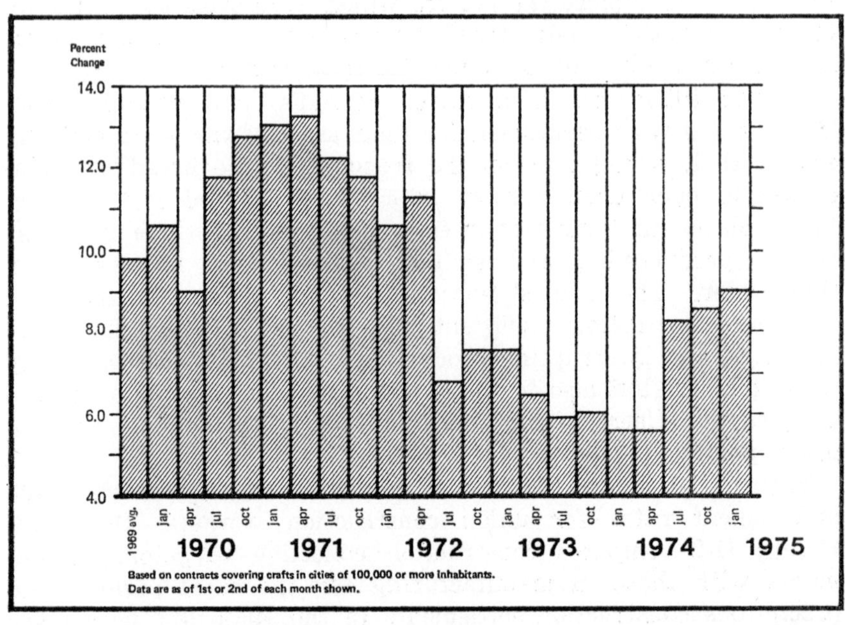

Source: Data, U.S. Bureau of Labor Statistics; Chart, *Contractors Mutual Association News* (February, 1975), p. 5.
Note: Union wage and benefit rates for the year ending January 2, 1975, increased 9.2 percent. The rate of increase has risen in each quarter since the termination of wage controls. (These figures do not include legally required payments such as social security).

The impact of union work rules is less ambiguous—in direction if not in magnitude. There are jurisdictional demarcations which often require unskilled work to be performed by high paid journeymen, or which result in delays because work cannot be assigned to employees who are immediately available at the site. There are usually restrictions on working hours, so that interruptions because of weather or materials shortages must be made up at overtime rates. There may be limitations on the number of machines a worker can operate in a day, or requirements that automatic equipment be manned. The terms "featherbedding" and "productivity" crop up again and again. Although it is impossible to say precisely how much these work rules add to labor costs, it is difficult to escape the conclusion that it is

FIGURE II-2
*Negotiated Wage and Benefit Changes—
Construction and Manufacturing
Negotiated Percent Increase-Annual Rate*

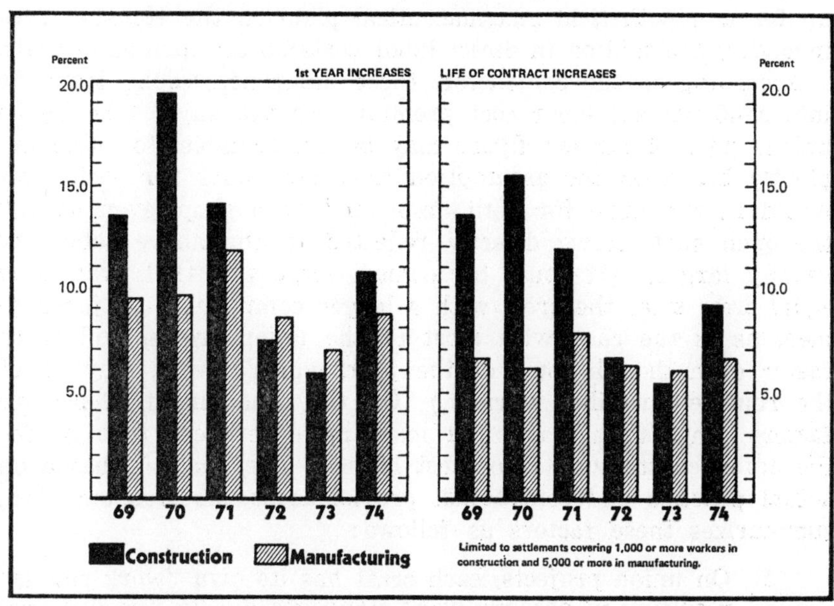

Source: Data, U.S. Bureau of Labor Statistics; Chart, *Contractors Mutual Association News* (February, 1975), p. 6.

Note: During 1974 the wage and benefit settlements in new construction contracts provided for a 10.8 percent increase in the first year of the contract and an annual average of 9.2 percent over the life of the contract. The corresponding increases in manufacturing settlements for 1974 were 8.7 and 6.6 percent. Wage controls, established in the construction industry in 1971, were terminated in 1974. 1971 was the last year, prior to 1974, in which construction increases exceeded those in manufacturing.

not negligible. Paradoxically, therefore, the very work rules which were demanded by the unions to preserve jobs may now be playing an important part in causing them to be lost to nonunion competitors.

Hypothetical Cost Comparisons

The economics of open shop construction have not been adequately studied, and we have really only scratched the surface here. In any event, however, open shop contractors are beginning to market aggressively the cost advantages of nonunion construction. One large firm, for example, prepares cost comparisons between union and nonunion operations for various types of projects for which it seeks contracts. These comparisons reflect both the wage differentials and differences in manning requirements. Table II-1 summarizes one comparison drawn up for a hypothetical pharmaceutical plant in the Houston area involving $15 million in direct labor costs on an open shop basis.

According to the contractor, these differences alone translate into a 40 percent labor cost premium for the buyer who builds union. The 40 percent figure may be questionable, for it is implicitly based on the assumption that man-hours for each crew would be the same for both union and open shop, even though the open shop crews directly reflected in the above table are usually larger. (It could be argued, moreover, that even with equal crew sizes the crew with a larger complement of journeymen, as is the case with most of the union crews, will work faster even though some of the journeymen's work may be of the routine, unskilled variety.) On the other hand, there are factors other than wage and manning differences that render the union contractor's labor cost higher. The analysis, based on actual practice and contractual provisions in the Houston area, summarizes these factors as follows:

1. On union projects, each craft has its own "work claims" resulting in possible work stoppages due to jurisdictional disputes. In open shop work a worker may be used temporarily in another craft, if expedient.

2. On union projects, any work in excess of 8 hours per day is on an overtime basis. On open shop projects, overtime is calculated in excess of 40 hours per week. Normally our open shop projects operate 10 hours Monday through Thursday. This allows us to make up on Friday and Saturday any time lost due to weather at straight time.

3. Second shift work is normally at a premium rate on a union project, i.e., 7½ hours work for 8 hours pay. There is no premium pay for shift work on an open shop project.

4. On a union project, work assignments between crafts cannot be varied in case of manpower problems or workloads.

5. Union weekend work (Saturday afternoon and Sunday) is at double time. Open shop work allows incorporation

TABLE II-1
Cost Comparison for Houston Area
Hypothetical Pharmaceutical Plant 1973

Craft	Union Shop						Open Shop					
	Foremen		Journeymen		Apprentice		Foremen		Journeymen		Apprentice	
	No.	Wage	No.	Wage	No.	Wage	No.	Wage	No.	Wage	No.	Wage
Carpenters	1	$8.55	7	$7.80	3	$5.85	1	$6.40	6	$5.90	6	$4.43
Pipefitters	1	9.40	6	8.65	3	6.49	1	6.60	5	6.10	5	4.58
Millwrights	1	8.85	8	8.10	2	6.08	1	6.60	7	6.10	3	4.58
Electricians	1	9.45	8	8.70	1	6.53	1	6.60	6	6.10	6	4.58
Iron Workers	1	8.90	6	8.15	1	6.11	1	6.50	5	6.00	3	4.50
Insulators	1	8.75	10	8.00	2	6.00	1	6.60	5	6.10	5	4.58
Painters	1	8.40	8	7.65	1	5.74	1	6.25	6	5.75	4	4.31
Cement Masons	1	8.20	10	7.45	0	0.00	1	6.40	5	5.90	5	4.43
Laborers	1	6.15	10	5.40	0	0.00	1	5.15	10	3.75	0	0.00
Bricklayers	1	9.20	5	8.45	2	6.34	1	6.75	12	6.25	10	4.69
Operators	1	8.45	4	7.70	1	5.78	1	6.50	26	6.00	0	0.00

Source: Comparison supplied by open shop contractor.
Note: Union apprentice wages were calculated at 75 percent of the journeymen wage.

of Saturday and Sunday as part of a four-day, 10-hour shift if expedient. This is generally done for painting crews in areas where they would be unable to operate during normal working hours and it is impractical to utilize a second shift.

6. On union work each individual craft has a steward to provide representation. This means that a certain percent of his time is spent in nonproductive work. Depending upon the specific situation, up to 25 percent of his time can be expected to be lost.
7. Most union crafts receive vacation and holiday fringes. Open shop workers are paid only for hours actually worked.
8. The insulators, boilermakers, and pipefitter crafts receive a travel allowance and travel time depending on the distance to the worker's home.

Another open shop contractor provided a cost comparison based upon a power plant construction job in the Southeast. Table II-2 shows the relative wage costs by crafts, claiming nearly $40 million savings over a 347 week period. The open shop contractor calculated additional savings in premium pay of $8.3 million based upon union rules. These are spelled out in Table II-3, and include such items as nonwork time of job stewards, check-in and check-out time, use of craftsmen for laborer work (loading and unloading), excessive labor, and overtime.

Again it is likely that these comparisons exaggerate the advantages of the open shop. They do, however, point to the basic economic fact that both in direct compensation and in labor utilization, open shop operators have the potential of tremendous economic advantages which the union wage escalation since the late 1960's has exacerbated.

The Strike Problem

The cost of work stoppages is particularly hard to measure. Construction is a relatively strike-prone industry, accounting in 1972 for about 12 percent of all unionized workers, 14 percent of all strikes, and 28 percent of all man-days lost.[6] A stoppage means, of course, idle plant and equipment, foregone investment return to partially completed structures, and the possible income

---

[6] Data from U.S. Bureau of Labor Statistics strike statistics.

TABLE II-2
Hypothetical Power Plant, Southeast Area
Manual Labor Cost Comparisons
1973

Craft	Manual Man-hours	Percent Total	Open Shop: 1973 Crew Rate[a]	Open Shop: Craft Total	Closed Shop: 1973 Crew Rate[b]	Closed Shop: Craft Total
Boilermakers	1,598,000	13.1	$6.20	$ 9,907,600	$ 8.44	$ 13,487,120
Carpenters	1,452,000	11.9	5.19	7,535,880	8.48	12,312,960
Electricians	1,500,000	12.3	5.72	8,580,000	10.19	15,285,000
Ironworkers	1,404,000	11.5	6.06	8,508,240	8.52	11,962,080
Laborers	1,525,000	12.5	3.23	4,925,750	5.30	8,082,500
Millwrights	488,000	4.0	5.90	2,879,200	8.40	4,099,200
Operators & Mechanics	769,000	6.3	5.06	3,891,140	7.97	6,128,930
Pipefitters	1,891,000	15.5	6.38	12,064,580	9.15	17,302,650
Miscellaneous	1,573,000	12.9	5.06	7,959,380	7.85	12,348,050
Subtotal	12,200,000	100.0	$5.43	66,251,770	$ 8.27	101,008,490
Payroll Taxes and Insurance 12%				7,950,212		12,121,018
Totals @ 1973 Wage Rates				74,201,982		113,129,508

Source: Open shop contractor.
[a] Rates recognize mix of foremen, journeymen and journeymen helpers.
[b] Rates recognize mix of foremen, journeymen and apprentices. Rates include fringe benefits, but exclude travel or subsistence allowances.

TABLE II-3
Hypothetical Power Plant, Southeast Area
General Premiums

1. Job Stewards

Union regulations provide that a job steward be provided whenever 20 members are employed on an individual job. An estimate of this cost that would have been paid by the owner is as follows:

Boilermakers	282 wks @ 334.00=	94,188
Carpenter	347 wks @ 335.00=	116,245
Millwright	247 wks @ 332.00=	82,004
Plumber-Pipefitter	330 wks @ 362.00=	119,460
Ironworker	273 wks @ 337.00=	92,001
Electrician	330 wks @ 404.00=	133,320
Oper. Engineer	308 wks @ 315.00=	97,020
Mason	234 wks @ 310.00=	72,540
Painter	213 wks @ 310.00=	66,030
Laborer	347 wks @ 208.00=	72,176
Total	944,984	

Assume 50% production & 50% as steward lost cost:

Savings (50% x 944,984)=$472,492

2. Check-In and Check-Out Penalty

Closed shop projects require that the workmen be allowed five to ten minutes in the morning on company time to report, pick up tools, and get to his place of work, This period is also customary at the end of the work day when a similar period is allotted for cleanup, checking-in tools, etc. On the basis of an eight-hour work day, this loss represents a conservative labor loss of 4.16%.

Total labor: .0416 x $101,008,490=$4,201,953.00

Assume 50% of this cost to cover any lost time which might normally develop.

Savings (50% x 4,201,953.00=$2,100,976.00

3. Warehousing

Under closed shop operations, the union rules specify that craftsmen **unload all materials relating to their work.** We can assume that under union rules, we would have had the following warehousemen:

1 Storekeeper	347 wks @ 420.00=	145,740.00
1 Electrical Warehouseman	312 wks @ 415.00=	129,480.00
1 Mechanical Warehouseman	312 wks @ 375.00=	117,000.00
4 Electrical Journeymen	312 wks @ 404.00=	504,192.00
4 Mechanical Journeymen	312 wks @ 362.00=	451,776.00
2 Laborers	347 wks @ 208.00=	144,352.00
		$1,492,540.00

TABLE II-3
General Premiums (continued)

Under Open Shop conditions, we would require:

1 Storekeeper	347 wks @ 265.00=	91,955.00
1 Electrical Warehouseman	312 wks @ 229.00=	71,448.00
1 Mechanical Warehouseman	312 wks @ 255.00=	79,560.00
6 Laborers	347 wks @ 130.00=	270,660.00
		$513,623.00
	SAVINGS:	$978,917.00

4. Operating Engineers

Union regulations provide that operating engineers must be employed for the operation of hoist, pumps and air compressors.

Under Union Conditions:

1 Foreman	312 wks @ 335.00=	104,520.00
4 Oper. Engrs-Compressors	312 wks @ 315.00=	393,120.00
6 Oper. Engrs-Pumps	177 wks @ 315.00=	334,530.00
5 Oper. Engrs-Hoists	233 wks @ 315.00=	366,975.00
	Total	1,199,145.00

Under Open Shop Conditions:

1 Mechanic	312 wks @ 300.00=	93,600.00
1 Helper	312 wks @ 202.00=	63,024.00
5 Hoist Operators	233 wks @ 202.00=	235,330.00
		391,954.00
	SAVINGS:	$807,191.00

5. Overtime Savings

Past experience indicates 3% of total payroll as premium time contributing to the timely execution of the Project.

DCC Normal Premium Time (as time & ½ rate)=3% of total payroll

$66,251,770.00 x .03=$1,987,553.00

Union Equivalent (Doubletime)=99,788,490 x .06=5,987,309.00

Savings:	5,987,309	Union Premium Time
	1,987,553	DCC Premium Time
	3,999,756	

Savings $3,999,756

Summary of General Premium savings:

1)	Job Stewards	$ 472,492
2)	Check-in and Check-out Penalty	2,100,976
3)	Warehousing	978,917
4)	Operating Engineers	807,191
5)	Overtime Savings	3,999,756
		$8,359,332

Total Savings $8,359,332

Source: Open shop contractor.

loss to salaried as well as hourly employees of struck firms. There is, moreover, a cost to the buyer in the delay in utilizing his purchase.

Strikes, of course, are a contingency in any unionized industry. But the situation is exacerbated in construction by the large number of strikes that occur during the term of a contract, most of which grow out of craft jurisdictional disputes. These strikes are especially troublesome and costly for the contractor, largely because of their unpredictability and the relative helplessness of the contractor in dealing with their root causes. Of all the complaints communicated regularly by contractor groups to the unions, jurisdictional strikes are invariably near the top of the list. Open shop contractors, of course, do not have to contend with this difficulty, and are thus in a better position to assure buyers that a fixed completion deadline can be met.

Advantages of Union Shops

Subsequent chapters will explore all these issues in greater detail. We shall also be examining features of the labor market in which open shops may operate at a disadvantage. Recruitment of manpower is one such area; training is another. Because of the long experience in the union sector with referral services and apprenticeship programs, union contractors are often in a better position to adjust to changing manpower needs. The open shop contractor will usually seek to minimize these adjustments by maintaining as large a steady work force as he can, sometimes even at an appreciable cost to him. This point is perhaps best illustrated by nascent efforts by open shops and their associations to develop arrangements with regard to recruitment and training which in some key respects emulate long established practices and institutions in union construction. These developments still have some way to go, however, and the cost advantages of the open shop delineated above must be somewhat tempered by these and other considerations discussed in Parts Two and Three.

METHODOLOGY

Most of the information described and analyzed in the ensuing chapters was gathered through field interviews, telephone conversations, and written correspondence with literally hundreds of contractors, association executives, and staff personnel of various organizations connected with open shop construction. About one-half of the interviews were conducted by the authors, the rest by staff members of the Industrial Research Unit. The interviews were relatively unstructured, although they usually included a common set of questions which are reproduced in Appendix C. Most of the material in Part Three (Labor Markets In Open Shop Construction) was obtained directly from contractors themselves, while that in Part Two (Extent of Open Shop Construction) was mainly derived from association spokesmen who usually had a broader view of the extent and character of nonunion construction work in their localities than did individual employers.

Interviews were conducted in most of the major regions in the country, although constraints on time and resources precluded direct visits to the West Coast. The interviewer usually began by making contacts with key association executives in an area (particularly the Associated Builders and Contractors and the Associated General Contractors) who would then put them in touch with individual contractors who had an active role in local industry affairs. Because of its concentration of open shop activity, the South received the most intensive coverage, with visits to Texas, Oklahoma, Louisiana, Florida, South Carolina, North Carolina, Georgia, Virginia, District of Columbia, and Maryland. Heavy coverage was also obtained in all Northeastern and Great Lakes states where unions are very strong.

At the national level, we received considerable helpful cooperation from the headquarters of the major contractors' associations, again most notably the AGC and the ABC. Approximately two-fifths of the AGC members operate open shops. In addition, we conducted wide-ranging interviews with officials of a number of the largest open shop contractors whose operations extend over broad geographic areas. Brown & Root, Daniel International, and H. B. Zachry deserve special mention in this regard.

In some instances, interviews were also conducted with major construction users. In a number of cases we discovered that important breakthroughs for open shop construction grew out of decisions by large customers to abandon policies of dealing exclusively with unionized contractors. Especially significant in this connection are some petroleum and chemical companies and public utilities, whose capital building budgets often run into the hundreds of millions of dollars.

Wherever possible, we sought to supplement the information supplied verbally by interviews with documentation. In a number of instances we were able to obtain private studies of open shop activity conducted by unions and by contractors' associations. As we note where appropriate, many of these efforts had important methodological deficiencies, but they were nevertheless useful in developing some rough gauges of open shop construction, and occasionally the results were both surprising and dramatic. In the area of labor market behavior, we attempted both to assemble written descriptions of various plans on such subjects as training programs, referral services, wage structures, and fringe benefit arrangements and to develop quantitative estimates of the extent to which these plans were actually used. In those cases where the numbers are at some variance with the formal descriptions issued by the sponsors of various programs—that is, where the activities seemed to have been more thoroughly developed on paper than in practice—we have so noted.

Although there is very little previously published material on the nonunion construction sector, the federal government has conducted studies dealing generally with one or another aspect of construction labor from which certain data on open shops can be extracted. These are summarized in their appropriate places below. Also, we have tried to utilize any prior scholarly work which sheds light on the topic, such as two earlier volumes published by the Industrial Research Unit,[7] and an unpublished study under the direction of Professor Sherman Dallas of the Georgia Institute of Technology.[8] In short, we have tried to canvass as thoroughly as possible all available written material both within and without the public domain, including, in addition to the sources mentioned above, the published academic literature, the trade journals, and *Construction Labor Report,* a

[7] Howard G. Foster, *Manpower in Homebuilding: A Preliminary Analysis*, Manpower and Human Resources Study No. 3; and Richard L. Rowan and Lester Rubin, *Opening the Skilled Construction Trades to Blacks*, Labor Relations and Public Policy Series, No. 7 (Philadelphia: Industrial Research Unit, The Wharton School, University of Pennsylvania, 1974 and 1972 respectively).

[8] Joel H. Penick, "Building Construction Awards in Atlanta: 1961-1972," mimeographed report prepared by the Georgia Institute of Technology, Atlanta, Georgia, 1973.

weekly information service issued by the Bureau of National Affairs, Inc.

Throughout this book, the material gathered from our field work and literature search are supplemented by the results of a questionnaire survey conducted by the Industrial Research Unit. A copy of the questionnaire may be found in Appendix B. Responses were solicited from members of several contractors' associations, including AGC, ABC, the Associated Road Builders of America, the National Electrical Contractors Association, The Associated Independent Electrical Contractors, and the Mechanical Contractors Association. The questionnaires were sent to every other member (with the other one-half receiving a separate questionnaire on the Davis-Bacon Act), about 10,000 contractors in all. Usable responses were received from over 1,500 firms, almost equally divided between union and nonunion. About 68 percent of the union respondents and 61 percent of the nonunion respondents were general contractors, with the rest scattered among various subcontracting specialties. About two-thirds of the subcontractors were in the electrical, heating, or plumbing fields.

The mechanics of administering the questionnaire unfortunately led to an unrepresentative sample of respondents. Since larger firms are more likely to be association members in the first place, and since the larger firms among such members are more likely to have the staff resources to respond, small establishments were grossly underrepresented in our final compilations. For example, according to the *1967 Census of Construction Industries*, less than 5 percent of all firms had gross receipts in excess of $1 million; such firms, however, constituted some two-thirds of our responses. Similarly, firms with twenty or more employees comprised about 70 percent of our sample but less than 10 percent of all establishments in 1967.[9] As a consequence, the results of the questionnaire will be applied cautiously as indicators of the practices and views of major contractors, rather than as a basis for precise statistical analyses of the industry.

Finally, it should be noted that two important sources of information were not tapped in this study. The first, of course, is the workers themselves. On certain subjects, such as skill acquisition, intersector mobility, and job search, worker input

---

[9] U.S. Department of Commerce, *1697 Census of Construction Industries* (Washington, D.C.: Government Printing Office, 1971), Vol. 1, Tables 5, 6.

would have been invaluable. Unfortunately, a comprehensive canvass of any meaningful sample of workers is far beyond the resources of any nongovernmental body. The second untapped source is the building trades unions. In some cases, we were able to obtain internal letters and documents relating to local unions' concerns with open shop competition, and in other cases we have utilized speeches, position papers, convention proceedings, officers' reports, and the like from the public record. In addition, we had at our disposal the ample literature, both academic and governmental, dealing with unionized construction. We also asked the national offices of twelve unions to respond to various questions on the extent and character of nonunion competition in their respective industry segments, and to indicate what kinds of steps they had taken in response. Only the Painters union replied.

The remainder of this volume is divided into three parts. Part Two describes and analyzes the extent and patterns of open shop activity in the several subdivisions of the industry and within each of the major geographical regions of the country. The section ends with an examination of the variety of ways that the building trades unions have sought to stem the growing penetration of open shops into other unionized areas. Part Three deals with various labor market issues and practices in the open shop sector. Part Four presents a summary of the findings and conclusions of the study.

PART TWO

Extent Of Open Shop Construction

CHAPTER III

Residential Construction

Residential construction historically has had a significant open shop component. Even in areas where unions remain firmly entrenched in other segments of the industry, the erection of homes and apartments is, in many cases, performed almost exclusively with nonunion labor. There are, to be sure, important distinctions to be made within the residential sector. In some large cities, and in a few scattered small communities, the unions have maintained their strength throughout all of construction, including residential. In many areas, moreover, union contractors have dominated the market for large, high rise residential structures (apartments, hotels, dormitories), even while being virtually shut out of the construction of single-family homes, small apartments and town houses, and repair and remodeling work generally. In this context, the separation usually occurs when an elevator is required in the building, usually above three or four stories.

EXTENT OF OPEN SHOP

There is as yet no universally accepted estimate of the amount of residential building currently performed open shop, but a figure of 80 percent has been often used. This was the estimate offered in a 1972 interview with Mr. John Riley, Labor Counsel of the National Association of Home Builders. Mills writes: "certainly some branches of the industry are more fully organized than others. Residential construction . . . is probably the least organized; perhaps 80 percent of the workers are nonunion."[1] The Construction Employers Labor Relations Association in New York State, in a 1971 survey of open shop construction work, assumed residential work to be 80 percent

---

[1] Daniel Quinn Mills, *Industrial Relations and Manpower in Construction* (Cambridge: MIT Press, 1972), p. 17.

nonunion. As shall be argued later, however, union strength in the residential sector, may be even scantier at the present time.

Systematic attempts to estimate the extent of union representation in construction generally, or in residential construction in particular, have been few and far between. There is some evidence that housing has at one time been more heavily unionized than it is now. In 1936, the U.S. Bureau of Labor Statistics surveyed the records of 5,450 contractors in 105 cities employing 186,145 workers.[2] The Bureau estimated that the sample included 25 to 30 percent of all building trades workers in the cities covered. Although the survey was concerned primarily with wages and hours, information was also gathered on union status. About one-third of the workers in the sample were engaged in residential construction. Of these less than 57 percent were union members, compared to over 72 percent in nonresidential.[3] In larger cities (over 250,000), union workers constituted 62 percent of the residential work force but only 41 percent in smaller cities.

Estimates of unionism in residential construction were made two decades ago by Richard Scheuch[4] and by William Haber and Harold M. Levinson.[5] Scheuch argued that the BLS survey overstated the incidence of unionism nationally, since the areas and employers in its sample were not representative of the industry as a whole. His conclusion was that "prior to World War II, single-family dwelling construction, with the exception of certain urban areas, was generally carried on in an essentially nonunion milieu. Since 1940, however, there has been a persistent increase in the unionization of the labor force."[6]

Relying on union membership reports to the AFL Building and Construction Trades Department, Scheuch calculated that in 1947 the industry was 67.9 percent unionized, and that the

[2] Edward P. Sanford, "Wage Rates and Hours of Labor in the Building Trades," *Monthly Labor Review*, XLV (August, 1937), p. 283.

[3] The reader is reminded that residential construction includes apartment building. The figure for homebuilding would doubtless be lower.

[4] Richard Scheuch, "The Labor Factor in Residential Construction," Ph.D. dissertation, Princeton University, 1951.

[5] William Haber and Harold M. Levinson, *Labor Relations and Productivity in the Building Trades* (Ann Arbor: Bureau of Industrial Relations, University of Michigan, 1956), esp. pp. 34-37.

[6] Scheuch, *op. cit.*, p. 2.

growth of organization since the 1930's was concentrated largely in the residential sector. In an interview with Scheuch in 1950, William Tobin, Industrial Relations Director for the National Association of Home Builders, estimated that some 65 percent of workers employed by member firms were union members. Scheuch's own estimates of the extent of organization in twenty-seven areas throughout the country, based largely on personal interviews and congressional testimony, estimated that thirteen of the areas were almost entirely union, and six of these had changed from a predominantly nonunion character during and after the war. He noted further that even in many of those areas which were nonunion in the late 1940's, certain individual trades were heavily organized.

The Haber and Levinson study was based on a 1952 survey of sixteen cities, ranging in size from 49,000 (Battle Creek) to 3.6 million (Chicago). The authors conducted a total of 268 interviews primarily with local contractors and union representatives, and they concluded that union organization in both residential and nonresidential construction had grown considerably since 1936.

> In all sixteen cities surveyed in the summer of 1952, union strength in commercial, industrial, public, and semipublic work was close to 100 percent, with large apartment buildings only slightly weaker.[7]

The estimates for homebuilding were less uniform among the cities, although there was "substantial agreement" among those persons interviewed within each city, ranging from virtually complete organization in Chicago, St. Louis, and Cleveland to less than 25 percent in most of the smaller communities.

A major limitation of the Haber and Levinson estimates is that they are based on a relatively small and somewhat unrepresentative sample. The authors note that:

> As compared to what was probably a somewhat high estimate of 57 percent made by the Bureau of Labor Statistics in 1936, it is perhaps reasonable to estimate that approximately two-thirds of the homes being built in the early 1950's were under union control.[8]

Yet eleven of their sixteen cities are in regions identified by the BLS as relative union strongholds and none of the larger cities in the South were included. Nevertheless, however much Haber

---

[7] Haber and Levinson, *op. cit.*, p. 35.

[8] Haber and Levinson, *ibid.*, p. 36.

and Levinson may have over estimated the extent of unionized residential building in 1952, it would appear highly unlikely that the actual nonunion component even approached the 80 percent figure commonly used twenty years later. The Haber and Levinson estimates for specific cities, as well as the earlier ones of Scheuch, are presented in Table III-1.

The period between World War II and the Korean Conflict probably represents the highwater mark of union representation in homebuilding for the past four decades. The years after World War II witnessed an explosive expansion in the demand for all kinds of construction, particularly residential, and the building trades unions for a sustained time had a congenial environment for their organizational efforts. Between 1954 and 1965, however, the average annual unemployment rate for construction workers never fell below 10 percent, and although the picture changed for the better in the late 1960's, it had already begun to darken again in 1970. Furthermore, residential building had already begun to move increasingly away from the central cities, making it progressively more difficult for the unions to maintain control in some areas.

NAHB Surveys

The only recent efforts to estimate the extent of union representation in housing have been undertaken by the National Association of Home Builders. The Association's quinquennial membership surveys ask respondents to identify themselves as either union, nonunion, or open shop. The most recent canvass, taken in 1969, found that 18.6 percent were union employers, 32.7 percent were strictly nonunion, and remainder were open shop, using union workers or subcontractors in some trades only.[9] Only 45 percent of the NAHB members responded to the survey, and it is probable that the larger and hence mostly union builders are somewhat more apt to respond. Thus, these figures on nonunion and open shop operations can be regarded as conservative estimates.

The NAHB also conducts periodic surveys of its local executive officers to gather information on both union status and wage rates. Table III-2 summarizes the responses to the two most re-

[9] Michael Sumichrast and Sara A. Frankel, *Profile of the Builder and His Industry* (Washington, D.C.: National Association of Home Builders, 1970), p. 202.

TABLE III-1
Estimates of Union Strength in Residential Construction By Scheuch and Haber/Levinson, by Selected Areas

Area	Scheuch 1949	Haber/Levinson Percent Range 1952
Atlanta, Ga.	mostly nonunion	—
Baltimore, Md.	open shop	—
Battle Creek, Mich.	———	0-25
Boston, Mass.	strongly unionized	50-75
Buffalo, N.Y.	unionized after war	75-90
Cape Cod, Mass.	nonunion	—
Charleston, S.C.	———	75-90
Charlotte, N.C.	———	0-25
Chicago, Ill.	strongly unionized	95-100
Cincinnati, Ohio	———	0-25
Cleveland, Ohio	———	95-100
Columbus, Ohio	open shop	0-25
Dallas, Tex.	mostly nonunion	—
Denver, Colo.	unionized after war	—
Detroit, Mich.	unionized after war	75-90
Grand Rapids, Mich.	———	0-25
Hartford, Conn.	strongly unionized	—
Indianapolis, Ind.	open shop	0-25
Kalamazoo, Mich.	———	0-25
Little Rock, Ark.	mostly nonunion	—
Long Island, N.Y.	unionized after war	—
Lynn, Mass.	mostly nonunion	—
Memphis, Tenn.	30 percent all union; rest union in some crafts	—
Milwaukee, Wis.	strongly unionized	—
New York, N.Y.	strongly unionized	—
Oklahoma City, Okla.	open shop	—
Philadelphia, Pa.	strongly unionized	—
Pittsburgh, Pa.	———	25-40
Portland, Oreg.	unionized after war	—
St. Louis, Mo.	strongly unionized	95-100
San Antonio, Tex.	open shop	—
San Francisco, Calif.	strongly unionized	—
Washington, D.C.	mostly open shop; some closed shop	25-40

Source: Richard Scheuch, "The Labor Factor in Residential Construction," Ph.D. dissertation, Princeton University, 1951, Chapter V; and William Haber and Harold M. Levinson, *Labor Relations and Productivity in the Building Trades* (Ann Arbor: University of Michigan, 1956), p. 252.

TABLE III-2
Unionization in Single-Family Building
As Estimated by NAHB Local Executive Officers
1969 and 1971

City	Percent of Single-Family Nonunion 1969	Percent of Single-Family Nonunion 1971	City	Percent of Single-Family Nonunion 1969	Percent of Single-Family Nonunion 1971
Birmingham, Ala.	100	100	Ames, Iowa	90	100
Gadsen, Ala.	—[a]	98	Des Moines, Iowa	100	—
Montgomery, Ala.	100	—	Iowa City, Iowa	95	100
Tucson, Ariz.	98	—	Sioux City, Iowa	90	100
Phoenix, Ariz.	5	5	Hutchinson, Kans.	100	—
Ft. Smith, Ariz.	100	100	Wichita, Kans.	—	100
Mt. Home, Ariz.	—	100	Lexington, Ky.	100	100
Harrison, Ariz.	100	—	Louisville, Ky.	100	100
Hot Springs, Ariz.	100	—	Lafayette, La.	100	100
Pine Bluff, Ariz.	100	—	Shreveport, La.	75	—
Los Angeles, Calif.	0	0	Baltimore, Md.	100	100
Sacramento, Calif.	0	—	Silver Spring, Md.	100	—
San Diego, Calif.	2	5	Boston, Mass.	100	100
San Francisco, Calif.	0	0	Worcester, Mass.	100	—
San Mateo, Calif.	0	—	Ann Arbor, Mich.	0	—
Modesto, Calif.	—	100	Detroit, Mich.	0	—
Colorado Springs, Colo.	n.a.	90	Grand Rapids, Mich.	100	100
Denver, Colo.	—[b]	30[b]	Midland, Mich.	90	—
Hartford, Conn.	100	—	Davison, Mich.	—	80
Mystic, Conn.	100	—	Kalamazoo, Mich.	—	100
Washington, D.C.	100	—	Duluth, Minn.	100	—
Gainesville, Fla.	95	100	Minneapolis, Minn.	2	2
Tampa, Fla.	95	100	Columbus, Miss.	90	—
W. Palm Beach, Fla.	50	75	Hatiesburg, Miss.	100	—
Albany, Ga.	90	—	Kansas City, Mo.	0	—
Valdosta, Ga.	100	100	St. Louis, Mo.	0	0
Atlanta, Ga.	—	98	Billings, Mont.	50	80
Honolulu, Hawaii	n.a.	95	Norfolk, Nebr.	100	—
Alton, Ill.	90	—	Dover, N.H.	—	95
Chicago, Ill.	1	0	Merrimack, N.H.	—	100
Quincey, Ill.	100	—	Lakewood, N.J.	0	—
Indianapolis, Ind.	100	—	Basking Ridge, N.J.	—	100
Seymour, Ind.	90	—	Binghamton, N.Y.	100	100
Bloomington, Ind.	—	95	Spring Valley, N.Y.	50	—
Elkhart, Ind.	—	100	Buffalo, N.Y.	—	95

TABLE III-2 (continued)

City	Percent of Single-Family Nonunion 1969	1971	City	Percent of Single-Family Nonunion 1969	1971
Syracuse, N.Y.	—	100	Sioux Falls, S. Dak.	75	100
Charlotte, N.C.	100	100	Chattanooga, Tenn.	—	90
Goldsboro, N.C.	100	—	Austin, Tex.	100	100
Greensboro, N.C.	100	100	Beaumont, Tex.	1	0
Rocky Mt., N.C.	100	—	Dallas, Tex.	100	—
Wilkesboro, N.C.	100	—	Victoria, Tex.	100	—
Fargo, N. Dak.	—	90	Lubbock, Tex.	—	100
Canton, Ohio	97	95	Wichita Falls, Tex.	—	100
Ashtabula, Ohio	100	—	Salt Lake City, Utah	100	—
Cleveland, Ohio	5	10	Ogden, Utah	100	95
Norwalk, Ohio	100	—	Petersburg, Va.	100	—
Toledo, Ohio	0	2	Hampton, Va.	—	95
Ardmore, Okla.	—	100	Lynchburg, Va.	—	100
Stillwater, Okla.	100	—	Roanoke, Va.	—	100
Portland, Oreg.	10	—	Kennewick, Wash.	25	50
Salem, Oreg.	100	—	Seattle, Wash.	0	—
Harrisburg, Pa.	100	—	Spokane, Wash.	100	100
Cresco, Pa.	—	95	Tacoma, Wash.	10	20
Providence, R.I.	n.a.	100	Morgantown, W. Va.	—	100
Anderson, S.C.	100	—	Fond du Lac, Wis.	100	—
Columbia, S.C.	100	100	Madison, Wis.	100	—
Hartsville, S.C.	100	—	Milwaukee, Wis.	0	0
Spartansburg, S.C.	100	100	Wausau, Wis.	—	100

Source: National Association of Home Builders Labor Survey, (mimeo) 1969 and 1971.

[a] Dashes indicate no response.

[b] Our field work indicates that homebuilding in Denver is heavily nonunion. We question these figures.

cent surveys taken in 1969 and 1971. Certain features of the table merit special note. First, the cities with extensive union coverage are almost entirely limited to major metropolitan areas, although even some large cities, such as Baltimore, Boston, and Washington, are all nonunion. The few small and medium-sized cities with high union representation are mostly on the West Coast. Thus, in either the 1969 and/or the 1971 surveys, 89 of the 105 localities were reported to be at least 90 percent nonunion in single-family building.

The table also offers some clues as to what has been happening over time. Buffalo, for example, was estimated earlier by Scheuch as solidly union; there is now virtually no union representation in single-family building. The case of Boston is even more illuminating. Scheuch called the city "highly unionized;" Haber and Levinson put union strength there at 50-75 percent, noting that "while [Scheuch's characterization] is true for the city itself, a very large volume of homes is constructed in suburbs where union strength was reported to be much weaker." [10] In 1971, according to the NAHB, Boston was totally nonunion. But perhaps the more noteworthy changes are those within the table itself, covering only the short time period between 1969 and 1971. A total of thirty-five cities were surveyed in both 1969 and 1971; sixteen reported some change in single-family unionization over the two years. In all but three of these cases, involving small reductions in nonunion work in Chicago, Canton, Ohio, and Ogden, Utah, the changes were in the direction of more open shop building. Moreover, some of the increases were substantial; notice especially the figures for West Palm Beach, Fla., Billings, Mont., Sioux Falls, S.D., and Kennewick, Wash.

The NAHB surveys also verify that single-family housing is more likely to be built on a nonunion basis then is high rise apartment construction. Table III-3 summarizes the responses of executive officers in those cities where high rise and single-family building were reported to be different in terms of their respective proportions of union representation. The table also includes the single-family estimates for comparative convenience. In all but two of the twenty cases, high rise building was reported to be more unionized, and usually significantly more unionized than single-family, and in the case of Denver, our field surveys indicate that residential is both much more open shop than the NAHB reported and more open shop than high rise. It is not clear, unfortunately, whether the designation "none" means no nonunion high rise or no high rise at all. In some cities, such as Boston, it is certainly the former but in Denver it may be the latter, although our observations also question that. But for the cases where there are numerical estimates for both single-family and high rise, it seems sufficient to make the point that in the aggregate, high rise apartments tend more to be built by union workers than do single-family homes.

---

[10] Haber and Levinson, *op. cit.*, p. 36, note 11.

TABLE III-3
Unionization in High Rise Residential Building as Estimated By NAHB Local Executive Officers, Selected Cities 1969 and 1971

City	Percent High Rise Nonunion	Percent Single-Family Nonunion	Year
Birmingham, Ala.	0	100	1969
Tucson, Ariz.	10	98	1969
Colorado Springs, Colo.	70	90	1971
Denver, Colo.	50	30	1971
Gainesville, Fla.	50	100	1971
W. Palm Beach, Fla.	25	75	1971
Honolulu, Hawaii	100	95	1971
Indianapolis, Ind.	25	100	1969
Seymour, Ind.	0	90	1969
Iowa City, Iowa	0	95	1969
Wichita, Kans.	90	100	1971
Silver Spring, Md.	95	100	1969
Boston, Mass.	0	100	1969
Worcester, Mass.	0	100	1969
Davison, Mich.	20	80	1971
Billings, Mont.	0	80	1971
Basking Ridge, N.J.	10	100	1971
Binghamton, N.Y.	0	100	1969
Canton, Ohio	0	97	1969
Columbia, S.C.	80	100	1971

Source: National Association of Home Builders, Labor Surveys, 1969 and 1971 (mimeo).

There are a few further observations that need to be made about these NAHB estimates, or indeed about estimates of this kind generally, especially as they relate to the situation in very large cities. It can be observed in Table III-2 that most local NAHB officials estimated the extent of nonunion residential construction at either very close to zero or very close to complete. Reports of total unionization of single-family housing, however, may be misleading for two reasons. First, in many of these large cities the NAHB itself has contracts with the basic building trades unions. Thus, a home builder who opts to operate open shop may not be a member of the Association at all. In Detroit, for example, where unionization is reported by the NAHB to be virtually complete, a number of open shop builders belong instead to the Associated Builders and Contractors. An official of the ABC in Detroit estimates that 40 to 50 percent of residential work in the area is nonunion. In short, an estimate of 100 percent unionization by the NAHB may not fully account for builders who are not association members.

Furthermore, union contracts usually apply to a specific geographic jurisdiction in and around the central city. As suburban land becomes fully utilized, residential building may move into exurban areas outside the NAHB's territory. A good example is Cleveland, where the 1971 survey put the nonunion residential sector at 10 percent. Even if this estimate is accurate, it relates only to the city and its immediate environs. Yet an increasing amount of building, mostly nonunion, is taking place on the periphery of the metropolitan area.

On the other hand, NAHB estimates of zero union building do not always take account of the various subcontractors to whom the builder assigns work. In Houston where virtually all homebuilding is open shop, there are nevertheless one or two contractors operating who have national agreements with the Carpenters union, as will be discussed below. Also, although the builders themselves may not be signatory to any union contracts, some of them will utilize union subcontractors in many areas for one or another of the specialty functions. These specialties will vary from locality to locality and even among builders in a single locality. Thus in Buffalo, builders subcontract work to union firms in the electrical and mechanical fields; in New Hampshire to masonry contractors, and in the Detroit area to rough carpentry and drywall contractors. And, as will be detailed below, this phenomenon is not uncommon in other branches of construction.

Industrial Research Unit Survey

The Industrial Research Unit questionnaire, which was sent to principal contractor association members, but not to members of the NAHB, sought to obtain estimates from contractors as to the proportion of nonunion work performed in their localities for each sector of the industry. Not surprisingly, union respondents tended to estimate nonunion work at an appreciably lower level than did open shop respondents. In the low rise residential sector (homes, town houses, and garden apartments), however, the responses from union and open shop firms were relatively consistent, after allowing for the larger number of union respondents who declined to answer this question. Table III-4 sum-

TABLE III-4
Percent Distribution of Respondents' Estimates of the Proportion of Open Shop Work in Low Rise Residential Construction, by Region and Union Status 1974

Region	Number	DK[a] NR	0-20 Percent	21-40 Percent	41-60 Percent	61-80 Percent	81-100 Percent
Union Respondents							
Not reported	89	41.6	10.1	4.5	4.5	5.6	33.7
New England	27	22.2	3.7	0.0	0.0	14.8	59.3
Middle Atlantic	125	33.6	1.6	0.8	4.8	5.6	53.6
E.N. Central	147	33.3	12.2	6.8	3.4	8.2	36.1
W.N. Central	60	33.3	15.0	3.3	3.3	11.7	33.3
S. Atlantic	68	17.6	0.0	0.0	8.8	8.8	64.7
E.S. Central	32	31.3	6.3	6.3	0.0	0.0	56.3
W.S. Central	45	13.3	4.4	2.2	2.2	8.9	68.9
Mountain	52	38.5	7.7	5.8	7.7	7.7	32.7
Pacific	133	44.4	15.8	6.0	10.5	9.0	14.3
Total	778	33.6	8.7	4.0	5.4	7.8	40.5
Open Shop Respondents							
Not reported	83	22.9	2.4	2.4	4.8	7.2	60.2
New England	63	17.5	1.6	0.0	1.6	7.9	71.4
Middle Atlantic	134	25.4	2.2	0.7	1.5	8.2	61.9
E.N. Central	75	16.0	2.7	2.7	1.3	9.3	68.0
W.N. Central	45	24.4	4.4	4.4	0.0	2.2	64.4
S. Atlantic	220	23.7	5.0	0.9	0.9	6.4	63.2
E.S. Central	45	8.9	0.0	0.0	0.0	8.9	82.2
W.S. Central	92	20.7	1.1	0.0	3.3	2.2	72.8
Mountain	21	19.0	4.8	4.8	9.5	14.3	47.6
Pacific	6	0.0	0.0	16.7	16.7	33.3	33.3
Total	784	21.1	2.9	1.4	2.0	7.0	65.4

Source: Industrial Research Unit Questionnaire.
[a] DK/NR—Do not know or not reported.

marizes the proportion of open shop low rise residential work reported by the contractors surveyed. Since the figures in Table III-4 are somewhat distorted by the "no responses", Table III-5 is presented to indicate the proportion of those actually responding to the question who estimated open shop work in their areas at over 80 percent.

Since the union and open shop respondents do not necessarily represent the same local areas, the differences in their responses

TABLE III-5
Proportion of Those Responding to Questionnaire Who Put Open Shop Work at over 80 Percent, by Region 1974

Region	Union Respondents	Open Shop Respondents
New England	76.2	86.5
Middle Atlantic	80.7	83.0
E.N. Central	54.1	80.9
W.N. Central	50.0	85.2
S. Atlantic	78.5	82.8
E.S. Central	82.0	90.2
W.S. Central	79.5	91.8
Mountain	53.2	58.8
Pacific	25.7	50.0
Total	61.0	82.9

Source: Industrial Research Unit Questionnaire.

may reflect actual differences in open shop housing in various areas within a region, as well as conflicting perspectives between the two groups of respondents. In any event, however, the overall picture remains clear, for even the responses of union firms show low rise residential building to be predominantly the province of the open shop. With the exception of the Pacific and Mountain states, housing construction appears predominantly nonunion throughout the nation. And, with three-fifths of the responding union contractors estimating open shop building at over 80 percent, the common use of that figure as described earlier may well be an underestimation.

The level of open shop work in high rise housing construction is agreed, by both union and nonunion respondents, to be appreciably lower than in low rise building. The estimates of the two groups, however, differed markedly. The median response among union contractors was about 29 percent, compared to about 68 percent for the open shop firms. About one-quarter of the difference is attributable to the varying distributions of respondents among regions. Thus, if the nonunion respondent totals by region are applied to the union respondent percentage distribution, the resulting median response is about 39 percent. This disparity precludes making precise estimates of the nonunion share of high rise construction. It would be hazardous to say that the overall proportion is more than one-third to one-half. But even this estimate is significant in light of the unions' traditional strength in the high rise housing sector. Note again, for example, the observation of Haber and Levinson two decades ago: "In all sixteen cities surveyed in the summer of 1952, union strength in commercial, industrial, public, and semipublic work was close to 100 percent *with large apartment buildings only slightly weaker.*" [11]

The growth of open shops in residential building generally was also explored in the Industrial Research Unit questionnaire. Contractors were asked whether their current estimates of nonunion work were different from what they would have been a few years earlier. Since the responses indicated 20-point ranges (i.e., 0-20 percent, 21-40 percent, etc.), the estimates of change were tabulated in terms of the movement of ranges over this period. Thus a change to a different range may be thought to represent, on average, a movement of some 20 percentage points. Table III-6 summarizes the responses for both low rise and high rise housing construction.

The responses in Table III-6 show a significant movement, considering the brief time span involved, in the direction of more open shop activity in both low rise and high rise residential building. Perhaps most noteworthy is the substantial agreement among union and open shop respondents in terms of both the amount and direction of change. The relative propensity of open shop firms to respond "no change" in low rise building is doubtless attributable to their judgment that low rise was already overwhelmingly open shop and thus the open shop share could not rise any further. It should be especially noted that about 13 percent of all union respondents reported a significant increase in open shop apartment building. Since these projects have long been thought to be within the unions' domain, open shop penetration there would appear to signal a significant development.

ANALYSIS OF TRENDS

The historical patterns outlined in the pages above show a clear picture of declining union influence in both low rise and high rise residential construction. In the case of large apartment construction, the phenomenon is a relatively recent one. Homebuilding, however, has always had a significant nonunion component, although its size has varied over the years and among localities. Still,

[11] Haber and Levinson, *ibid.*, p. 35. Emphasis added. It will be remembered that these authors' survey covered small as well as large cities.

TABLE III-6
Respondents' Estimates of Change in Proportion of Open Shop Residential Construction Over Past Three Years, by Region and Union Status
1974

	Union								Nonunion							
			Change in Designated Range								Change in Designated Range					
Region	Total	Number Reporting Change	—3	—2	—1	+1	+2	+3	Total	Number Reporting Change	—3	—2	—1	+1	+2	+3
Low Rise Building																
New England	27	7	0	0	1	1	4	1	63	5	0	0	0	3	1	1
Middle Atlantic	125	16	0	0	3	10	1	2	134	15	1	1	2	7	4	0
E.N. Central	147	21	0	2	1	12	5	1	75	7	0	0	1	4	1	1
W.N. Central	60	6	0	0	0	3	3	0	45	2	0	0	0	2	0	0
S. Atlantic	68	21	0	0	4	13	4	0	220	13	0	0	1	7	5	0
E.S. Central	32	2	0	0	0	1	0	1	45	6	0	0	2	2	2	0
W.S. Central	45	4	0	0	0	2	2	0	92	10	0	0	1	7	0	2
Mountain	52	8	0	0	2	5	1	0	21	3	0	0	0	1	2	0
Pacific	133	18	0	1	2	7	4	4	6	2	0	0	0	1	1	0
Not reported	89	10	0	0	0	7	1	2	83	9	0	0	0	7	2	0
Total	778	113	0	3	13	61	25	11	784	72	1	1	7	41	18	4

TABLE III-6 (continued)

High Rise Building																
New England	27	9	0	0	1	4	3	1	63	13	0	0	2	6	2	3
Middle Atlantic	125	27	1	0	2	18	5	1	134	13	0	0	3	7	3	0
E.N. Central	147	18	0	1	1	11	5	0	75	11	0	0	1	5	4	1
W.N. Central	60	9	2	1	2	3	1	0	45	4	0	0	0	4	0	0
S. Atlantic	68	19	0	1	4	8	6	0	220	28	0	0	5	16	4	3
E.S. Central	32	7	0	0	0	5	1	1	45	11	0	0	1	7	1	2
W.S. Central	45	8	0	0	2	2	4	0	92	12	0	0	1	9	1	1
Mountain	52	6	0	0	1	4	0	1	21	2	0	0	0	1	0	1
Pacific	133	7	0	0	1	3	3	0	6	0	0	0	0	0	0	0
Not reported	89	9	0	0	0	7	1	1	83	11	0	0	0	7	4	0
Total	778	119	3	3	14	65	29	5	784	105	0	0	13	62	19	11

Source: Industrial Research Unit Questionnaire.

it is fair to say that whatever period or area one wishes to examine, homebuilding will be found to have a lower level of unionization than virtually any other branch of the construction industry.

Several factors contribute to the decline of unionization and its exceptionally low level in homebuilding. Residential contractors tend to be smaller than firms performing other construction work. In 1967, homebuilding establishments averaged about four employees compared to approximately nine employees for all construction.[12] Many "establishments" are one-man operations, and it is not at all unusual for a builder to subcontract all phases of the work. In Houston, for example, the average home builder has at most one or two direct employees, and many have none. This was the typical case in many cities visited. Small, inconspicuous firms are very difficult and costly for the unions to organize and police.

A related factor alluded to earlier is the growing geographic dispersion of residential building. Housing construction has moved progressively away from the centers of large cities where the unions are strongest. Few local unions have the resources to pursue hundreds or even thousands of firms scattered throughout an area of hundreds of square miles.

The small local builder can enter the business, subcontract most of his work, and compete effectively with larger firms that may have union contracts. As a result, the region becomes increasingly nonunion as it both expands in area and increases in the number of individual entrepreneurs involved. This dispersion, moreover, must be kept in mind in evaluating estimates of union strength in certain cities. Both union and industry spokesmen may assert that their "area" is completely union, but the jurisdiction involved may encompass only a portion of the applicable market.

This move from the city is illustrated by what has occurred in Denver, where such movement involves many miles of travel for anyone in center city who wants work in homebuilding. There, single-family home building is virtually all open shop, with an occasional union subcontractor or a national builder who has an agreement with the Carpenters' union. Denver has been a boom building city almost continuously since World War

---

[12] U.S. Bureau of the Census, *1967 Census of Construction Industries* (Washington, D.C.: Government Printing Office, 1970), Vol. 1, p. 26-3.

II until recently, thus reducing the interest of the unions in pursuing organization and jobs in homebuilding. Even if this interest had been high, however, the sheer cost of attempting to unionize the myriad of building contractors and subcontractors in the area involved would be enormous.

The increasing tendency of the homebuilding sector to go open shop since the Korean War is also closely related to the wage escalation in construction and the difficulties of the unions in adapting their wage policies to fit the needs of the homebuilding sector. In most areas, the industrial building scale has become much too high for the homebuilder to accept. Construction unions have recognized this in many instances and have established separate, lower rates for the homebuilding sector. Such rates in practice, however, do not work to the advantage of homebuilders. When the labor market is tight, union men gravitate toward commercial and industrial work where the wages are higher and homebuilders have difficulty obtaining needed labor; when the opposite is true, homebuilders receive a surfeit of employees whose experience in homebuilding is limited and who are dissatisfied with the compensation received.

Our interviews also revealed a strong feeling among homebuilders against the employment of personnel who traditionally were employed or trained on union commercial and industrial work. The homebuilders felt that such personnel, besides being unfamiliar with homebuilding construction techniques, were used to working at a more deliberate pace and were too insistent on observing narrow craft jurisdictional lines. Such reactions are perhaps in part merely a reflection of the very strong feeling against unions exhibited by small nonunion contractors. Moreover, the reactions indicate another reason why the homebuilding industry has trended more and more toward operating on an open shop basis. Homebuilders use their labor across craft lines, particularly having carpenters do some cement work and various incidentals in other trades which speed the ability of carpenters to do their basic job. There is just not enough of other craft work in small home construction to make employment of specialists financially viable. A literal application of union jurisdictional demarcations is considered by most homebuilders to be an impossible burden for them to bear.

Subcontractors who specialize in housing construction also tend to be smaller than their counterparts in other branches of the industry. Many are family arrangements, or small partnerships or proprietorships. In southern or western areas, or in the nonurban areas generally, such groups often farm or do other work on the side. They are paid weekly by the homebuilding contractor, with whom they have a close working arrangement, often following him in many areas and over long periods of time. They see little to be gained by unionization, indeed they often fear that to be unionized would jeopardize their work arrangements.

The subcontractors most likely to be unionized in homebuilding are those in the electrical, plumbing, or mechanical trades. Craftsmen in these trades are more likely to be trained under union conditions and nonunion firms are not as available as in carpentry, for example. Nevertheless, the homebuilding industry features a surprisingly large number of small, often one- or two-man firms in these trades who specialize in homebuilding erection and repair, and who make a very comfortable living operating on a nonunion or open shop basis. When interviewed, such subcontractors pointed to the continuity of employment and to the satisfaction of self-employment as more than compensating for their often former union status.

Especially in the South, many of the open shop subcontractors were black, or in the Southwest, Mexican-American. Some of these, under the aegis of civil rights programs or contractor association affirmative action activities, were expanding out of homebuilding to commercial building. Nearly all emphasized that discriminatory union policies had encouraged their move into homebuilding and self-employment. In the South, and in other areas as well, individual subcontractor units, including the subcontractor as well as his employees or partners, were often members of a single racial or ethnic group. This enhanced their cohesion as a working group, their interdependence, and their disinterest in seeking union membership or support.

Finally, small scale residential construction is characterized by a high degree of specialization by contractors.[13] A builder or subcontractor in housing is much less likely to do significant amounts of work outside his specialty than are firms which concentrate in other kinds of construction. The upshot is that residential builders often do not pose a direct competitive threat

---

[13] See Howard G. Foster, *Manpower in Homebuilding: A Preliminary Analysis*, Manpower and Human Resources Studies, No. 3 (Philadelphia: Industrial Research Unit, The Wharton School, University of Pennsylvania, 1974), Chapter 2.

to union standards in other sectors of the industry. To the extent that unions are content to consolidate their strength in nonresidential construction and that housing contractors do not venture into commercial or other building, the unions can afford to acquiesce in a predominantly open shop residential sector. It may offend their sensibilities, but it does not imperil their existence or compromise their power elsewhere. Large apartment building, on the other hand, is more often done by contractors who also erect commercial structures. This work, moreover, has traditionally been more apt to be located in or near large cities where union strength is concentrated, and it requires a scale of operation frequently beyond the resources and expertise of most homebuilding contractors. For these reasons, the relatively smaller penetration of open shops into apartment construction (which has been found consistently), is to be expected.

Nevertheless, the open shop is moving into the larger home structures. This began with garden type apartments of three stories or less. Such buildings do not require elevators or heavy foundation work; in both the subcontractors are highly unionized. Moreover, such apartments spread early to the suburbs and beyond.

The current boom in town house construction, again low level multiple dwellings, has aided the movement of open shop contractors into apartment building. These homes are being built in city, suburbs, and exurbia. In the Philadelphia area, for example, they are being constructed in the suburbs and outlying areas both by open shop and union contractors, but the former appear to be making considerable gains. In New York, an open shop contractor from nearby Connecticut is building a virtual new town of such residences in the previously union area of Westchester County, fifty miles from the center of Manhattan. In Denver, the open shop has captured at least one-half of all apartment construction, including high rises. In Indianapolis, open shop has all low rises (three stories and under), union shop the high rises. In Texas, where space is not at a premium, high rise apartments are found only in a few center cities, and these not in large numbers. Open shop contractors build most apartments there. Numerous other examples could be given.

Apartments today are thus being built both by predominantly commercial and industrial concerns and by homebuilders. For unions, the danger exists that more homebuilders will first move into apartment construction and then gravitate into nonresidential work, as some indeed have. Since labor used in residential and nonresidential work is interchangeable to some degree, it can, and probably does, provide a pool of manpower for open shop construction generally. Although high rise apartment construction is predominantly union, there seems to be a definite trend for a greater open shop share of the work. Low rise apartment building is already well into the open shop domain.

In periods of extensive labor surplus, the housing sector is, at least for some unions, an inviting source of job opportunities for unemployed members. In recently launching Operation CHOP (Coordinated Housing Organizing Program), the Carpenters union, which has lost the most from the erosion of union strength in homebuilding, acknowledged the growing cancer in the building trades.

> We must invade the housing construction industry's tremendous pool of nonunionism, and we must do the organizing job which is so necessary and vital to our survival. The greater the degree of organization which we accomplish in the construction industry overall, the greater the impact of our Brotherhood, its district councils and its local unions. The stronger we become, the better we will be able to secure job protection and benefits for our members.[14]

There is as yet no evidence that Operation CHOP has made any significant inroads into the housing sector.

Finally, it must be borne in mind that residential construction is not merely an appendage to the industry; in recent years it has constituted from one-third to two-fifths of all building work.[15] The preponderance of residential building, moreover, takes the form of single-family homes. The point here is that even though open shop may be concentrated in small projects, these projects in the aggregate may account for a substantial amount of expenditure and, concomitantly, a significant number of jobs. If the open shop sector had 80 percent of the residential work in 1973, it would have needed barely one quarter of nonresidential work to capture the lion's share of all construction.

---

[14] Carpenters President William Sidell, quoted in Bureau of National Affairs, *Construction Labor Report,* No. 951 (January 2, 1974), p. A-9.

[15] *Construction Review,* (April, 1974), p. 11.

NATURE OF UNION REPRESENTATION

Union strength in homebuilding today is concentrated in a few geographic areas and in isolated cities. It remains strong in the New York City metropolitan area, in the Chicago SMSA and much of Illinois, in much of Arizona, and California, in selected cities of Florida, and in several cities where unionization is strong (see Table III-2). Its strength in California and Arizona towns and cities derives from the tremendous population explosion in these areas, and the advent of large builders who have mass-produced houses. Such builders have found it advantageous to deal with unions, which, in turn, have organized other builders.

In some smaller cities, such as Peoria, Illinois, where factory workers are highly unionized, the construction unions remain strong, and also have been able to maintain a tight grip on the homebuilding labor force. Nevertheless, in many other cities which have industrialized work forces, this is not the case; e.g., Louisville, Kentucky, Midland, Michigan, or Indianapolis. There seems to be no rationale for these variations.

Likewise, New York and Chicago unions have managed to maintain a reasonably strong hold on residential construction in their suburban areas. This is not the case in the Philadelphia or Boston areas, or indeed in most other metropolitan regions.

Variations in the Nature of Union Representation

Characterizing the residential construction industry in a locality as either "union" or "nonunion" tends to obscure several intermediate situations which may exist in different areas. The extent and impact of unionization in residential labor markets varies along a spectrum. At one end, both builders and subcontractors operate under contracts with the building trades unions which are based upon, or identical to, those negotiated in other sectors of the industry. At the other end, where most areas are situated, there is virtually no union representation among either builders or subcontractors. In-between, some builders may be organized, some subcontractors may be organized, but in either case the residential work standards may differ from those in commercial building construction.

A few examples will illustrate the diverse forms of organization alluded to here. In some areas, unions in the basic trades negotiate directly with the local Home Builders Association (HBA), and builders may be bound by the terms of the agreement by virtue of their membership in the Association. In some cases the agreements provide for somewhat different conditions from those in nonresidential construction: wage rates may be lower and/or certain work rules relaxed. In other cases there are no differences; in Cleveland, for example, the contracts negotiated with the commercial employers association are applied in their entirety to members of the HBA. The homebuilders themselves are not directly represented in the bargaining process. In Detroit, the builders do participate in negotiations and one contract is executed for both residential and nonresidential contractors.

Even where negotiations do take place between a union and an HBA, not all member builders are necessarily covered. In some areas, the HBA negotiates only in behalf of those members who wish to operate on a union basis. Since residential wage rates are typically lower than those in other sectors, this arrangement generally can be maintained only if the agreement provides for a special residential rate. The agreement between the Carpenters union and the HBA in Rhode Island, for example, covers only a relatively small number of the Association's members, and provided for a lower wage rate than that negotiated by commercial contractors. Nevertheless, a survey by the Rhode Island HBA revealed that the residential rate for carpenters was still substantially higher than that actually paid by nonunion builders.

Occasionally a union may maintain a relationship with an individual builder without any formal bargaining through the HBA. In Buffalo, New York, the last agreement between the Carpenters union and the Niagara Frontier Builders Association expired in 1962. Since then, a handful of builders have operated under individual agreements with the union which provide for no special residential rate, as there had been under the old HBA agreement. The number of both employers and workers involved in this arrangement are exceedingly small, and it applies principally when the buyer specifies for his own reasons that the home be built by union workers.[16] There is no way to ascertain just how common such individual agreements are in other communities.

---

[16] Occasionally, a single home may be built by union labor under somewhat different circumstances. Some commercial contractors start out as homebuilders and are asked to erect homes by friends or customers. Again, the number of units thus built is very small.

In Houston, where homebuilding is virtually all open shop, there are, nevertheless, one or two national builders who maintain agreements with the Carpenters union. Such agreements permit the builder to utilize nonunion labor if the union cannot supply union employees, and apparently do not require unionized subcontractors or laborers. Again, it is difficult to ascertain how common such arrangements are, but they do not appear to be widespread.

CONCLUSION

The homebuilding sector is the least unionized of any construction sector. The small size of the homebuilding contractor, the movement to suburbia and exurbia, and the inability of the homebuilding sector to operate under union wages and conditions have all contributed to a twenty year trend of declining unionism. It is difficult to envision a reversal of the situation in the near future.

Multiple family dwelling construction is much more unionized, but a differentiation must be recognized between low and high rise structures. The latter require talent that is highly unionized, and the management organization that is found in the commercial and industrial sectors which commonly deals with unions. Moreover, high rises are more likely to be located in the unionized urban areas.

Low rises, on the other hand, are more analogous to family residential building and can be handled by homebuilding labor and contractors more easily. Town houses, increasingly popular today, are low rise structures which both union and open shop contractors are building. The open shop penetration of these dwellings, especially outside of cities, appears strong and may herald a still greater open shop dominance in the homebuilding sector.

CHAPTER IV

Commercial Construction

Commercial construction is a heterogeneous mix, with projects varying greatly in size, type of building, and value. The next chapter will discuss the union status in the construction of some of the largest industrial structures, such as oil refineries, chemical plants, and power generating facilities. The remaining components of the commercial sector cover a broad range. They include such diverse buildings as retail stores, warehouses, factories, office buildings, nursing homes, hospitals, shopping centers, schools and post offices. These projects may represent expenditures from a few thousand dollars to tens of millions.

There is little doubt that, both historically and presently, commercial construction is less hospitable to the incursions of the open shop contractor than residential building. The early studies described in the previous chapter all made this point. In part, the relative persistence of union strength in the commercial sector is attributable to factors of size and location. Since many of these projects represent large concentrations of job opportunities, unions have the incentive to expend effort and resources to keep them organized; and since, because of their size, they are conspicuous, it is less likely that they will escape the unions' attention. Moreover, commercial buildings, more than housing, traditionally have been in, or near, metropolitan centers where the unions' economic and political strength is greatest.

It should not be inferred, however, that union control over commercial building was once complete. Smaller structures like service stations, individual stores, small warehouses or modest professional offices are especially prone to open shop competition even in the most tightly organized locality. But is it not with the small job that the significant challenge to the union lies. It is rather the spread of open shop competition into the market for buildings in the range of several million dollars and up, which has alarmed many spokesmen for union contractors and a few union officials. One local leader of the Sheet Metal Workers union, in an unusually frank communication to the membership, entitled "The Honeymoon is Over," described it this way:

> In Syracuse they started with a 4½ million dollar Shopping Center. The Building Trades took them on and made a full scale effort to get the job switched to Union. The Trades put pickets on the project for 9 months. When injunctions were issued another Trade would proceed to picket. Unfortunately the Building Trades did not remain strong and eventually some unions even went in there to work. Needless to say, the project was completed without going too far beyond the anticipated completion date. As a matter of fact the job went so well A.B.C. went to the other side of Syracuse and built a 6½ million dollar Shopping Center and this job went that much easier. They use each completed project as advertisement and leverage to gain the next. They are presently involved in a Students Housing project on one of the Universities in the Syracuse area. The final estimate of this project will exceed 30 million dollars. You can see where it would be relatively easy for them to convince an owner to have his construction done by them especially when they have built up such an impressive track record.[1]

In a similar vein, the Iron Workers Employers Association of Washington, D.C., commented in mid-1974 in an "Open Letter to All Members of Local #5" of the International Association of Bridge, Structural and Ornamental Iron Workers:

> The total construction volume in the United States last year was 109 billion dollars. Of that total, members of the Associated Builders and Contractors, commonly called the ABC, did 45 billion. Most of you know that ABC is a strong, growing open-shop group. When you add to this the large volume of housing and other residential work done by non-union contractors not affiliated with any organization, you can quickly see that the building business in the United States is fast becoming predominantly non-union.
>
> In the Washington, D.C. area the situation is worse. Statistics prove that union construction represents a smaller percentage every year. Only the Davis-Bacon Act with its artificial price supports on government work keeps union construction alive.
>
> There are many reasons for the growth of non-union companies. Practically all of these relate to the higher cost and the lack of productivity union contractors are experiencing. Much has been said about the cost of living. Figures available from your International will show that the rate of pay for Local #5 members over the last ten years has increased twice as fast as the cost of living, even taking into account the inflation of the last year.

---

[1] Communication in authors' possession from Henry Landau, President-Business Manager, Local #83, Sheet Metal Workers International Association, Albany, New York, to membership, October 5, 1972.

> Some costs are not tied directly into wages. The recent increases in Workmens Compensation for the District of Columbia extend to Maryland and Virginia for union contractors only. The recent rate increases initiated by the insurance companies because of the increased benefits have cost companies erecting structural steel the equivalent of a raise of $1.40 per hour for every employee. This one item alone is turning more and more of your work in the suburbs to the nonunion companies because we cannot compete.[2]

The description of the Syracuse, New York, and Washington, D.C., situations could be given with change of only names and details to many areas. To be sure, union control remains very tight in most center cities, but as soon as the city limits are reached, the proportion of open shop commercial construction tends to rise. Since considerable major construction (office buildings, warehouses, shopping centers and industrial plants) has moved outside the cities, the opportunities for the open shop contractor have grown substantially.

Nearly everyone interviewed, including both union and open shop contractors, date the big jump in open shop construction in the commercial area to the construction wage inflation of the late 1960's. Prior thereto, the dispersion of living and work to suburbia and exurbia, and the growing industrialization of the South and West, permitted open shop contractors to establish themselves. But it was the high building costs of the late 1960's and early 1970's, described by the Washington, D.C., iron work contractors, that gave the open shop its big economic advantage and consequent opportunity. And as the Sheet Metal Workers' business agent's letter so vividly portrayed, each opportunity created another. A successful $200,000 job puts a contractor in a position to bid on a $500,000 one; when he completes that, he can raise his sights to $750,000 or $1,000,000; and then, perhaps double that, etc. The larger the job, the larger the capability and the better the track record to sell. With users looking for cost relief, and with a growing cost gap between union and open shop, both the size of projects and the number of projects in the commercial sector have grown substantially for the open shop contractor since 1968.

---

[2] Letter in authors' possession not dated, but obviously written in mid-1974. *The $45 billion reference is clearly hyperbole.* For analysis of Davis-Bacon impact, see Armand J. Thieblot, Jr., *The Davis-Bacon Act,* Labor Relations and Public Policy Series, Report No. 10 (Philadelphia: Industrial Research Unit, The Wharton School, University of Pennsylvania, 1975).

The previous statements would probably evoke little disagreement. Union presidents have said as much.[3] Supportive data, however, are another matter, both historically and at present. There are, nevertheless, a number of fragmentary studies, each lacking in many ways to supply proof of a trend; but when taken together the studies point decidedly to open shop gains.

EARLIER STUDIES

There have been only two earlier comprehensive efforts to gauge the magnitude of open shop activity in commercial and industrial construction; both studies were cited in the previous chapter. The 1936 U.S. Bureau of Labor Statistics survey put the proportion of union workers in nonresidential building construction at 72.2 percent.[4] The later study by Haber and Levinson offered no precise estimate, but nevertheless concluded: "there is no doubt that the strength of union organization in all branches of the industry was considerably greater in the postwar period than it had been in 1936. In 1950 union membership was approximately three times its 1936-37 level, whereas the number of persons employed in contract construction has somewhat more than doubled."[5] These same authors surveyed sixteen cities in 1952 and put commercial work at "close to 100 percent" union. Although the overall focus of their study was on the residential sector, they do not specify whether there were open shop contractors among their sources of information.

CONTRACTOR ASSOCIATION AND UNION SURVEYS

Except for the Atlanta survey and our own questionnaire, both described below, there have been no recent academic studies comparable to the Haber and Levinson one. Nor has the U.S. Bureau of Labor Statistics, or another federal government

[3] See, for example, the comments of Hunter P. Wharton, President of the Operating Engineers, and Frank Bonadio, President of the Building and Construction Trades Department, AFL-CIO, as reported in the *Construction Labor Report*, No. 865, (April 26, 1972), pp. A-13-16.

[4] Edward P. Sanford, "Wage Rates and Hours of Labor in the Building Trades," *Monthly Labor Review*, XLV (August, 1937), p. 297.

[5] William Haber and Harold M. Levinson, *Labor Relations and Productivity in the Building Trades* (Ann Arbor: Bureau of Industrial Relations, University of Michigan, 1956), p. 35.

agency, examined the extent of open shop construction, although the Bureau is now publishing a series on construction wages that includes open shop rates. There have, however, been useful attempts by contractor, union, and user groups to estimate the extent of open shop activity. Although these studies are not explicitly limited in focus to commercial construction, they are largely directed to that branch.

These studies are scattered and their results fragmentary; nevertheless, together with our field work and questionnaire, they can be put into perspective. Some of the studies amount to little more than a listing of jobs won by open shop contractors, but even these lists can serve to dispel the notion that open shop commercial construction is limited to small jobs in which the unions have little interest.

A few cautionary remarks are in order before examining the results of contractor and union surveys of open shop work. To the extent that such a survey purports to go beyond a simple listing of nonunion projects, it must attempt to gauge open shop activity in relation to some measure of the total volume of construction in an area. Obtaining comparable and meaningful measures of nonunion construction and total construction is not an easy task. A common approach is to ascertain the union status of contractors who, according to Dodge Reports [6] for an area, are awarded contracts. The problem is that coverage of construction work in these reports is not exhaustive. Smaller projects, which are more likely to be built open shop, are underrepresented. Projects which are negotiated, rather than bid, are not represented at all. There is, unfortunately, no way to know whether negotiated building contracts are more, or less, unionized than those awarded to the lowest bidder. Further, the Dodge Reports identify only prime contractors—those who are responsible directly to the purchaser—and thus complicate the task of measuring the union status of the entire job. Since the situation where a union general contractor uses open shop subcontractors is much less common than its converse, the net effect of this factor is probably to understate the aggregate magnitude of union representation in an area.

---

[6] The F. W. Dodge Company issues regular reports on the status of construction projects put out for bid. These "Dodge Reports" are made for individual localities and are a widely used source of information in the construction industry.

Another factor which must be considered is that a single large project awarded in any one year in an area can distort the area trend for that period. Consequently, if the volume of union shop projects in an area increased in one year, for example, from $300 million to $325 million, this could be the impact of just one award and not indicate any trend.

Nevertheless, Dodge Reports are widely used to develop measures of total construction activity because of their convenience. The alternative—to trace the value and the identity of the contractor for every project—is usually beyond the capacity of the individual researcher or analyst. Thus, the findings of the studies described below should be taken only as gross approximations, with due regard for the methodological and practical obstacles which stand in the way of precise and rigorous estimates.

Associated General Contractors of America

For several years questionnaires sent to its membership by the national office of the Associated General Contractors of America (AGC) have included questions relating to the union, open shop or "double-breasted" status of the contractor members. Through the courtesy of AGC national staff, the Industrial Research Unit obtained data for the years 1969 and 1973 from these surveys. It was felt that a comparison of these years would be very meaningful, since it was in this period that our field interviews indicated that the open shop sector experienced considerable growth.

The results of the AGC surveys must be evaluated with some caution for several reasons. First, the AGC does not include all general contractors within its membership, although it is the largest of all contractor groups. The AGC is, therefore, unrepresentative of all general contractors in at least two ways. Smaller firms, which are more likely to be open shop than larger outfits, are more likely to belong to the Associated Builders and Contractors, or to no association, than to the AGC. On the other hand, many very large union contractors hold membership in the National Constructors Association, although they may belong to the AGC as well. In addition, many AGC chapters make no provision for nonunion members, and even provide that all members must give the association power of attorney to negotiate for them in labor relations matters. Where such AGC chapters exist, a contractor who wishes to operate open shop will of necessity eschew membership in the AGC. These factors may well cause an understatement of the percentage of open shop contractors.

Two other caveats relate to the old story of possible response bias. The 1969 survey elicited a total of 3,044 responses; the 1973 one 5,938 responses. These numbers represent, respectively, approximately 38 percent and 72 percent of the total AGC membership in the two years covered. There is no way to assess definitely whether there was, in fact, any response bias or, indeed, what direction it might have taken. The usual plausible guess is that smaller members with meager managerial and administrative staff, will be less likely (generally) to respond to surveys, and that these firms are the ones more apt to be nonunion. If this reasoning is accurate, the effect again will be to understate open shop activity.

In addition, the much larger proportional response in 1973 could mean many things, including the possibility that open shop members of AGC, by then accorded much greater recognition in the Association, were less reluctant to state their status; or that being on the defensive, contractors operating union were anxious to assure a good response for their views. All of this is purely speculative, of course, but any such event—no matter what the cause—could possibly bias the results.

The data do, however, offer some clues as to the relative strength of the unions in commercial building among the various regions of the country, as well as to recent trends pertaining to the growth of nonunion competition. A contractor is defined as a commercial builder if he reported any volume in that category during 1969 or 1973. Data on total volume, however, are limited specifically to that work which falls within the commercial building classification. Table IV-1 summarizes the union/nonunion breakdown by individual contractors, as well as by total dollar volume. (Dollar volume data were obtained only in the 1969 survey.)

There are several noteworthy features of the findings in the table that merit mention. First, the relative percentages of dollar volume and number of contractors suggest that union contractors in 1969 worked, on average, smaller projects than their open shop counterparts. This result is at variance with every other indication of the relationship between union status and job size encountered in this study, and we can offer no explanation for it. Second, the breakdowns show the familiar pattern of union strength in the northern and western states with substantial

TABLE IV-1
Union Status of AGC Members Engaged in Commercial Building Construction, By Region, 1969 and 1973

Region	1969 Number of Contractors by Dollar Volume Percent Union	1969 Number of Contractors			1973 Number of Contractors		
		Union	Nonunion	Percent Union	Union	Nonunion	Percent Union
New England	58.7	153	34	81.8	158	74	68.1
Middle Atlantic	98.4	141	3	97.9	342	45	88.4
E. N. Central	99.4	367	11	97.1	536	47	91.9
W. N. Central	82.7	165	84	66.3	275	183	60.0
S. Atlantic	57.9	107	178	37.5	159	496	24.3
E. S. Central	20.1	78	49	61.4	80	136	37.0
W. S. Central	50.8	159	49	76.4	199	216	48.0
Mountain	98.6	108	21	83.7	169	67	71.6
Pacific	95.3	219	13	94.4	409	49	89.3
Total United States	72.2	1,497	442	77.2	2,327	1,313	63.9

Source: Associated General Contractors of America.

open shop activity in the South.[7] Finally, and perhaps most significantly, the change from 1969 to 1973 is dramatic and in the direction of a substantially greater open shop presence. (Unfortunately, the dollar volume figures for 1973 which would enable us to assess the change in greater depth are not available.) The reduction in the percentage of contractors who operate exclusively union is across-the-board, although especially marked in the South. It might also be noted that in 1973, some chapters of the AGC were just beginning to admit open shop members; the open shop membership percentages are undoubtedly affected by such organizational policies, as distinct from the actual participation of nonunion contractors in the commercial building market. Still, the bottom line is that over one-third of the association's commercial building members were open shops in 1973. A statistical bias or error cannot account for this very strong trend, especially since it conforms not only with the other data presented in this chapter, but also with our field interview findings.

General Building Contractors Association of Philadelphia, Inc.

Since 1966, the Philadelphia Builders Chapter of the AGC has compiled information on the union status of contracts awarded in the Philadelphia area. The projects covered are those reported in the Dodge Reports and valued at $50,000 or more. Table IV-2 summarizes the figures separately for the City of Philadelphia and four surrounding counties (Bucks, Chester, Delaware, and Montgomery) for the years 1966-1972. There appears to be three major conclusions to be drawn from Table IV-2, all reflecting situations or phenomena noted earlier: (1) open shop work represents a larger proportion of projects than of volume, demonstrating again that open shops operate more freely in the small job market; (2) open shop work is much greater in suburban Philadelphia than in the city itself (although it is far from dominant in the suburbs); and (3) the open shop share of all building appears to be growing in recent years.

The last point is particularly noticeable since 1970 in the outlying counties, where the proportion of open shop jobs doubled and the open shop volume of work increased by 50 percent. In the city proper, where union political and economic strength is very great, unions have, by and large, held their own. Never-

[7] For a detailed discussion of these geographic variations, see below, Chapter VII.

TABLE IV-2
Nonresidential Building Construction by Union Status
Philadelphia Area 1966-1972

	Union				Nonunion			
Year	Volume[b]	Per-Cent	Number of Jobs	Per-Cent	Volume[b]	Per-Cent	Number of Jobs	Per-Cent
Philadelphia								
1966	238.8	95.9	194	89.8	10.1	4.1	22	10.2
1967	257.5	99.0	265	94.6	2.5	1.0	15	5.4
1968	601.4	99.3	239	92.6	3.9	0.7	19	7.4
1969	329.7	93.5	236	93.3	22.9	6.5	17	6.7
1970	529.3	99.0	213	93.8	5.6	1.0	14	6.2
1971	560.4	99.6	194	94.6	2.4	0.4	11	5.4
1972	392.2	98.9	161	92.0	4.5	1.1	14	8.0
Surrounding Counties[a]								
1966	237.1	84.7	306	65.1	42.9	15.3	164	34.9
1967	188.3	88.9	232	66.3	23.4	11.1	118	33.7
1968	246.4	87.4	218	63.2	35.6	12.6	127	36.8
1969	283.2	83.9	493	76.1	54.3	16.1	155	23.9
1970	308.5	85.9	150	52.6	50.6	14.1	135	47.4
1971	335.3	81.7	126	45.8	74.9	18.3	149	54.2
1972	269.7	77.4	146	51.8	78.8	22.6	136	48.2

Source: General Building Contractors Association of Philadelphia, Inc.
[a] Bucks, Chester, Delaware, and Montgomery.
[b] In millions of dollars.

theless, in both city and surrounding counties, our field interviews indicated a higher proportion of open shop work than the analysis supported by the Dodge Reports. If all work in commercial construction could be surveyed, the open shop sector in the city would be shown to have a sizable additional percentage of the jobs in the outlying counties and somewhat more in the city. The significance both of the Philadelphia contractors' study, and of our estimate, becomes much greater if one realizes that Philadelphia is considered one of the strongest construction union cities in the nation.

Associated General Contractors, Central Ohio Division

Since 1972, the Central Ohio Division, AGC, has compiled data on the inroads of open shop contractors into the commercial construction market. It begins with the projects reported in the Dodge Reports for the Columbus area, and on a monthly basis identifies the union or nonunion status of each general contractor. The projects surveyed are purposely limited to commercial and industrial building only, so that the results would not be distorted by work (homebuilding and small apartments) which have traditionally been dominated by open shop contractors. The findings for the years 1972 through 1974 are given in Table IV-3.

The figures in Table IV-3 show a steady nonunion share of about 40 percent over the period covered (actually about 36 percent when the very large union jobs are included), a period which may well have succeeded the years of the most dramatic open shop gains. But perhaps the most significant feature of the numbers was expressed by the AGC in a communication to its members: "The alarming figures are not the Open Shop dollar totals but the drop in the number of jobs they required in 1972 to produce $130 million in contracts as compared to the much smaller number of jobs required to produce $136 million in 1974." Clearly, open shops in the Columbus area are beginning to compete effectively on the larger jobs which have long been the heart of the unions' domain.

Construction Employers Labor Relations Association (Upstate New York)

In June 1972, the New York State Building and Construction Industry held an "emergency conference" to consider, among other things, the growing threat of open shop competition. Both contractor and union representatives attended the conference, which commissioned the Construction Employers Labor Relations Association (CELRA) to conduct a study of open shop work in forty-two upstate New York counties. Open shop projects were identified through personal contact with industry leaders, and then compared with aggregate construction figures compiled on a county-by-county basis in the Dodge Report. Unfortunately, these comparisons were rendered less meaningful by the inclusion of negotiated projects in the open shop figures. As a result, the open shop volume for some counties exceeded the total construction figure compiled in the Dodge Report.

TABLE IV-3
Nonresidential Building Construction in the Columbus, Ohio Area, 1972-1974, by Union Status

	Union[a]				Nonunion			
Year	Volume[b]	Percent	Jobs	Percent	Volume[b]	Percent	Jobs	Percent
1972	190.4	59.3	276	39.4	130.5	40.7	425	60.6
1973	155.7	60.2	256	44.7	103.0	39.8	317	55.3
1974	220.1	61.7	258	48.7	136.8	38.3	272	51.3

Source: Associated General Contractors of Ohio, Central Ohio Division.
[a] Figures exclude five projects each amounting to over $20 million in order to factor out the influence of a few large jobs. The effect is to lower the union share by three or four percentage points.
[b] Volume in millions of dollars.

The study found a total of $307 million of nonresidential construction work performed on an open shop basis, $189 million of which was classified as "commercial." According to the Dodge Report, nonresidential construction in the forty-two counties totalled almost $1.6 billion. Proceeding on the assumption that 80 percent of the $972 million worth of residential building was nonunion, the Association arrived at the overall estimate of 42.5 percent as representing the open shop share of all construction. It was recognized, however, that "with respect to non-residential building, only that work which was specifically identified [as open shop] is used for comparison. This figure is accordingly very much lower than that actually being performed on a nonunion or open shop basis by several hundred million dollars." [8]

Despite its methodological weaknesses, the CELRA study provides some revealing insights into the scope of open shop competition in the commercial construction market. The survey uncovered sixty-three commercial projects valued at one million dollars or more, with nineteen of them at three million dollars or more. In much of upstate New York, the building trades unions were being challenged for jobs which are large by any standard, including a $25 million shopping mall, a $20 million dormitory, and an $11 million marina. Sizable shopping centers, nursing homes, sewage treatment plants, hotels/motels, and substantial additions to factories were widely found to be done open shop.

[8] Copy of the CELRA study results, dated April 18, 1973, in authors' possession.

And even in Buffalo, perhaps the strongest union area north of the New York suburban Westchester County, an open shop firm was awarded the initial phase, at over $10 million, of a massive sewage treatment project. Whatever the precise share of open shop activity in New York State, it is clearly not limited to the scraps of the commercial construction market, and it is obviously growing.

AGC, New Orleans

On October 16, 1974, the chairman of the Labor Committee of the Associated General Contractors of America, Inc., New Orleans Chapter, composed exclusively of union contractors, wrote the building trades unions in the New Orleans area as follows:

> From time to time we have advised you of the growing influence of open shop contractors in the New Orleans area. We would like now to furnish you with a list of jobs which have been awarded to open shop contractors in our area during the months of January through September 1974, which totals $105,097,541. The list encompasses those types of jobs or projects which have heretofore been performed by union contractors.
>
> Our contractors feel that open shop contractors have a distinct competitive advantage over them in that they, the open shop contractors, are not required to abide by the restrictive and costly conditions contained in our collective bargaining agreements. This information is being sent to you in the hope that you will recognize this situation and agree to modify the respective agreements in order to make our contractors more competitive. If the present conditions are allowed to continue, open shop contractors will eventually dominate the construction market as we have known it and union contractors will, for the most part, cease to exist.
>
> We will, of course, be delighted to discuss this subject further with you, including any of the projects contained in the enclosed list. We would like to point out that the information contained in the list was obtained by us through the reporting services which we subscribe to and, consequently, there may be other projects which have been awarded to open shop contractors of which we are not aware. We would also like to point out that the contractors included in the list were classified by your office as being primarily open shop contractors.[9]

Included in the list, which ran seventeen pages, were contracts as low as $3,000 and several over one million. The largest was a $7 million apartment development, and several were large highway jobs. The bulk, however, consisted of every imaginable

[9] Copy of letter and survey in authors' possession.

commercial construction project: offices, stores and shopping centers, alterations of existing buildings, service stations, warehouses, banks, factories, schools, college buildings, churches, etc. Our interviews in New Orleans revealed that just a few years ago, the open shop contractor could barely handle a $500,000 job. Now the limit is close to $10 million and going higher with each job.

Of interest also is the fact that the ABC chapter in New Orleans is growing at a rapid rate. A majority of those on the AGC list of successful bidders are ABC members. The New Orleans ABC chapter is also one of those with a flourishing training program.

National Environmental Systems Contractors Association (NESCA)

NESCA, a small 2,500 member organization, surveyed its members in mid-1974 and received a 45 percent response.[10] Almost 70 percent of these contractors had a gross annual volume of under one million dollars, with the largest concentration between $250,000 and $500,000. Only 8.3 percent grossed over $3 million.

Total annual volume of all NESCA contractors was estimated at $1,384,600,000, of which 44.5 percent was performed open shop, 50 percent union shop, and 5.5 percent "operating mixed shops, employing both union and non-union personnel." Unfortunately, these results were not broken down by project size. They are significant in that most of the work of NESCA is in the plumbing and mechanical areas where unions have traditionally been very strong.

IBEW, Local #58, Detroit

In mid-1974, the International Brotherhood of Electrical Workers, Local #58, which has jurisdiction over Detroit and southeastern Michigan, and the Southeastern Michigan Chapter of the National Electrical Contractors Association, made a study to determine the amount of work being done nonunion within Local #58's jurisdiction.

> Essentially, the survey consisted of examining every electrical permit issued by some 123 municipalities in our [Local #58] wage

[10] "NESCA Member Profile Study," memorandum dated September 16, 1974, in authors' possession.

area during the period May, 1973, through May, 1974. Approximately 88,000 permits were examined and classified as residential, commercial, institutional and industrial. Also it was determined whether they were drawn by union or nonunion contractors.[11]

In this period, the total electrical contracting was $249,623,500 for the area, of which $135,619,400 or 54.3 percent was classified as union, and $114,004,100, or 45.7 percent as nonunion. Local #58 broke down the data as set forth in Table IV-4.

TABLE IV-4
Building Permits by Union Status and Type of Construction Southeastern Michigan May 1973-May 1974

Number and Percent	Number of Permits Classified	Residential (Excluding homeowner)	Commercial	Industrial	Institutional
Number of permits	74,163	63,407	8,684	1,125	947
Percent union	25.3	20.2	55.1	57.7	58.2
Percent nonunion	74.7	79.8	44.9	42.3	41.8

Source: *Construction Labor Report,* No. 1000 (December 11, 1974), p. A-3.
Note: Of the 88,000 permits, only 74,163 disclosed name of company. These did, however, provide information on type of work.

In a letter to the membership, Jack Jones, Business Manager of Local #58, stated that considerable business had been lost to ABC contractors who "can guarantee a prospective customer that there will be no jurisdictional work stoppages, no strikes . . . and can generally provide his services at a substantially cheaper price." He also felt that Local #58 had "lost much small work to non-union firms that belong to no organization and we obviously lost much change-over and renovation types of work to inplant forces, some of whom are organized and some of whom are not."[12] Certainly, this penetration of more than 40 percent in commercial, industrial and institutional work in a unionized area as southeastern Michigan, and moreover, in electrical work, one of the strongest union trades, is a major penetration indeed. It is further evidence of the growth of the open shop,

[11] Letter of Jack Jones, Business Manager, Local #58, IBEW, to membership, September 23, 1974. Copy in authors' possession, and reproduced in *Construction Labor Report,* No. 1000 (December 11, 1974), p. A-3.

[12] *Ibid.* p. A-4.

even if, as discussed in Chapter VII, it does exaggerate that penetration.

ABC Membership Trend

As already noted, the key organization for open shop contractors since its incorporation in 1950 has been the Associated Builders and Contractors. Membership in the ABC, again as already noted, is open both to general and to specialty contractors and to materials suppliers and construction related personnel. The largest segment of ABC is, however, composed of general contractors engaged in commercial construction. The growth of ABC's membership, as set forth in Table IV-5, is thus another rough barometer of the growth of the open shop movement.

Table IV-5 shows that ABC's membership grew slowly in the 1950's and early 1960's, not reaching 1,000 until 1962. It then tripled by 1969, and rose to 8,000 in 1974, almost tripling again. Of special significance is that much of these latest membership gains have been in areas where union shop construction was once considered impregnable, such as San Diego, San Francisco, Kansas City, and parts of Oregon and Illinois. ABC is not strong in the South, except in Florida and the Washington, D.C. area of Virginia, and to a lesser extent, in Louisiana and Texas. The southeast areas, and particularly the Carolinas, are the least unionized areas in the construction industry. In these states, the chapters of the Associated General Contractors are likely to be dominated by the open shop and since AGC existed long before ABC, contractor loyalties have remained with AGC. The Carolinas AGC, the largest and one of the strongest AGC chapters, dominates the construction scene in those two states with a militant open shop program, and ABC has never gained a foothold there. Only in 1974 did ABC establish chapters in Alabama and Arkansas. In many other southern states where it exists, its chapters are relatively small. Thus ABC's principal gains have been in traditionally unionized areas, and its recent surge in membership is another indication of open shop expansion.

Contractor—Union Studies: Final Comment

As noted, any of the aforementioned studies standing alone would not provide definitive evidence of a trend. Yet they all

TABLE IV-5
Membership in Associated Builders and Contractors Selected Years 1951-1974

Year	Number of Members
1951	52
1952	210
1953	365
1954	500
1959	670
1961	925
1962	1,000
1969	3,080
1971	3,759
1972	5,000
1974	8,000

Source: *The Contractor*, (January, 1975).

point in the same direction. Moreover, they confirm the evidence which our field interviews invariably obtained: a growing incursion of the open shop into the commercial building sector, with increasing capability of open shop contractors to handle larger jobs each year since the mid-1960's. The studies also point to the increasing importance of the open shop in the subcontract areas of electrical iron working, plumbing and mechanical work, which have traditionally been union strongholds.

It is thus obvious that open shop contractors, although a minority, are a formidable force in commercial construction. This is reflected not only in the aforementioned studies, but in developments throughout the country. Meetings of the AGC's Open Shop Department in 1974 in such highly unionized areas as Seattle, Phoenix and San Diego, have attracted a large number of interested contractors. The ABC has established chapters in key unionized areas. In New York City, an open shop contractor won a $3 million renovation job in a federal government building, dramatizing the spread of the open shop in this type of work in the highly unionized metropolis, where in late 1974, 20 percent of the unionized construction workers were reported to be unemployed.[13] The spread of the open shop is further supported by the study made at the Georgia Institute of Technology and by the results of the Industrial Research Unit questionnaire, which are summarized below.

THE ATLANTA STUDY

Perhaps the most detailed and comprehensive study of open shop activity in one area to date was done in Atlanta by Joel H. Penick, under the direction of Professor Sherman Dallas of the Georgia Institute of Technology.[14] The study examined building permits for projects valued at $80,000 or more in the city of Atlanta over the period 1961-1972. These limitations, of course, (excluding the suburbs and small jobs generally) doubtless serve to understate the overall extent of nonunion construction. The union status of firms identified in building permits was ascertained through consultations with a nonunion contractor and an official of the local building trades council.

In a number of cases, the union status of the job could not be specified, either because the work was performed entirely by subcontractors and/or individuals unattached to the general contractor (day labor) or because the general contractor was unknown to either of the author's consultants. For the years covered, this proportion ranged between 14 and 40 percent of all jobs, accounting for 7 to 31 percent of total volume. Since the building trades council spokesman believed that most day labor work was nonunion and that contractors unknown to him were most likely open shop, Penick calculated the union-nonunion distribution with the assumption that 90 percent of the "unknown" category was open shop.

Table IV-6 summarizes the study's findings for the 1961-1972 period. With the exception of 1963 and 1972, the data show a steady increase in nonunion activity. Penick explains the 1963 jump in the open shop share of building in terms of a sharp increase in apartment construction, whose volume was about 3.5 times that of either 1961 or 1965. The 1972 increase in the union construction share was attributed to a few exceptionally

---

[13] "New York Unions Protest Open Shop," *Engineering News-Record*, (December 19, 1974), p. 19.

[14] Joel H. Penick, "Building Construction Awards in Atlanta, 1961-1972," mimeographed report prepared by Georgia Institute of Technology, Atlanta, Georgia, 1973.

TABLE IV-6
Percent Distribution of Union and Open Shop Construction in Atlanta 1961-1972

	All Projects						All Projects[a]			
	Volume			Number of Projects			Volume		Number of Projects	
Year	Union	Open Shop	Unknown	Union	Open Shop	Unknown	Union	Open Shop	Union	Open Shop
1961	73.7	19.7	6.6	59.0	27.1	13.9	74.7	25.3	60.4	39.6
1963	51.9	25.0	23.2	38.7	32.0	29.3	54.2	45.8	41.6	58.4
1965	72.8	15.7	11.5	53.4	23.3	23.3	73.9	26.1	55.7	44.3
1967	67.7	12.1	20.2	46.3	25.0	28.7	69.7	30.3	49.2	50.8
1969	57.4	13.1	29.5	40.0	27.0	33.0	60.3	39.7	43.3	56.7
1971	50.3	19.1	30.6	34.6	25.7	39.7	53.4	46.6	38.6	61.4
1972	70.9	10.9	18.3	36.2	27.1	36.7	72.7	27.3	39.9	60.1

Source: Joel H. Penick, "Building Construction Awards in Atlanta: 1961-1972," mimeographed report prepared by Georgia Institute of Technology, Atlanta, Georgia, 1973.
[a] Assumes unknown to be 90 percent nonunion.
Note: Percents may not add to 100.0 because of rounding.

large projects, including a $36 million office, hotel, and apartment complex, as well as a substantial decline in apartment construction. The years 1965-1971, however, show a substantial and steady decline in the proportion of union work. Furthermore, since this decline was somewhat more precipitous in terms of dollar volume than in number of projects, it may be suggested that during this period open shop contractors were becoming more successful in competing for larger jobs. Thus again using the assumption of 90 percent nonunion status for the unknown category, the study shows that, among projects valued at $500,000 or more, the nonunion share of jobs rose from 25.2 percent in 1965 to 53.6 percent in 1971. Even among the very largest jobs, there is a nonunion presence. Thirty percent of the $2 million and over projects (which include large apartment complexes) during all seven years of the study were nonunion, including three of the twenty-four which were valued at over $5 million.

Since much of the change in the aggregate figures is attributable to fluctuations in apartment construction, it may be useful to examine the study's breakdown by type of project. Since most of the projects whose union status was unknown may be considered nonunion, then we shall regard the specifically identified union share as reasonably representative of the total proportion of union construction. In order to neutralize the effects of major year-to-year fluctuations, we present in Table IV-7 the union share of work in each of several categories, averaged for the periods 1961-1965 and 1969-1972. Table IV-7 reveals that during the 1961-1972 period, open shop construction was far from negligible in the nonresidential commercial sector, with especially noteworthy inroads in the building of offices, warehouses, and churches. The data also reflect, again, the relatively greater nonunion influence among the smaller projects.

Inexplicably, Penick concludes that "although union contractors have been obtaining fewer jobs, they have generally maintained their dollar share of the market."[15] His own data, partially reflected in Table IV-6, appear to contradict such a conclusion. Except for what Penick himself notes to be the unusual year of 1972, his findings reveal a fairly steady decline in the union share of commercial building, even among projects valued at $500,000 or more. For smaller jobs ($80,000 to $500,000), the

[15] *Ibid.*, p. 63.

TABLE IV-7
Percent Distribution of Specified Union Share of Construction in Atlanta By Type of Project 1961-1965 and 1969-1972

	Union Share			
	1961-1965		1969-1972	
Type of Project	Volume	Projects	Volume	Projects
Office Buildings	91.8	75.0	73.8	49.5
Schools	86.3	77.8	80.7	47.4
Apartments	16.9	7.0	16.4	7.8
Hospitals/Nursing Homes	54.8	50.0 [a]	84.2 [b]	66.7
Warehouses	62.0	55.3	38.0	22.6
Churches	79.8	63.2	14.4	18.2
Retail Stores	73.8	52.9	76.9 [c]	39.4

Source: Joel H. Penick, "Building Construction Awards in Atlanta, 1961-1972," mimeographed report prepared by Georgia Institute of Technology, Atlanta, Georgia, 1973.
[b] Includes two large projects at over $10 million each, both union.
[a] Total includes only four projects.
[c] One store, built union, accounted for 60 percent of the total.

union share was virtually cut in one-half (to 26 percent in 1972), and these data do not include the predominantly open shop market below $80,000. These "small" jobs, moreover, become significant in the aggregate; in the years covered by the survey they constituted from about one-third to over one-half of all building construction. And finally, as observed earlier, the limiting of the data to Atlanta itself almost certainly serves to understate the penetration of open shop construction in the metropolitan area.

Atlanta Project Agreement

Confirmation that union contractors' share of work in the Atlanta area is declining has come from the unions themselves. In June 1974, unions affiliated with the North Georgia Building and Construction Trades Council signed a new productivity agreement calling for "the elimination of featherbedding, illegal strikes and nonworking stewards," and dealing also with "employer hiring prerogatives, overtime, safety, jurisdictional disputes and grievance procedures."[16] Previous agreements along these lines had been negotiated one year earlier covering the electrical, mechanical, plumbing, and steamfitters trades. According to the article reporting these agreements, open shop contractors were doing 10 to 30 percent of the work in Atlanta in 1973, but as high as 51 percent in mid-1974.[17] Loss of work is, of course, the key factor which induces unions to grant such concessions as were noted here.

INDUSTRIAL RESEARCH UNIT QUESTIONNAIRE

Responses to the Industrial Research Unit questionnaire corroborate the findings that the open shop is gaining in the commercial building sector, but that the union shop remains strong in most areas. Moreover, as in the case of the homebuilding sector, there were some differences and some similarities in the response of union and nonunion contractors.

Table IV-8 shows respondents' estimates of the proportion of open shop work in the commercial sector, by region and union status. Since the percentages in Table IV-8 are somewhat distorted by the inclusion of nonrespondents, Table IV-9 more accurately illustrates the disparity by showing, by union status, the proportion of those actually responding who put open shop commercial work at over 60 percent.

There are several possible explanations of the differing responses offered by union and open shop contractors. First, and perhaps most obvious, is the different perspective brought to the question by members of the two groups. They are likely to belong to different associations, have different business acquaintances, and generally travel in different circles. In short, they are more likely to be aware of work being done by contractors like themselves. Second, the respondents surely do not proportionately represent the same market areas within the broad regions. Open shop respondents from New England are more representative of the northern New England states than of the metropolitan Boston area. Open shop respondents in the Midwest are more likely to be referring to Columbus, Indianapolis and Grand Rapids, than to Chicago, Milwaukee, or Cleve-

[16] "Atlanta Building Trades Offer Productivity Agreement," *Engineering News-Record*, (June 13, 1974), p. 43.

[17] *Ibid.*

TABLE IV-8
Percent Distribution of Respondents' Estimates of the Proportion of Open Shop Work in Commercial Construction, by Region and Union Status
1974

Region	Union							Nonunion						
	Number	NR/DK[a]	0-20	21-40	41-60	61-80	81-100	Number	NR/DK[a]	0-20	21-40	41-60	61-80	81-100
Not reported	89	36.0	29.2	7.9	15.7	6.7	4.5	83	20.5	4.8	12.0	22.9	18.1	21.7
New England	27	29.6	11.1	11.1	25.9	7.4	14.8	63	11.1	1.6	7.9	31.7	30.2	17.5
Middle Atlantic	125	28.8	20.0	18.4	19.2	9.6	4.0	134	26.1	6.0	8.2	22.4	17.9	19.4
E.N. Central	147	27.9	37.4	14.3	12.9	4.1	3.4	75	13.3	4.0	17.3	25.3	22.7	17.3
W.N. Central	60	28.3	36.7	11.7	16.7	1.7	5.0	45	22.2	6.7	6.7	15.6	13.3	35.6
S. Atlantic	68	17.6	10.3	19.1	36.8	11.8	4.4	220	20.4	2.3	4.1	15.9	24.1	33.2
E.S. Central	32	15.7	18.8	12.5	37.5	9.4	6.3	45	8.9	2.2	8.9	6.7	33.3	40.0
W.S. Central	45	6.6	24.4	22.2	28.9	13.3	4.4	92	16.3	8.7	13.0	21.7	23.9	16.3
Mountain	52	34.7	34.6	9.6	9.6	11.5	0.0	21	23.8	19.0	9.5	19.0	9.5	19.0
Pacific	133	40.6	42.9	11.3	3.8	1.5	0.0	6	50.0	33.3	16.7	0.0	0.0	0.0
Total	778	29.0	29.6	13.9	17.2	6.7	3.6	784	19.2	5.0	8.9	20.0	22.1	24.7

Source: Industrial Research Unit Questionnaire.
[a] NR/DK—Do not know or not reported.
Note: Percents may not add to 100.0 because of rounding.

TABLE IV-9

Proportion of Those Responding to Questionnaire Who Put Open Shop Commercial Work at over 60 Percent by Region, 1974

Region	Union	Nonunion
New England	31.6	53.6
Middle Atlantic	19.1	50.5
E. N. Central	10.4	46.1
W. N. Central	9.3	62.8
S. Atlantic	19.7	72.0
E. S. Central	18.6	80.5
W. S. Central	19.0	48.0
Mountain	17.6	32.2
Pacific	2.5	0.0
Total	14.5	57.9

Source: Industrial Research Unit Questionnaire.

land. Third, the distribution of the two groups of respondents among regions is very different, clearly reflecting varying proportions of nonunion firms in the regional populations of contractors. If the regional distribution of union respondents is applied to the percentage estimates of nonunion activity given by nonunion respondents, the median response falls from 66 percent to 56 percent. Finally, there may have been some tendency for union and open shop contractors to interpret the question differently. In our interviews with industry spokesmen, those representing open shop firms would frequently estimate open shop activity in terms of the proportion of jobs; whereas those representing union contractors would speak in terms of total volume. Since open shop construction is still relatively more prevalent among smaller projects, these respective approaches will result in markedly differing estimates.

These factors preclude any precise conclusions as to the overall proportion of open shop commercial construction in the nation. The figures do suggest, however, that this proportion is far from negligible. In the southern states, over 59 percent of the union firms responding to this question put open shop activity at over 40 percent of all commercial building. Only in the West does commercial work appear to have resisted substantial open shop incursions into this previously strong union market, but as noted, even there, interest in the open shop appears to be growing. Both union and nonunion respondents, moreover, agree that any changes having taken place recently are in the direction of more open shop competition for commercial building work.

As noted earlier, the survey solicited respondents' views on whether the amount of open shop activity in their areas had changed over the past few years. Of all the types of construction specified on the questionnaire, the commercial sector was seen as the one having undergone the most change. Table IV-10 summarizes respondents' estimates of the change in the proportion of open shop commercial work.

As before, the change is expressed in terms of movement from one percentage range to another, with the ranges covering twenty percentage points. Eighteen percent of the union respondents believed that the open shop share had increased substantially, whereas less than 4 percent felt that the nonunion share had actually fallen. The comparable figures for nonunion respondents were 23 percent and 2.5 percent respectively. The remaining respondents estimated that there had been no change—or at least not enough of a change to move the proportion to a different percentage range.

The responses reflected in Table IV-10 are perhaps most significant in terms of the relative agreement between union and open shop contractors. Although the two groups differed markedly in their estimates of the current share of open shop commercial activity, many among them concurred in the view that there has been some appreciable increase in the penetration of open shop firms into the commercial building market, a view consistent with the findings of the studies described above. It appears, both from these studies and from our interviews with spokesmen for both union and open shop contractors, that open shops in many areas have not only consolidated and augmented their hold on the small job market, but that they have also moved increasingly into the market for larger commercial projects. When asked about the extent to which nonunion contractors have captured commercial work, a respondent will often answer in terms of a monetary cutoff point; that is, that open shops are active among jobs costing less than $1 million, but are not likely to compete for bigger projects. As already noted, however, this cutoff point appears to be rising steadily.

TABLE IV-10
Respondents' Estimates of Change in Open Shop Share of Commercial Construction over Past Few Years By Region and Union Status

Region	Total	Total Indicating Change[a]	Lower by 3	Lower by 2	Lower by 1	Higher by 1	Higher by 2	Higher by 3
Union								
New England	27	11	0	0	1	3	7	0
Middle Atlantic	125	36	0	1	5	25	5	0
E.N. Central	147	30	1	2	2	16	9	0
W.N. Central	60	10	0	1	3	5	1	0
S. Atlantic	68	23	1	0	4	12	6	0
E.S. Central	32	12	0	1	1	8	1	1
W.S. Central	45	15	1	0	2	7	4	1
Mountain	52	9	2	0	0	4	3	0
Pacific	133	8	0	0	1	5	2	0
Not reported	89	15	0	0	0	11	2	2
Total	778	169	5	5	19	96	40	4
Nonunion								
New England	63	23	0	2	1	12	7	1
Middle Atlantic	134	31	0	0	5	20	6	0
E.N. Central	75	29	0	1	3	18	6	1
W.N. Central	45	7	0	0	0	5	2	0
S. Atlantic	220	37	0	0	4	24	8	1
E.S. Central	45	20	0	0	1	15	2	2
W.S. Central	92	30	0	0	2	22	4	2
Mountain	21	5	0	0	0	3	1	1
Pacific	6	0	0	0	0	0	0	0
Not reported	83	19	0	0	1	14	3	1
Total	784	201	0	3	17	133	39	9

Source: Industrial Research Unit Questionnaire.
[a] Change expressed in terms of movement between ranges of 20 percentage points (i.e., 0-20, 21-40, etc.).

Our inquiries also suggest that open shop commercial construction is more prevalent among certain types of projects. Such structures as apartments, nursing homes, and shopping centers seem especially prone to open shop incursions, more so than in the case of office buildings or factories. Two major reasons for these differences may be postulated. First, the role of the purchaser may be significant. A governmental agency or large industrial corporation is likely to be more sensitive to economic and political pressures exerted by organized labor. Second, there is doubtlessly a connection between the location of a project and its union status. Whereas major shopping centers tend to follow residential populations toward the peripheries of metropolitan areas, large office buildings are more likely to favor central locations. As noted, in virtually every branch of construction, union strength wanes with distance from the central city.

CONCLUSION

Despite these limitations and those of other studies noted herein, it is clear that the open shop sector has been gaining in all aspects of commercial construction. This specifically includes the largest projects, which are still largely union dominated, but for which a few open shop firms have developed increasing capability. The next chapter examines the industrial sector of the industry in which these projects are found.

CHAPTER V

Industrial Construction

Large scale industrial construction of huge office buildings, major industrial plants, dams, refineries, and power plants has, at least since World War II, been the special domain of the biggest unionized construction companies, such as Bechtel, Ebasco, Lummus, Morrison, Kaiser Engineers & Constructors, and several others. The largest of these companies operate throughout the country, and often, all over the free world as well. They usually have design and engineering divisions or affiliated companies and can bid and execute a major job (for example, a nuclear power plant), from drawing board to the last construction detail. About forty of such companies are members or associate members of the National Constructors Association, have contracts that gross from $40 million to $3.5 billion, and have national agreements with all or several of the building trades unions.

Today, major industrial construction remains the stronghold of unionism, but beginning in the 1960's, the hegemony of the unions has been challenged. The challenge has come from five sources: (1) the increasing capacity of the two largest open shop contractors, Brown & Root and Daniel International, to win major industrial jobs, not only in the South where they originally rose to prominence, but elsewhere as well; (2) the growth of other open shop contractors and their capability to take on even larger jobs; (3) the industrialization of the South where large open shop contractors have long been concentrated; (4) the strength of open shop contractors in such specialties as offshore oil drilling rigs, petroleum refineries and chemical plants; and (5) the increasing willingness of large industrial users to permit open shop contractors to bid on jobs. We shall explore these causal factors as we examine the data relevant to the open shop penetration of industrial construction.

SOME INDICATIONS OF OPEN SHOP GAINS

The fact that the open shop contractors have garnered a growing and significant share of heavy industrial and commercial construction was shown in all our field interviews, and in the responses to our questionnaire. Examples of open shop gains were given in all parts of the country, with numerous ones similar to those noted in Chapter IV dealing with smaller size commercial construction. Again we must depend upon incomplete studies and our questionnaire for statistical verification, but again the data in these studies, although incomplete, all point in the same direction—important gains by the open shop sector in recent years.

The AGC Survey of 1973

In Chapter IV we examined the national Associated General Contractor's 1969 and 1973 survey to demonstrate the expansion of the open shop in the commercial (building) sector. The 1973 survey, but unfortunately not the 1969 one, had a separate tabulation for industrial construction. Table V-1 shows the results by region. Not surprisingly, the open shop penetration in industrial work—29.7 percent—is less than that in commercial—36.1 percent (Table V-1). The surprising element is that the two figures are so close, or to put it another way, that the open shop penetration in industrial is as high as it is.

On a regional basis, the industrial and commercial figures do not differ greatly. The presence or absence of a large open shop contractor or two can have a powerful impact on the regional data given the relatively small number of industrial contractors covered by the sample. Nevertheless, the data do affirm that in this key sector, the open shop is a significant factor.

The Engineering News-Record "400"

For a number of years, the *Engineering News-Record* has annually compiled a list of the 400 largest construction firms (excluding homebuilders), based upon value of contracts held. Identification of the union *vs.* open shop status of the companies on the list is difficult because there is no central clearing house for such information, and also because many companies operate "double-breasted," having both union and open shop affiliates. Thus, although Brown & Root and Daniel Interna-

TABLE V-1
Union Status of AGC Members Engaged in Industrial Construction by Region, 1973

Region	Number of Replies	Number Union	Percent Union	Number Open Shop	Percent Open Shop
New England	37	23	62.2	14	37.8
Middle Atlantic	117	103	88.0	14	12.0
E.N. Central	164	152	92.7	12	7.3
W.N. Central	84	56	66.7	28	33.3
S. Atlantic	100	25	25.0	75	75.0
E.S. Central	36	17	47.2	19	52.8
W.S. Central	76	35	46.1	41	53.9
Mountain	41	31	75.6	10	24.4
Pacific	85	78	91.8	7	8.2
Total United States	740	520	70.3	220	29.7

Source: Associated General Contractors of America.

tional are primarily (70-90 percent) open shop, they do accept jobs where the user insists they operate union. Primarily union firms, such as J. A. Jones of Charlotte, North Carolina, which had $442.7 million in contracts in 1973, or Catalytic, Inc., of Philadelphia, which had contracts of $255 million in that year, have open shop concerns. Jones's affiliate is Metric Constructors, Inc.; Catalytic's affiliate is called Amway Construction, Inc. On the other side, Brown & Root's union firm is known as Mid-Valley. Many other examples could be given.

Within these limitations we have identified the primarily open shop firms listed among the "400" for 1973, and in Table V-2, compared that list with the ones for 1972 and 1971. Not all of the open shop contractors so identified are primarily industrial constructors; some for example, are principally in the highway and heavy branch. Most of both the union and open shop ones on the "400" are, nevertheless, in the industrial group and therefore, the comparisons noted do give a good rough sketch of the open shop progress in this area.

Table V-2 shows that in 1973, thirty-one primarily open shop firms identified by the authors were listed in the "400." Of these,

TABLE V-2
Engineering News-Record "400" List
Open Shop Contractors, 1971-1973

Company Headquarters	1973		1972		1971	
	Rank	Contracts in $ millions	Rank	Contracts in $ millions	Rank	Contracts in $ millions
Brown & Root, Houston, Texas	1	4,740.4	4	1,466.8	3	1,491.5
Daniel International, Greenville, S.C.	4	1,882.8	3	1,603.8	5	888.0
J. Ray McDermott & Co., Inc., New Orleans, La.	24	452.0	9	498.7	20	346.0
H. B. Zachry Co., San Antonio, Texas	43	214.6	77	100.1	40	164.3
B. E. & K., Inc., Birmingham, Ala.	64	131.0	285	33.1		
Yeargin Construction Co., Greenville, S.C.	100	86.3	117	69.5	75	83.5
Ruscon Corp., Charleston, S.C.	123	73.0	126	64.9	94	72.2
Nello L. Teer Co., Durham, N.C.	124	72.8	217	41.4	140	51.4
Joe M. Rodgers & Assoc., Inc., Nashville, Tenn.	137	66.6	102	80.2	262	32.0
Blythe Brothers Co., Charlotte, N.C.	149	62.2	144	56.1	151	48.9
Ballenger Corp., Greenville, S.C.	164	55.1	230	39.8	108	65.0
Dickerson, Inc., Monroe, N.C.	187	49.9	182	46.7	141	51.1
McCrory-Sumwalt Construction Co., Columbia, S.C.	198	46.7	207	42.1	226	35.7
Vecellio & Grogan, Inc., Beckley, W. Va.	216	43.9	268	35.5	270	30.5
M. B. Kahn Construction Co., Columbus, S.C.	217	43.8	114	71.0	179	42.2

TABLE V-2. (continued)

Company Headquarters	1973		1972		1971	
	Rank	Contracts in $ millions	Rank	Contracts in $ millions	Rank	Contracts in $ millions
Delta Engineering Corp., Houston, Texas	223	43.2	228	39.9	384	22.1
Dargan Construction Co., Inc., Myrtle Beach, S.C.	227	42.5				
Hardaway Construction Co., Inc., Nashville, Tenn.	239	41.7	250	37.1	301	27.8
George W. Kane, Inc., Durham, N.C.	249	40.6	224	40.8	276	30.3
Allen M. Campbell Co., Tyler, Texas	303	34.5				
Thomas P. Harkins, Inc., Silver Spring, Md.	315	33.0				
Gulf Contracting Inc., Sarasota, Fla.	319	32.7				
Cianbro Corp. Pittsfield, Me.	323	32.1				
Capeletti Bros., Inc., Hialeah, Fla.	329	31.4			342	25.1
Paul N. Howard Co., Greensboro, N.C.	331	31.3	375	24.7	344	25.0
Charles E. Brohawn & Bros., Inc., Cambridge, Md.	339	30.3				
Seaward Const. Co., Inc., Portsmouth, N.H.	352	28.3	314	30.2		
The Arundel Corp., Baltimore, Md.	363	27.0	238	38.6	138	51.9
D. R. Allen & Son, Inc., Fayetteville, N.C.	375	26.2				
Demetree Builders, Orlando, Fla.	389	25.0				
N. C. Monroe Construction Co., Greensboro, N.C.	396	24.5	319	29.9		

Source: *Engineering News-Record*, (April 11, 1974), pp. 49-58; (April 12, 1973), pp. 51-67; (April 6, 1972), pp. 49-63.

twenty-five were headquartered in the South, three in Maryland, birthplace of ABC, one in West Virginia and two in New England. The significance of the South as a stronghold of the open shop and the area where open shop firms have grown with industrialization, is clearly demonstrated by this list.

Most of the open shop firms listed in Table V-2 are concentrated in the lower, or smaller end of the group, with only five having contracts over $100 million, four over $200 million, three over $400 million and two over $1 billion. These open shop contractors held almost $9 billion in contracts in 1973 (Table V-3), but $6.6 billion, or 77.5 percent of the total was accounted for by the two giants, Brown & Root and Daniel International, and 85.3 percent by the top four, the first two plus J. Ray McDermott and H. B. Zachry. The share of open shop industrial work for the top four remained relatively constant over the three year period (Table V-3), but that of the top two rose to a new high between 1972 and 1973, largely as a result of Brown & Root's big gains. This distribution of work within the large open shop contractors leads one to the conclusion that, except for the top few open shop concerns, the capability of the open shop industrial contractors to tackle the biggest jobs remains to be developed.

Comparing the three years listed on Table V-3, we find substantial increase in the volume held by open shop contractors. Examining the performance of just those contractors appearing on all three lists, we find their volume increased by almost $1 billion between 1971 and 1972, and then doubled to $8 billion the following year. The bulk of the gains, however, were registered by the two giants. Daniel doubled in size between 1971 and 1972, and advanced $200 million the following year. Biggest gainer was Brown & Root, in 1973 the country's largest contractor, which after a small decline between 1971 and 1972, jumped from $1.5 billion in 1972 to $4.7 billion in 1973, accounting for about 75 percent of the gains of all the open shop group listed in 1973. The bulk of the open shop contractors on the list seem to have remained within a fairly stable range, given the variations which can be caused by rising prices and/or the receipt, or failure to receive, a single large contract.

Table V-4 examines whether open shop contractors on the "400" list have increased their share of work faster than all "400" contractors.

The results show a substantial gain for the open shop. Whereas the value of all "400" contracts increased 52 percent during

TABLE V-3

Engineering News-Record "400" List

Distribution of Contractors Among Largest Open Shop Contractors

1971-1973

Group	1973		1972		1971	
	Contracts in $ Millions	Percent of All Open Shop Contractors on list	Contracts in $ Millions	Percent of All Open Shop Contractors on list	Contracts in $ Millions	Percent of All Open Shop Contractors on list
All Open Shop Contractors on List for Year	8,545.4	100.0	4,490.9	100.0	3,584.5	100.0
Open Shop Contractors on List for all three years	8,073.9	94.5	4,397.7	97.9	3,559.4	99.3
Largest two Open Shop Contractors[a]	6,623.2	77.5	3,070.6	68.4	2,379.5	66.4
Largest four Open Shop Contractors[b]	7,289.8	85.3	3,669.4	81.7	2,889.8	80.6

Source: Derived from Table V-2.

[a] Brown & Root and Daniel International.

[b] Brown & Root, Daniel International, J. Ray McDermott, and H. B. Zachry.

TABLE V-4

Engineering News-Record "400" List,
Amounts, Growth, and Percent of the Total Contracts
for Open Shop Contractors, 1971-1973

Group	1973		1972		1971		Growth, 1971-1973	
	Contracts in $ millions	Percent of Total	Contracts in $ millions	Percent of Total	Contracts in $ millions	Percent of Total	Amount	Percent
Total "400"	$55,600.7	100.0	40,678.9	100.0	36,600.7	100.0	19,000.0	51.9
Open shop contractors on list for year	8,545.4	15.4	4,490.9	11.0	3,584.5	9.8	4,960.9	138.4
Open shop contractors on lists all three years	8,073.9	14.5	4,397.7	10.8	3,559.4	9.7	4,514.5	126.8
Largest two open shop contractors[a]	6,623.2	11.9	3,070.6	7.5	2,379.5	6.5	4,243.7	178.3
Largest four open shop contractors[b]	7,289.8	13.1	3,669.4	9.0	2,889.8	7.9	4,400.0	152.3
Open shop contractors except largest two	1,922.2	3.5	1,420.3	3.5	1,205.0	3.3	712.2	59.5
Open shop contractors except largest four	1,255.6	2.3	821.5	2.0	694.7	1.9	560.9	80.7
Open shop contractors on list all three years except largest two	1,450.7	2.6	1,327.1	3.3	1,179.9	3.2	270.8	23.0
Open shop contractors on list all three years except largest four	784.1	1.4	728.3	1.8	669.6	1.8	114.5	17.1

Source: See Table V-2.
[a] Brown & Root and Daniel International.
[b] Brown & Root, Daniel International, J. Ray McDermott, and H. B. Zachry.

these years, open shop contracts rose 138 percent, those of the two open shop giants, 178 percent, and those of the largest four open shop contractors, 152 percent. Moreover, the gains were not concentrated at the top. If the largest two open shop contractors were excluded, the other open shop contractors showed a gain of 60 percent in value of contracts; excluding the largest four, the percentage gain is 190 percent.

Table V-4 also has tabulations comparing those open shop contractors who were on the list all three years to the total—actually an unfair comparison since this open shop group is compared to union contractors regardless of whether the latter were on the list all three years. Again the results are impressive for the open shop. Those on the list three years increased the value of their contracts 127 percent; excluding the two largest, the gain was 23 percent; and excluding the four largest, 17 percent.

In terms of the open shop share of all contractors of the "400," the 1971-1973 period saw a jump from 9.8 percent to 15.4 percent, an increase of 57 percent. The lion's share of this went to the two largest contractors; but if these two were excluded, the other open shops increased their share from 3.3 to 3.5 percent; or excluding the four largest, from 1.9 to 2.3 percent. The open shop contractors other than the four largest have a long way to go before they can compete on very large jobs, but they have made a start. A continuation of their growth will inevitably add to the competitive problems of NCA and other large union contractors.

The 1974 Engineering News-Record Data

The 1974 "400" data were published in April 1975,[1] too late to be subject to detailed analysis for this study. Brown & Root slipped to the 2 spot in 1974, although its contracts increased slightly; and Daniel fell to the 5 spot despite a billion dollar contract growth. J. Ray McDermott, however, jumped from position 24 to 12, while H. B. Zachry's position went from 43 to 44. Some open shop contractors who made the list in 1973 did not do so in 1974, but we also identified some newcomers to the list.

Fortunately, the editors of *Engineering News-Record* published their own analysis of open shop participation in their list between 1970 and 1974:

[1] *Engineering News-Record,* (April 10, 1975), pp. 52-67.

> The number of open shop contractors on The ENR 400 has increased from 19% of 300 contractors responding to the question in 1970 to 31% of 264 respondents in 1974. Of the total 57 open shop contractors in 1970, 22 or 39% were only open shop and 61% reported they did some portion of their work on an open shop basis. Last year [1973], the 82 contractors doing some or all of their work open shop was split into 35% working solely open shop and 65% or 53 companies that do only some part of their work open shop.
>
> More than three quarters of the exclusively open shop contractors are in the South, and among The ENR 400 there are none that say they work only open shop in the far western states. Of the 53 open shop companies that do some of their work using union labor, 22 do so through a separate operating unit, and 11 of the 53 do at least 50% of their work on an open shop basis.
>
> Geographically, the 82 contractors on the 400 that work open shop are divided as follows: New England, 5; Middle Atlantic, 7; Midwest, 9; South, 37; Mississippi to the Rockies, 18; and Far West, 6.[2]

This analysis confirms the continued growth of open shop activity among the largest contractors, as well as the geographic dispersion of open shop strength which we shall examine in detail in Chapter VII.

The NCA Data

Since 1961, the National Constructors Association (NCA) has examined the extent to which open shop contractors have won contracts which this Association believes would otherwise have gone to NCA members. The NCA data, which are set forth in Table V-5, show a steady rise between 1961 and 1972 in number of jobs and listed dollar volume (and listed dollar volume can be much less than actual) of work which the NCA believed would ordinarily, or in the past, be done by its members, but which instead went open shop. To be sure, the great bulk of these jobs were in the Gulf Coast or southeast regions where the open shop is dominant and where, as we have just found, the largest open shop contractors are mostly concentrated. Yet this decade saw also a slow but steady increase of large open shop jobs elsewhere.

The data for 1971-1973, which seem to indicate a lessening of the open shop incursions into these once union controlled major projects, need to be interpreted with caution. The NCA data

---

[2] *Ibid.*, pp. 52-53.

TABLE V-5

National Constructors Association
Survey of Jobs Lost by NCA Members to Open Shop by Project Type and Region[a]
1961-1973

Period	Number of Jobs Lost	Dollar Volume (in $ billions) of Jobs Lost (when listed)[b]	Types of Projects Lost			Projects Lost by Region					
			Petro-Chemical	Power Plant	Other	East Coast	Great Lakes	Mid-continent	Gulf Coast	South-east	West Coast
1961-1963	75	$1.4	40	3-5	32	1	3	1	33	36	1
1963-1965	90	$2.5	54	5	31	2	3	2	40	40	3
1965-1967	100	$4.2	63	12	25	1	2	2	48	43	4
1967-1969	150	$7.6	72	37	41	1	3	2	92	47	5
1969-1971	181	$8.5	97	37	47	4	3	4	98	65	7
1971-1973[c]	78	$7.2	22	25[d]	31	2	6	4	37	24	3

Source: National Constructors Association.

[a] Regions are defined as follows:

East Coast: New England states, New York (east of Rochester), Pennsylvania (Altoona and East), Delaware, Maryland, and District of Columbia.

Great Lakes: Balance of New York and Pennsylvania, Ohio, Kentucky, Indiana, Illinois, Wisconsin, Minnesota, Michigan, and West Virginia.

Mid-Continent: Montana, Wyoming, North Dakota, South Dakota, Colorado, Iowa, Missouri, Kansas, Nebraska.

Gulf Coast: Texas, Oklahoma, Arkansas, Louisiana, and Mississippi.

Southeast: Florida, Georgia, South Carolina, North Carolina, Tennessee, Alabama, Virginia.

West Coast: Washington, Oregon, California, Idaho, Nevada, Utah, Arizona, New Mexico, Hawaii, and Alaska.

[b] If all job volumes were listed, the amounts would obviously be much larger.

[c] Incomplete data.

[d] Includes 6 nuclear power plants.

for this period were marked "preliminary" and did not include all projects. In addition, during this time, large open shop contractors were in many cases so extended by increased business that they were turning down some jobs. Union contractors had a temporary respite in cost escalation by the 1971-1973 wage-price freeze and preceding restraints on construction wage increases. Although the largest open shop contractors have remained overburdened with excess business opportunities, our field work, supported by communications both with NCA and major open shop contractors, indicates that the latter had continued to expand and increase their market share through 1974. This, of course, is further supplemented by the *Engineering News-Record* "400" data.

As the NCA data show, a major source of the open shop incursion into large industrial projects has occurred in the construction of petroleum refineries, chemical and petro-chemical plants, and additions and/or modifications thereto. Because the Gulf Coast area has been historically open shop, and because of the prevalence and great growth of the industries there, open shop contractors have been able to develop and to expand their capabilities in this area; and to take work, not only in this field, but in other industrial construction applications, or to expand their work into other geographic areas. Such companies include, of course, first and foremost Brown & Root, but also H. B. Zachry, the Hudson Engineering Division of J. Ray McDermott, Delta Engineering, and many not on the *Engineering News-Record* "400" list.

The increased capability of such companies, combined with sharply increased wages in the union sector, as discussed in Chapter XI, has induced a number of major chemical and petroleum concerns to reexamine their construction policies and to give serious consideration to utilizing open shop contractors. In one specialty area, offshore oil rig and platform construction, one company, J. Ray McDermott of New Orleans, the already noted third largest open shop contractor, has a commanding position operating not only in the Gulf Coast but all over the world. It has constructed its own shipyard; and by purchasing Hudson Engineering of Houston, the company is now a strong factor in chemical process plant construction as well. It operates strictly open shop.

The Houston Area Data

The strength of the open shop in large industrial construction in the Gulf Coast area, as well as some problems faced by open shop contractors, are well illustrated by the Houston area situation. A survey (as of June 14, 1974), was made by the Employers' Council of the Houston Gulf Coast Area, a users' group. The survey covered not only Houston, but such contiguous locations as Baytown, Freeport and Texas City. Forty-two chemical and petroleum companies and company divisions were included in the study, and requested to list the number of employees working on contract construction and contract maintenance. The survey found that the construction work force on projects under construction for these companies numbered 11,694, of whom 6,853 (or 59 percent) were employed under open shop conditions; and 4,841 (or 41 percent) under union shop conditions. In contract maintenance for these firms, of 5,261 then on the jobs, 3,695 (or 70 percent) were under the open shop, 1,566 (or 30 percent), union shop.[3]

A contractor association official in Houston told one of the authors that the open shop percentage, particularly on new construction in Houston, would have been larger if the open shop firms could have stretched their resources further. He pointed out a number of specific jobs on which open shop contractors had declined to bid because of managerial and manpower shortages, and expressed the belief that the NCA national constructors would increase the union share of work in the area because of the open shop limitations.[4] This, of course, emphasizes a problem of the open shop contractors to which we shall return several times. Nevertheless, in Houston today, large union shop contractors now have flourishing "double-breasted" open shop concerns, which are growing and which can be expected to expand the open share in the long run, if present trends continue.

The DuPont Shift

E. I. du Pont de Nemours & Company, the largest chemical concern in the United States, for many years operated its own construction company. During World War II, DuPont went union

---

[3] "Houston Gulf Coast Business Roundtable Manpower Survey" August 27, 1974. Copy in authors' possession.

[4] Based on a series of personal and telephone interviews, July 1973-January 1975.

in construction and continued to operate on a union basis until the early 1970's. DuPont did not sign union contracts, but entered into verbal agreements with some unions, and operated through subcontractors with others. The jobs, no matter how they were handled, were strictly union. Engineering and design was done by DuPont; and the labor, except that of subcontractors, was put directly on DuPont payrolls. Construction labor received all union benefits plus company benefits.[5]

By 1970, DuPont felt that its costs and productivity were so out of line that significant changes were required. It gradually withdrew from direct employment of construction labor, and then began awarding contracts in some areas to three open shop contractors, Brown & Root, Daniel International, and H. B. Zachry. By late 1974, about 50 percent of DuPont's huge construction jobs—employing approximately 10,000 employees—were on an open shop basis. This, of course, has meant a major gain for the industrial sector of the open shop, and has encouraged other chemical companies to move in the same direction. The nearly 350 chemical plants lost to NCA contractors between 1961 and 1973, as shown in Table V-5, are indicative of shifts by DuPont and other concerns.

The Edison Electric Institute Study and Public Utility Construction

Power plant construction, and particularly, the building of nuclear power plants, requires the largest and most sophisticated work of the big industrial contractor. In recent years, the top two open shop contractors, Brown & Root and Daniel International, have been major forces in this work. H. B. Zachry has entered the field and won several contracts. A few other open shop contractors are attempting to gain entrance, and one company, Duke Power, has developed its own work force for the job. Another company, Dayton Power and Light, has its own construction subsidiary. Table V-5 above shows that NCA contractors lost about 120 public utility jobs to open shop contractors between 1961 and 1963, of which six were nuclear facilities.

---

[5] This section is based upon talks by Trumbull Blake, Director, Construction Division, E. I. du Pont de Nemours & Company before the Associated Builders and Contractors convention, Freeport, Grand Bahamas, November 9, 1973, and before the Business Roundtable Conference, St. Louis, November 14, 1974, and upon personal interviews.

In the first quarter of 1973, the Construction Problems Subcommittee of the Industrial Relations Division, Edison Electric Institute,[6] completed a survey that indicated the degree of union and open shop in construction for new powerhouses, transmission and distribution facilities. Table V-6 summarizes the results of this study.

As usual, a number of cautionary points must be made in evaluating the data. The questionnaire responses were not always clear on the degree of open shop; hence we placed the category where most of the work was done ignoring minor variations. Second, in the transmission and distribution area, many in-house forces are unionized, some are nonunion and often they are both. Moreover, some of the work could be overhaul and maintenance, not new construction. On the other hand, the construction of power plants by in-house forces on the part of a southern utility undoubtedly refers to Duke Power, which is unique in that its forces have the capacity to build nuclear power plants.

By the first quarter of 1973, open shop concerns were being used to build, according to the Edison Electric survey, only six facilities: five in the South and one unidentified; plus the Duke Power arrangement. In addition nine utilities were utilizing open shop contractors on transmission and distribution construction, and others, like Duke Power, were utilizing nonunion in-house forces for this work.

The Midwest utility, reported in Table V-6 as using in-house personnel for construction facilities, is probably Dayton Power and Light. The company established a special subsidiary, UCON, Inc., to handle its construction "more efficiently, with better productivity and obviously at a lower cost . . . to better meet our construction schedules, which formerly were not met by most contractors except at extreme cost and the utmost pressure by us."[7] UCON at first signed a contract with the Utility Workers Union, AFL-CIO, which represents Dayton Power and Light's operating employees. But under pressure from the building trades unions supported by the AFL-CIO, the Utility Workers withdrew and were replaced by an independent union. The AFL-

---

[6] The Edison Electric Institute is the trade association of the electric power utilities.

[7] The information on UCON, Inc., is based on a talk by Lawrence J. Renas, Vice-President, Construction Management, Dayton Power and Light Company, Business Roundtable Conference, St. Louis, November 14, 1974.

TABLE V-6

Edison Electric Institute Power Facility Construction Survey by Facility Type, Union Status and Region, [a] *1973*

	Power Plants				Transmission and Distribution			
		Type of Labor				Type of Labor		
Region	Number of Responses	Union	Open Shop	In-house Forces [b]	Number of Responses	Union	Open Shop	In-house Forces [b]
United States	87	79	6	2	89	26	9	54
New England	2	2			4	1	1	2
Middle Atlantic	15	15			15	3	1	11
Midwest	28	27		1	27	11		16
South	28	22	5	1	26	5	6	15
West	12	12			14	4		10
Unidentified	2	1	1		3	2	1	

Source: Edison Electric Institute, Industrial Relations Division, Construction Problems Subcommittee.

[a] Regions are defined as follows:
New England: Maine, New Hampshire, Massachusetts, Connecticut, and Rhode Island.
Middle Atlantic: New York, New Jersey, and Pennsylvania.
Midwest: Ohio, Indiana, Michigan, Illinois, Iowa, Wisconsin, Minnesota, Kansas, Missouri, and West Virginia.
South: Virginia, North Carolina, South Carolina, Georgia, Florida, Arkansas, Kentucky, Mississippi, Texas, and Oklahoma.
West: California, Washington, Oregon, Montana, Idaho, Utah, Nevada, Colorado and New Mexico.

[b] In-house forces are either union, nonunion or some of each.

CIO building trades' unions are attempting to organize UNCON's employees, offering each worker membership in the craft union of his work. Meanwhile the company is proceeding with its plans to construct a fossil power plant (coal, oil or gas burning), with the labor of its UCON subsidiary.

Duke Power Company, operating in the Piedmont of North and South Carolina, has had its in-house construction division since 1925. In the construction of fossil power plants, it utilizes its own forces plus those of contractors. The latter are generally specialty types, particular boiler installation, high pressure piping, heat insulation, etc., all of which they usually purchase from major suppliers on an erected basis. Generally Duke Power attempts to maintain stable employment, and its use of contractors is also geared to that objective. Contractor labor utilized, as described here, has usually been union.[8]

When Duke Power went into nuclear power, it decided to eliminate contract labor because of the rising costs, and the problems beginning to develop over jurisdiction and work rules. Since Duke Power has its own design and engineering departments, it was felt that company labor would be able to provide better integration with engineering. Two nuclear plants were in operation in early 1974, eleven more are in progress. The construction force numbered 5,000, in addition to 550 engineers and designers.

Several other utility companies have in-house construction forces, but they do not take on the major projects, that is, power plant construction. For example, Pennsylvania Power and Light does its own construction, except power plants and large office buildings, with an in-house company which it purchased soon after it was formed by the consolidation of many small companies. The employees of this company are represented by an independent union. Arizona Public Service Company's in-house force is similar, but it is unionized by the AFL-CIO construction trades.

Overall, the Edison Electric Institute survey shows that open shop construction has made some gains, but power plant building remains overwhelmingly the province of the major union shop contractors, most of whom are members of NCA. There is, however, reason to believe that this survey understates open shop penetration. Table V-5, based on NCA data, lists 120

---

[8] This section is based on interviews with Duke Power personnel, Charlotte, North Carolina, February 7, 1974.

power plant jobs lost to NCA contractors in 12 years including 25 for 1971-1973 when only partial data were available. It does not appear likely that all of these were in the South. In addition, the authors know that power plants are being constructed in the Rocky Mountain area and in the Midwest on an open shop basis. These facilities may have been begun after the Edison Electric survey.

It is, of course, still true that the construction of power plants remains very heavily within the union purview. The open shop sector has made gains, but more open shop contractors in addition to Brown & Root, Daniel International, and H. B. Zachry will have to achieve the capability of building these projects before the open shop sector can accomplish a major increase in its share of such work.

The Industrial Research Unit Questionnaire

Responses to the Industrial Research Unit questionnaire again support the findings that open shop contractors have made gains in the industrial sector, and also confirm the strength of the union shop in this sector. As was the case with commercial construction, there were also some differences and some similarities in the responses of union and nonunion contractors. Table V-7 sets forth the responses.

Not surprisingly once more, the open shop contractors believe, for reasons already set forth, that their own constituency is larger than the union shop contractors, and vice versa. Within each region, there are both agreements and major discrepancies in their answers. But again the responses demonstrate the surprisingly strong showing of open shop contractors in this sector, even though the nonunion contractors themselves acknowledge less impact in the industrial sector than in commercial or residential.

As in the case of residential and commercial construction, we asked respondents to the Industrial Research Unit questionnaire whether they believed that the open shop penetration was changing; and if so, to express their idea of that change between ranges of 20 percentage points. Table V-8 summarizes the results of this inquiry divided among union and nonunion respondents.

TABLE V-7
Percent Distribution of Respondents' Estimates of the Proportion of Open Shop Work in Industrial Construction by Region and Union Status

Region	Number	NR/DK[a]	0-20	21-40	41-60	61-80	81-100
Union							
Not reported	89	42.7	36.0	9.0	6.7	1.1	4.5
New England	27	29.6	37.0	7.4	7.4	11.1	7.4
Middle Atlantic	125	31.2	36.8	14.4	10.4	3.2	4.0
E. N. Central	147	26.5	53.7	8.2	4.8	2.7	4.1
W. N. Central	60	30.0	41.7	11.7	6.7	5.0	5.0
S. Atlantic	68	25.0	33.8	17.6	14.7	2.9	5.9
E. S. Central	32	18.8	28.1	25.0	9.4	9.4	9.4
W. S. Central	45	22.3	46.7	13.3	11.1	2.2	4.4
Mountain	52	36.6	44.2	5.8	1.9	5.8	5.8
Pacific	133	43.6	50.4	3.0	1.5	0.0	1.5
Total	778	32.4	43.1	10.3	6.8	3.1	4.4
Nonunion							
Not reported	83	33.7	16.9	8.4	16.9	18.1	6.0
New England	63	20.6	12.7	15.9	23.8	19.0	7.9
Middle Atlantic	134	32.8	16.4	14.2	11.9	12.7	11.9
E. N. Central	75	17.3	24.0	21.3	10.7	17.3	9.3
W. N. Central	45	35.5	13.3	11.1	8.9	11.1	20.0
S. Atlantic	220	33.6	9.1	8.6	14.5	13.2	20.9
E. S. Central	45	8.9	11.1	13.3	15.6	24.4	26.7
W. S. Central	92	23.9	21.7	17.4	17.4	12.0	7.6
Mountain	21	28.6	28.6	4.8	28.6	0.0	9.5
Pacific	6	50.0	33.3	16.7	0.0	0.0	0.0
Total	784	28.4	15.4	12.8	15.1	14.4	13.9

Source: Industrial Research Unit Questionnaire.
[a] NR/DK—Do not know or not reported.

TABLE V-8
Respondents' Estimates of Change in Open Shop Share of Industrial Construction Over Past Few Years by Region and Union Status

Region	Total	Total Indicating Change[a]	Lower by 3	Lower by 2	Lower by 1	Higher by 1	Higher by 2	Higher by 3
Union								
New England	27	5	0	0	0	3	2	0
Middle Atlantic	125	23	0	0	4	17	2	0
E. N. Central	147	11	1	0	1	9	0	0
W. N. Central	60	8	1	1	1	3	1	1
S. Atlantic	68	13	1	1	2	6	3	0
E. S. Central	32	8	0	1	0	4	2	1
W. S. Central	45	5	1	0	1	2	0	1
Mountain	52	4	0	0	0	4	0	0
Pacific	133	7	0	1	0	3	3	0
Not reported	89	8	0	0	1	5	1	1
Total	778	92	4	4	10	56	14	4

TABLE V-8. (continued)

Region	Total	Total Indicating Change[a]	Lower by 3	Lower by 2	Lower by 1	Higher by 1	Higher by 2	Higher by 3
Nonunion								
New England	63	20	0	1	1	10	5	3
Middle Atlantic	134	24	0	0	7	15	2	0
E. N. Central	75	21	0	0	2	15	2	2
W. N. Central	45	3	0	0	0	3	0	0
S. Atlantic	220	30	2	1	5	15	6	1
E. S. Central	45	17	0	0	1	11	2	3
W. S. Central	92	26	1	1	1	17	5	1
Mountain	21	4	1	0	0	2	0	1
Pacific	6	0	0	0	0	0	0	0
Not reported	83	13	0	0	2	8	3	0
Total	784	158	4	3	19	96	25	11

Source: Industrial Research Unit Questionnaire.
[a] Change expressed in terms of movement between ranges of 20 percentage points (i.e., 0-20, 21-40, etc.).

Not surprisingly, more open shop contractors believed that the open shop was gaining than did union contractors, and felt also that the gain was somewhat greater. Nevertheless, we again find surprising agreement that the open shop is gaining, in this case not greatly (up to 20 percent) by most of both groups who thought it is gaining, and 21-40 percent by about one-fourth as many respondents of both categories. Significantly, only 8 union and 7 nonunion respondents of a total of 1,562 believed that open shop industrial construction was losing ground.

Thus, despite different geographic concentrations and certainly different locations within geographic areas, it appears that the respondents to our questionnaire, both union and open shop, support the general findings in this section of this chapter—that open shop contractors have made important inroads into industrial construction, but that union firms still dominate this sector.

CONCLUSION

The major source of strength of the construction unions is, and always has been, the erection of commercial and industrial buildings and structures. Now for the first time since World War II, these unions and the unionized builders have serious competition in these sectors of the industry. Open shop firms are gaining strength, and the larger ones are growing faster than their unionized counterparts. If this trend continues, the capacity of more open shop firms to build larger, and more sophisticated structures will be enhanced. The result will be greater penetration on their part, not only into commercial but also into industrial building, at the expense of the unionized sector.

CHAPTER VI

Highway And Heavy Construction

Highway and heavy construction activities are generally considered together because of the similarity of the equipment, labor, and methods of work. Highway construction is, of course, self-explanatory. It involves the construction of roads, which includes earth moving and site preparation, concrete, asphalt, or other road material laying; and often the construction of bridges, tunnels, or other accesses through, under, over, and around natural and man-made obstacles. Heavy work includes site preparation for large construction projects, the building of dams, airports, underground facilities, missile sites, etc.

Both highway and heavy work requires large numbers of heavy equipment and truck drivers and laborers, some carpenters, plus iron workers, electricians, and other crafts for special jobs. Where the work is unionized, the largest craft is the Operating Engineers International Union, representing the equipment operators and the oilers or helpers, with the Laborers' Union and the Teamsters also well represented. Carpenters are involved for form and related work, and iron workers may be used for rod setting. Special contractors are likely to perform bridge, tunnel, electrical, and sewer work and have agreements with specialty crafts.

Open shop contractors organize their labor quite differently. Oilers are not utilized. Equipment operators are expected to lubricate their own machines, assisted where necessary by laborers. Laborers work up to helper, and then to operating smaller machines or trucks; and if qualified, they continue up the ladder to the larger equipment. Laborers, or those upgraded to helper, do much of the form work under supervisors or lead carpenters. Laborers and helpers do the rod setting work, and assist journeymen in the other crafts. As in commercial construction, the labor force is compensated over a wide range within a smaller number of classifications, and journeymen are not employed to do unskilled or semiskilled work—for example, rod setting or very rough carpentry.

FACTORS AFFECTING THE EXTENT OF OPEN SHOP

Before we attempt to analyze the degree and nature of open shop competition in highway and heavy construction, it is necessary to recognize explicitly certain salient features of that sector of the industry. Some features work toward greater open shop penetration, while others serve to neutralize what might place the union contractor at a disadvantage. In the first place, unlike most residential and commercial work, much highway construction is performed away from major centers of population. As we have noted before, union strength tends, on the whole, to wane with distance from the metropolitan areas. Thus, the construction of highways, especially new highways connecting metropolitan areas rather than serving any one of them, might be expected (other things equal) to represent a particularly attractive market for the nonunion contractor.

On the other hand, the very remoteness of these projects raises questions about the ability of open shop contractors to man them. As we have noted earlier, the union contractor has historically had an advantage in his ready access to large pools of manpower which can be assembled by the unions on relatively short notice from many distant areas. Without this extensive network of contacts with different labor markets, the open shop contractor must: rely on less systematic means of recruitment; or seek to maintain a steady work force willing to travel; or (actually most common) some combination of the two. Moreover, the task of maintaining a steady work force is difficult for highway contractors because of the extreme seasonality of the work in colder climates.

The problem is to some degree abated in highway construction by the relatively heavy reliance in that sector on unskilled and semiskilled labor. Against the standards of the construction industry as a whole, highway projects typically employ a disproportionate number of laborers, helpers, truck drivers, and operators of small equipment.[1] Even within the skilled ranks,

[1] U.S. Bureau of Labor Statistics, *Labor and Materials Requirements for Construction of Federally Aided Highways, 1958-1961, and 1964*, Report No. 299 (Washington, D.C.: Government Printing Office, 1966), p. 7. Compare with data shown in Table II-1.

moreover, there are many jobs (such as cement masonry and concrete form building) which require less skill and training than others (such as electrical and mechanical work). These are more predominant in building construction. Wages for unskilled labor on highway work are substantially higher than those for unskilled labor in other industries (owing in part, as we shall see later, to the effects of the Davis-Bacon Act and similar state prevailing wage laws); and it is presumably easier to recruit unskilled workers than trained craftsmen. Because of these wage and recruitment factors, the open shop highway contractor often finds it less troublesome to assemble a crew capable of performing the work, compared with his open shop counterparts operating in the commercial sector.

Davis-Bacon Impact

Another important feature of highway construction is that it is virtually all publicly financed, and much of it is supported by the Federal Highway Administration. As a consequence contractors are subject to the provisions of the Davis-Bacon Act, or other prevailing wage statutes which require that employers pay the equivalent of union wages. The exception is those areas, such as Texas or the Carolinas, where open shop contractors are represented by a vigilant association that regularly provides irrefutable wage surveys to the administrators of these laws.[2] Indeed, in no segment of the industry is the Davis-Bacon Act more significant in maintaining union power. This was recognized early by the construction unions, particularly the Operating Engineers, and they have utilized it to the full, even employing a former U.S. Department of Labor staff member, previously involved in Davis-Bacon administration, to coordinate their organizing activities.[3] According to the historian of the Operating Engineers, Professor Garth L. Mangum:

> The major organizing tools were federal prevailing wage laws. The procedure was to approach a contractor with whom one or more of the unions already had contractual relationships, usually either an interstate contractor or one who was also engaged in building work. Here the engineers took the lead because the scar-

[2] See, in general, Armand J. Thieblot, Jr., *The Davis-Bacon Act,* Labor Relations and Public Policy Series, Report No. 10 (Philadelphia: Industrial Research Unit, The Wharton School, University of Pennsylvania, 1975).

[3] Garth L. Mangum, *The Operating Engineers: The Economic History of a Trade Union,* Werthering Publications in Industrial Relations (Cambridge: Harvard University Press, 1964), p. 257.

> city of skilled operators often brought them into contractual relationships before the other crafts. Laborers and truck drivers could be obtained where operating engineers could not. The state committee would agree to whatever concessions were necessary to allow the union contractor to become successful bidder on a heavy or highway project. These agreements also promised no stoppages.
>
> The Davis-Bacon Act provides that a wage rate common to the majority of the employees in a particular classification in an area (or 30 per cent if there is not a majority paid at the same rate) shall be determined as the prevailing rate which all in that classification must be paid. This being the case, once the Joint Heavy and Highway Construction committee was successful in signing the employers of a majority of the members of their crafts in an area, they could appeal to the Department of Labor and have those wage agreements become binding upon all other employers upon construction projects in which the federal government was involved. The unions then suggested that the contractors form a statewide association, if they had not already done so, and bargain as a group. Whatever wages were negotiated became the prevailing rate, and, since the contractors were more interested in relative than absolute costs as long as they were established in advance of the bidding, rates could be increased to a level more acceptable to the union member.
>
> Once the union scale became prevailing, there were advantages to using the union as a labor supply source which usually brought in the nonunion contractor. If not, interrelations between union and nonunion contractors could be used as a lever for organization. The familiar pattern of persuading a union contractor to break off relations with a nonunion subcontractor is well known. An example of a more direct technique was one case where union engineers refused to hoist some quick-drying concrete which a nonunion subcontractor was attempting to pour.[4]

This same author gives the Davis-Bacon Act substantial credit for unionizing much of the nation's highway work which prior to the establishment of the federal program in the early 1950's was substantially open shop.[5] Thus, he states that "Heavy and highway construction were reasonably well organized in twenty states by 1954. By 1958, four more which had been partially organized and four more which had little or no organization in 1954 were well organized. Seven had progressed from little or no organization to partial organization. Little progress was made in the other thirteen states." [6]

---

[4] *Ibid.,* pp. 257-258.

[5] There are apparently no early studies of the degree of unionism in highway work such as we cited in the chapters on homebuilding, commercial, and industrial construction.

[6] Mangum, *op. cit.,* p. 258.

The Mangum book carries the story of the Operating Engineers to 1958. Since then the Davis-Bacon Act has continued to aid the unions in maintaining a strong position in highway construction, as the Thieblot volume makes clear.[7] In heavy construction, the situation is similar since much of the work either is federally funded and thereby covered by the Act,[8] or supported by other public funds and hence often covered by state legislation that is similar in content and administration to the Davis-Bacon Act.

The Davis-Bacon Act does have a few supporters among the open shop highway contractors. Thus two large such contractors, one in North Carolina, the other in New York State, told the authors that they can win jobs under Davis-Bacon provisions because they then know their competitors' labor costs and can deploy manpower more cheaply. This is a limited asset, however, because the Davis-Bacon regulations require that the open shop contractor follow union job designations unless, as in Texas or the Carolinas, the open shop job titles have been found "prevailing." Thus potential labor saving manpower utilization by open shop contractors can be limited.[9]

The public character of highway construction may have other consequences with respect to the prospects of open shop contractors for obtaining the work. Since the laws of many states require that contracts be awarded to the lowest qualified bidder, the political influence of the unions with governmental agencies is theoretically somewhat neutralized. Furthermore, bidding procedures will sometimes provide that various segments of a project (grading, paving, bridge building) be contracted separately rather than through a single general contractor, so that the awarding of the main portion of a project to a union contractor does not necessarily preclude open shop bidders from winning some work. In fact, however, union pressures, including refusal to work with nonunion concerns, the threat and actual acts of violence against the easily exposed highway contractors' equipment and men, and the political power of the

[7] See particularly his descriptions of the "Metro Segment C-7" and "Delta Electric" cases, *op. cit.*, pp. 109-120, 126-129.

[8] See Thieblot's description of the "Mountain Park Dam" case, *op. cit.*, pp. 121-126.

[9] For general reactions of contractors to the Davis-Bacon Act, and their negative view of it, see Thieblot, *op. cit.*, Chapter IX.

crafts, all tend to reduce open shop work on predominantly union jobs.[10]

Some public agencies do perform their own highway work, especially repair and maintenance on their own account. Since these jobs tend to be smaller projects for which open shop contractors are usually most competitive, such activity probably invades the market of open shop more than that of union contractors. In recent years, municipal employees have become increasingly unionized, either by the Teamsters or the American Federation of State, County, and Municipal Employees.

District 50

Rival unionism is especially significant in highway construction in Pennsylvania, West Virginia, Kentucky, and in other eastern coal field regions. There is a significant number of highway construction workers who have been unionized by District 50, which was organized by the late John L. Lewis originally as a home in the United Mine Workers for coal and coke by-product workers, and later as a catchall conglomerate union. District 50 agreements are of an industrial type, permitting the contractor to employ whom he chooses and to align the work as he desires, but providing for layoff and recall by seniority. Wage rates, if not set by Davis-Bacon standards, are likely to be lower than those of the AFL-CIO crafts. District 50 operated independently for many years, first under an affiliation with the Mine Workers, then without any ties to other unions.

Open shop contractors have found District 50 policies closer to their usual way of operations than those of the standard crafts and frequently operate "double-breasted" with District 50 contracts where the latter is a factor. In 1973, however, District 50 merged with the United Steelworkers of America. Since then, several open shop contractors have told the authors that District 50 is more stringent in its requirements, and that its seniority-layoff procedures and pension-welfare requirements have become onerous. Discussions with Steelworker officials, moreover, indicate clearly that, although they have no plans to disband the former District 50's construction locals, they plan no expansion in this industry and expect their membership there-

---

[10] See Mangum, *op. cit.*, pp. 256-259, for some union pressure tactic examples, and Chapter VIII, below, for violence and other tactics.

in to decline and eventually to disappear. Obviously, the Steelworkers believe that their construction locals are an unnecessary source of friction with the standard construction unions. Hence, contractors are likely to find former District 50 locals less and less available as a sort of halfway house between union and open shop operations.

EXTENT OF OPEN SHOP SURVEYS

There has never been an all encompassing study of the extent of open shop and/or unionized segments in the highway and heavy sectors by the federal government or any one else. The earlier studies noted in the homebuilding and commercial sections did not cover these sectors. It is quite clear from the already noted work of Mangum, and from our discussions in the field, that prior to the 1950's, highway work was not well unionized except in and around major cities. The passage of the Federal Highway Act, the administration of the Davis-Bacon Act, and the success of the Operating Engineers and other unions changed this rapidly, so that by 1958, Mangum could report twenty-eight states completely organized, seven partially organized, and thirteen largely open shop.[11] Since then, two well organized states, Hawaii and Alaska, have joined the Federal Union.

Because of the pervasive impact of the Davis-Bacon Act, we can hypothesize that the heavy sector will be as well unionized as the highway sector. This means that by approximately 1960, although both the highway and heavy sectors were considerably more unionized than homebuilding, they were both also much less unionized than the commercial sector. This broad generalization is concurred by Mills, writing about 1970.[12] The surveys in our possession confirm this for more recent years, plus a growing open shop trend.

Associated General Contractors—Highway Sector Data

The 1969 and 1973 surveys of the Associated General Contractors, utilized in the three previous chapters, also included questions of union status for highway and heavy contractors. Thirty percent of the 3,044 respondents in 1969 reported that they were engaged in highway construction, and 39 percent of the 5,938 respondents so signified in 1973.

---

[11] Mangum, *loc. cit.*

[12] Daniel Quinn Mills, *Industrial Relations and Manpower in Construction* (Cambridge: The MIT Press, 1972), p. 17.

Before examining the AGC data, it should be noted that AGC has a rival association among highway contractors, the American Road Builders Association (ARBA). Some highway contractors belong to both, but many who have joined one are not members of the other. Thus, a survey by the AGC may not be inclusive in some areas, for example New England, where the ARBA is strong.

Table VI-1 shows union status of AGC members engaged in highway construction by region as reported by the two surveys and the percentage union (by dollar volume) in 1969, the only year in which it was available. Table VI-1 shows that open shop highway construction among the various regions of the country, tended to follow much the same pattern revealed in our previous discussions of other sectors. Open shop operations predominate in the South generally, while union representation remains highest in the eastern, east central, and western states. Since the rate of response in 1973 was apparently much higher than in 1969, any assessment of change must be made with caution. Nonetheless, the overall growth of open shop highway building seems to have been concentrated in those regions where the unions have traditionally been strongest. In other words, it appears to reflect an expansion of open shop activity into areas of union strength, rather than a continued erosion of union representation in regions where the building trades have historically met substantial open shop competition.

The union percentage undoubtedly reflects not only the contractors that dealt with the standard AFL-CIO crafts, but also those that had District 50 agreements. Without District 50's inclusion, the union percentage in the Middle Atlantic area especially, but also in the East North Central area, could well be less. Likewise, the decline in union strength in these areas could also be attributable to decisions of open shop contractors to abandon District 50 contracts, as well as those with the crafts.

Changes from union to open shop operations between 1969 and 1973 were less pronounced, according to the AGC surveys, for highway contractors than for all contractors covered. Thus, in 1969, 43.8 percent of the highway contractors were open shop as compared with 46.3 percent in 1973. The percentages for all contractors were 31.1 in 1969 and 41.7 in 1973. This would confirm our previous findings of major open shop gains in commercial and industrial construction, and indicate more stability of status in the highway sector. Federal funding and the

TABLE VI-1
Union Status of AGC Members Engaged in Highway Construction, by Region, 1969 and 1973

Region	Percent Union[a]	Number of Contractors					
		1969			1973		
		Union	Nonunion	Percent Union	Union	Nonunion	Percent Union
New England	73.0	26	18	59.1	18	47	27.7
Middle Atlantic	98.1	53	4	93.0	185	44	80.8
E.N. Central	91.6	122	14	89.7	345	72	82.7
W.N. Central	24.3	83	127	39.5	149	280	34.7
S. Atlantic	20.6	6	47	11.3	50	217	18.7
E.S. Central	55.3	12	20	37.5	28	41	40.6
W.S. Central	5.1	8	123	6.1	37	255	12.7
Mountain	78.9	73	46	61.3	138	94	59.5
Pacific	99.1	135	5	96.4	312	38	89.1
Total United States	44.0	518	404	56.2	1,262	1,088	53.7

Source: Associated General Contractors of America.
[a] Calculated by using the dollar volume of contracts granted in 1969.

impact of the Davis-Bacon Act could account for maintenance of union strength in the highway sector. Although the highway sector remains less unionized than commercial, the differences have considerably narrowed for AGC members. Thus, the 1973 survey showed commercial contractor respondents 63.9 percent unionized (Table IV-1), as compared with a highway contractor ratio of 53.7 percent. In 1969, the respective percentages were 77.2 for commercial, 56.2 for highway.

In most regions of the country, union contractors appear to operate on a larger scale than their open shop competitors. The 1969 survey (but unfortunately not the one in 1973) solicited information on the volume of work performed by respondents in the various industrial categories. Among those doing some highway construction, average highway volume was higher, and usually substantially higher, for union shops in all geographical regions except the West North Central and West South Central states. In fact, the large number of open shops reported in the survey was attributable to a significant degree to the number of responses from these two regions (almost two-thirds of the open shop total). The responses from union shops were considerably more dispersed.

Associated General Contractors—Heavy Construction

Only 18 percent of the 3,044 respondents to the 1969 AGC survey reported that they were engaged in heavy construction as compared with 38 percent of the 5,938 who replied in 1973. This, of course, raises the question of whether the respondents answered the question in the same manner. Nevertheless, the trends in Table VI-2, which contains the results of the two surveys for the heavy sector, follows that for other types of construction. Thus, we find that the overall union ratio declined from 67.6 percent in 1969 to 59.8 percent in 1973, and that the open shop was especially strong in the South Atlantic, East South Central, and West South Central regions. Moreover, between 1969 and 1973, the open shop sector gained in all regions including the most highly unionized ones.

District 50 has been much less a factor in heavy work than in the highway sector. Thus, changes in the heavy sector's degree of unionization between 1969 and 1973 probably do not reflect to a significant degree any gains or losses other than those of the standard crafts.

TABLE VI-2
Union Status of AGC Members Engaged in Heavy Construction, by Region, 1969 and 1973

Region	Percent Union[a]	Number of Contractors					
		1969			1973		
		Union	Nonunion	Percent Union	Union	Nonunion	Percent Union
New England	96.5	21	11	65.6	32	38	45.7
Middle Atlantic	96.1	47	3	94.0	174	21	89.2
E.N. Central	98.5	55	2	96.5	351	48	88.0
W.N. Central	33.6	51	41	55.4	141	166	45.9
S. Atlantic	47.6	16	26	38.1	63	201	23.9
E.S. Central	71.4	9	13	40.9	25	58	30.1
W.S. Central	6.6	21	63	25.0	63	275	18.6
Mountain	90.3	31	12	72.1	147	77	65.6
Pacific	55.2	122	8	93.8	383	42	90.1
Total United States	43.4	373	179	67.6	1,379	926	59.8

Source: Associated General Contractors of America.
[a] Calculated by using the dollar volume of contracts granted in 1969.

Heavy construction respondents to the AGC questionnaire were more highly unionized than highway ones, not only nationally but in virtually every region both for 1969 and 1973. One reason is that heavy work is concentrated in metropolitan areas (subways and airports, for example) or in remote locations where only the largest contractors, or a consortium thereof, are qualified to work and where union recruiting can supply manpower (dams or mountain tunnels, for example). On the other hand, as noted, many highway projects are either in rural areas or involve small projects, both situations in which the smaller open shop contractors can compete more readily. Although more highly unionized than highway construction according to the AGC data, the heavy sector remains less unionized than commercial construction, falling between the latter and the highway sector in this respect. Overall, the percentage of highway contractors in the AGC who are open shop is very close to that of all contractors who answered the surveys both for 1969 and for 1973. Thus in 1969, this percentage for heavy contractors was 32.4; for all contractors, 31.1. In 1973, the figures were 40.2 percent for heavy contractors; 41.7 percent for all contractors.

In terms of type of projects, the union constructors did the largest, more costly projects in 1969 in most regions, but not in the highly open shop areas. Again, the heavy responses from the southern regions affected the overall results.

American Road Builders Association

The American Road Builders Association (ARBA) has not made a survey of its membership similar to that of the Associated General Contractors. At the request of the authors, however, the managing director of the ARBA Contractors Division did provide information on the union status of its state and regional councils. In New England, the ARBA Council is composed of union contractors, although the area is trending heavily open shop. In other areas, however, the makeup of the ARBA groups corresponds with the AGC survey.

Thus all ARBA southern councils, plus those in the border states of Maryland, Kentucky, Oklahoma, and West Virginia are open shop; those in the Great Lakes states are union, as are the ones in Delaware, District of Columbia, Pennsylvania, and California. Open shop highway contractors in the unionized areas who have association membership may belong to AGC. In

Pennsylvania, however, both AGC and ARBA groups are unionized, and some open shop highway contractors are members of the Associated Builders and Contractors (ABC).

Federal Highway Administration

The Federal Highway Administration, pursuant to its enabling legislation, requires that highway contractors provide training for a percentage of their labor forces. Such training may be on the job, or through apprentice programs. We shall examine this training and its impact on minorities in Chapters X and XII. Here we are interested in the training data as an indication of union status of contractors.

Training by open shop contractors is heavily of the on-the-job type. The unions generally prefer, and usually insist upon, apprenticeship training over which they exercise considerable control. However, the Operating Engineers, as well as other unions, sponsor some on-the-job training. As we shall see in Chapter X, open shop operators are increasingly sponsoring apprenticeship training. Nevertheless, an examination of the relative importance of on-the-job in comparison with apprenticeship training under Federal Aid Highway Projects, does give a reasonable indication of union status. Table VI-3 presents such data by region for July 31, 1974.

The data in Table VI-3 generally confirm the findings of the Associated General Contractors' survey. Thus in Region 1 (New England), nearly 70 percent of all trainees are on-the-job, and this is an area that we have found to be largely and increasingly open shop. Region 4, the Southeast, Region 6, the Southwest, and Region 7 (Iowa, Kansas, Missouri, and Nebraska) are heavily open shop except for St. Louis and Kansas City, eastern Iowa and parts of Missouri.

The high percentage of trainees in Region 3 reflects the open shop status of Virginia and Maryland, of the rural areas of Pennsylvania and West Virginia, and the fact that District 50 (now the United Steelworkers), which is strong in this region, has also accepted trainees and has not stressed apprenticeship programs. This more than offsets the unionized areas of Pennsylvania, Delaware, West Virginia, and District of Columbia.

On the other hand, Region 9 (California, Arizona, and Nevada) is highly unionized and under an Operating Engineers' local jurisdiction. That local has refused to accept on-the-job trainees

TABLE VI-3

Apprentices and On-the-Job Trainees as Indicators of Union Status by Region,[a] *Under Federal Aid Highway Projects, July 31, 1974*

Region	Total Both Types of Trainees	Apprentices	Percent of Total	On-the-Job Trainees	Percent of Total
1	496	155	31.2	341	68.8
3[b]	689	207	30.0	482	70.0
4	667	71	10.6	596	89.4
5	1,206	662	54.9	544	45.1
6	377	46	12.2	331	87.8
7	325	69	21.2	256	78.8
8	282	133	47.2	149	52.8
9	471	461	97.9	10	2.1
10	242	127	52.5	115	47.5
All Regions	4,755	1,931	40.6	2,824	59.4

Source: Office of Civil Rights, Federal Highway Administration.

[a] Regional definitions: (1) Maine, New Hampshire, Vermont, Massachusetts, Rhode Island, and Connecticut.
(3) Delaware, District of Columbia, Maryland, Pennsylvania, Virginia, and West Virginia.
(4) Alabama, Florida, Georgia, Kentucky, Mississippi, North Carolina, South Carolina, and Tennessee.
(5) Illinois, Indiana, Michigan, Minnesota, Ohio, and Wisconsin.
(6) Arkansas, Louisiana, New Mexico, Oklahoma, and Texas.
(7) Iowa, Kansas, Missouri, and Nebraska.
(8) Colorado, Montana, North Dakota, South Dakota, Utah, and Wyoming.
(9) Arizona, California, and Nevada.
(10) Alaska, Idaho, Oregon, and Washington.

[b] There is no Region 2.

who comprised only 3 percent of the total persons in training on July 31, 1974.

The other areas show a fairly close division between apprentices and trainees, reflecting in large part the split between union and nonunion contractors. In such states as Colorado and those in the Northwest, it reflects the growth of the nonunion contractors. We repeat that the presence of on-the-job trainees or apprentices is not a definitive measurement of union status. It is, however, a strong indication and the data in Table VI-3 support our previous findings of the strength of open shop in highway construction throughout much of the country.

The Industrial Research Unit Survey

The Industrial Research Unit survey, referred to in previous chapters, included within its coverage both Associated General Contractors and American Road Builders Association members, as well as those of other associations. As in the case of other construction sectors, highway and heavy contractors who operated union differed markedly with those who operated nonunion in their estimate of the extent of open shop activity in the highway and heavy sector. Table VI-4 shows that over 50 percent of the nonunion contractors who were able to offer an estimate put the open shop share of highway work at 60 percent or more, but more than one-half of the union contractors responding to the question estimated it at 20 percent or less. (We have already noted several possible explanations for this discrepancy in previous chapters.) Table VI-5 shows the same relationship for the heavy sector, with both union and open shop contractors indicating a higher proportion of union strength in the heavy than highway sectors.

To the extent that respondents saw a change in open shop highway work over the past few years, that change was predominantly in the direction of greater open shop competition. On the whole, however, both union and nonunion respondents perceived less overall change in highway and heavy construction than in other branches of the industry. This finding is largely consistent with the results of the 1969 and 1973 surveys by the AGC.

These responses are summarized in Table VI-6 and Table VI-7. Since a relatively small proportion of the respondents could be classified as highway or heavy contractors, we attempted to determine whether the differences between the perceptions of union shops and open shops could be attributable to a lack of direct knowledge on the part of many respondents. If anything, however, union and nonunion highway and heavy contractors (those with at least one-half of their volume in such construction) were even more inconsistent in their views on the open shop share of highway building. For example, about 58 percent of the union highway firms felt that open shops had captured

TABLE VI-4
Percent Distribution of Respondents' Estimates of the Proportion of Open Shop Work in Highway Construction, by Region and Union Status

Region	Number	NR/DK[a]	0-20	21-40	41-60	61-80	81-100
Union							
Not reported	89	53.9	34.8	6.7	1.1	2.2	1.1
New England	27	66.6	18.5	0.0	3.7	0.0	11.1
Middle Atlantic	125	39.2	29.6	12.0	11.1	4.8	3.2
E.N. Central	147	29.2	50.3	8.8	5.4	2.0	4.1
W.N. Central	60	38.4	21.7	10.0	6.7	6.7	16.7
S. Atlantic	68	36.8	8.8	7.4	11.8	4.4	30.9
E.S. Central	32	28.1	31.3	12.5	6.3	3.1	18.8
W.S. Central	45	31.2	11.1	4.4	6.7	6.7	40.0
Mountain	52	36.5	36.5	15.4	1.9	5.8	3.8
Pacific	133	48.1	44.4	4.5	0.8	0.8	1.5
Total	778	40.1	33.3	8.4	5.5	3.3	9.4
Nonunion							
Not reported	83	44.6	15.7	8.4	9.6	3.6	18.1
New England	63	39.7	12.7	14.3	11.1	9.5	12.7
Middle Atlantic	134	47.0	23.1	6.0	9.0	6.7	8.2
E.N. Central	75	33.3	25.3	12.0	13.3	8.0	8.0
W.N. Central	45	20.0	6.7	8.9	6.7	17.8	40.0
S. Atlantic	220	45.5	6.8	3.2	5.0	10.0	29.5
E.S. Central	45	37.7	8.9	8.9	4.4	8.9	31.1
W.S. Central	92	33.7	8.7	2.2	5.4	7.6	42.4
Mountain	21	33.3	14.4	14.3	9.5	9.5	19.0
Pacific	6	16.6	66.7	16.7	0.0	0.0	0.0
Total	784	40.2	13.8	6.9	7.7	8.5	23.0

Source: Industrial Research Unit Questionnaire.
[a] NR/DK—Not reported or do not know.

TABLE VI-5
Percent Distribution of Respondents' Estimates of the Proportion of Open Shop Work in Heavy Construction by Region and Union Status

Region	Number	NR/DK[a]	0-20	21-40	41-60	61-80	81-100
Union							
Not reported	89	59.6	34.8	0.0	2.2	2.2	1.1
New England	27	69.2	22.2	7.4	0.0	0.0	11.1
Middle Atlantic	125	40.0	37.6	7.2	8.8	2.4	4.0
E.N. Central	147	34.7	51.7	5.4	2.0	1.4	4.8
W.N. Central	60	36.6	30.0	8.3	3.3	6.7	15.0
S. Atlantic	68	39.7	13.2	8.8	14.7	2.9	20.6
E.S. Central	32	31.2	31.3	9.4	6.3	6.3	15.6
W.S. Central	45	37.8	13.3	2.2	6.7	4.4	35.6
Mountain	52	42.4	38.5	9.6	1.9	3.8	3.8
Pacific	133	46.6	47.4	3.8	0.0	0.0	2.3
Total	778	42.5	36.8	5.7	4.4	2.4	8.4
Nonunion							
Not reported	83	49.4	12.0	9.6	4.8	7.2	16.9
New England	63	38.1	23.8	11.1	1.6	9.5	15.9
Middle Atlantic	134	49.2	24.6	7.5	6.0	5.2	7.5
E.N. Central	75	36.0	33.3	12.0	8.0	4.0	6.7
W.N. Central	45	26.7	11.1	4.4	8.9	15.6	33.3
S. Atlantic	220	47.8	7.7	4.5	4.1	9.5	26.4
E.S. Central	45	46.7	13.3	2.2	4.4	4.4	28.9
W.S. Central	92	39.1	12.0	1.1	2.2	10.9	34.8
Mountain	21	38.1	19.0	14.3	4.8	14.3	9.5
Pacific	6	16.7	50.0	33.3	0.0	0.0	0.0
Total	784	43.5	16.5	6.8	4.7	8.3	20.3

Source: Industrial Research Unit Questionnaire.
[a] Not reported or do not know.

TABLE VI-6

Respondents' Estimates of Change in Open Shop Share of Highway Construction Over Past Few Years, by Region and Union Status

Region	Total	Total Indicating Change[a]	Lower by 3	Lower by 2	Lower by 1	Higher by 1	Higher by 2	Higher by 3
Union								
New England	27	0	0	0	0	0	0	0
Middle Atlantic	125	17	1	0	4	8	4	0
E.N. Central	147	10	0	0	2	7	1	0
W.N. Central	60	4	1	0	1	1	1	0
S. Atlantic	68	6	1	0	1	2	2	0
E.S. Central	32	5	0	0	1	3	0	1
W.S. Central	45	5	0	0	0	3	1	1
Mountain	52	4	0	0	2	2	0	0
Pacific	133	2	0	0	0	1	1	0
Not reported	89	4	0	0	1	3	0	0
Total	778	57	3	0	12	30	10	2

TABLE VI-6 (continued)

Nonunion								
New England	63	7	0	0	0	7	0	0
Middle Atlantic	134	10	1	2	0	5	2	0
E.N. Central	75	10	0	1	0	9	0	0
W.N. Central	45	8	0	0	2	5	0	1
S. Atlantic	220	9	0	0	2	6	1	0
E.S. Central	45	7	0	0	1	4	2	0
W.S. Central	92	8	0	0	1	3	3	1
Mountain	21	2	0	0	0	1	0	1
Pacific	6	1	0	0	0	1	0	0
Not reported	83	5	0	0	1	4	0	0
Total	784	67	1	3	7	45	8	3

Source: Industrial Research Unit Questionnaire.
[a] Change expressed in terms of movement between ranges of 20 percentage points (i.e., 0-20, 21-40, etc.).

TABLE VI-7
Respondents' Estimates of Change in Open Shop Share of Heavy Construction Over Past Few Years, by Region and Union Status

Region	Total	Total Indicating Change[a]	Lower by 3	Lower by 2	Lower by 1	Higher by 1	Higher by 2	Higher by 3
Union								
New England	27	0	0	0	0	0	0	0
Middle Atlantic	125	15	0	1	3	8	3	0
E.N. Central	147	7	0	0	2	4	1	0
W.N. Central	60	4	1	0	1	1	1	0
S. Atlantic	68	6	1	0	2	2	0	1
E.S. Central	32	4	0	0	1	2	0	1
W.S. Central	45	3	0	0	0	2	0	1
Mountain	52	4	1	0	2	1	0	0
Pacific	133	1	0	0	0	1	0	0
Not reported	89	4	0	0	1	2	1	0
Total	778	48	3	1	12	23	6	3

TABLE VI-7 (continued)

Nonunion								
New England	63	6	0	0	0	6	0	0
Middle Atlantic	134	8	1	1	1	3	2	0
E.N. Central	75	8	1	0	1	6	0	0
W.N. Central	45	7	0	0	1	5	0	1
S. Atlantic	220	9	1	0	0	5	3	0
E.S. Central	45	7	0	0	1	4	2	0
W.S. Central	92	5	0	0	0	3	2	0
Mountain	21	1	0	0	0	0	0	1
Pacific	6	2	0	0	0	2	0	0
Not reported	83	4	0	0	0	3	1	0
Total	784	57	3	1	4	37	10	2

Source: Industrial Research Unit Questionnaire.
[a]Change expressed in terms of movement between ranges of 20 percentage points (i.e., 0-20, 21-40, etc.).

no more than 20 perecnt of the work, while a like proportion of the open shop firms put the percentage at 80 or more.

CONCLUSION

Perhaps because of the impact of federal funding and the Davis-Bacon Act, highway and heavy construction have probably exhibited a smaller move toward open shop construction than the commercial and industrial sectors. On the other hand, highway and heavy construction were less unionized to begin with, and some shift to the open sector has indeed occurred. An unknown factor for the future is the impact of the probable decline of the former District 50 in the Appalachian area states, now that it has merged with the United Steelworkers. Given the determination of the Steelworkers to ease controversy with the construction unions, a gradual phasing out of old District 50 relationships could either open up new territory for the standard craft unions, or induce contractors to abandon District 50's brand of unionism in favor of the open shop. Because of the large number of open shop contractors who have had "double-breasted" relationships with District 50, the latter appears more likely. This could increase the trend toward the open shop in the highway sector in areas where District 50 has been prominent.

CHAPTER VII

Regional Variations

Having discussed the extent of open shop penetration by industry sector, we now turn to its geographic variations. This will permit us to bring the whole into focus, and thus to summarize our findings by sector while emphasizing the geographic variations which, of course, have been noted in part in the four previous chapters.

BACKGROUND AND EARLY STUDIES

Patterns of open shop construction activity tend to vary along two major dimensions. The first, discussed at length in Chapters III through VI, is the size and character of the construction project. The second is its location. Although these two factors are not completely unrelated, they do, nevertheless, appear to exert independent influences on the propensity for open shop contractors to capture construction work. Thus, certain branches of the industry exhibit relatively less unionization (homebuilding is the prime example) throughout the country, and certain geographic regions tend to be more hospitable to open shop activity (e.g., the Southeast) than others across most or all categories of building. Although union strength, in the aggregate, may grow or ebb over the years, the rankings along both these dimensions have been discernibly stable.

The influence of geography on the degree of open shop competition takes two somewhat related forms. One is reflected in variations in unionization among broad geographic areas, and among different states within those areas. The major concentrations of union strength have historically been found in two regional swaths: one ranging from southern New England southward through Pennsylvania and westward along the Great Lakes, and one along the West Coast. Open shops, on the other hand, have traditionally prospered most in the southern and border states, from Maryland to Texas. As we shall see, however, these generalizations must be viewed as statements of aggregate trends and not unvarying patterns across entire multistate regions. Even in the South, for example, there are still islands where the challenge to union dominance has been relatively limited (e.g., the Beaumont, Port Arthur, and Orange areas, called the "Golden Triangle" of Texas).

The second form of geographical variation relates to the extent of urbanization of construction labor markets. As a general proposition, open shop penetration varies inversely with the size of a metropolitan area and with the degree of proximity to it. (There is, of course, a connection between the regional patterns noted above and the urbanization factor cited here, with key states in the Northeast, Midwest and West having relatively high levels of population concentration.) Even in the case of heavily unionized metropolitan centers, nonunion contractors are often active in the fast-growing suburban and exurban communities growing around them. Although there is relatively little building work in rural areas, what remains often is predominantly open shop. And among the cities themselves, open shops have had substantial success in winning even the largest projects in small and medium-sized communities.

GEOGRAPHIC VARIATIONS IN THE 1970'S

The variations just described were evident nearly four decades ago, and although open shop contractors have recently made discernible inroads across-the-board, the basic configurations do not appear to have changed. In 1936, the U.S. Bureau of Labor Statistics survey, discussed in previous chapters, found that the proportion of union workers in building construction ranged from 41 percent in the West South Central states, (Texas, Oklahoma, Louisiana, and Arkansas), to 82 percent in the Middle Atlantic states (New York, New Jersey, and Pennsylvania). Similarly, the proportion of union workers was significantly higher in larger cities than in smaller ones. The result of the BLS survey are summarized in Table VII-1.

These basic geographic configurations of open shop construction have been regularly acknowledged in the literature. Thus, Haber and Levinson state that "geographically, the centers of greatest (union) strength are in the larger cities of the North,

TABLE VII-1
Union and Nonunion Workers, Building Construction, by Region and Size of City, 1936

Region	Union Workers	Nonunion Workers	Percent Union
United States	126,014	60,131	67.7
New England	8,832	4,390	66.8
Middle Atlantic	37,783	8,123	82.3
E.N. Central	30,796	10,384	74.8
W.N. Central	8,817	4,840	64.6
S. Atlantic	12,223	13,455	47.6
E.S. Central	3,743	4,955	43.0
W.S. Central	4,609	6,669	40.9
Mountain	3,288	1,457	69.3
Pacific	15,923	5,858	73.1
City size			
1,000,000 and over	44,042	12,231	78.3
500,000-1,000,000	34,738	8,515	80.3
250,000-500,000	21,741	13,555	61.6
100,000-250,000	14,969	15,214	49.6
50,000-100,000	6,928	7,031	49.6

Source: Edward P. Sanford, "Wage Rates and Hours of Labor in the Building Trades," *Monthly Labor Review*, XLV (August, 1937), Tables 1 and 5.

East, and Far West; the smaller cities, particularly in the South, are very weakly organized."[1] Mills, writing sixteen years later, echoes the point: "Geographically, union organization is greatest in major cities, least in suburban and rural areas and the South."[2] What is largely missing in the literature, however, is an explicit analysis of the factors which account for these patterns. Yet, since the patterns themselves have

[1] William Haber and Harold M. Levinson, *Labor Relations and Productivity in the Building Trades* (Ann Arbor: University of Michigan, Bureau of Industrial Relations, 1956), p. 34.

[2] Daniel Quinn Mills, *Industrial Relations and Manpower in Construction* (Cambridge: MIT Press, 1972), p. 17.

been remarkably stable over time, the relative success of open shop contractors in certain types of localities and regions is surely not randomly determined. Such an analysis is attempted later in this chapter, but it will be facilitated by preceding it with a detailed examination of the current state of the building trades unions across the nation. The discussion will be based on the findings of various recent contractor association surveys as well as the interviews and questionnaire of the Industrial Research Unit.

Open Shop Activity in the Northeast[3]

In the Northeast, perhaps more than elsewhere, an especially sharp distinction must be drawn between the populous, highly industrialized areas surrounding major cities and the large stretches of territory in-between. Our inquiries into the experience of various localities revealed a recurrent pattern: a systematic diminution of union strength as one moves further away from large population centers. Perhaps even more important, there is increasing, although still scattered, evidence of open shop incursions into the perimeters of union strongholds.

In sparsely populated northern New England, unions have witnessed the preponderance of construction work taken over by open shop contractors. In New Hampshire, for example, only six of the forty-seven members of the Associated General Contractors were signatory to labor agreements in the summer of 1973.[4] In Vermont, the unions have become so weak that their apprenticeship programs could not be sustained; AGC contractors were obliged to initiate and develop unilateral training programs. Vermont contractors have also been able to mount a few successful challenges of Davis-Bacon wage determinations by showing that the union rates were by no means "prevailing." The picture for the unions has been equally bleak in Maine. Even the largest projects were likely to go nonunion unless the buyer, for his own purposes, insists on running the job with union workers. That proviso has resulted in two major paper mills being built union in 1974.

---

[3] For purposes of this discussion, the Northeast includes the New England states, plus New York, New Jersey, and Pennsylvania.

[4] It is important to remember here that even jobs performed by open shop general contractors may include the services of one or more unionized subcontractors. In some areas of New Hampshire, for example, the Bricklayers union has maintained much of its strength with masonry firms which themselves contract with nonunion generals.

In southern New England, union strength is concentrated, not surprisingly, in the Boston area. The Boston labor market is ringed by two highways: Route 128 about 10 miles from the city, and Route 495 about 25 miles away. The area in-between, which represents perhaps the fastest growing section of the metropolitan region, has seen a number of large projects won by open shop contractors. Some open shops confided to us that they are reluctant to take on jobs within the Route 128 perimeter because of anticipated confrontations with unions. One open shop contractor, a national leader in the Associated Builders and Contractors, told us that he had performed several major nursing homes and hospital construction jobs within the city of Boston itself.

On the whole, the area within Route 128 is still predominantly unionized; beyond it open shops appear to be making significant inroads. In the first half of 1973, members of the Yankee Chapter of the Associated Builders and Contractors obtained $167 million in construction work and then nine one-million-dollar-or-more, projects in July of that year alone. Recently, and for the first time, the Massachusetts Associated General Contractors Chapter admitted three nonunion firms to membership. In addition, according to one prominent open shop contractor, thirty to forty AGC members operate "double-breasted," working union within the Route 128 perimeter and nonunion outside it. Nor is the phenomenon confined to Massachusetts. In Woonsocket, Rhode Island, the local building trades organization announced a demonstration against a nonunion contractor in a communication to its members with the provocative heading "Concerned Hard Hats: Protect Your Future Now." [5]

The growth of open shop construction in New England is reflected in both the 1969 and 1973 membership surveys of the AGC and the Industrial Research Unit questionnaire. Over 76 percent of the 1969 AGC respondents identified themselves as unionized in 1969; the proportion fell to under 60 percent in 1973. (It should be noted, moreover, that the vast majority of nonunion general contractors do not belong to the AGC.) In the Industrial Research Unit survey, the median estimate by union contractors of the open shop share of all construction was about 47 percent; the median estimate by nonunion contractors was about 65 percent. Twelve percent of the respond-

[5] Reproduced in "ABC Merit Shop Bulletin," Yankee Chapter, July 1973.

ents felt that the open shop share had grown significantly in recent years; only about 2.5 percent believed that it had declined.

The picture drawn above of union predominance becoming increasingly confined to a few strongholds is equally true in New York State, where the unions are beginning to view the situation as critical. Between New York City in the southeast and Buffalo in the northwest, the inroads of open shop firms have shaken the industry. One statewide meeting between union and contractor representatives was dubbed an "Emergency Conference." In October 1972, a communication from an upstate union leader described the problem in unmistakably blunt language, and is worth quoting at some length.

> You have undoubtedly heard a lot of talk recently, concerning A.B.C. (Associated Building Contractors) and the Open Shop movement, which is spreading throughout the country. It's only human when you hear about a subject such as this, to say to yourself, "we don't have to worry, it won't happen here."
>
> Well, let us assure you it's so close to happening here that it's a threat to your livelihood.
>
> If you're not familiar with the open shop movement, let's take a minute to bring you up to date. This anti-union movement is designed to eventually destroy Organized Labor. They make their program attractive to any owner contemplating construction of a new building project by relating they have a battery of attorneys that can counter any move the unions make to stop a job. They do not have any jurisdictional disputes on their jobs because their personnel can do any type of work. One day they may be doing carpenter work, the next day electrical. There are no arguments or work stoppages over who owns what work. They also relate the job can be done much cheaper because the men do not receive Pension and Welfare Fringe Benefits or Room and Board or Transportation Expenses. Their pitch is effective because statistics prove that better than half of Construction work in the U.S. last year was performed by the open shop or non-union contractors. Right next door to us in the Utica, Syracuse and Rochester areas, this movement is growing at astonishing speed.
>
> The third largest construction firm in the U.S. is Brown & Root, an open shop contractor. They are presently in a Nuclear Power Complex somewhere out in the mid west. This is a multi-million dollar job. They have relatively little trouble completing a project and what's worse we understand they are turning business away.
>
> We now have four A.B.C. jobs going within remote areas of our jurisdiction and we were recently shocked to hear there are three A.B.C. contractors on the bidding list for the Schenectady Waste-Water Project. This is a 14 million dollar job, and it proves they are getting bold when they bid a project that close to a metropolitan

> area. Fortunately, it went to a union contractor. It also proves we better wake up real quick or our entire industry will be lost for good.
>
> Conclusion—if you are a sincere Union Tradesman you will realize something has to be done. What you are about to read may be unpopular and probably not the kind of statements a Union Representative should make if he likes his job but to be perfectly honest the situation has gone beyond the point where we can pussyfoot or sweep it under the rug. It's a reality and we have to be big enough to face it.[6]

Many employer spokesmen in New York speak in equally dramatic terms. The findings of a 1972 study by an organization called Construction Employers Labor Relations Association were described in Chapter IV; suffice it to say here that they reveal a significant erosion of union strength across the state, especially in medium-sized upstate communities like Binghamton, Syracuse, and Utica. And perhaps most important, there is budding evidence of open shop activity in the strongest union localities. Recently, a $200 million nonunion condominium project in Westchester County, just north of New York City, evoked a demonstration by 10,000 building tradesmen. It was reported in *Engineering News-Record,* a construction trade journal, as "the first major penetration of the open shop into what has been a strong union area."[7] And in Buffalo, the state's second largest city and a "union town," the unions have watched with growing consternation as an Ohio-based open shop contractor has won a series of large public construction projects, including a $14 million dike, a $10 million garbage removal job, and $10 million in suburban sewer work. Even more ominous for the unions is that several of these projects represent initial phases of truly major works which will ultimately run into the hundreds of millions of dollars. Despite active picketing by the Operating Engineers union (later declared unlawful by the National Labor Relations Board[8]) the work has progressed smoothly. Interestingly, some public officials have been almost apolo-

---

[6] Open letter from Henry Landau, Business Manager, of the Sheet Metal Workers Local #86 (Albany, New York), October 5, 1972. It will be recalled that we quoted another part of Mr. Landau's letter in Chapter IV.

[7] *Engineering News-Record,* (November 7, 1974), p. 3.

[8] *I.U.O.E. Locals 17, 17A, and 17B* v. *Firelands Sewer and Water Construction Co., Inc.,* 210 NLRB No. 30 (1974).

getic in awarding contracts to the open shop firm, noting that they are obliged by state law to favor the lowest responsible bidder.

The growth of open shop activity in New York State is also reflected within the major contractors' associations. The Heavy and Highway division of the AGC had, in the summer of 1973, 35 nonunion members out of a total membership of 200, and the division's director acknowledged to us that many open shop highway contractors were not members of his group. In addition, the statewide General Building Contractors, an AGC affiliate, recently amended its bylaws to permit the entrance of nonunion firms and formed an open shop committee to coordinate the services to be provided by the association to nonunion members.

The situation in New Jersey varies largely with the distance from New York City. In southern New Jersey, the picture is much the same as in upstate New York. The major locus of union strength is in those counties which form part of the metropolitan Philadelphia area, although even there, open shop activity is significant. The unions are stronger in the northern part of the state, especially in those counties included in the New York City metropolitan area. Yet even there, open shop firms are sufficiently numerous to have recently formed a chapter of the Associated Builders and Contractors. Spokesmen for unionized contractors in New Jersey have publicly called notice to the burgeoning threat of open shop competition.[9]

In Pennsylvania, not surprisingly, union strength is greatest in the metropolitan centers of Pittsburgh and Philadelphia. Although low rise residential construction in and around both major cities is almost entirely open shop, nonresidential building activity has remained largely within the union domain, with nonunion work limited predominantly to small scale building and renovating. As in other areas, open shop competition varies directly with distance from the center cities. Earlier, we reported the results of a Dodge Report study by the Philadelphia AGC which found the nonunion share approaching one-quarter of all construction in the Philadelphia suburbs. Because of the underrepresentation of small jobs—especially residential—in the study's sample, this estimate is almost certainly an understatement of the actual magnitude of open shop penetration. Estimates of open shop work by a spokesman for the Delaware chapter

[9] See, for example, statement of Paul Brienza, Managing Director of the New Jersey Building Contractors Association in *Construction Labor Report*, No. 860 (March 22, 1972), pp. A-5, 6.

of the AGC ranged from 40 percent in Chester and Delaware counties, to 85 percent in Bucks and Montgomery counties. Whatever the true figures, the hypothesis that the open shop challenge is real indeed is lent credence by the notorious experience of the Altemose Construction Company, an open shop contractor whose jobs have been systematically sabotaged in one of the most egregious examples of union inspired violence.[10]

Our inquiries in Philadelphia also require repeating a caveat noted elsewhere in this chapter: the union status of a general contractor does not necessarily reflect the union status of an entire project. Because unions in certain crafts tend to control a larger share of their jurisdiction than do other trades, many open shop jobs are completed with the participation of one or more unionized subcontractors. The ABC director in suburban Philadelphia estimates that "open shop" jobs under $3 million tend to be about 30 percent union, with larger projects as much as 70 percent union. On the other hand, contractual restrictions usually prevent a unionized general contractor from utilizing nonunion subcontractors. In a number of instances, however, union generals have gone "double-breasted," using their nonunion operation to exploit the increasing inability of the unions to stem open shop competition in the city's environs. This approach appears to be preferred over simply withdrawing from the union contract when it expires, partly because of legal questions raised by the latter and partly because of possible exclusion from projects still largely under union contract. The open shop operations of "double-breasted" contractors tend to be relatively small, although if the erosion of union strength continues, they will undoubtedly grow.[11]

The situation in Pittsburgh is somewhat complicated by the presence of industrial unions which have organized construction workers. One is District 50 (now merged with the United Steelworkers of America), which is heavily engaged in highway construction; another is a largely black organization called the Associated Trades and Crafts. The industrial unions' agreements tend to be much less onerous for the contractor than those of the AFL-CIO craft unions, with significantly lower

---

[10] We shall discuss violence in Chaper VIII.

[11] This statement, of course, excludes Brown & Root, whose "double-breasted" company is union and much the minor part of its business.

wage rates, no jurisdictional demarcations, and few restrictions on manpower deployment. They do, however, have fairly rigid seniority provisions, largely absent in craft union agreements, which contractors often find troublesome. Many of the contractors with industrial type agreements belong to the Pittsburgh area ABC.

The AGC building chapter in Pittsburgh, like the one in Philadelphia, is comprised entirely of unionized contractors.[12] As in Philadelphia, according to a spokesman for the ABC, there is some "double-breasted" activity (although for obvious reasons this is not the kind of information a union contractor prefers to publicize). According to the executive director of the AGC, however, open shop competition has not reached significant proportions; his assertion was that no major building project in the area has gone nonunion. This conclusion is supported by the fact that in 1972 the 86 members of the ABC's Western Pennsylvania Chapter accounted for only $54 million worth of construction work, or well under one million per contractor. There is no information, however, on the amount of building work done by nonunion contractors who are not members of the ABC.

The extent to which open shop activity tends to grow with distance from the metropolitan center was revealed in a survey by the AGC Heavy and Highway Division. Between 1970 and the first seven months of 1973, the nonunion share of highway work in Allegheny County (Pittsburgh) was only 10.2 percent. In the three suburban counties (Beaver, Washington, and Westmoreland) included in the Pittsburgh SMSA, the proportion was 21.3 percent. And in the twenty-nine counties comprising the rest of western Pennsylvania, open shops captured fully one-third of the work. AGC spokesmen note that nonunion firms are especially competitive in the construction of sewage and water treatment facilities, even those in the metropolitan Pittsburgh area. Union concern in this sector of the industry is illustrated in the growing willingness of the Operating Engineers union, among others, to relax some of their contractual provisions on an *ad hoc* basis when a job is bid by one or more open shop contractors.

Although, as might be expected, one receives conflicting reports from various industry spokesmen as to the extent of open shop penetration, it seems fair to conclude that in the two

---

[12] In the case of Pittsburgh, the term "union" shall hereafter refer exclusively to the AFL-CIO craft unions.

metropolitan centers of Pennsylvania, open shop contractors are barely beginning to make their presence felt, probably more so in Philadelphia than in Pittsburgh. In-between, however, the challenge to the unions is much more pervasive. The Keystone Chapter of the ABC, based in Lancaster, is one of the Association's oldest and largest with 281 members in 1973. Some 20 percent of the membership is unionized, although their agreements are negotiated on an individual basis rather than through an association. The union firms tend to operate over a wide area, and their union status helps them to compete in other areas where local unions are somewhat stronger, such as Harrisburg, Reading, and Philadelphia. The ABC estimates that only about 10 percent of all construction in Lancaster county is performed under union contract, and that not a single general contractor in the county is unionized. An indication of the lack of union strength in the area is that the ABC has been able successfully to challenge prevailing wage determinations based on union scales.

The foregoing should not be construed to suggest that Lancaster is necessarily representative of smaller cities throughout the heartland of Pennsylvania. Most probably the unions have been more successful in maintaining some strength in cities whose economies are dominated by heavily organized firms and industries, such as coal mining and steel fabrication, although here District 50 has been a problem for the standard unions. At the same time, the overall picture appears to be similar to that of New York, with open shops competing strongly in the relatively sparsely populated areas spanning the metropolitan centers. Despite the fact that the major AGC chapters in Philadelphia and Pittsburgh are all union, the 1973 survey of AGC members had over 10 percent of the Pennsylvania respondents reporting themselves as open shops, compared to only 2.5 percent in 1969, and these numbers do not include most of the members of the several ABC chapters based in the state.

In sum, although the Middle Atlantic states have historically constituted one of the most strongly unionized areas of the nation, they have not been immune to the trends which have seen an erosion of union strength across the country. The 1973 AGC survey found almost 20 percent of the respondents in New York and New Jersey to be open shop. In the questionnaire study of the Industrial Research Unit, more than one-half of the union respondents from the Middle Atlantic area (not including those who offered no opinion) estimated open shop work at over 40 percent of the total. (Among non-union respondents, the proportion was over 4 out of 5). On the question of the recent growth of open shop activity, about one-fifth of the union respondents felt that open shop work had increased significantly, compared to only about 3 percent who believed that it had declined. Thus, although precise magnitudes cannot easily be measured, it seems clear that the building trades have been placed under a stiff challenge even in those geographic and industrial sectors where they have been relatively secure.

Open Shop Activity in the Midwest[13]

The Midwest comprises a markedly heterogeneous region economically, ranging from the predominantly agricultural states of the nation's heartland, to the heavily industrialized states along the Great Lakes. In the rural and farm states, open shop construction has historically had a substantial presence; as we saw in Table VII-1, the East North Central region—from Ohio to Wisconsin—was appreciably more unionized in 1936 than the less industralized West North Central states. The recent membership surveys by the AGC tell much the same story. The vast majority of respondents from Ohio, Michigan, Illinois, Indiana, Wisconsin, Minnesota, and Missouri were union contractors, but those from Iowa, Kansas, Nebraska, North Dakota, and South Dakota were preponderantly open shop. The data summarized in Table VII-2 show not only this, but also a swing to the open shop between 1969 and 1973 in both predominantly unionized and open shop states. The sole exception was North Dakota in which the number of respondents was too small to be meaningful.

Given the kinds of national trends outlined in foregoing chapters, it seems safe to conclude that the building trades unions have not made significant organizational inroads into areas where their strength has long been modest. Our concern here, therefore, will be with those states and areas where unions have traditionally been strong. Our most detailed information comes from Ohio and Michigan, but field work was

---

[13] The Midwest includes the following states: Ohio, Michigan, Indiana, Illinois, Wisconsin, Minnesota, Iowa, Missouri, Kansas, Nebraska, North Dakota, and South Dakota.

TABLE VII-2
Proportion of Union Respondents in AGC Membership Survey, 1969 and 1973

State	1969 Total Number	1969 Percent Union	1973 Total Number	1973 Percent Union
Ohio	80	98.8	267	86.9
Michigan	114	89.5	151	84.1
Indiana	85	95.3	135	84.4
Illinois	161	98.1	273	90.5
Wisconsin	60	96.7	101	90.1
Minnesota	99	82.8	172	74.4
Iowa	125	34.4	220	28.6
Missouri	79	92.4	173	85.5
Kansas	81	49.4	173	31.2
Nebraska	40	42.5	n.a.	n.a.
North Dakota	38	7.9	59	11.9
South Dakota	33	12.1	68	10.3

Source: Associated General Contractors of America.

also conducted in Indiana, Illinois, Iowa, and Missouri. Although it is always hazardous to attempt to generalize from a limited base, we have no reason to believe that these states, and the major metropolitan areas within them, are significantly different from other states in the Midwest whose populations are largely concentrated in one or a few major urban centers. It is in these states that much of the significance of recent open shop growth lies. They are not only where much construction work is being performed, but also where the unions have exercised their strongest influence. Thus, a nascent erosion of union strength in Detroit almost certainly signifies a broader expansion of nonunion competition in the rest of Michigan. And if open shop contractors in Detroit are beginning to make their presence felt, it seems quite likely that the process is being repeated (or about to be repeated) in Minneapolis, Milwaukee, St. Louis, and Kansas City.

There are seven important metropolitan centers in Ohio: Cleveland, Columbus, Cincinnati, Toledo, Akron, Dayton, and Canton. In general, open shop construction has made its greatest inroads in the southern portions of the state, especially Columbus, the capital and second largest city. In the northern areas, particularly Cleveland and Toledo, nonunion competition is much more modest. Even in Cleveland, however, there is some fragmentary evidence of budding open shop penetration. The residential sector, long a union province through agreements with the local homebuilders association, is seeing more open shop building as the population moves further from the city and its immediate suburbs. There is an increasing amount of residential construction at and beyond the Cuyahoga County limits. As we have seen in earlier discussions, this trend is usually accompanied by a burgeoning of open shop activity in the ancillary commercial building, such as shopping centers, that residential development generates. At the least, there is enough nonunion building in the Cleveland area for the ABC, headquartered in Columbus, to have opened a small satellite office there. As yet, however, we have uncovered no evidence of a major open shop breakthrough in Cleveland.

The case is different in Columbus. The ABC in Columbus has become an important force in the industry, with about 260 contractor members; some 50 to 60 have union contracts. (Most of the union contractors, however, operate on a "double-breasted" basis.) The ABC estimates that a little more than one-half of all open shop contractors in the Columbus area are members of the association, although the proportion is very much lower throughout the rest of the state. As is generally the case, open shops in Columbus have made substantially greater inroads in residential and small scale commercial construction, although there is no universal agreement on just what constitutes "small scale." According to an ABC spokesman, the only specialties which open shops have not penetrated are glazing and elevator construction.

Representatives of both union and nonunion contractors associations in Columbus agree on the fact that open shops have mounted a significant challenge to union influence; they disagree, however, on the extent of it. The executive director of the ABC's Central Ohio Chapter estimates that 50 to 60 percent of all commercial work in Ohio, and 65 percent in Columbus, is done open shop, with open shops in Columbus capturing a "majority of jobs in the three to four million dollar range." His assessment of the nonunion share of industrial and heavy construction was on the order of 25 to 50 percent, and even lower for public works because of their typically large scale and because of prevailing wage laws. Residential building is, of course, almost entirely nonunion, a statement disputed by no one.

The executive director of the AGC Building Chapter in Columbus places the extent of nonunion penetration at a somewhat lower level, although he is quick to acknowledge that it is growing, particularly in light commercial work. He puts the open shop share of commercial building under $1.5 million at about 50 percent, with industry, public, and large commercial construction still mostly union. He notes further that "double-breasted" operations are common and growing, and that unionized subcontractors are frequently engaged to work on projects of open shop general contractors. The AGC Building Chapter is entirely union, and in the most recent negotiations (1973) it experienced discernible concern on the part of the building trades about open shop competition. A number of onerous work rules, relating particularly to restrictions on certain mechanical devices, the employment of nonworking foremen, and travel pay, were substantially relaxed.

An apparently significant factor in the willingness of the Columbus unions to make these concessions was the AGC's survey of union and open shop work during the first few months of 1973, reported earlier in Chapter IV. In the period February to May, open shop contractors captured over one-third of the total volume and over five-eighths of the jobs, proportions appreciably higher than those pertaining to the same period in 1972. These figures, moreover, exclude work, particularly residential (including low rise apartments), which has long been entirely open shop. Since ABC spokesmen often regard apartment building as "commercial," the discrepancy between the overall estimates of nonunion activity by the ABC and AGC executives may thus be largely explained. The upshot, in any event, is that building construction in Columbus can by no means be said to be dominated by the building trades. We have no reason to believe that the picture is significantly different throughout southern Ohio.

Heavy and highway contractors in Ohio are organized statewide through the Ohio Contractors Association, an AGC affiliate.

About one-quarter of the association's 500 members are open shops, a few of them are "double-breasted." The executive director of the OCA estimates that 10 percent of the state's highway work, and 20 percent of its site development, and water and sewage treatment facilities is nonunion, virtually all of it in jobs valued at under a million dollars. Still, the industry has not been immune to open shop inroads; recently, for the first time in the executive director's memory, a power plant project near Cincinnati was awarded to an open shop contractor from out of state. It will also be remembered that the nonunion contractor who has won a number of large public works projects in the Buffalo area is based in Ohio. On balance, however, it appears that open shop competition in this sector is still spotty in the state as a whole, and is not yet regarded by the unions as a serious threat. There is no hard evidence that—unlike some of their counterparts elsewhere, most notably the Operating Engineers—the highway unions have been willing to make significant changes in their work rules in response to open shop gains, although they have done so in other states.

Michigan, unlike Ohio, has only one really major metropolitan center. Detroit is an archetypical "union town," with its economy heavily reliant on durable manufacturing related to the production of automobiles. Outside the Detroit SMSA, open shop construction is widespread. The labor relations director for the Detroit Chapter of the AGC estimates the nonunion share of construction work "outstate" to be perhaps one-half of the total. Some unionized general contractors in Detroit have open shop arms which operate outside the jurisdiction of the Detroit-based unions. Recently, a nonunion firm from Texas was engaged by the Shell Oil Company to construct a large refinery in the upstate town of Kalkaska. The event struck so close to the heart of the unions' industrial domain that it precipitated a massive protest, often violent, by union members some of whom travelled some 200 miles for the occasion, as will be recounted in the next chapter. As yet, however, there has been no comparable breach of union hegemony over the most sizable projects in the Detroit area itself.

Spokesmen for unionized contractors in Detroit do not acknowledge any serious penetration of open shop activity in the area. The executive director of the local homebuilders association, comprised of unionized builders, asserts over 90 percent of the residential construction in his jurisdiction is performed on a union basis. The Detroit labor market, however, includes four counties outside that jurisdiction in which there is virtually no union organization. Since in most metropolitan areas there is now significant residential building in their outer reaches, and since there is actually little in Detroit itself, the 90 percent estimate is of questionable import.

The fact that open shop activity is beginning to be felt in Detroit is reflected in the existence of a small, but growing ABC Chapter based in the suburbs. The chapter has about 110 contractor members, many of whom are specialty firms doing electrical and mechanical work. Only about one-quarter of the members are general contractors. The ABC estimates that only about 10 percent of the open shops in the area belong to the association. As we shall see momentarily, nonunion work is probably furthest advanced in electrical contracting, with a sizable electrical contractor currently serving as the president of the ABC itself.

In general, however, ABC officers in Detroit are more modest in their claims of open shop penetration than those in other cities. Its executive director places the nonunion share (including residential) at 25 to 35 percent; its president estimates the nonunion share of electrical work at 40 percent. Both stress that the proportion of open shop work varies directly with the size of the project and its proximity to the city. Presently, both individuals estimate that open shops have gained perhaps one-fourth of the commercial market (mostly jobs under $1 million) and at best only a very small fraction of industrial work. Residential building is said to be at least 50 percent open shop. Recent growth among nonunion firms has been concentrated in the residential and small commercial building sectors, with relatively little in the large jobs.

The labor relations director of the AGC, an association comprised entirely of union contractors, sees even less open shop activity. His assertion to us was that 98 percent of the work within forty miles of Detroit is union, with virtually all nonunion work limited to residential building. There has been, he notes, some union concern about the prospect of nonunion activity outstate spreading to the area, but it has not happened yet. This concern, however, is reflected in the recent execution of a special agreement covering power plant construction, in which the unions agreed to relax a number of important restrictions otherwise applicable through the regular contract language.

Our interview with the AGC director took place in the summer of 1973. His sanguineness must have been jarred by the study jointly conducted a year later by the union and union contractors of the electrical contracting industry, which was reported at length in Chapter IV. It excluded homeowner construction, yet it put the percentage of nonunion construction permits in southeastern Michigan at 79.8 percent for nonhomeowner, residential construction, 44.9 percent for commercial, 42.3 percent for industrial, and 41.8 percent for institutional, with 74 percent of all permits issued to open shop contractors.

This study undoubtedly overstates the extent of open shop work because it probably includes considerable maintenance and repair. Certainly if nonunion electrical contractors have captured three-fourths of the jobs and nearly one-half of the volume in the Detroit area, it is inexplicable that there has been no greater overt sense of urgency among the building trades or their employees. It should be remembered that contractual restrictions often preclude unionized general contractors from engaging a nonunion subcontractor. Thus, the jobs and volume reflected in the IBEW-NECA study should represent work undertaken by open shop general contractors, although they may also include industrial maintenance work contracted directly to electrical firms. In short, the nonunion activity represented in these numbers transcends the relatively modest claims made by the ABC itself, and if the figures are even moderately accurate, the threat to union influence in the Detroit area is apparently greater than anyone in the industry had heretofore imagined.

Illinois remains a heavily unionized state. In the Chicago SMSA, including the outlying counties, even residential construction is unionized. In the southern part of the state, the unions have moved out from their east St. Louis base to maintain an equally strong control. Peoria, in central Illinois, and Moline, farther north and west, are completely union towns, again with residential construction included. Unions and union contractors in this state are prime supporters of the state's dominant political organization, contribute heavily to it, and in turn receive strong support from it.[14] Throughout the state, highway and heavy construction is highly unionized.

---

[14] Chuck Neubauer, "$203,000 for Daley Since Primary Vote," *Chicago Tribune*, March 19, 1975, Sec. 1, p. 5. The bulk of these contributors were

Indiana is a more mixed situation. Gary and the other communities near Chicago are heavily union, as is Evansville on the southern border. Indianapolis, however, is union for commercial and industrial, but open shop for homebuilding and garden (under four stories) apartments and many small towns and rural areas are entirely open shop. Highway and heavy work is divided, with the major jobs union.

Iowa's union condition varies with the distance from Illinois. Mississippi River towns like Davenport and Burlington are heavily union, but as one moves westward, union strength declines heavily in all branches of work.

Missouri boasts two of the country's strongest union cities in Kansas City and St. Louis, but the area in-between has seen a rising open shop movement. Recently, the ABC established a chapter in Kansas City. It is still small in numbers and job size, but has considerable support from investors, architects, and others who have been concerned about the excessive wage costs, low productivity and long strikes there. Its establishment presages a serious effort to provide a competitive alternative to unionized construction in a major union stronghold.

The Dakotas and Nebraska—primarily agricultural except for Omaha—are also largely open shop. The installation of a missile site or similar major government construction project brings in a union job, but the union status does not remain. Highway work is usually open shop in these states also.

In the Midwest generally, the respondents to the Industrial Research Unit survey were again divided on the extent of open shop penetration. The median estimate by union firms of the nonunion share was about 29 percent; among open shop respondents the median estimate was 60 percent. Among both groups, most of those perceiving any significant trend (about 12 percent of the total) saw it moving in the direction of a larger open shop share in recent years. This view, of course, is very consistent with the more objective and systematic evidence addressed earlier in this section.

Although much of our evidence about the extent of the open shop in the Midwest is fragmentary and suggestive rather than conclusive, the inferences about open shop growth are

---

contractors and unions and others who did business with the city. For background on these relationships, see Barbara Warne Newell, *Chicago and the Labor Movement* (Urbana: University of Illinois Press, 1961).

strong, and not without objective support. There is no obvious reason for a union leader in Detroit to exaggerate the threat he perceives in burgeoning nonunion competition, as reflected in a systematic study; it is hardly plausible that his surprising report to the brothers was fraudulent. And if open shops are encroaching to that extent in Detroit, it is a good bet that there are similar experiences in and around other industrialized urban centers. To the extent that the security of the building trades unions is founded to a substantial degree on their holds in major cities in the Midwest, their prospects in at least some of these cities are beginning to look uncertain.

Open Shop Activity in the Southern and Border States

That the South is the most open shop area in construction is indisputable.[15] Throughout the previous chapters we have presented data from various sources all of which point to the weak union penetration in the South. Moreover, the South is the home of the great bulk of the largest open shop contractors—Brown & Root, Daniel International, J. Ray McDermott, H. B. Zachry, and others—who have grown strong in that region and then branched out elsewhere.

Nevertheless, there are union enclaves in the South just as there are open shop ones in the East or West. Thus the central city areas of Atlanta, Richmond, New Orleans, Houston, Dallas, Miami, and other major cities, and much of Alabama and Louisiana are usually union for commercial and major apartment construction. Sherman in North Texas, Galveston on the Gulf, and the great industrial complex known as the "Golden Triangle", the Beaumont, Port Arthur, and Orange areas, are union even in homebuilding. These, however, are as we described them, enclaves of union power in an open shop dominated region.

On a state-by-state basis, there is also variation. Virginia remains a heavily open shop area, particularly away from the Norfolk and Richmond SMSAs. The area around Washington, D.C., is overwhelmingly open shop even for large office building and apartment construction. As in most southern states where recent industrial progress has been rapid, manufacturers building plants sometimes insist on union contractors, but high

[15] The South is defined as Virginia, North Carolina, South Carolina, Georgia, Florida, Tennessee, Alabama, Mississippi, Arkansas, Louisiana, and Texas.

costs in recent years have tended to reduce such happenings. Virginia Electric Power Company, in which the major National Constructors Association member, Stone and Webster, has an ownership interest, began opening up its work to open shop contractors in recent years, thus ending one area of strong union control. Du Pont, on the other hand, has maintained a union contractor in Richmond primarily because of its satisfaction with his work.

Small commercial construction and homebuilding is largely open shop throughout the state, and highway work is heavily open shop also. In Virginia, our field work and all available data pointed to a decline in an already low union influence in recent years.

The Carolinas are without doubt the most completely open shop states in the United States. Moreover, in recent years, unions have suffered significant losses. Du Pont, which had a large number of plants in the Carolinas built union, has now turned this construction over to open shop firms, and this practice has been followed by other major concerns, such as Firestone Tire and Rubber and General Electric in recent expansions. Two of the major utilities—Carolina Power and Light, and South Carolina Light and Power—traditionally gave their work to Ebasco, also a large National Constructors Association member, since both this contractor and the utilities were once subsidiaries of the Electric Bond and Share Company, a former utility holding company. In recent years, however, this tie has been broken and considerable such work has gone to Daniel and other open shop concerns. Duke Power Company has divided its work on fossil fuel plants between its nonunion in-house construction crews and union contractors, but now the in-house forces perform virtually all nuclear plant construction.

In commercial and industrial construction, Charlotte, the largest city in the two states, has four large union contractors, but within the Carolinas, they build with "double-breasted" open shop firms. Virtually all highway and homebuilding in these states is also open shop. A sizable number of large electrical and mechanical contractors in the state operate open shop, thus adding to the potential of open shop firms.

A feature of the Carolinas is the militant open shop AGC chapter. Unlike most AGC chapters, its jurisdiction extends throughout both states, and covers all sectors of construction.

Moreover, it works very closely with specialty trade associations. It is militantly open shop and encourages users to build open shop. As the largest AGC chapter in the nation, it has had a significant impact on the AGC national organization. It has contributed materially to altering the policies of the national AGC from one dedicated almost solely to serving union contractors, to its present policy of service to both union and open shop contractors.

Georgia is also heavily open shop, but has strong union contractors, especially in and around Atlanta. As we noted in Chapter IV, however, the open shop has made gains in this city and is quite strong in the suburbs and in much of the rest of the state. Georgia Power Company gave a major contract to one of the big open shop construction companies in recent years, altering a strong past practice of dealing with union firms only. Homebuilding and highway construction in most of Georgia are also open shop.

Florida is less of a southern state than a national vacationland. The open shop-union mix in construction exemplifies this. Thus, before the construction of "Disney World," "Sea World," and "Circus World," the central Florida area around Orlando was heavily open shop. Disney brought the unions in under a project agreement.[16] Because of the amount of work, union workers migrated to the area, open shop firms signed union agreements and the area went heavily union. Once, however, the major work was completed, union work began to wane and today the open shop is again in the ascendency there. The changeover has been accompanied by considerable violence, as discussed in the following chapter. The decline in union work in central Florida exacerbated the situation for the unions because space work at nearby Cape Canaveral had fallen precipitously, and this also was heavily union.

The west coast of Florida, including Tampa, is heavily open shop in the highway and residential areas, including condominiums, apartments, and in smaller commercial work; but heavy industrial, power plant, and large commercial work is likely to be union. Southeast Florida has seen considerable open shop encroachment on what was once strong union territory. Today unions still control one-half of the condominiums and apartments and 80 percent of the highway and heavy work, but buildings below four stories have gone largely open shop.

[16] Project agreements are discussed in Chapter VIII.

Of all the southern states, the ABC has made its strongest inroads in Florida. In southeast Florida, the ABC has led the fight against the union violence discussed in the following chapter, and has benefited considerably from this activity. Thus, not only have open shop contractors joined ABC, but others have decided to turn open shop as a result of ABC's efforts. The ABC has two other Florida chapters—one on the west coast, and another in the central area. Both are growing rapidly and helping to stimulate open shop activity in their areas.

Alabama is one of the more unionized areas of the South, particularly in the Birmingham-Gadsden industrial sectors. Construction unions enjoy a close rapport with the dominant politician, Governor George Wallace, and benefit from it. Daniel International generally builds union in Alabama, indicating a union environment. Small commercial, homebuilding, and some highway is, however, open shop. Mississippi, on the other hand, is strongly open shop except in a few isolated areas such as Pascagoula, where strong plant unions exist.

Tennessee unionism owes much to the Tennessee Valley Authority (TVA) which brought construction union strength to that state and has nurtured it with wages that are set high ever since. Knoxville and Chattanooga are union towns, but Nashville (especially) and Memphis have in recent years seen unions lose heavily. Key contractors there have broken with unions and the ABC has a strong foothold in the state now. Recently, ABC established an office in Knoxville, indicating inroads there for the open shop. Highway and heavy are largely union, but less so in the central and western sector. Arkansas is largely nonunion, and becoming more so now that Memphis on its eastern border is shifting.

Louisiana is a mixed picture, with Baton Rouge and Lake Charles two of the strongest union controlled areas in the country. Other parts of the state vary considerably, with a few union enclaves like Bogalusa, but much of the state is open shop.

New Orleans is a mixed situation. Chapter IV presented evidence that open shop contractors had made substantial gains in this city. J. Ray McDermott is headquartered there, and is the leading off-shore oil rig and platform contractor. Brown & Root does considerable business there also, and an enterprising ABC chapter exists. The AGC is all union, but a sizable number of contractors now operate "double-breasted." Downtown construction remains union, but the area, formerly all union for commercial work, now has seen many contracts over one million dollars go to open shop firms. Louisiana State University, New Orleans, was in part built open shop.

Homebuilding, as in other cities, is completely open shop for single homes and garden apartments (one to three stories). High rises are union built. Highway and heavy work is union within New Orleans, but open shop prevails outside of the city, often with "double-breasted" companies.

Texas has several strong union enclaves, as already noted, but overall it is one of the more complete open shop states. The Texas statewide highway and heavy chapter of the AGC is strictly open shop, and is one of the chapters which prepares detailed wage surveys for Davis-Bacon and state prevailing wage law purposes that maintain open shop rates as prevailing ones. Dallas and Houston, outside of center city, have become increasingly open shop, and Waco almost totally so in recent years. The huge Dow complex at Freeport has turned over much of its construction in recent years to open shop contractors by letting contracts on a bid basis, and many other firms in the burgeoning Gulf Coast petro-chemical complex have followed suit. With Brown & Root, and numerous smaller but sizable open shop contractors in the Houston and Gulf Coast areas west of the "Golden Triangle," the area has substantial open shop capacity. Yet so great has been the demand that, as noted in Chapter V, a large share of work is being won by unionized national contractors who can supply the talent that the area open shop contractors cannot.

The border states[17] are also heavily open shop. The ABC was spawned in Maryland. Baltimore is less unionized than any major city to the north; large buildings in its center have been ABC built, although unions have a large share of this work. Throughout the state, which has three ABC chapters, the open shop is dominant in all but major commercial and industrial work. Delaware, on the other hand, is unionized in its northern sectors which border the Philadelphia SMSA, but tends toward open shop to the south.

The District of Columbia and the Washington SMSA are 80 percent open shop. Only government buildings, particularly in the heart of the city, remain union; highway and heavy

[17] Defined here as Maryland, Delaware, District of Columbia, West Virginia, Kentucky, and Oklahoma.

work is union within the city, open shop outside. Nonfederal housing is open shop, and the city is now ringed on both the Maryland and Virginia sides with high rises often built open shop.

West Virginia and Kentucky have both highly unionized and open shop sectors, plus District 50 strength in highway work. Strong mining and industrial unions support the construction unions (or District 50); yet the open shop areas are significant, particularly in the less populated areas and in smaller construction projects.

Oklahoma has become increasingly open shop in recent years with Brown & Root and Zachry taking over power plant and other utility work. In the Oklahoma City area, all work is open shop except nonpower plant industrial and commercial jobs over one million dollars. In the Tulsa area, unions are stronger and control the power plant work, but highway, sewer, small commercial, and homebuilding is generally open shop throughout the state. Moreover, several of the larger union firms have recently established "double-breasted," open shop companies.

Open Shop Activity in the West [18]

The western states, especially those along the Pacific Coast, are among the most strongly unionized in the nation. Even residential building, which tends to be almost entirely open shop in most other regions, still has an appreciable union component in many parts of the West. The strength of the unions here was reflected in the Bureau of Labor Statistics study nearly four decades ago, and again in the AGC membership surveys in 1969 and 1973. During this four year period, however, the AGC surveys show some diminution of union representation in most of the states in the region, although the differences in the rates or response for the two surveys preclude attaching much significance to this change. The AGC fiindings are given in Table VII-3.

Union strength in many of the mountain states tends to be concentrated in a single metropolitan area (Albuquerque in New Mexico, Phoenix in Arizona, Denver in Colorado, Las Vegas in Nevada) in which the preponderance of the state's

---

[18] The West includes the mountain states (Arizona, New Mexico, Colorado, Utah, Wyoming, Montana, Idaho, and Nevada) and the Pacific states (California, Oregon, Washington, Alaska, and Hawaii).

TABLE VII-3
Union Status of AGC Members in Western United States, by State, 1969 and 1973

	Union Contractors		Nonunion Contractors		Percent Union	
State	1969	1973	1969	1973	1969	1973
Mountain States	168	281	65	153	72.1	64.7
Arizona	44	64	2	16	95.7	80.0
Colorado	46	63	8	30	85.2	67.7
Idaho	18	43	7	17	72.0	71.7
Montana	27	31	5	10	84.4	75.6
Nevada	6	29	2	3	75.0	90.6
New Mexico	11	28	8	22	57.9	56.0
Utah	11	17	12	21	47.8	44.7
Wyoming	5	6	21	34	19.2	15.0
Pacific States	425	727	22	80	95.1	90.1
Alaska	17	30	0	1	100.0	96.8
California	220	386	3	23	98.7	94.4
Hawaii	3	15	2	3	60.0	83.3
Oregon	56	91	7	23	88.9	79.8
Washington	129	205	10	30	92.8	87.2

Source: Associated General Contractors of America.

population resides, although there are smaller communities where the building trades also exercise influence (Colorado Springs, Pueblo, and Fort Collins, Colorado, for example). As a result, building construction is generally more apt to be unionized than highway construction, much of which is carried out at some distance from metropolitan centers. In the 1973 AGC survey, 71.6 percent of the building contractors in the region were union, compared to 59.5 percent of those doing highway work.

Nevertheless, highway and heavy work is also strongly unionized in the West. As was pointed out in the previous chapter, one strong local of the Operating Engineers (#3) holds sway in California, Hawaii, Utah, and Nevada, and it has been strong enough, as we noted in the last chapter, virtually to preclude the use of trainees on Federal Highway Aid projects in its vast territory.

Staff members of the Industrial Research Unit conducted detailed interviews with industry spokesmen in Albuquerque, Phoenix, and Denver. In Albuquerque, nonresidential building construction is heavily unionized, with only six of sixty AGC member firms operating on an open shop basis, and even these are very small. Homebuilding, on the other hand, is virtually all nonunion, as it has been for about the past fifteen years. There is a considerable amount of open shop highway construction in New Mexico, particularly outside of Albuquerque. According to an AGC spokesman, only fourteen of thirty-three members of the New Mexico highway chapter have union contracts. Finally, there is recent evidence of open shop activity in large scale heavy construction. In one power plant project in the Farmington area, two of the four generating units were, at the time of our interview, being designed by Brown & Root.

Phoenix was the first city in the western states to establish a chapter of the ABC, itself a sign of a growing movement toward the open shop. Perhaps a significant factor in this regard is that the local Home Builders Association, one of the few in the country, negotiates with the building trades for its unionized members. As a result, many open shop residential developers and builders have looked for a new organizational home (although others belong to the Home Builders Association nevertheless) and found it in the ABC. Within the next few years, however, according to a spokesman for the Home Builders of Central Arizona, the association will cease to represent its unionized members at the bargaining table (undoubtedly in anticipation of growth in the open shop component of its membership). At the same time, there is still, by all accounts, considerable subcontracting by nonunion developers to unionized specialty firms.

Commercial and highway building in the Phoenix area is predominantly unionized, a situation which has been little affected by Arizona's right-to-work law. In recent years, however, the AGC highway chapter has opened its rolls to open shop firms who now comprise about 10 percent of the membership. According to an AGC spokesman, the large wage increases negotiated in the late 1960's engendered a tendency for new firms to operate on an open shop basis, a tendency reflected in the AGC membership surveys (see Table VII-3). Power plant construction is performed mostly with union tradesmen, although much of it is done by the in-house work force of the Arizona Public Service Company. In sum, the strength of the building trades in Arizona is still substantial, but the trends appear to point toward an increasingly important open shop presence.

Residential building in the Denver area is predominantly open shop. Homes and small apartments are almost entirely nonunion, while high rise apartments and condominiums are about equally divided between union contractors and open shops. There has been no recent attempt by the building trades to organize the housing sector, although in recent years there was a series of fires of suspicious origin which invariably occurred as the rough carpentry work was being completed.[19]

Commercial construction, on the other hand, tends to be done with union labor; the local AGC chapter has no nonunion members. An AGC spokesman estimates that, within the five county metropolitan Denver area, some 70 percent of commercial construction volume is unionized, a figure which may include some apartment building as well. The building trades are also strong in some smaller communities "outstate," although open shop have apparently made greater penetration in the recreational areas of the state such as Vail, Aspen, and Steamboat Springs. There, according to the AGC official, open shop work may be as much as one-half of the total volume. The recent establishment of an ABC chapter in Denver may presage more open shop activity.

As elsewhere, open shop firms in Denver appear to subcontract a considerable amount of work to unionized subcontractors, especially in the electrical and mechanical specialties where there is a dearth of nonunion subcontractors. High rise apartment construction is particularly prone to be subcontracted to union firms.

Highway construction in Colorado finds a greater representation of open shop contractors, especially away from the Denver metropolitan area. In the 1973 AGC survey, 59 percent of the highway respondents identified themselves as open shop, compared to 81 percent of those doing building work. Heavy construction, particularly in power plants, has seen virtually no open shop penetration in the state.

---

[19] On this situation, see Chapter VIII.

The responses to the Industrial Research Unit questionnaire from the Mountain states were too few to permit any conclusions to be drawn from it as to the overall level of open shop activity. Among these few, however, there was again a marked difference between the views of union and nonunion respondents. At the same time, there appeared to be little sense of a major change in the open shop share over the past few years among either group of respondents, a picture which seems to us roughly consistent with the results of our interviews. In short, there has for some time been an appreciable open shop construction component in this area, especially in residential and (to a lesser extent) highway building, but recent years have not seen a dramatic diminution of union strength. The exception may be in Wyoming where Brown & Root is constructing a power plant—a first for it in the area.

The Pacific states have always been strongly unionized. Aided by this strong labor movement and rapid expansion, even homebuilding has been unionized. These states still are at the top of those in which the construction unions are dominant. We have already noted the overall strength of Local #3 of the Operating Engineers which, with other unions, has organized nearly all highway work in its jurisdiction. The situation is similar in the Northwest. Industrial, commercial, and heavy work are all strongly unionized. Both the AGC and the Industrial Research Unit surveys support our field impressions that the Pacific states are among the most highly unionized.

Even here, there are chinks in the union armor. The ABC has a new chapter in Southern California and promises to open one in the San Francisco SMSA. Our field researchers talked with companies that have used open shop builders to construct small or medium-sized commercial buildings in the San Francisco and Los Angeles SMSA's. Open shop forums sponsored by the AGC's Open Shop Section have been held throughout these areas and drawn large contractor audiences. With such interest, the potential for change exists.

REGIONAL VARIATIONS: CONCLUDING REMARKS

Although the preponderance of the evidence outlined in the foregoing pages shows a broad diminution of union strength across the nation, there are still substantial differences among states, regions, and individual labor markets as to the magnitude of open shop activity in the construction industry. The broad geographic patterns, moreover, appear to have changed little in the past four decades. The South has historically been, and still is, a region where open shop contractors compete effectively. Most of the really large nonunion firms are headquartered in the South. On the other hand, the Middle Atlantic, East North Central area of the Midwest, and Pacific Coast states have long been union strongholds, and although there is growing evidence that this strength is eroding even here, really significant open shop penetration is still more the exception than the rule in some key areas.

Many of the factors which affect the strength or weakness of the building trades unions among regions clearly go beyond the specific characteristics of the construction industry. The areas in which the building trades exercise the greatest influence tend also to be areas where unionization generally is relatively high. The rank correlation coefficient between union members as a percentage of all nonagricultural employment in 1970 (the latest year available) and the proportion of union firms in the 1973 AGC membership survey is .798.[20] A breakdown of these data by states and regions is given Table VII-4, where the parallel regional differences, with respect to both unionism generally and construction unionism in particular, stand out starkly.

One must not, of course, draw too many inferences from such a high correlation. Nonunion contractors are often not represented in AGC chapters. Homebuilders are also outside of AGC's pale. On the other hand, AGC does not include highly organized specialty contractors. Thus the data in Table VII-4 must be considered indicative, not conclusive.

The broader question raised by these observations—that of why certain regions are more generally hospitable to unionism than others—carries beyond the scope of this study. The answer undoubtedly embraces a complex interdependence of political orientation, demographic structure, industry base, and even random historical events. Without attempting to disentangle this web, we can nevertheless try to outline the salient features of the more unionized regions and the ways in which

---

[20] Union membership data from U.S. Bureau of Labor Statistics, *Directory of National Unions and Employee Associations*, 1971, Bulletin 1750 (Washington, D.C.: Government Printing Office, 1972), p. 84.

TABLE VII-4

Union Membership as a Percentage of Total Nonagricultural Employment, 1970, and Proportion of Union Firms in 1973 AGC Membership Survey, by State

State	Percent Union Members	Percent AGC Union Contractors	State	Percent Union Members	Percent AGC Union Contractors
New England	26.3	59.6	E. S. Central	24.0	36.0
Maine	22.0	10.0	Alabama	22.6	28.8
Vermont	20.9	4.3	Kentucky	32.2	56.0
New Hampshire	21.2	24.1	Mississippi	14.9	34.9
Massachusetts	27.2	83.7	Tennessee	24.0	21.6
Connecticut	27.5	88.9	W. S. Central	17.1	29.1
Rhode Island	28.0	87.1	Arkansas	19.5	15.9
Middle Atlantic	38.5	85.2	Louisiana	19.3	56.7
New York	40.2	81.0	Oklahoma	18.6	31.8
Pennsylvania	40.0	89.4	Texas	15.7	22.0
New Jersey	31.2	83.5	Mountain	25.1	64.7
E. N. Central	38.6	87.5	Arizona	21.4	80.0
Illinois	27.3	90.5	Colorado	25.0	67.7
Indiana	37.5	84.4	Idaho	22.1	71.7
Michigan	43.5	84.1	Montana	34.3	75.6
Ohio	38.9	86.9	Nevada	36.5	90.6
Wisconsin	33.3	90.1	New Mexico	18.8	56.0
W. N. Central	29.2	47.1	Utah	26.2	44.7
Iowa	24.5	28.6	Wyoming	24.8	15.0
Kansas	21.1	31.2	Pacific	36.7	90.1
Minnesota	31.9	74.4	Alaska	34.4	96.8
Missouri	37.5	85.5	California	35.7	94.4
Nebraska	21.0	n.a.	Hawaii	30.3	83.3
North Dakota	21.5	11.9	Oregon	36.7	79.8
South Dakota	14.7	10.3	Washington	45.3	87.2
S. Atlantic	18.6	23.5			
Delaware	25.7	55.0			
D.C.-Maryland	25.2	72.9			
Florida	16.2	38.2			
Georgia	17.5	19.4			
North Carolina	9.4	6.3			
South Carolina	11.6	7.7			
Virginia	18.9	11.7			
W. Virginia	46.8	57.9			

Source: The union membership percentages were calculated from U.S. Bureau of Labor Statistics, *Directory of National Unions and Employee Associations, 1971,* Bulletin 1750 (Washington, D. C.: Government Printing Office, 1972), Table 18; and *Manpower Report of the President, 1974* (Washington, D.C.: Government Printing Office, 1974), Table D-1. The percentages are not entirely consistent with those reported in the BLS Directory. Separate calculations were necessary to obtain regional totals. AGC data are from the 1973 membership survey.

they operate to preserve the holding power of the building trades.

One obvious variable is urbanization. The most broadly unionized states tend generally to be those with large proportions of their populations concentrated in a few metropolitan areas. We saw repeatedly in the foregoing pages that the building trades, despite some exceptions, are strongest in major cities, particularly older ones. Larger cities are organizationally congenial to the building trades for several reasons. Projects often tend to be expansive, enhancing the importance of the union as a mechanism for mobilizing large numbers of workers. Their concentration, moreover, facilitates the unions' ability to identify and combat nonunion operations as well as to police those that are undertaken with union labor. It is no accident, therefore, that the centrifugal expansion of urban areas has frequently been associated with a diminution of union strength. It is also no accident that the three regions where unions have historically been most influential—Middle Atlantic, East North Central, and Pacific—are the three with the largest proportions of their populations living within SMSAs.[21]

The passing reference in the above paragraph to the timing of urbanization deserves a bit more comment. Certain southern states are becoming much more urbanized: Virginia, Florida, and Texas are cases in point. These states, nevertheless, have considerable open shop construction activity. Throughout the South, however, increasing urbanization (and industrialization) has been accompanied by a growing proportion of the unionized work force generally. In every southern or border state except Maryland and Arkansas, union membership as a percentage of total employment rose between 1964 and 1970.[22] Much of this growth, however, has clearly been attributable to the movement of national market manufacturing firms which were already unionized into the metropolitan areas of the South. Since construction is predominantly a local market industry, this "transfer effect" is largely absent, and with open shop contractors firmly established in the region, the building trades unions

---

[21] U.S. Bureau of the Census, *Statistical Abstract of the U.S.*, 1974 (Washington, D.C.: Government Printing Office, 1974), Table 18.

[22] U.S. Bureau of Labor Statistics, *Directory of National Unions and Employee Associations, 1965 and 1971*, Bulletins 1493 and 1750 (Washington, D.C.: Government Printing Office, 1966 and 1972), Tables 9 and 18, respectively.

do not appear to have benefitted significantly from the changes in the South's basic economic and demographic character.

The implication here is that the level of industrialization in a state or region is more of a factor in helping to maintain union strength where it already is high rather than augmenting it. Large, unionized manufacturing establishments may be reluctant to incur the enmity both of the building trades and of the industrial unions with which they deal. This pressure, moreover, can operate even in relatively open shop areas. In one case, Daniel International is building a major paper mill in Maine with union labor because of pressure from the customer. In union strongholds, industrial and commercial purchasers are sometimes willing to absorb higher costs in order to ensure labor peace. At other times they may have no choice since there may not be any open shop contractors operating in the area equipped to handle sizable or highly specialized building projects. On the other hand, where the unions are not strong enough to mount an effective protest and where there are open shop contractors available, these factors obviously do not apply, and the unions have lately been unable to make significant organizational inroads into the open shop sector.

A related factor in regional differences is the degree of political influence exercised by the labor movement, which may be seen as both a cause and an effect of union power. A political environment favorable to unions can affect the fortunes of the building trades on at least three levels: through the promulgation of specifications for awarding public contracts; through laws and executive decisions either encouraging or hampering union activity; and through the enforcement of these policies. Where local political leaders have considerable labor support, their aggressiveness in dealing with mass picketing and demonstrations, or even violence, may be tempered. They may also be instrumental in persuading private construction purchasers to build union in the interest of stability. In areas where local authorities have historically been antagonistic to union organization—the South is the best example—the forces which nationally have contributed to a weakening of the unions' base are not checked by favorable political alliances.

Public policy formulation affects open shop competition in a number of areas. Elsewhere in this volume we discuss the impact of "prevailing wage" laws and state apprenticeship regulations. Here we may add still another factor: right-to-work laws. These state statutes, which outlaw the negotiation of union security agreements, have special significance for the construction industry, where relatively little organization is affected through representation elections, and where the unions historically enforced their control over labor supply through the closed shop and later through exclusive hiring halls.[23] Of the twenty states ranking at the bottom of the 1973 AGC survey in terms of proportion of unionized contractor members, sixteen are among the nineteen right-to-work states. Only Nevada (rank 3) and Arizona (rank 18) fail conspicuously to fit the pattern. Again, of course, the existence of a right-to-work law is both the cause and consequence of relative union weakness. Such laws exist only where unions are weak, but they may well help to maintain the status quo.

It must also be understood that these factors cannot entirely explain the various regional and market-wide conditions found around the country. The variables here, either because of their conceptual basis or because of lack of data, do not admit such neat quantification. Furthermore, some cities, some local unions, some crafts, and some individual projects defy the general patterns outlined here, and many of the explanations are undoubtely idiosyncratic. The building trades have continued strong in Peoria, Illinois, a highly unionized industrial city; but in highly unionized Utica, New York, construction unionism is weak. Many such examples could be cited.

There is a final point that should be stressed. The open shop has gained throughout the country because of various factors, including the movement to the suburbs and the increasing industrialization, and therefore rising construction volume, in the South. But the big gains came in the late 1960's and early 1970's. The reason seems clear: the unions have been pricing themselves out of the market. Economics remains a powerful force, and the market will exert itself despite many obstacles.

[23] See Philip Ross, "Origin of the Hiring Hall in Construction," *Industrial Relations*, XI (October, 1972), pp. 366-379.

CHAPTER VIII

The Union Reaction

As the studies and comments quoted in the previous chapters clearly demonstrate, construction union officials have been well aware of the increasing expansion of open shop contractors. They have moved to offset these open shop gains by three approaches: (1) by economic moves, either by adjusting contracts, diminishing demands, or by "project agreements"—making special deals to set aside usual contractual conditions for particular projects or even a particular area; (2) by utilizing the legal "weapons of conflict"—picketing, boycotts, or economic power of a similar nature or by political pressure; and (3) by utilizing illegal weapons of conflict—violence, or threats thereof, intimidation or other such unsavory activities. This chapter surveys the three approaches.

ECONOMIC RESPONSES

By the end of 1974, the unemployment rate among construction workers exceeded 12 percent nationally and in many areas it was double this.[1] Nevertheless, wage concessions by the construction unions have been more the exception than the rule, although it appears likely that 1975 will see unions in many locations modify or reduce demands.

Frequently cited examples of union wage modifications have been of the Operating Engineers in western Pennsylvania and eastern Ohio, who announced a $1.50 lower rate for residential construction; the Laborers in Chicago who extended their contract for one year without a wage increase;[2] and the construction unions in Westchester County, New York, who accepted

[1] Data used herein are based upon those released by the U.S. Bureau of Labor Statistics and by the Contractors Mutual Association.

[2] James C. Hyatt, "Construction Workers, Despite Dearth of Jobs, Still Seek Wage Boosts," *Wall Street Journal*, April 9, 1975, pp. 1, 19.

work at below union scales.[3] In regard to the first situation, we noted in Chapter III that special, lower rates for homebuilding did not usually increase union strength because homebuilders still found union labor expensive and unaccustomed to their needs; and that when employment increased, union members left homebuilding and sought work in the higher paying sectors of the industry. The Chicago Laborers' action reflects the serious situation for construction work in a highly unionized area where, at least until now, open shop construction has not been a serious threat.

The Westchester County situation also reflects serious unemployment in a unionized area where the open shop has, however, made at least some progress. The workers involved there are employed under Title 6 of the Comprehensive Employment and Training Act (CETA), and have reduced their wages to stay under the annual limit of $10,000 to make them eligible for CETA sponsored work. This put their rates below Davis-Bacon ones but this was justified "because of the emergency nature of the program and because all the workers have volunteered for employment."[4] In addition to this very interesting interpretation of the Davis-Bacon Act, about which the Department of Labor allegedly expressed "some misgivings,"[5] the Westchester County administrators promised that subsequent allocations of funds would be divided between union and nonunion employees.[6]

Acceptance of a lower rate is rare among unionized employees. More common, as Dr. John T. Dunlop pointed out many years ago, is the retention of the rate on paper, but "concealed reduction" instead.[7] Undoubtedly, this has occurred in many areas of the country, where construction employment is sharply below levels of previous years. Such actions include waiving overtime rules, permitting work to be done in a more efficient manner, or simply accepting a lower than contract rate

---

[3] James Feron, "Westchester Unions Accept 'WPA' Jobs," *New York Times*, April 10, 1975, p. 1.

[4] "Union Workers Take Pay Cut to Get County Building Jobs," *Engineering News-Record*, (April 17, 1975), p. 13.

[5] Feron, *loc. cit.*

[6] *Ibid.*

[7] John T. Dunlop, *Wage Determination Under Trade Unions* (New York: The Macmillan Company, 1944), p. 67.

for a job. Where such arrangements are formalized, they are known as "project agreements" and are discussed in the following section. Besides such formal arrangements, however, periods of unemployment spawn many informal arrangements to reduce costs in return for employment. In addition, of course, many unions have modified demands, or like the Chicago Laborers union, agreed to forego upward adjustments.

Sometimes these concealed reductions are implemented selectively. In the Pittsburgh area, for example, and undoubtedly elsewhere, the Operating Engineers union has been willing to ignore various costly contractual provisions (although not the basic wage rate) on projects on which open shop contractors have shown a desire to bid. In these cases, the union has negotiated side agreements with the Western Pennsylvania Highway Chapter of the AGC, enabling union contractors to bid more competitively on those jobs. In other areas, some unions have agreed, in advance, to maintain existing wage scales for the life of projects on which there are likely to be open shop bidders, thus foregoing increases scheduled to take effect later.

The extent to which the various signs of union restraint are caused by open shop competition is difficult to ascertain. In Chapter XI, we shall demonstrate that union wage rates are substantially above those of open shop workers in addition to the many other cost advantages enjoyed by open shop contractors, and that the union-open shop wage rate differential seems to have widened since the mid-1960's. This is also the period of the open shop's greatest growth spurt, and obviously the two phenomena must be related. Certainly open shop gains also add to the unemployment problems of unionized workers. Thus, although it is unemployment *per se,* not the loss of jobs to open shop contractors, which spurs unions to examine their wage and related policies, the increase in open shop work can often be a factor in the overall situation. As a union official for Operating Engineers Local 382 in Arkansas, which recently agreed to wage cuts of up to $2.82 an hour, put it, "your contract wage rate may be $10 or $12 an hour, but that doesn't mean anything if the contractor isn't competitive and there isn't any work for our members." [8]

We do not imply, however, that either unemployment or open shop competition has imbued an overall sense of re-

[8] "Some Arkansas Workers Agree To Take Pay Cuts," *Wall Street Journal,* April 21, 1975, p. 3.

straint in construction union wage policies. Where neither is an immediate threat, as in the state of Washington, fabrication headquarters for the Alaskan pipeline, early 1975 saw the electrical workers negotiate a $6.42 per hour increase, raising their rate to $20 per hour. In San Francisco, plumbers won a $1.62 per hour increase on top of an hourly rate in excess of $13.[9] In other cases, increases have been large while employment has fallen sharply. Obviously, union wage policy is predicated for the most part on the assumption that construction employment will not be radically affected by wage costs except for short periods, that the demand is inelastic, and therefore, that wage reductions will prove more costly than helpful to the union worker. Where difficult situations ensue, some restraint may occur, or off-rate adjustments may be made on an informal or temporary basis. Where a large construction project is at stake—that is, when the issue is either whether it will be built by union or open shop contractors—then a formal, but temporary "project agreement" may solve the immediate problem for the unions without prejudicing future gains.

Project Agreements

Project agreements are usually entered into by large industrial contractors and unions to cover such major buildings as power plants, petro-chemical complexes, etc. In an unusual case discussed below, such an agreement was worked out for the Houston, Texas, area.

Not all project agreements are spurred by open shop competition. Thus one exists for the Alaskan pipeline project where no such threat appeared; the need for uninterrupted construction, special problems, etc., can all result in a project agreement. There is no question, however, that open shop competition has been a decided spur in recent years for project agreement consummation.

Daniel International will operate union only under project agreements. The fact that this company has the capability to work open shop (and does 80 percent of the time) on the largest of projects, places unions in a frame of mind to "make a deal."

Project agreements do not usually affect wage rates, although one in Niagara Falls, New York, covering the con-

[9] Hyatt, *loc. cit.*

struction of a convention center reportedly provided for wages 15 percent below prevailing scales. It, however, excluded two key trades—carpenters and electricians.[10] Often the agreements purport to reduce labor costs by: banning jurisdictional dispute interruptions; including provisions for no strikes and arbitration of disputes arising from a contract; reducing the number of nonworking union stewards; reducing or eliminating coffee break periods; permitting management to select its supervisors; reducing the overtime rate from double-time to time-and-one-half; eliminating travel time, standby crews, etc. Most project agreements do not, however, make changes in basic craft rules —that is, who performs what work—and therefore do not permit one craft to do incidental work in another craft that is necessary to perform a job.

One of the most unusual project agreements is the one signed by the National Constructors Association and the Houston Building and Construction Trades Council, November 6, 1973. It applies to "all industrial construction work on projects with a value of $2 million or more . . . in the Houston area." Its provisions (among others) give employers "the unqualified right to select and hire directly all supervisors without such persons being referred by the unions;" establishes trainee classifications as set forth below; forbids jurisdictional strikes, slowdowns and work stoppages, limits on production, restrictions on the use of tools and equipment, and "coffee breaks, rest periods, or other non-working time established during working hours;" gives the employer "the right to determine crew sizes, including partial crews during inclement weather;" and includes these paragraphs:

> Trainee classifications should be included in all skilled crafts. Such classifications shall be considered a training classification and the rate of pay will be at the equivalent apprentice rate of pay. The trainee may be over age for apprentice training, but will have the necessary qualifications to become a skilled craftsmen. Training period will be at least the same length as the apprentice. The trainee will be assigned by the Employer to perform any work which is normally performed by his craft and which is within the capability of the trainee.
>
> The trainee will remain in training until qualified to become a journeyman. Trainees and/or apprentices shall comprise from 20

---

[10] *Engineering News-Record,* (January 17, 1974), p. 3.

to 30 percent of each craft's work force at any time and the composition of this ratio shall be at the craft's discretion.[11]

Another significant project agreement was negotiated in 1973 by the Building and Construction Trades Councils of Detroit and the State of Michigan and AGC contractors engaged in the construction of power generating units. The agreement is a nine page document which provides several important modifications to the applicable local contracts. It covers fourteen large projects, worth billions of dollars, for the Consumers Power Company and the Detroit Edison Company. Several of the more significant provisions are:

1. There shall be no limit on production by employees nor restrictions on the full use of tools or equipment. There shall be no restriction, other than may be required by safety regulations, on the number of employees assigned to any crew or any service. [(Certain rules regarding Ironworker rigging crews are excepted.)]
2. A steward shall be a qualified employee performing work of his craft and shall exercise no supervisory function. There shall be no non-working stewards.
3. Shift work may be performed at the option of the Employer(s), but when performed it must continue for a period of not less than five (5) consecutive work days. Saturday and Sunday, if worked, can be used for establishing the 5-day minimum shift work period. In the event the second or third shift of any regular work day shall extend into a holiday, employees shall be paid at the regular shift rate.
4. High time and other so-called hazardous premiums where they now exist in the local and national Union(s) agreements will be frozen at the present level of payment and any reduction through future contract negotiations will be reflected in this Agreement . . . . Any so-called hazardous premiums that apply exclusively or predominantly to the construction work covered by this agreement will not be recognized.
5. The Employer(s) shall not recognize any guaranteed overtime negotiated in the local Union(s) agreements.
6. On equipment operated by Operating Engineers, Employer(s) shall be allowed to make two (2) complete equipment changes per shift.

[11] Copy of agreement in authors' possession.

7. There shall be no 40-hour work guarantee for any employees on this Project(s), except for general foremen and foremen of these local Union(s) which have a negotiated 40-hour guarantee in their local Union(s) agreements on the initial date of this Agreement.
8. The starting time of the work day may be changed at the discretion of the Employer(s) to take advantage of daylight hours, weather conditions, shift or traffic conditions. The variation of the starting time will not exceed one hour without mutual consent of the parties involved.
9. Subsistence, travel allowance, mileage or pay on travel time will be paid in accordance with provisions existing in each respective Union(s) collective bargaining agreement on the initial date of this Agreement. These rates shall not be increased for the life of this Agreement and any reduction through future contract negotiations will be reflected in this agreement.[12]

Project agreements thus return to construction management many managerial rights which have been negotiated away or usurped by unions over the years. The Houston one provides a greater return to management than most, undoubtedly spurred by the strength of Brown & Root and other open shop contractors in the area. As noted in Chapter VI, the inability of open shop contractors to supply sufficient management and manpower to cope with the great petro-chemical boom in the Gulf Coast area, has given the unionized national constructors an opportunity to obtain major contracts there that they might otherwise have been unable to do, and the project agreement improves their competitive position.

Nevertheless, project agreements do not meet open shop competition in a number of key respects. For example, the trainee classification gives the Houston union builders a virtual helper category and thus permits considerable saving on work crews. But whereas his open shop competitor can use, for example, one journeyman, one helper, and three laborers on a five man plumbing crew, the union shop builder will have two or three journeymen and the rest helpers. Open shop laborers will still unload and move materials, whereas union shop craftsmen perform these tasks; open shop workers will cross craft lines

[12] Copy of agreement in authors' possession.

without concern; and open shop wage rates and benefits are likely to be considerably less.

Moreover, despite ironclad rules, jurisdictional strikes do occur. It takes just one ambitious business agent "to pull the men." Although such walkouts may be quickly settled, time and money are lost.

The project agreement thus recognizes a practical situation and moves to meet it by reducing nonproductive, costly practices. Wage rates and basic jurisdictional lines remain largely unaffected, however. As a result, the project agreement is likely to reduce the economic differential between union and open shop operations, but at the same time some very fundamental economic advantages remain with the latter. It is possible, through excellent management, high productivity, and skilled manpower, for union operations to eliminate this differential. Such key characteristics, however, are also found on the open shop side. The Houston union builder, competing with Brown & Root, H. B. Zachry, Delta Engineering or the Hudson division of J. Ray McDermott has a hard competitive task indeed.[13]

UTILIZING THE LEGAL WEAPONS OF CONFLICT

Construction unions have tremendous bargaining power and leverage. By striking, they can bring contractors to their terms since the lost time is so expensive to the contractor. With picketing, they can shut down a job by keeping materials from entering a job, or even induce or prevent employees from working. By boycotting, they can prevent a product from being used on a job, thus causing severe losses to suppliers, contractors, and owners.

Taft-Hartley: Interpretations and Practices

The nation's labor laws attempt to regulate this power in a manner that balances contending forces in the interests of the public good. Twice Congress—in the Taft-Hartley Act in 1947

---

[13] A unique opportunity to compare work by a national constructor company and Brown & Root on virtually identical projects will soon be possible. Lummis designed virtually identical ethylene plants for ARCO and Gulf. Both are being constructed in reasonable proximity in the Houston area, ARCO's by Brown & Root, Gulf's by Lummis. Unfortunately, construction was not far enough advanced for such a comparison to be included in this study.

and in the Landrum-Griffin Act of 1959—enacted amendments to the National Labor Relations (Wagner) Act of 1935 which were designed, in part, to restrict union power in the use of strikes, picketing, and boycotts. As a result of interpretive difficulties and rulings by the National Labor Relations Board and the courts favorable to the union point of view, construction unions have considerable latitude to utilize these "weapons of conflict" and do so in their drive to restrict open shop builders.[14]

Thus unions are allowed to publicize a dispute by keeping pickets before an open shop construction site. They must claim no organizing interest or the picketing becomes organizational picketing and can be enjoined in due course. Since the unions would be most happy to remove pickets if the job becomes union, this distinction between "publicity picketing" and "organization picketing" is, to the layman, often more fictional than factual.

The consequences of publicity picketing varies from area to area and job to job. In some areas, it can seriously retard deliveries, cause customer hardship, and induce employee separations. In open shop areas, its impact can be slight at most. Certainly, this impact is a factor considered by users and open shop builders in determining whether it is possible to build in an area.

Boycotts are attempts to apply pressure on one party by economic action against a second party. In turn, the second party is induced to pressure the first party to accede to the unions' demands in order to relieve himself of a dispute to which he (the second party) is not directly involved. In a construction setting, for example, a union that picketed a supplier, or refused to handle that supplier's materials on construction sites, because the supplier sold materials to an open shop builder, would be engaged in secondary boycott activity.

Whether such boycotting was illegal, however, would depend on the supplier's relationship, if any, to the open shop builder,

---

[14] This section is based primarily upon Ralph M. Dereshinsky, *The NLRB and Secondary Boycotts*, Labor Relations and Public Policy Series, Report No. 4 (Philadelphia: Industrial Research Unit, The Wharton School, University of Pennsylvania, 1972). See this monograph for a complete analysis of the issues discussed in this section. For additional cases, background, etc., see *The Developing Labor Law*, ed. by Charles J. Morris (Washington, D.C.: Bureau of National Affairs, Inc., 1971), Chapters 21-24. Annual supplements to this work are also available from the publisher.

plus any of various other relationships, proof of union directed actions and motives, and other interpretations by the NLRB and the courts. Moreover, the lack of clarity of these decisions often tends to induce third parties to avoid such disputes by refraining from dealing with open shop builders while at the same time encouraging unions to act and to inflict damage on open shop builders while the law is being tested. Dereshinsky points out that various NLRB and court interpretations of Section 8(b)(4)(B) of the Taft-Hartley Act, which many thought outlawed secondary boycotts, "works to divest secondary employers of their neutrality and thereby makes them a party to the primary dispute." He also notes that the NLRB and court case-by-case approach "undermine[s] the clear and predictable administration of the Act," and in some cases appears" to be evolving a doctrine that greatly expanded union rights at the expense of the neutral employer." [15]

Finally, unions are permitted by language of Section 8(b)(4)(i) and (ii)(B) of the Act to appeal to consumers to support a boycott which they cannot enforce themselves. Thus the unions can call upon consumers to cease doing business with a company, but pursuant to judicial decisions, they can also make this appeal, under certain circumstances, by picketing if the picketing is not "coercive." The effect is to draw the neutral third party into the dispute and inevitably enhance union power.[16]

Practice and Pressure

In practice, union power of this nature is often exerted behind the scenes. A supplier told quietly by a union business agent that he might have trouble if he delivered concrete to an open shop builder is likely not to test the question. As a result, open shop builders often have difficulty in obtaining key materials because suppliers are "sold out," "have no trucks for delivery," or the order "gets lost." Similarly, the comment of a business agent to a user that he "will not be responsible for any trouble that might arise" if a contract is awarded to a nonunion builder often is sufficient to achieve results.

Unions often call upon their friends for support. Large additions to paper manufacturing facilities in Maine, begun in

[15] *Ibid.*, p. 72.

[16] *Ibid.*, p. 94.

1974, were awarded by two giant companies with the requirement that they be build on a union basis despite the fact that the areas involved had long been strictly open shop territory and that one of the contractors was Daniel International. The companies feared pressure by their plant unions if construction was open shop.

Construction unions have considerable political power in many localities, a point to which we shall return below. Open shop contractors can be left off bid lists or pressured not to bid by public authorities. One also wonders if the U.S. Department of Labor would waive Davis-Bacon requirements because of an "emergency" and because workers were "volunteers," as was apparently done in Westchester County, New York, if nonunion employees were involved. And of course elsewhere in this volume, and more completely in a companion study, is discussed the pro-union impact of prevailing wage laws.[17]

Unions also put considerable pressure on their political friends when the job market is low. Sometimes this pressure borders on violence. This occurred in New York City on February 17, 1975, when 10,000 construction workers rallied for jobs around City Hall, halting traffic for several hours, hurling curses at the Mayor, and generally causing a disruption.[18] The issue here was jobs *per se,* not open shop competition, but smaller rallies elsewhere have been aimed at both during the 1974-1975 construction recession.

"Double-Breasted" Operations

Unions have become increasingly concerned in stopping "double-breasted" operations—that is, common ownership of firms, one of which operates union shop, the other open shop. They have attacked such arrangements by maintaining that the separation is artificial and that, therefore, companies have violated Section 8(a)(5) of the Taft-Hartley Act by not bargaining in good faith concerning conditions in the open shop company and/or not adhering to union conditions therein. If the union charge can be sustained, then they are free to picket and to

---

[17] Armand J. Thieblot, Jr., *The Davis-Bacon Act,* Labor Relations and Public Policy Series, Report No. 10 (Philadelphia: Industrial Research Unit, The Wharton School, University of Pennsylvania, 1975).

[18] Fred Ferretti, "10,000 Construction Workers Block Traffic Near City Hall in Job Protest," *New York Times,* February 18, 1975, p. 24.

boycott the open shop company. If not, however, such picketing and/or boycotting can be enjoined.

For the NLRB, the critical factor is the degree of separation in management, particularly the management of labor relations. If such management is, in fact, separate, and if employees do not transfer back and forth, the NLRB will find that under the law there exists separate companies that picketing and boycotting of the open shop company is secondary activity and therefore is illegal.[19]

Mixed Crews

Wherever unions are strong, they are usually able to insist that jobs be wholly union—that is, the general and all subcontractors must be union. This is done by refusing to work with nonunion subcontractors. Often, regardless of the legal rights involved, an open shop subcontractor is simply forced off the job because the unionists will not work with his crews. Where the general contractor is open shop, union subcontractors will often work without problems because they need each other. This is not likely to occur, however, in strong union areas because the crafts are more likely to work together to keep the area union. As noted in Chapter IV, however, as open shop general contractors win more of the business, the union specialty trades can no longer afford to refuse their work.

Contractors and users can sometimes avoid excessive trouble on a mixed crew job by establishing separate gates for open shop and union shop subcontractor employees. If a union pickets an open shop employee gate, the employees may simply cross it; if it pickets a union shop one, it is putting pressure on secondary employers—union contractors or the building owner—because of its dispute with an open shop contractor, and this has been construed to be illegal if various conditions are met.[20]

Subcontractor Clauses, the NLRB and Antitrust Laws

A key demand of unions in negotiating with general contractors is a provision requiring that all subcontracted work

---

[19] See, for example, *Gerace Construction, Inc., et al.*, 193 NLRB No. 91; *Frank N. Smith Associates, Inc., et al.*, 194 NLRB No. 34; *Carpenters District Council of Houston, et al., and Baxter Construction Company, Inc.*, 201 NLRB No. 16.

[20] See Dereshinsky, *op. cit.*, Chapter II, especially pp. 29-32.

be given to union subcontractors or to subcontractors that meet "union conditions." Section 8(e) of the Taft-Hartley Act, which was added to this law in 1959 as part of the Landrum-Griffin Act amendments thereto, outlaws so-called "hot cargo" agreements but provides that "nothing in this subsection (e) shall apply to an agreement . . . in the construction industry relating to the contracting or subcontracting of work to be done at the site of the construction, alteration, painting or repair of a building, structure or other work. . . ." Then by a series of court and NLRB decisions, application of the other Taft-Hartley antiboycott clauses have been weakened by drawing distinctions between what has been determined to be "lawful subcontracting clauses, which have as their object the protection and preservation of [bargaining] unit work, and unlawful clauses which only forbid subcontracting to nonunion subcontractors." [21] The result has been "a gradual watering down of a statutory proscription in favor of union interests." [22]

Some unions have developed additional techniques to eliminate open shop subcontractors. Thus they have required that general contractors subcontract only to signatories of a special agreement. Other unions have picketed general contractors who were not signatories to a labor agreement and demanded that they agree not to do business with subcontractor firms who do not have agreements with that union. In both the latter two cases, contractors that refused to accede to these unions have, after vainly seeking remedies pursuant to the Taft-Hartley Act, attacked these clauses as violating the antitrust laws. In a reverse twist to these situations, a group of unions have brought suits charging independent unions and contractors in Pittsburgh and Ohio with restraint of trade. These cases are now all in litigation, but worth reviewing because of the importance of the outcome to the ability of open shop contractors to operate in many areas.

The Morse Bros., Inc. Case.[23] Local 701 of the Operating

---

[21] *Ibid.*, p. 110.

[22] *Ibid.*, p. 113. The work preservation issue is discussed again in Chapter IX. Essentially, unions now can refuse to handle prefabricated materials if they once constructed them on the site.

[23] *Morse Bros., Inc.* v. *International Union of Operating Engineers, et al.*, Civil No. 71-515, U.S. D.C. (Dis. Ore.). *Daily Labor Report*, No. 229, (November 26, 1974), pp. D-1 to D-6.

Engineers negotiates an agreement with the Oregon-Columbia Chapter of the Associated General Contractors covering five counties in Oregon and five counties in southwest Washington. Signatories are required to subcontract paving and material supply, if they do so, only to signatories of the agreement or companies which have reached agreement with the union. Rejecting the union claim that its agreement was exempt from the antitrust laws, the U.S. District Court, District of Oregon, ruled that this agreement amounted to a union-management conspiracy and was violative of the Sherman Antitrust Act.

The Connell Case.[24] Connell Construction Company is a Dallas, Texas, general contractor which employs no plumbers, and has subcontracted plumbing work both to union and open shop plumbing subcontractors. Local 100 of the Plumbers' Union demanded that Connell sign an agreement which specifically did not recognize the union as a bargaining agent, but would commit Connell to subcontract work within the jurisdiction of Local 100 "only to firms that are parties to an executed current bargaining agreement with Local Union 100. . . ." When the company refused, Local 100 picketed Connell projects and forced it to sign the required agreement, which was done under protest.

In a previous case, the NLRB and the courts found a limited violation of the Taft-Hartley Act because the picketing was deemed to be organizational in purpose.[25] Local 100, by specifically stating that it wanted no recognition to bargain and by picketing contractors who had no employees who could be covered by its bargaining agreement, avoided this type of charge.[26]

Other Dallas area general contractors filed charges with the NLRB against Local 100's picketing, but the NLRB general counsel refused to entertain them. There is no appeal from such lack of action, although the Court of Appeals, Fifth Circuit, was highly critical of the general counsel's action which it deemed "may constitute an abuse of discretion." Connell therefore sought relief under the antitrust laws. He lost in the district court and court of appeals, but the latter decision

---

[24] *Connell Construction Company* v. *Plumbers and Steamfitters Local No. 100, et al.*, 483 F.2d 1154 (CA-5, 1973), *cert. granted*, 94 Sup. Ct. 2381C; reversed and remanded, June 2, 1975.

[25] *Dallas Building Trades* v. *NLRB*, 396 F.2d 677 (CA-D.C., 1969).

[26] Section 8(b)(7) of the Taft-Hartley Act limits organizational picketing to 30 days.

was accompanied by a strong dissent.[27] The U.S. Supreme Court granted certiorari, and in an historic decision, ruled June 2, 1975, that such union conduct may be subject to the antitrust laws and treble damages. This decision could well limit effective union action against open shop subcontractors and therefore increase the share of work of the latter. On the other hand, unions can still engage in "information picketing" to "protest area standards." Hence the impact of the decision, although it will undoubtedly be significant, cannot be immediately ascertained.

Independent Union-Association Cases.[28] AFL-CIO construction unions have brought antitrust charges against two independent unions in eastern Ohio and western Pennsylvania charging collusion with employers. In both cases, contractors were members apparently both of the union and contractor association. One union, the Associated Trades and Crafts, is a black organization. In both cases, the courts have held antitrust issues in abeyance while referring the matters to the NLRB for possible unfair labor practice violations.

These independent unions have won a sizable amount of work in areas that were once standard craft union strongholds. Obviously, however, their members are vulnerable both to unfair labor practice and antitrust violations if they attempt to operate both as an employer association and a trade union.

Weapons of Conflict and Organizing Methods

This summary of laws and practices is not meant as definitive, but rather as illustrative of some of the legal and tactical methods utilized by unions in their drive against open shop expansion. Many of these union policies stem from their in-

---

[27] The dissent stated in part: ". . . where a union bypasses the congressionally sanctioned methods of organizing the employer whose employees it seeks to unite (here, the individual subcontractors) and illegally brings pressure on a neutral, secondary source of work for all such employers within an area (Connell) to force that unrelated economic entity to execute a contract which requires that all directly involved subcontractors bring their work forces into the membership of that local or starve for lack of work, then that union has passed beyond the scope of antitrust immunity."

[28] *Carpenters' District Council of Mahoning, et al.,* v. *United Contractors Association of Ohio, et al.,* 484 F.2d 119 (CA-6, 1973); and *International Association of Asbestos Workers, et al.,* v. *United Contractors Association of Pittsburgh, Pa., Inc.,* 483 F.2d 384 (CA-3, 1973).

ability to organize open shop contractors by winning the votes of their employees. In part this is attributable to the nature of the industry. Workers are often on one company's payroll for a relatively short period, and therefore are not easily solicited for the typical NLRB bargaining rights election that is found in most other industries.

Actually, however, open shop contractors, particularly larger ones, maintain a larger permanent payroll than most union contractors, as we discuss in Chapter IX. But the construction unions, as a policy, generally avoid NLRB election procedures, and follow instead their traditional route of using the weapons of conflict to compel the employer to accept a union contract and thereby to obtain his work force from the union hiring hall. Since this means that the unions will supply personnel, and that the personnel on the open shop contractor's payroll may be replaced or may not even be put on the union rolls, it can readily be understood that employees of open shop contractors are often unlikely to vote for union representation if given the opportunity.

Thus conflict and power, not election procedures, are the organization techniques in the construction industry. If the union wins, a different group of employees are likely to receive work on a given project. More than likely, a different set of contractors will also be involved. Given both the extent of what is at stake, and the failure of the more democratic—and indeed more civilized—procedures to govern which set of employees and employers will be the victors, it is perhaps not surprising that the legal weapons of conflict, and the judicial determination of enforcement of the extent of their legality and appropriateness in given situations, have given way in other instances to the raw use of violence.

VIOLENCE

The use of violence to compel contractors to accept unionism has a long history. At the turn of the century, officials of the Ironworkers' union were convicted of dynamiting nonunion construction jobs.[29] Montgomery's classic history of industrial relations in the Chicago construction industry makes repeated

---

[29] Luke Grant, *The National Erectors' Association and the International Association of Bridge and Structural Ironworkers* (Washington, D.C.: United States Commission on Industrial Relations, 1915).

references to bombings and other violence;[30] Ryan recounts one strike alone in San Francisco in which "over three hundred cases of violence occurred;"[31] Seidman's study of labor racketeering is replete with instances of violence perpetrated against construction union members and contractors;[32] and the McClellan hearings of the 1950's contain numerous similar accounts.[33] Even such a sympathetic historian of a construction union as Mangum recounts the violence accompanying union organizing drives.[34]

That the increased penetration of open shop firms since the mid-1960's has led to a resurgence of violence seems incontrovertible. In 1972, the *Engineering News-Record* reported:

> Violence is the gut reaction of unions in some areas to counter the open shop. In recent years violence and property damage have hit nonunion projects in Florida, Maryland, Tennessee, Georgia, Ohio and Pennsylvania.[35]

In May, 1973, the Associated Builders and Contractors filed complaints with the National Labor Relations Board against seventeen AFL-CIO building trades unions and numerous other state and local affiliates charging a conspiracy to initiate and to commit violence on a national scale. After a year's consideration, the general counsel of the NLRB issued complaints against four international unions (Laborers, Carpenters, Roofers, and Ironworkers), plus state and local union bodies of the Operating Engineers (Ohio, Michigan, New Jersey, and Pennsylvania), Ironworkers (Michigan and Massachusetts), Laborers (Ken-

---

[30] Royal E. Montgomery, *Industrial Relations in the Chicago Building Trades* (Chicago: University of Chicago Press, 1927). In the index, the word "violence" is followed by twelve separate citations.

[31] Frederick L. Ryan, *Industrial Relations in the San Francisco Building Trades* (Norman, Oklahoma: University of Oklahoma Press, 1936), p. 191.

[32] Harold Seidman, *Labor Czars: A History of Labor Racketeering* (New York: Liveright Publishing Corporation, 1938).

[33] Useful summaries of the McClellan hearings, in which the Teamsters and Operating Engineers were featured, are found in John Hutchinson, *The Imperfect Union: A History of Corruption in American Trade Unions* (New York: E. P. Dutton & Co., Inc., 1970); and Robert F. Kennedy, *The Enemy Within* (New York: Popular Library, 1960).

[34] Garth L. Mangum, *The Operating Engineers: The Economic History of A Trade Union* (Cambridge: Harvard University Press, 1964), e.g., pp. 181-195.

[35] "Open Shop, A Growing Force and a Catalyst for Change," reprint from *Engineering News-Record* (November 2, 1972).

tucky), Plumbers (Michigan), and Roofers (Pennsylvania), and the Building and Construction Trades Councils of the State of Michigan and of subdivisions thereof, and of Middlesex County, New Jersey. The allegations of a national conspiracy were dismissed, as were charges against the Baltimore and Orlando, Florida, Building and Construction Trades Councils and several local unions affiliated with each.[36] Since then the Michigan case was settled by a consent stipulation in which the unions involved there agreed to refrain from violence, as will be discussed below, and a NLRB administrative law judge has found locals of the Laborers union (but not the international) and the Operating Engineers guilty of violence designed to restrain and coerce employees of an open shop highway firm. This case is now before the NLRB on appeal.[37]

Besides these NLRB cases, violence has provided considerable additional litigation in various parts of the country. As examples of the scope and character of such violence, we have set forth below summaries of events which have occurred in the Denver, Philadelphia, and Michigan areas, and comment more briefly on the situation elsewhere.

Denver [38]

Fires which destroyed principally apartment houses and condominiums under construction, but also some other buildings and lumber yards supplying them, have plagued a number of areas, but particularly Denver since the early 1970's. About forty such fires doing an estimated $10 million damage have occurred there, most of them involving open shop builders or contractors who had a dispute with unions. Usually, the fire occurred after a building was closed in, but before internal walls and ceilings were in place—the period when fire can do maximum damage.

---

[36] This summary is based on the General Counsel's press release and *Order Consolidating Cases, Consolidated Complaint* and *Notice of Hearing* in Cases Nos. 8-CB-2112, 22-CB-2598, 1-CB-2316, and 7-CC-757, 7-CB-2834).

[37] *Laborers' International Union, et al.,* Case No. 8-CB-2112, Administrative Law Judge Decision, March 27, 1975.

[38] The Denver fires story has appeared regularly in the press there, and was, of course, discussed in our field visits. See *Rocky Mountain News,* July 27, 1972; May 13 and December 14, 1974; and April 10, 1975; and *Denver Post,* July 28 and 31, August 8 and 28, September 7, October 10, and December 29, 1972; March 1 and 2 and June 13, 1973, and December 15, 1974, January 9 and April 14, 1975. Also *Rocky Mountain News,* June 26, 1975.

Investigators were stymied for about one year while attorneys for the Northern Colorado Building and Construction Trades Council vainly sought to suppress evidence allegely obtained by wiretap in accordance with Colorado law, appealing all the way to the U.S. Supreme Court.

In December 1974, Anthony Charles Mulligan, business agent for the Colorado Building and Construction Trades Council (the northern and southern branches have been merged) and William F. Swanson, a business representative for Cement Masons Local 577, were indicted for arson. In April, 1975, Edward L. Urioste, Executive Secretary of the New Mexico Building and Construction Trades Council, Albuquerque, was indicted for conspiracy to commit arson, plus several other crimes, after Colorado Bureau of Investigation undercover agents flew with him from New Mexico to Denver in a private plane in which he carried dynamite and other explosives. Swanson was convicted of conspiracy to commit arson in June 1975, and trials of the others were then pending.

Philadelphia [39]

Philadelphia, as we have noted in previous chapters, is a "union town." The construction unions have been key supporters of the current and previous mayors and enjoy a close relationship with City Hall. Philadelphia is also a city where construction union violence has been endemic.

Much publicity has been given to the Altemose case. In the words of the U.S. Court of Appeals, Third Circuit:

> This case arises out of highly unusual circumstances. In the background is the history of an intense and violent labor dispute between Altemose and the Building and Construction Trades Council of Philadelphia, over Altemose's refusal to sign a "subcontractor's agreement" which would obligate it to let subcontracts exclusively to firms using only unionized labor. The dispute reached a climax during the summer of 1972, after Altemose had been

[39] The material for this section, unless otherwise noted, is based on numerous press stories and articles collected over the years. See, particularly, for the Altemose Case, the (Philadelphia) *Evening and Sunday Bulletin,* June 5, 11, 12, 14, 15, 18, 20, and 22, July 16 and 17, August 19, 20, 21, 22, 24, and 29, September 15, 18, 19, 20, 21, and 28, October 18, and 24, 1972; February 18, June 28, July 19, 24, 25, 27, and 28, September 11, October 23, November 8, 10, 11, 22, and 30, and December 1, 5, and 28, 1973; January 20, February 6 and 9, March 3, April 4, 7, 11, and 14, September 8, October 2 and 20, and November 1 and 29, 1974; and January 14, 17, 21 and 22, and March 12, 1975. For other aspects of Philadelphia violence, see notes 38-41, below, and *Philadelphia Inquirer,* May 26 and June 7 and 14, 1972.

> awarded the general contract for the construction of a hotel and office building complex in King of Prussia, Pennsylvania, known as the Valley Forge Plaza. In the morning of June 5, 1972, approximately 1,000 men from the Trades Council arrived at the Plaza construction site in buses chartered by one of the Council's member unions and proceeded to destroy vehicles, equipment and other property belonging to Altemose, causing damage in excess of $350,000. Although Altemose immediately obtained a preliminary injunction in state court prohibiting picketing by members of the Trades Council within one mile of any Altemose site or its office building, a second mob descended the following day on the office of Altemose Enterprises and threatened to burn it down. Violence was prevented only through the combined efforts of state and local police. Subsequently, on August 17, J. Leon Altemose was attacked and beaten by members of the Trades Council in broad daylight, while attempting to enter a bank in downtown Philadelphia.
>
> Members of the Trades Council also put pressure on the employees at the construction site to cease working for Altemose. Edward Fitzpatrick, a business agent for one of the member unions in the Trades Council, called one of the subcontractors on the site, Richard Czeiner, and told him that the unions would prefer that he not work there. Czeiner refused to quit, however, and subsequently several of his vehicles were destroyed or damaged by fire bombs. Despite strong security measures taken by Altemose, construction on the project was plagued by sabotage.
>
> As a result of the violence and threats, many subcontractors withdrew from the site and Altemose and Energy had considerable difficulty in obtaining qualified workers willing to risk work there.[40]

About two weeks after the Altemose destruction, vandals registered at the Sheraton Hotel in Philadelphia—the same chain for which Altemose was constructing a hotel—and caused serious damage in a number of rooms. Since then at least one other Altemose project has been bombed and other violence has occurred.

Despite a battery of lawyers and the estimated expenditure of $300,000 for the first trial alone by the Philadelphia Building and Construction Trades Council, eighteen unionists, most of them from Local 30 of the Roofers' union, were convicted of multiple accounts of violence and related crimes in two trials held in Norristown, Montgomery County. They are now on bail while appealing. The attack on Mr. Altemose in broad daylight in downtown Philadelphia brought no conviction to some of the same Local 30 members.

---

[40] *Altemose Construction Company, et al.,* v. *National Labor Relations Board,* U.S. Court of Appeals, Third Circuit, March 14, 1975. *Daily Labor Report,* No. 67 (April 7, 1975), pp. D-1 to D-5.

The union attack on Altemose has been total, apparently in an endeavor to drive him out of business. Thus, two plumbers sought employment with him and, after being discharged, filed charges with the NLRB. The NLRB hearing was ringed with demonstrators who threatened the Altemose participants. Yet the NLRB regional director did not order a change of venue and the administrative law judge credited the discharged plumbers, discredited the company witness, and found Altemose guilty of an unfair labor practice, to which the NLRB concurred.

In a decision that was about as critical of NLRB procedure as any ever written, the Court of Appeals, Third Circuit, reversed, castigating the Board for permitting a hearing under such circumstances, pointing out numerous discrepancies which reflected upon the credibility of union witnesses, and questioning several key rulings of the administrative law judge.[41] A clear point brought out by the court decision was that the unions expressed no interest in organizing Altemose's employees, reinforcing a point made earlier, that they want jobs for their members, not unionization of open shop workers.

Besides these activities, Altemose's suppliers and creditors have been pressured to cease doing business with him. Users have been warned not to put him on their bid list. (To their shame, several church groups have removed his company from bidding.) He completed the project where the huge vandalism occurred, but the going since then, partly because of the recession, has been difficult. His future as a builder is not assured as of mid-1975. Meanwhile, the unions have maintained their pressures on all fronts, recently inducing the governor of Pennsylvania, the host for the next Governor's Conference, to move it away from Valley Forge so that the Altemose built hotel would not receive the patronage.

Violence in the Philadelphia area seems to be the special province of Local 30 of the Roofers. Its business agent rented the bus for the Altemose attack. Open shop builders and workers have been smashed with baseball bats bearing the Local 30 name, or otherwise brutalized in Philadelphia and in the suburbs. Local 30 has had injunctions issued against it; it is the subject of one of the NLRB charges emanating from ABC's several complaints; and it has been written about in the (Philadelphia) *Evening Bulletin* and in feature articles

---

[41] *Ibid.*

in the *Philadelphia Magazine,* all with remarkable specificity.[42] Yet the violence goes on, and is being emulated by other crafts. On April 9, 1975, for example, members of Local 699, Cement Masons, were arrested after a nonunion construction site was vandalized.[43]

A former mayor of Philadelphia once remarked that the ABC would never get into Philadelphia while he was mayor.[44] The situation has not changed. Union officials are represented on all key city agencies which deal with housing, zoning, or building codes. In the fall of 1974, the mayor of Philadelphia was not invited to sit on the dais of a Democratic Party dinner because of a dispute with a city party chairman. Here is how one report described the scene that follows:

> While over 4,000 Democrats were gathering at Civic Center to dine and hear speeches, a flying squad of roofers burst into the hall. They overturned tables, beat up a 60 year old . . . [opposition member] and a number of deputy sheriffs who were serving as ushers, while the police looked the other way.
>
> A few minutes after the roofers had set the tone, [the mayor] . . . pulled up in his city limousine. McCulloch [Business Agent of the Roofers], Magrann [President of the Building and Construction Trades Council] and Battone [Business Agent of Teamsters Local 107] were riding with him.
>
> Led by a fife and drum corps, . . . [the mayor] and 500 union toughs stormed into the Civic Center, completely upstaging the Democratic politicians and scaring hell out of everyone there.
>
> . . . They encircled the diners and dignitaries, chanting obscenities . . . and knocking people down along the way. The union chiefs formed a phalanx around the . . . [mayor], who boasted that it was the greatest night in his life.[45]

Michigan

In earlier chapters we noted that Michigan was heavily open shop outside of Detroit and that even in the Detroit suburbs unions were losing strength. Michigan has also been a center

---

42 See Jim Riggio, "The Hardhat's Holy War," *Philadelphia Magazine,* LXIII (August 1972), pp. 55-61, 126-138; and the series by L. Stuart Ditzen, *Evening Bulletin,* July 15-18, 1974.

43 *Evening Bulletin* (Philadelphia), April 10, 1975, p. 6.

44 Gaeton Fonzi and Greg Walter, "Plumbers' Friend," *Philadelphia Magazine,* LVIII (October 1967), pp. 46-49, 134-144.

45 Mike Mallowe, "You Got a Friend in the Business," *Philadelphia Magazine,* LXV (September, 1974), pp. 118-123, 200-213.

of union construction violence, climaxed by the ABC charge and the decision of the Michigan State Building and Construction Trades Council, and several other construction councils and unions to sign a consent decree foreswearing violence. Before that happened, however, violence in Michigan certainly prevalent enough in former years, reached a crescendo at Kalkaska[46] and Midland.[47]

In July 1971, Shell Oil Company announced plans to build a national gas processing plant in Kalkaska, a community of 1,600 inhabitants in the northern sector of Michigan's southern peninsula. Shell awarded the contract to Delta Engineering of Houston, a large open shop builder with considerable experience in this type of construction. Violence began early, and in February 1973, 400 "demonstrators" did $100,000 of damage at Kalkaska and another open shop construction site, injuring two state troopers in the process. Moreover, the construction unions began a series of demonstrations at Shell service stations across the state, aided in some cases by members of the Teamsters and Auto Workers unions. A threatened injunction stopped the service station picketing, but 200 to 500 construction workers continued literally to create terror and damage in Kalkaska until July 1973. The State of Michigan stationed 350 state troopers in this town of 1,600—20 percent of its total force. It cost Michigan taxpayers $30,000 per day to protect Delta Engineering's labor force from the demonstrators, most of whom were from Detroit. Repeated efforts by Shell and Delta to obtain enforceable injunctions were unsuccessful. Finally, in June 1973, at their request, the NLRB moved in

---

[46] The Kalkaska story is based upon the following press stories (all 1973): *Detroit Free Press*, February 20, 21, and 27, April 27, May 2 and 3, June 14, 15, 17, 19, 20, 21, 24, 26, 29 and 30, July 12, 17, and 18; *Detroit News*, June 16, 17, and 21, and July 17, 1973; *Bay City Times*, February 20, May 15 and 20, June 2, 19, and 24; *Midland Daily News*, June 15, 16, 20 and 28, July 13, 17 and 18; *Jackson Citizen Patriot*, June 18 and 19; *Traverse City Eagle*, July 11, 12, and 17; *Grand Rapids Press*, July 26; *New York Times*, March 25 and July 22; *Business Week*, July 7, 1973; *Construction Labor Report*, No. 929, July 25, 1973, pp. A-6 to A-7; *Solidarity*, June 1973; *Building Tradesman*, June 22 and 29.

[47] The Michigan material, exclusive of the Kalkaska situation, is based upon stories in the *Midland Daily News*, September 4, 5, 6, 14, 15, 17, 18, 20, 21, 27, 28 and 29, October 2, 6, 8, 9, 10, 13 and 17, November 1 and 11, 1973; January 21, February 12, March 5, September 24, October 30 and 31, and November 1974; and *Michigan State Building and Construction Trades Council et al.*, NLRB Decision and Order, Cases No. 7-CB-2897, *et al.*, February 7, 1974.

federal district court for an injunction against the secondary boycott activities and coercion of individuals on the part of the unions and scheduled a hearing for July to hear the issues.

The U.S. District Court Judge involved was a former labor mediator. Instead of granting an order, he pushed the parties into mediation sessions. The unions were demanding that Delta pay money into their welfare funds as a condition of settlement; Delta refused but offered to employ fifty union men in its work force. Under prodding of the judge and of the governor of Michigan, Delta and Shell agreed to donate $250,000—the estimated cost of union welfare programs—to the Kalkaska Township and to try to employ more workers from a 100 mile radius. The union called off the violence, and the operation remained open shop, but Shell and Delta suspended all legal action. According to one press report:

> . . . the union said they felt the publicity given to the often violence-marred dispute will reap long-range benefits for union members.
>
> "I don't think anybody else will try to do this again in Michigan," one union source said. "There's no doubt about that."
>
> He predicted "a hell of a lot of construction in the future in the oil industry in Michigan and I bet it's all going to be union." [48]

According to another union official, "There is no doubt it [the settlement] was good for the union movement. In the last three weeks we signed up 20 to 25 companies." [49] As one press article put it, neither Shell nor Delta were ever given the NLRB hearing or court injunction to which they were entitled. Instead they "were coerced by the federal judge and the state government into negotiating with a union organization not involved in their project," [50] or it might be added, which did not represent their employees.

The judge's rationale for mediating instead of issuing the injunction (that one was warranted is indisputable) was that it would not be enforced; and that he always preferred mediation. Such an approach by a federal judge is troubling.

> Somehow . . . we cannot help but have misgivings about a settlement which, in effect, has been arrived at because members of the

---

[48] *Traverse City Record-Eagle,* July 17, 1973.

[49] Edward J. Doherty, "Union Trouble in Kalkaska, Court Bows to Extortion," syndicated story for North American Newspaper Alliance, August 1973.

[50] *Ibid.*

> Building Trades Council—in order to achieve their ends—were willing to commit acts of violence and vandalism. . . . That such repugnant methods should be rewarded in any way is troubling indeed.[51]

Having considered that they won a victory at Kalkaska, the Michigan construction unions turned their attention to Dow Chemical Company, Midland. Dow lets construction contracts for its huge complex on the basis of bids and provides separate gates for union and open shop builders. Between September 1973 and January 1974, the open shop gate at Dow's complex was picketed by 50 to 200 building tradesmen. Dow received fairly good police protection, but entering workmen were severely harrassed. Dow sued the unions for $500,000 and filed charges with the NLRB. It won a stipulation, approved by the Board which can be enforced by any court of appeals upon NLRB application, and which ended the mass picketing and attendant violence there, but not in Michigan.

Collinson Construction Company, one of Dow's contractors, and a major open shop builder in Michigan, has long been beset with violence. After the unions were forced to desist the illegal picketing at Dow's gates, Collinson received additional threats. In addition, bombs damaged its construction projects at the Chippewa Indian Reservation, Mt. Pleasant, and at a high school in Coleman.

With this background, it is little wonder that the Michigan construction trades did not want a public trial. Hence after the NLRB had issued its complaint, the Michigan State Building and Construction Trades Council and its agents, Stanford D. Arnold, Eugene D. Tolot, John W. Sims, and Carl Bryer; the Southwestern Michigan Building and Construction Trades Council; the Greater Lansing Building and Construction Trades Council; Local 388 of the Plumbers; Local 324 of the Operating Engineers; and Local 340 of the Ironworkers consented to a settlement stipulation with the NLRB, which, like the Dow order, can be enforced upon application of the NLRB by any court of appeals and to which enforcement defense is waived in advance. The stipulation includes these paragraphs, which rather conclusively indicate the tactics that the Michigan trades have utilized:

---

[51] Editorial, *Grand Rapids Press*, July 26, 1973.

A. Respondents, Michigan State Building and Construction Trades Council, AFL-CIO, its officers, agents, successors, and assigns, and Stanford D. Arnold, Eugene D. Tolot, John W. Sims, Carl Bryer, and Fred J. Veigel, shall:

1. Cease and desist from:

(a) Restraining or coercing the employees of J. D. Parish Company, Inc., Schierbeek Construction Co., Tri-Cities Construction, Inc., Long Development, Inc., Shell Oil Company, Hastings Aluminum Products, Austin Oil Company, or any other employer or person, engaged in interstate commerce, or an industry affecting interstate commerce, by and through its agents, demonstrators, pickets or such labor organizations as may be acting in common cause with it, by participating in, directing, authorizing, ratifying, condoning or causing acts of property destruction and vandalism, mass picketing and obstruction of ingress and egress, threats of violence and bodily harm, and similar coercive conduct.

(b) In any other manner, or by any other means, restraining or coercing employees in the exercise of their rights guaranteed by Section 7 of the Act.

(c) Picketing at or in the vicinity of the gates, entrances and accesses reserved for the exclusive use of the employees, customers, and suppliers of Hastings Aluminum Products at Hastings, Michigan.

(d) In any manner or by any means, including picketing, vandalism, orders, directions, instructions, requests, or appeals, however given, made or imparted, or by any like or related acts or conduct, or by permitting any such to remain in existence or effect, engaging in, or inducing or encouraging any individual employed by Granger Interiors, Hastings Aluminum Products, Hector Bourrie & Son, Inc., or by any other person engaged in commerce or in any industry affecting commerce, to engage in, a strike or a refusal in the course of employment to use, manufacture, process, transport, or otherwise handle or work on any goods, articles, materials, or commodities or to perform any service, or in any manner or by any means, threatening, coercing, or restraining, Granger Interiors, Hastings Aluminum Products, or Hector Bourrie & Son, Inc., or any other person engaged in commerce or in any industry affecting commerce, where in either case an object thereof is to force or require Granger Interiors, Hastings Aluminum Products, or Hector Bourrie & Son, Inc., or any other person, to cease using, selling, handling, transporting, or otherwise dealing in the products of or to cease doing business with J. D. Parish Construction, Inc., Schierbeek Construction Co., Tri-Cities Construction, Inc., Anderson Plumbing and Heating, Inc., or any other person engaged in commerce or in an industry affecting commerce when doing business with J. D. Parish Construction, Inc., Schierbeek Construction Co., Tri-Cities Construction, Inc., and Anderson Plumbing and Heating, Inc.[52]

---

[52] *Michigan State Building and Construction Trades Council, AFL-CIO, et al.*, Settlement Stipulation, NLRB Case No. 7-CB-3030 (February, 1975).

It remains to be seen whether the quiet in effect after this stipulation was signed will endure.

Violence—Summary

The accounts of violence in Denver, Philadelphia, and Michigan are illustrative of what has occurred in many areas. Maryland, Tennessee, Florida, Ohio, and Louisiana are areas where violence has been especially bad, and other incidents have been reported in New York, Massachusetts, and Rhode Island. The *Reader's Digest* published three articles detailing such violence; [53] the ABC has an illustrated booklet with names, dates, and locations involved; [54] and many other incidents have appeared in the press or were pointed out during our field surveys.

The purpose of the violence is clear: to frighten contractors and employees from working open shop in some areas, and to frighten users from awarding contracts to open shop builders. To the question of how they determine where they will bid on work, large open shop contractors readily reply: "Where we can be reasonably sure of police protection." Many users consider the same thing before letting contracts. Violence has thus been effective in many areas in maintaining the union shop.

For the first time, however, there is an organization geared to fight such violence on the national scene and capable of supporting that fight. The ABC has made this task its urgent priority, and it has had support from the Business Roundtable, the organization of large corporate construction users. For both the open shop and for honest law and order, the existence of such groups, plus increased interest and activity on the part of federal law enforcement agencies, is the main hope that violence in construction may be curbed.

CONCLUSION

The union reaction to open shop gains has thus entailed a variety of tactics designed either to make union contractors more competitive or to discourage open shops from venturing into traditional union markets. Its effects have been both constructive, as where restrictive or inefficient practices are eliminated

---

[53] Charles Stevenson, "The Tyranny of Terrorism in the Building Trades," *Reader's Digest* (June, July, and August, 1973).

[54] Associated Builders and Contractors, Inc., *The National Press Reports on Violence in Construction,* n.d.

or modified, and ugly, as where the rule of law has given way to the law of the jungle. Our detailed accounts of violence in several localities are not offered as evidence of a general breakdown of civilization, but neither are they so isolated as to be considered a sporadic catharsis brought on by the frustrations of desperate men. (Indeed, nearly one-fourth of the open shop respondents to the Industrial Research Unit survey reported some experience with violence. Interestingly, however, over one-sixth of the union respondents had also been so beset.) The graphic descriptions in the foregoing pages are not to suggest that violence has been a more common or pervasive response than changing stances at the bargaining table, but rather than when the unions decide to react in truly dramatic ways, it is less likely to be peaceful. In short, one finds more examples of major violence than of massive overhauls of collective bargaining agreements.

At the same time, contract modifications and violence are really opposite poles of what may be regarded as a spectrum of union behavior. In-between lie the utilization of traditional union weapons of conflict, impassioned speeches and exhortations by union leaders propounding the necessity to "do something," and what is probably the most common reaction of all—doing nothing. Some unions have agreed to concessions which, however modest, nevertheless reflect a recognition that there are competitive restraints on their behavior. Some unions have engaged in violence in an effort to circumvent those restraints. But for many unions it appears to have been business as usual, negotiating wage increases to be paid on nonexistent jobs and maintaining or tightening restrictions on contractors whose competitive status has already been severely compromised. As the natural outgrowth of these policies, in the form of further open shop incursions into the unions' domain, continues to develop, one should expect to see more affirmative responses from those unions which are not content to see their status erode. It remains to be seen to which end of the spectrum these responses will lean.

The extent to which open shop builders can capitalize on their advantages will be determined by many factors. Not the least is their ability to recruit, deploy, train, and compensate manpower so as to be able to provide a competent work force to handle increasing business. The next part of our study examines these issues.

PART THREE

Labor Markets In Open Shop Construction

CHAPTER IX

Manpower Recruitment And Deployment

There are few industries in the United States whose labor market operations are as extensively influenced by unions as construction. Through both formal contractual mechanisms and informal pressures, the building trades unions share broadly in the rule-making process which regulates manpower flows and assignments, both among and within employing units. There will be debate, to be sure, on whether these various regulations and restrictions are, on balance, socially benign, malignant, or neutral. But these questions need not detain us here; let it suffice to observe that they exist and, for better or worse, serve to constrict the decision-making latitude of construction managers in the recruitment and deployment of their workers.

To the present, no researcher has seriously asked how labor market decisions are made by construction contractors who are unfettered by the strictures of collective agreements. How, for example, do they go about finding needed employees for replacement or expansion? How do they augment and contract their work forces in response to abruptly changing manpower requirements? How do they distribute the jobs to be done to workers of varying skills and capabilities? How, in sum, does a construction labor market operate where the guiding principles are the unilateral judgments of employers rather than the provisions of union-management contracts, which themselves are products of an essentially adversary process called collective bargaining?

The theoretical function of a factor market is to allocate resources to their most productive uses. If the market performs optimally, a given output will issue at the least possible cost. Resources will be neither underutilized nor overutilized. As needs change, resources must be shifted, and in the process workers are displaced. In weighing the social benefits of efficiency against the individual costs of displacement, American unions, and the building trades in particular, have traditionally emphasized the latter. The fear of job scarcity has, in many instances, led to bargaining goals which underscore the preservation of jobs, even though these jobs may be redundant in terms of the employer's production needs.

It is not universally accepted, even among detached observers, that the interests of society are invariably well served by the apotheosizing of economic efficiency. But the interests of the employer, however they may be defined, are certainly furthered by retaining flexibility in obtaining and allocating his work force. Indeed, open shop contractors will frequently argue that it is this flexibility more than anything else which gives them a competitive edge over their unionized counterparts. Moreover, even while pointing to competitive problems relating to high wages and strikes, unionized contractors often declare that loss of the right to manage is their most serious problem.

How, then, is this right to manage exercised by open shop contractors, and how are the results different? This chapter is concerned with a variety of labor market practices, all of which relate ultimately to manning the job. We begin with the task of recruitment, an area where unions in their sector, either directly through hiring halls or indirectly through hiring restrictions, play a significant role. In this connection, also, it will be appropriate to explore the linkages between the union and nonunion sectors of construction, specifically with respect to the movement of workers between the two sectors.

The other major area of concern here is the allocation of workers within the employing unit, the deployment of labor at varying levels and kinds of skills. A central question in this context is how flexibility in making job assignments is exercised, in contrast to the union sector where the managerial role is circumscribed by such contractual guidelines as craft jurisdictions. A further question involves the redeployment of manpower in response to changing seasonal needs, a condition endemic to a greater or lesser degree to most branches of construction. A final issue is the effect of the absence of various job-creating requirements (e.g., crew sizes, journeymen-foremen ratios, and standby manning), remuneration for nonworking time (travel and showup pay), and restrictions on the use of materials, equipment, and technology. To many contractors, both union and open shop, all these issues are terminologically subsumed under the general rubric of "productivity."

MANPOWER RECRUITMENT

New manpower needs in construction are of both a short-term and long-term character. Over a period of years, the industry must provide both for secular growth of the work force and vacancies created by death, retirement, and industry mobility. Long-term needs, especially those for skilled labor, are met predominantly by the various training forms discussed in Chapter X. Training programs, however, require time, and the contractor who wins a large job or loses some key workers may not be able to afford the luxury of gradually upgrading his workers. He must enter the market. "Entering the market," however, means different things to the union and open shop contractor.

For the union contractor, it most likely means a call to the union hiring hall. As Philip Ross has pointed out, the term "hiring hall" is often used loosely, referring both to: (1) a system of job assignments in which participants are given preference over nonparticipants and; (2) a routine referral service in which the union is merely a brokerage of information between employers and workers.[1] The distinction, although an important one, is not immediately critical for our purposes. For whether contractors utilize union referral systems because they are convenient and useful, or because it is required in some form or in some circumstances by contract, the fact is that for many union contractors the "hall" is the primary source of labor. And even when its services are not contractually required, in times of job scarcity employers are invariably under great, if informal, pressure to use it.

To the union contractor, the hall is, in a real sense, a mixed blessing. For all its abuses, it often does provide a reasonably reliable source of labor, usually on comfortingly short notice. It is also tied into a network of other halls in distant areas, so that a manpower shortage in one locality can, when possible, draw upon a manpower surplus in another. Through the hall, the employer is thus plugged into a well organized flow of labor market information which makes him accessible to a broad range of job-seeking workers.

Although different hiring halls have varying degrees of flexibility, the system has its costs, in that it often means serious restrictions on the contractor's freedom of hire. Especially in

---

[1] Philip Ross, "Origin of the Hiring Hall in Construction," *Industrial Relations,* XI (October, 1972), p. 366.

times of high unemployment, he may be contractually obliged or informally pressured to hire a worker different from the one he wants, or he may be unable to obtain a craftsman with experience specific to the job he is doing. Moreover, in times of tight labor markets, the union may be either unable to supply personnel, or it may accept, or give permits to, unqualified workers whom the employer must try out at great cost. Finally, contractors reported to us that union locals have often used control of labor supply to restrict an employer's labor requirements in order to stretch out work, force up wages, compel the utilization of overtime at double the regular wage rate, or even to favor one contractor over another. These disadvantages of the hiring hall to the contractor and the user, have been starkly presented by a Business Roundtable Report:

> The day-to-day operation of hiring hall administered by a union official can be ruthless. Referral lists can be manipulated, contractors enticed to order men by name or specialty skill in order to avoid the next man on the list, dissident members or "permit" men referred constantly to jobs of short duration, and many similar injustices perpetrated.
>
> Control over the referral process also may have a direct impact upon the layoff of employees. For example, instructions from a union official to quit a job are quickly honored if a member hopes to obtain a referral to another job in the future. In reality, contractors who are dependent on the hiring hall have substantially lost the right to hire or terminate their employees.
>
> Union control of the administration of the hiring hall results in unions being the repository of virtually all available information concerning the quality and quantity of the construction manpower pool within a labor market. The same information is usually inaccessible to contractors or construction users, except for general information about total membership in local building trades unions. This imbalance in the availability of construction manpower information prevails throughout the organized segment of the construction industry, regardless of the form of the hiring hall, and places contractors at a severe disadvantage in performing their role as employers.
>
> Union control over the work referral system has also had some profound economic implications on contractors and the users of their services. An increase in demand for labor encourages an increase in supply in most industries. Not necessarily so in construction! A union-administered work referral system establishes an environment conducive to artificial shortages. These shortages, in turn, have enabled the unions to achieve stronger bargaining positions, and thereby to obtain inflationary wage increases, excessively restrictive work practices, and other costly conditions of employment. In his role as hiring hall administrator, a union offi-

> cial is often torn between the longer term interests of the industry and the union members on the one hand and the political appeal of maintaining a surplus of job opportunities and additional income through overtime.[2]

With much more latitude in hiring, the open shop employer nevertheless may have less access to local labor supply. Since there is no central agency which performs the brokerage function of the union hiring hall, a nonunion employer is obliged to rely upon a variety of other methods to inform prospective employees of his needs. Taken together, these methods may eventually get his message across to large numbers of available workers within the labor market, but they are unlikely to work as expeditiously or as thoroughly as a telephone call to a single source. The broader use of diverse methods of hire by open shop contractors is well illustrated in Table IX-1.

Table IX-1 is based on responses to the Industrial Research Unit survey both of union and open shop contractors. Employers were given a list of various hiring methods and asked to indicate whether they use each method always, often, occasionally, or never. The table shows the number and percentage of respondents who answered "always" or "often" to each of the methods listed. With the obvious exception of hiring halls and the less obvious one of contacting past workers directly, all other methods of hire were used more frequently by open shop contractors than by union contractors. The frequent use of contacting past workers by union contractors is attributable (apart from a normal desire to utilize a known quantity when possible), to provisions in many hiring hall arrangements encouraging, or indeed requiring, employers to recall previous employees before soliciting new workers from the hall.

All the hiring methods listed in Table IX-1, with the exception of taking on workers "off the street," are at the initiative of the employer. These methods may be generally divided into two groups which we designate as a "formal" approach and an "informal" approach. The informal approach includes methods in which solicitation is limited to the employer's circle of contacts. The formal approach includes methods which employ some outside agency which routinely performs some kind of placement function.

---

[2] "The Hiring Hall in the Construction Industry," in *Coming to Grips With Some Major Problems in the Construction Industry* (New York: The Business Roundtable, 1974), p. 17. The Roundtable is, as noted earlier, a organization of major users of industrial and commercial construction.

TABLE IX-1
Hiring Methods Employed Always or Often by Union and Nonunion Contractors, 1974

	Number of Contractors Reporting Use			
	Union [a]		Nonunion [b]	
Method of Hire	Number	Percent	Number	Percent
Ask current employees	298	38.3	464	59.2
Ask other employers	88	11.3	129	16.5
Contact past workers	393	50.6	262	33.4
Contact prior applicants	158	20.3	355	45.3
Hiring hall	517	66.5	4	0.5
Newspaper advertisement	53	6.8	330	42.1
State employment service	46	5.9	222	28.3
Vocational schools	31	4.0	126	16.0
"Off the street"	78	10.1	171	21.8

Source: Industrial Research Unit Questionnaire.
[a] N=778.
[b] N=784.

Informal Approach

These methods generally involve the employer "letting the word out" that he is in the market for workers. He may ask his incumbent workers if they are acquainted with anyone available for work. He may ask his business associates—subcontractors, suppliers, competitors—if they know workers who have recently been laid off. Among open shop contractors especially, workers are commonly "loaned" for a limited time. This practice benefits the borrower by providing him with a reliable worker and benefits the lender by enabling him to release a temporarily redundant worker while not losing him permanently. He may contact workers whom he has employed in the past to see if they are, or expect to be, available. Finally, he may keep a file on previous job applicants who could not be hired at the time of their application and contact them when help is needed.

On the whole, open shop contractors appear to utilize these informal methods more frequently than union employers. They also utilize informal methods more frequently than formal methods, suggesting that the formal methods available to nonunion contractors are not deemed wholly reliable or desirable, or at least that contractors will usually seek workers from close to hand before resorting to a broader search. Many union contractors (about 30 percent), by contrast, invariably use the hiring hall, by far the single most common exclusive use of any hiring method by either union or nonunion employers.

These informal methods manifestly rely upon a grapevine of information. As with any grapevine, there is no assurance that information will reach all those who may be interested. To work effectively, the system must channel the job-seeking initiatives of workers and the labor-seeking initiatives of workers into a common pool, so that the two can find each other. The grapevine will be successful only where the specific contacts of employers overlap with the specific contacts of workers. Since these contacts are many and dispersed, the probability of a crossing of information from the supply and demand sides is less than that where all, or most, information is routed through one, or a few, points.

Formal Approach

The parallel to the hiring hall in open shop construction—to the extent there is one—lies in the use of some formal method of advertising that job openings exist. Among the various agencies which offer referral, placement, or advertising services, union contractors utilize the hiring hall to the virtual exclusion of all others. Alternatives to the hiring hall may include newspaper want ads, an employment service or agency, or the placement office of a trade or vocational school. Although these alternatives are not relied on by open shop contractors to the extent that the union hall is used by organized firms, they do constitute a counterpart to hiring halls.

The figures in Table IX-1 speak largely for themselves. Four to six times the proportion of open shops than union shops reported using newspapers, state employment services, or vocational schools on a regular basis to recruit their workers. And even these differences do not tell the whole story. Among respondents who answered "occasionally" or "never" to questions about their use of placement or referral services other than hiring halls, most of the union shops said "never" while most of the open shops said "occasionally". For union shops, because of their requirement to use hiring halls, this is scarcely surprising. There is, moreover, some previous research evidence of the relatively infrequent use of these services by union contractors, as well as of the greater, though far from preponderant, use of them by (residential) nonunion firms.[3]

The picture thus drawn of present hiring practices may be summarized as follows: union contractors use hiring halls extensively, either because it is required or because it is convenient. Alternatively, they contact workers whom they have employed in the past or ask their present workers to look for potential applicants. Open shop contractors appear to prefer informal methods to formal ones, which may reflect a dissatisfaction with the formal methods available to them. These formal methods are not, however, ignored, with more than 40 percent of the respondents using newspaper advertisements regularly and more than one-fourth using the state employment service. The relative frequencies reported, however, suggest that an informal approach is a first choice among most open shop contractors, who will, nevertheless, use formal methods contemporaneously, or when the grapevine fails to produce the right workers.

Examples Of Open Shop Approaches

There are budding indications that more systematic hiring systems which are counterparts to hiring halls are being developed by open shops, or more specifically, by open shop associations. Many of these associations act as a referral service for their members, but only on a very limited and infrequent basis. Essentially, association staff members will inform contractors seeking workers about other contractors who are cutting back. There is, however, usually little contact arranged by the association between employers and workers directly. Association spokesmen report that although contractors will occasionally seek to hire through them, few workers approach them for employment.

In a few areas, however, contractors associations are beginning to develop more sophisticated referral services for their members. Records are kept both on employer and worker ap-

---

[3] Howard G. Foster, *Manpower in Homebuilding: A Preliminary Analysis*, Manpower and Human Resources Studies, No. 3 (Philadelphia: Industrial Research Unit, The Wharton School, University of Pennsylvania, 1974), pp. 103-108.

plicants, with the goal of enabling the system to match supply and demand expeditiously. The outcome, in large measure, is a hiring hall without restrictions on the employer (or what Ross would call simply a "referral service"). In one case, such a service has been established on a nationwide basis for contractors and workers in the homebuilding industry. With financial support from the U.S. Department of Labor, the National Association of Home Builders has since 1973 operated the National Construction Job Clearinghouse[4] through its headquarters in Washington, D.C. Contractors are invited to submit announcements of job openings for 22 occupational groupings. Workers submit a brief resume indicating their specific job interest, prior experience, date of availability, and their preferred geographic location. The service is provided free to both contractors and applicants. The clearinghouse sends the resumes to appropriate employers and helps to arrange interviews. Since its inception, the clearinghouse has experienced a steady growth in the demand for its services, with the number of applicants increasing from 2,512 in the last quarter of 1972, to 7,072 in the last quarter of 1973. Referrals grew from 1,527 to 5,248 during the same period.[5] Unfortunately, there are no data on the proportion of referrals which resulted in actual hires.

At the local level as well, contractor groups are beginning to explore avenues for centralizing the job matching process. What is perhaps the first of these efforts was outlined at a 1974 meeting of AGC committees. The impetus for it was described as follows:

> Our chapter has always had about 25 to 30% of its members operating on an open shop basis. In the last few years, we learned that more of our members would be operating open shop if they could locate skilled manpower. There has been no central place from which they could locate the skills necessary to man open shop operations. If they are on a union basis, they can call the union halls. Those who operate successfully open shop have developed a following of men over the years.
>
> To meet this open shop need, our chapter has decided as a part of its open shop services to set up an open shop Hiring Center.

---

[4] The clearinghouse was initially established in 1971 to service returning veterans. Since 1973 it has been open to all applicants.

[5] Numbers are from NAHB Manpower Development and Training Department, *Report to the Executive and Finance Committee* (Washington, D.C.: The Association, January 1974).

> This is not a recruiting thing or a training thing. You would probably call it a locating service.[6]

The referral service is provided through an independent corporation called Construction Workers' Register, which is legally distinct from the local AGC chapter. Worker registrants are sought through newspaper ads and word of mouth. Employers who subscribe to the service register their openings by telephone and in turn receive a list of workers in the desired trades who are known to be available for work. All direct contacts and actual hiring are done by the employers themselves. Employers and workers are expected to inform the Register when their needs have been met, and the Register's lists are accordingly updated each day. The service is financed by its sponsors, and there is no charge to the individual contractor or the worker. The success of this service has led to its being copied by several open shop groups in other parts of the same state.

Open shop referral services are still scattered and experimental. Local chapters of the Associated Builders and Contractors are just beginning to develop placement functions. The first pilot project was established in 1974 in the Tampa, Florida, area and was sufficiently successful that several other ABC chapters have decided to develop similar functions in 1975, with a national program in prospect for 1976. The ABC format is somewhat different from the Construction Workers' Register described above in that information on job openings is given directly to workers and contacts are made at their initiative rather than the employer's initiative. In this respect, the procedure is more analogous to nonexclusive referral services run by the building trades.

These nascent programs by open shop contractor groups are, in all likelihood, harbingers of more extensive efforts to counter the recruitment advantage enjoyed by union shop contractors through their access to centralized hiring halls. The very fact that open shop contractors are seeking to duplicate the service functioning of the hiring hall without becoming subject to their restrictions, demonstrates that the damnation expressed by industry spokesmen about union halls should not go unqualified. At the same time, it also demonstrates that their undesirable features are not inevitable concomitants to their beneficial functions. Thus, in some respects, as we shall see below, open shop contractors suc-

[6] "Construction Workers' Register," mimeo, n.d. (late 1974).

cessfully compete with the union sector by improving upon its labor market operations; in other respects—in some forms of manpower training as well as recruitment methods—they are beginning to do it by copying some features of the devices utilized by union shops while attempting to avoid aspects which they find unacceptable.

Union Background of Open Shop Workers

A worker hired by an open shop contractor may come from several sources. He may be a new entrant to the labor force taken on initially as a helper or trainee. He may be attracted from another industry such as manufacturing or farming, where his job provided him with some kind of building experience. He may, of course, have quit or been laid off from a job with a different nonunion contractor. But perhaps not as readily expected, the worker may have come from employment in the union sector of construction.

Since wage rates in union shops tend to be significantly higher than in open shops, it is tempting to view intersector migration as operating in only one direction. Union membership has, to be sure, been augmented by workers whose initial exposure to, and training in, construction work was with nonunion employers. These workers may become union members by soliciting employment during periods of high activity, or simply by having their employer organized by a union. There is evidence to show that this movement from nonunion to union status is significant.[7]

At the same time, however, movement between sectors is decidedly not one way. For a variety of reasons, union workers do seek work in open shops. The transition may be temporary or permanent, depending upon the circumstances and the reasons given by the worker who opted for a change. We may estimate the extent of this mobility from our survey of open shop contractors. Respondents were asked to indicate the approximate proportion of their men who were once or currently union members. The responses are shown in Table IX-2. As the table indicates, a substantial majority of the respondents reported having some workers with union membership in their background. These reported percentages, moreover, may actually understate the true magnitude of the movement. Union

[7] Howard G. Foster, "Labor Supply in the Construction Industry: A Case Study of Upstate New York," unpublished Ph.D. dissertation, Cornell University, 1968, pp. 264-267.

TABLE IX-2
Percentage of Employees of Open Shop Contractors Presently or Previously Union Members, 1974

Percentage Union Members	Contractors Reporting Number	Percent
Zero	206	26.3
1 to 10	241	30.7
11 to 25	128	16.3
26 to 50	92	11.7
51 to 99	25	3.2
100	5	0.6
Not reported	87	11.1
Total	784	49.4

Source: Industrial Research Unit Questionnaire.

workers seeking open shop employment may fear later discrimination by the union should they return to work in that sector, or they may regard their chances of hire by a nonunion contractor as lower if their union status were known. Thus, the percentages in Table IX-2 include only those past or present union members of which the respondents are aware.

Some union workers, of course, will migrate to the open shop only as a temporary expedient. Although we do not have the longitudinal data necessary to test this proposition, it is reasonable to conclude that the amount of movement varies directly with changes in unemployment among union workers. Whether the unemployment is occasioned by a general downturn in construction activity or by a shift of work from union to nonunion contractors, some union members will undoubtedly seek open shop work rather than remain unemployed while waiting for conditions to improve. In the latter case, of course, actual migration is likely to be greater, for it is then that displacement in the union sector is more evenly matched by job vacancies in open shops.

Another temporary circumstance is a strike. The weakness of union contractors in collective bargaining is frequently analyzed in terms of the job alternatives available to union workers while they are on strike. One of these alternatives is employment in an open shop. Even though many open shop contractors will be unwilling to take on a worker who will leave when the strike is over, others will be satisfied to obtain a skilled craftsman (who, after all, requires little real investment by the employer) even for a limited time, and still others may hire a union worker unknowingly.

There is also permanent movement from union shop to open shop. One avenue is a direct parallel to the unionization of a firm, whereby some incumbent employees are automatically admitted to the union. Similarly, a union contractor may decide to go nonunion or to set up a "double-breasted" operation and transfer some of his workers to the new nonunion component. The result, of course, is much the same as when a worker changes employers in the course of moving from union to nonunion status.

Some permanent moves may, or course, start out as temporary ones. Union workers who are forced to seek employment in open shops because of a scarcity of union jobs may initially expect to return to the union sector when openings materialize, but later decide to remain with the nonunion contractor even then. A commonly cited reason for some workers' preference for open shops is the relative stability of employment there.[8] Many open shop contractors assert that despite wide differences in wage rates, their workers earn, on an annual basis, as much or more than the average union member. Workers may also dislike the uncertainty engendered by the possibility of strikes, or the control by union officials over their job opportunities. Further, the tendency for nonunion firms to be smaller and have less worker turnover may lead to stronger personal and social ties among employees or between employer and employees. Our point here is not that employment conditions are objectively better in open shops than in union shops, but that different workers place greater or lesser importance on the various attributes of a job. Union adherents may regard the hiring hall as a desirable, indeed an indispensible service; higher wage rates worth the price of some unemployment; personal and social relationships irrelevant to job satisfaction; and the general protection of a strong union, through grievance procedures and other devices, as highly valuable. And there is, of course, substantial migration from open shops to union shops. The central point, given the lack of previous research on open shop construction, is that there are arguments on both sides, and that it is not at all impossible to un-

---

[8] See discussion of seasonality below.

derstand the preference of some for nonunion work and the phenomenon of job mobility from the union to the nonunion sector. In sum, the willingness of some union workers to migrate permanently to open shops is probably attributable both to positive qualities of open shop status and to negative qualities of union status.

MANPOWER DEPLOYMENT IN OPEN SHOP CONSTRUCTION

The most salient aspect of manpower deployment practices of open shop contractors is that the practice is a managerial function, subject only to the managerial judgment of the supervisor and various legal requirements. This flexibility is limited in a number of ways when the contractor is unionized. Job assignments must be made within occupational classifications defined by the jurisdictions of the various building trades. In some instances, assignments must be made even where the employer, even if it was within his discretion, would not assign anyone at all. In other cases, workers may not be assigned, except at premium rates, at certain hours of the day or on certain days of the week, regardless of the total number of hours worked. These restrictions and requirements have appreciable cost implications, and their absence serves to reduce the labor cost of open shops even where they are obliged—as, for example, under Davis-Bacon or state prevailing wage laws—to pay the same wages as union contractors.

Restrictive practices are not necessarily limited to the matter of manpower deployment. Three broad categories of union work rules which serve to impede efficiency are:

1. Onsite rules, requiring certain work to be done on the premises and prohibiting or limiting the use of prefabricated products;
2. Restrictions against the use of certain tools and devices;
3. Requirements for excessive manpower on the job, including what appears to be irrational limits on the variety of work certain categories of workers may perform, and the requirement that skilled craftsmen perform semiskilled or unskilled work.[9]

---

[9] This categorization is based upon the path-breaking work of the late Sumner H. Slichter, *Union Policies and Industrial Management.* (Washington, D.C.: The Brookings Institution, 1941), Chapters VI-IX.

Our central concern here is with the third category, and we shall examine in turn the questions of "irrational limits on the variety of work certain categories of workers may perform" (largely a matter of union prohibitions), "excessive manpower on the job" (usually termed featherbedding by contractors), and the use of skilled workers to do unskilled work. The evidence suggests that contractual limitations on production techniques and devices are much less serious and widespread than is commonly believed, and a considerably less onerous burden on the contractor than restrictions on manpower deployment. In a major study conducted over twenty years ago, Haber and Levinson concluded that "it is reasonably clear that the building trades unions have been more receptive to new techniques than has been widely believed. In the summer of 1952, the overwhelming majority of new techniques were found to be in wide use in all or nearly all of the cities surveyed." [10] The authors' findings with respect to manpower allocation, however, were somewhat less favorable.

A more recent study by the U.S. Bureau of Labor Statistics suggests that restrictions on techniques and tools are still the exception rather than the rule. The study encompassed 769 agreements covering 1.2 million workers, or about one-half of all unionized building tradesmen. Limitations on prefabricated materials and components were found in 15 percent of the agreements covering less than 12 percent of the workers.[11] Such restrictions were common only with plumbers and sheet metal workers.[12] Limitations on tools and equipment were even less common, as they were found in only 8 percent of the agreements covering less than 12 percent of the workers. The principal example of these restrictions was among painters (about one-half of the agreements and four-fifths of the workers), clearly involving limits on the use of spray guns and the widths of brushes and rollers.[13]

---

[10] Haber and Levinson, *op. cit.*, p. 153.

[11] U.S. Bureau of Labor Statistics, *Characteristics of Construction Agreements, 1972-73*, Bulletin 1819, (Washington, D.C.: Government Printing Office, 1974), Table 39, p. 27.

[12] Haber and Levinson found widespread restrictions on precut, prethreaded, and preassembled pipe, but a common use of prefabricated sheet metal work. *Op. cit.*, pp. 128-130, 141-145.

[13] U.S. Bureau of Labor Statistics, Bulletin 1819, *loc. cit.* Haber and Levinson make much the same observation, *op. cit.*, pp. 121-127. In practice, some restrictions on the use of prefabricated materials may have been enhanced by

The foregoing observations suggest an important caveat with respect to a comparison of manpower deployment practices in union shops and open shops. Construction is a large and diverse industry. The union sector consists of many different formal crafts. There are few statements which can be made to cover all crafts in all localities. There is an unfortunate tendency, at times, for any restrictive practice anywhere to be assumed to occur everywhere. One can be appropriately critical of chains on one contractor's arms and another's legs without asserting, hyperbolically, that there are chains on all eight limbs. Union restrictions, for example, are much more common in a union city like Philadelphia than in a heavily open shop area like Houston.

On the other hand, many restrictions exist which are not found in formal agreements. Construction unions can, and frequently do, force additional concessions on the job by direct action which restrict use of materials, equipment, or add excessive manpower. These restrictions find their way into practice and can become as binding and onerous as restrictive agreements.

Allocation of Workers

The issue here is the assignment of workers to specific jobs. The question of how many are to be assigned and whether the employer on his own would assign any at all are left to the following section; for the moment we assume that the work must be done and that the employer must assign someone to do it. There are, then, two broad areas of inquiry: (1) should the work be assigned to a skilled or an unskilled worker; and (2) if assigned to a skilled worker, must he belong to a specific craft?

Under normal circumstances, it may be expected that the contractor will prefer to assign work to employees who are just sufficiently skilled to perform it. The assumption, of course, is that wage levels are tied fairly closely to skill, so that workers assigned to tasks which require less training or experience than they have had, constitute an unnecessary cost to the employer. There are, to be sure, circumstances under which skilled workers may understandably be given unskilled work, such as when employers have no other tasks to be done, yet are reluctant to lay

---

the controversial decision of the U.S. Supreme Court in *National Woodwork Manufacturer's Association* v. *NLRB*, 386 U.S. 612 (1967). As noted in Chapter VIII, this decision permits a union to "preserve work" by refusing to handle prefabricated materials, thus negating what appeared to many as a clear prohibition against such action in the Taft-Hartley Act.

off their skilled people for fear of losing them permanently. But in typical situations, routine, undemanding jobs will be assigned to workers in the lower occupational classifications.

The union contractor, however, may be required to use skilled tradesmen for some kinds of unskilled or semiskilled work. The jurisdictional claims of the various building trades are typically grounded not on the skill requirements of the work, but on its relationship to other functional components of the job. The jurisdictions of most skilled craft unions, therefore, include work which requires appreciably less training than is required of the average journeyman. Haber and Levinson describe some examples:

> A large proportion of bricklayers' locals in the cities surveyed required that only members of the union could wash down and paint brick, a relatively unskilled task. The cement masons' locals often required that the cement finishing machine be operated by a skilled man, though a semiskilled worker would usually be satisfactory on work where the quality of finish was not of great importance. Most of the plumbers', electricians', and sheet metal locals demanded that the unloading and carrying of materials and fixtures be done by union members. In carpentry, a small number of locals insisted upon the right to strip wooden forms from concrete; in most cases, however, this task, as well as the unloading and carrying of lumber, was done by laborers. Finally, minor problems sometimes arose in the finishing trades, particularly in painting, because of the demand that cleaning up the job be done by skilled men.[14]

Since Haber and Levinson wrote nearly twenty years ago, such take-over of unskilled work by the skilled craft unions has expanded. Indeed a key feature of the period between World War II and the present has been this assumption of unskilled work by the skilled crafts. Thus, it is not infrequent to encounter jurisdictional disputes between the plumbers and the laborers as to which will carry and lay underground pipe; between the carpenters and laborers over work pertaining to rough forms; between the laborers and any one of several crafts over the handling of materials, etc. If laborers can do such work satisfactorily, it is difficult objectively to sustain a reason why a craftsman must do it at skilled wages.

Similarly, the period since World War II has seen the almost total elimination of the helper in union construction. In his place has come the single rated craftsman. Thus even though

---

[14] Haber and Levinson, *op. cit.*, p. 179.

the work may be only semiskilled and the worker a semicompetent "craftsman," if he is used in the union jurisdiction to perform that work, he must receive the full craftsman wage rate. This custom has been aided, abetted, and institutionalized by the U.S. Department of Labor's administration of the Davis-Bacon Act.[15]

A good example of what contractors are required to do under union contracts and can avoid doing when operating open shop, is found in the installation of electrical outlets and connections. A unionized contractor may utilize crews consisting of three to five persons, depending on the nature of the project, all paid journeymen's rates of $8 to $15 per hour or more. Yet much of the work is unskilled, or at best semiskilled, as for example attaching the conduit, inserting and pulling the wires, and nailing, screwing or bolting the conduit and boxes to the walls, after all this has been laid out. In fact, the crew will usually have one craftsman, or at most two, really first class craftsmen who will direct it and make the actual connections and installations, particularly where they are especially complicated.

In contrast, the open shop contractor will do the same work with crews of one craftsman, or perhaps on very large projects two, top rated craftsmen, one or two helpers and the balance laborers. The craftsmen may be paid as much or more than the union rate; the helpers are paid a lower rate, varying with their skill and experience, and the laborers, still less, again varying according to their experience and abilities. Given a large number of crews and similar differences in their composition and wage schedules, not only for electricians but for other skilled crafts as well, the savings to the contractor and customer by an open shop operation can thus be very significant indeed on this single aspect of manpower utilization and organization.

In addition to information obtained by field interviews, there are some indirect clues on the extent of the varying use of skilled personnel. For example, the Bureau of Labor Statistics has conducted several surveys of manpower requirements on various kinds of construction projects. These surveys have consistently found a higher proportion of unskilled labor used on building work in the South, where, as we have seen, union

---

[15] Armand J. Thieblot, Jr., *The Davis-Bacon Act,* Labor Relations and Public Policy Series, Report No. 10 (Philadelphia: Industrial Research Unit, The Wharton School, University of Pennsylvania), e.g., pp. 126-129.

contracts are distinctly less widely applicable than in the rest of the country. This point is illustrated in Table IX-3. Other factors may, of course, be responsible,[16] but it does seem likely that the extent of the open shop in the South is the major point of difference in skilled craft utilization.

In sum, the open shop contractor is free to divide work among his employees according to their skill rather than their organizational affiliation, and therefore enjoys a direct cost advantage over his unionized competitor. He may not only utilize his unskilled labor to the fullest, but he is also at liberty to assign his skilled workers to whatever jobs that need to be done when there is a temporary lull in their own work, thus preserving the stability of his work force and increasing employee loyalty.

The second ramification of craft jurisdictional lines involves the assignment of work among the various skilled trades. Since differences in the wages between two crafts tend to be significantly less than the difference between skilled and unskilled labor generally, it might be of relatively little concern to the contractor as to which is assigned the work. Nevertheless, even beyond the obvious costs associated with work stoppages growing out of jurisdictional rivalries,[17] contract requirements which prescribe job assignments to specific crafts may entail several costly practices. Three examples are: (1) some jobs, such as activating equipment or temporary heating and lighting devices could be done in a short time by many craftsmen with normal mechanical ability, but the contractor is required to bring in a specific type of journeyman and pay him for a full day's work even though there is no other work for him to do. (2) A small task associated with the work of one craft requires the temporary use of a worker in a different trade. Even if the workers at the site are capable of meeting the problem, they

---

[16] It could be charged, for example that the southern data indicate the use of skilled blacks who are given unskilled designations and therefore discriminated against. In fact, however, as we shall make clear in Chapter XII, the take-over of unskilled work by skilled craft unions, has involved the displacement of blacks by whites, and the elimination of the helper has also eliminated many minorities.

[17] Year after year, a significant proportion of work stoppages in construction stems from interunion disputes over jurisdiction. In 1972, for example, 38 percent of construction strikes involved jurisdiction, or what the government terms "interunion or intraunion matters." U.S. Bureau of Labor Statistics, *Analysis of Work Stoppages, 1972,* Bulletin 1813 (Washington, D.C.: Government Printing Office, 1974), Table A-12.

TABLE IX-3
Proportion of Unskilled Manpower Requirements, by Region and Type of Project, Various Years

Type of Project	Year	U.S.	Region			
			North-east	North Central	South	West
1. School	1959	29.1	27.8	27.2	38.7	23.0
2. Federal office building	1959	32.5	28.3	31.6	33.7	25.1
3. Hospital	1959-60	26.7	24.6	26.6	32.0	18.6
4. Public housing	1959-60	30.9	23.3	25.3	40.8	22.0
5. One-family house	1962	23.3	25.2	14.9	31.0	14.8
6. College housing	1960-61	31.8	24.9	29.5	40.5	24.7
7. Sewer works	1962-63	38.8	31.7	34.9	44.3	29.5
8. School	1964-65	30.9	24.6	24.3	42.7	22.3
9. Hospital/nursing home	1965-66	19.6	17.8	18.1	28.3	10.8
10. Public housing	1968	30.2	25.4	26.7	36.4	20.4

Source: U.S. Bureau of Labor Statistics Bulletins; 1-1299 (1961); 2-1331 (1962); 3-1340 (1962); 4-1402 (1964); 5-1404 (1964); 6-1441 (1965); 7-1490 (1966); 8-1586 (1968); 9-1691 (1971); 10-1821 (1974).

must delay until the other craftsman is brought in to handle it.[18] (3) A relatively simple job overlaps the jurisdiction of several crafts, and all must be utilized for a brief time but paid a full day's pay. Thus, it is possible that if a hospital table was moved which had fittings for gas, electricity, and water, a union contractor might have to utilize and pay a steamfitter, an electrician and a plumber to get it operable.

The extent and impact of these jurisdictional restrictions today cannot be readily measured. But their existence was corroborated by interviews with contractors and other industry spokesmen in this study. It is apparent, moreover, that the open shop con-

[18] Haber and Levinson found several instances of this practice. One illustration was that drilling holes for pipe and wire had to be performed by carpenters, although the plumber or electrician on the scene could easily do it. The authors note, however, that these kinds of practices were infrequently enforced because of the high level of employment at the time. They did, however, constitute contractual requirements, and could be activated by a local facing a scarcity of job. (*op. cit.*, pp. 179-180.) Again, however, we have found that more recent years have seen a proliferation of this type of featherbedding much more rigorously enforced.

tractor enjoys at least some cost advantage by being free to allocate work among his skilled tradesmen with a minimum of interruptions and friction. This is not to say, to be sure, that nonunion workers are perfectly interchangeable. The average bricklayer does not simply drop his trowel and begin stringing wire or laying pipe when the masonry work is done. The major difference appears to occur when there is a temporary need for a worker to perform routine tasks out of his normal occupational class. The freedom of the open shop worker to do that manifestly allows the job to continue more smoothly and less expensively than if the work has to be done in bits and pieces by several craftsmen.

Determination of Work Force Size

In addition to provisions requiring the assignment of certain kinds of work to specific crafts, union contracts often contain various clauses which, according to employer spokesmen, mandate the use of excessive manpower. Where the open shop contractor is free to try to ensure that, in his judgment, all workers are engaged in productive labor, the unionized employer is in several respects constrained in the number of workers he assigns to a particular function. It is difficult to evaluate the net effects of these provisions for at least two reasons. First, it is not easy to determine the extent to which the contractual obligations actually differ from the practices which would be voluntarily adopted by the employer—or, for that matter, the practices which are in reality adopted by contractors not subject to union rules. Second, it is not always clear that the restrictions are socially unjustifiable in themselves. Arguments, for example, that certain manpower requirements are necessary for safety considerations cannot be dismissed out of hand. In many cases, however, safety is not a factor, and the alternative rationalizations are much less persuasive.

Charges of excessive manpower requirements may be grouped broadly into three related categories: (1) those mandating minimum crew size; (2) those mandating assignment of workers to unnecessary jobs; and (3) those mandating a minimum number of foremen. Foremen requirements appear to be the most common. In the 1972-1973 Bureau of Labor Statistics survey of 769 construction agreements, 65 percent of them (embracing about 60 percent of the workers covered) specified the assignment of a foreman for a given number of workers (in most cases, only four or fewer). About one-quarter of the contracts also prescribed a ratio or foremen to workers, a provision found most commonly among electricians and plumbers.[19] Although the study does not specify how often the requirement is for nonworking foremen, agreements often prohibit foremen from working with the tools once the crew reaches a certain size.

Open shop contractors, of course, also utilize foremen, and it is not improbable that, in some instances, they would meet the union standards anyway. But not all situations are the same, and the use of foremen (especially nonworking foremen) should logically be predicated on the complexity of the work and the need for close supervision. A fixed formula does not distinguish between the routine job and the special case. The open shop contractor who is able to get along with fewer foremen saves money both in terms of saving the foreman's premium wage and obtaining more productive working time. On balance, however, this factor appears to constitute less of a cost advantage to the nonunion contractor than most other restrictive practices. When the open shop contractors and executives were interviewed we asked them to outline the reasons for the growth of open shop construction. Foremen assignments were seldom mentioned.

Employment of "unnecessary" workers by union contractors, on the other hand, was high on almost everyone's list. The operating engineers have traditionally come under the most criticism for these kinds of practices. One example is clauses mandating the assignment of a worker to a limited number of small machines such as pumps and compressors which, according to employer spokesmen, require no continuing attendance. Another is the specification of an oiler to work with the operator of each machine. Finally, many contracts limit the number of transfers of an individual from one piece of equipment to another. Although the operating engineers typically receive much of the attention in this connection,[20] other crafts are not immune. The Construction Roundtable has cited some illustrations:

> Examples of costly "standby" manning include: carpenters being required to stand by during the pouring of concrete even though

---

19 U.S. Bureau of Labor Statistics, Bulletin 1819, *op. cit.*, p. 13.

20 The reader may recall the reference in Chapter VIII to a practice of some unions to waive some of their contractual restrictions when a contractor is bidding for a job in competition with one or more open shops. It is significant that the operating engineers were frequently mentioned in this regard.

wooden forms are not used; cement finishers in some areas have to be on hand when concrete is being poured even though they are not actually needed or used; the union steward who must be on the job at all times work is performed even though he is not required and may not be able to perform any of the available work.[21]

The issue of crew size is, of course, closely related to the requirement of unnecessary workers. The BLS survey of construction agreements found references to crew size in 38 percent of the contracts examined.[22] Crafts for which over one-half of the agreements surveyed contained restrictions on crew size included boilermakers, ironworkers, electricians, operating engineers, and roofers. Some of these cases, to be sure, involve obvious safety considerations, as in the case of crane operators and ironworkers erecting structural steel.

It must again be emphasized that none of the practices described above are universal in the union sector, nor are they all necessarily in conflict with the prevailing norm in open shops. The evidence suggests, however, that they are sufficiently common to help explain the growing penetrations of open shops into previously union markets. It is significant that complaints from organizations of union contractors and their customers—the National Constructors Association, Associated General Contractors, Construction Roundtable—even during the period of explosive wage settlements, did not center as much on wage rates as on what is broadly described as "featherbedding." The open shop contractor, facing no jurisdictional restrictions or disputes, and no limitations on the size and allocation of his work force (other than those prescribed by building codes and other laws), has found himself in a position of increasing competitive advantage simply because of his greater flexibility in operations. The extent to which this flexibility is differently exercised may obviously vary considerably, and the differences, in practice, may indeed have been exaggerated by spokesmen for embattled union contractors. But even a phenomenon that is exaggerated is still one that exists, and in a competitive industry like construction all small advantages—and these are not necessarily small—may spell the difference between winning and losing an important con-

---

[21] "Restrictive Work Practices in the Construction Industry", mimeographed report prepared by the Construction Roundtable, New York, 1974, p. 14. The Construction Roundtable is now part of the Business Roundtable.

[22] U.S. Bureau of Labor Statistics, Bulletin 1819, *op. cit.*, p. 28.

tract. Other implications of this question will be further explored below.

SEASONALITY

One of the more significant burdens borne by the construction labor market is the necessity of adjusting to seasonally changing manpower needs. Although the magnitude of seasonal change varies along a number of dimensions—geographic region, type of construction, and function of the contractor or subcontractor are the most prominent of these—the aggregate swings in the industry's employment over a twelve month period are substantial. In the years 1970 to 1974, employment rose an average of 22.4 percent between February and August. The significance of these movements is obvious: from the winter low to the summer high the industry must somehow recruit some 800,000 workers, and then determine what to do with these workers during the subsequent downturn.[23]

Only part of the answer is found in the unemployment statistics: between February and August construction unemployment typically falls by only a fraction of the concomitant rise in employment. The major adjustment is made in the size of the labor force rather than simple fluctuations caused by the release of workers who go on the unemployment rolls and are absorbed again later. The latter alternative creates problems in both the union and nonunion sector. For the open shop contractor, the layoff of a regular employee runs the risk that he will be unavailable when he is needed again later and that a suitable replacement will be difficult to recruit. For the union contractor, this process is less troublesome, for the hiring hall usually provides a ready source of manpower for the upswing. But large numbers of unemployed members constitute serious political problems for the union, which will, therefore, normally seek to maintain its regular membership at a level somewhat lower than that needed to meet all peak season needs.

Seasonal labor force adjustments take place at both extremes of the cycle. The character of these adjustments have been described elsewhere[24] and need to be only briefly outlined here. During a seasonal upswing, some previously unemployed workers

---

[23] Data from U.S. Bureau of Labor Statistics monthly compilation. See Appendix A.

[24] Foster, *Manpower in Homebuilding, op. cit.,* Chapter III.

are recalled; in addition, other workers are recruited on a temporary basis to meet peakseason needs.[25] During the downswing, three main phenomena can be broadly identified: (1) the temporary seasonal workers return to their primary activity; (2) some regular workers are laid off; and (3) certain changes take place in the utilization of the remaining work force. Although many of these adjustments are common both to union and open shops, we propose to show that the relative extent and importance of certain adaptations tend to be somewhat different with the nonunion contractors.

It is common for construction contractors to supplement their regular work forces with seasonal help. These temporary workers are usually students or teachers taking summer jobs, though they may also include moonlighters from other industries. Respondents to the Industrial Research Unit survey were asked whether they "typically put on supplementary summer help (college students, etc.?" The responses, presented in Table IX-4 below, demonstrate that this practice is more frequently utilized by open shops, although most union contractors used it as well.

Perhaps the most persuasive explanation of the higher incidence of summer help among nonunion contractors lies in the relative wages which these workers can receive. Although some local unions permit students to be paid at the apprentice rate, others require a full journeyman wage for all workers (other than *bona fide* apprentices) in the union's jurisdiction. The open shop contractor, however, is free to pay all temporary workers according to their skill and experience. It has been shown elsewhere that summer workers are typically untrained or at least are less accomplished than the average worker with a full-time attachment to construction work.[26] For the union contractor who must pay the going rate to such a worker,[27] there is a real disincentive to utilize him. For the nonunion contractor who can peg the wage to the worker's productivity,

---

[25] Other adjustments may occur as well: workers are upgraded; job assignments are changed to make more intensive use of scarce skills; overtime is scheduled; supervisors and contractors do more work themselves; and, in the last analysis, jobs are either not accepted or postponed.

[26] Howard G. Foster, "Labor Force Adjustments to Seasonal Fluctuations in Construction," *Industrial and Labor Relations Review*, XXIII (July, 1970), pp. 528-540.

[27] It may be added that even an apprentice's wage for this worker may well exceed the entry level wage paid by nonunion firms.

TABLE IX-4
Constructor Use of Supplementary Summer Employment, Union and Nonunion, 1974

Response	Union Number	Union Percent	Nonunion Number	Nonunion Percent
Yes	473	60.8	614	78.3
No	290	37.3	162	20.7
Not reported	15	1.9	8	1.0

Source: Industrial Research Unit Questionnaire.

these workers can be a satisfactory alternative to higher paid skilled workers who are likely to be scarce during a busy season.

Open shop contractors are also apt to respond differently during the downswing. The Industrial Research Unit questionnaire asked contractors if they "have had to lay off any workers in the past three years because of seasonal slowdowns." As shown in the Table IX-5, open shop contractors were more likely to respond in the negative.

These responses were largely consistent with the assertions of spokesmen for open shop contractors to the effect that employment tends to be steadier in the nonunion sector. Since there is no reason to expect that union and nonunion employers differ in the extent to which their needs fluctuate over the seasons, the conclusion is suggested that open shops make more concerted efforts to avoid layoffs. These efforts, to be sure, are usually not represented as gratuitous or altruistic. In our personal interviews with contractors, they were more often represented as necessary and prudent, in part to offset relatively low wages paid, and in part as a recognition of the open shop's relative difficulty and uncertainty in finding suitable replacements later. A typical response would take the following form: "We keep our employees by offering them steady work, thus firming up their attachment and loyalty to the company." In short, the conventional premise that the construction worker forms a bond with his trade rather than his employer is less true of nonunion workers.

The open shop contractor seeks to ensure that his employees can be kept on during slow periods in a variety of ways, some

TABLE IX-5
Seasonal Layoffs by Union and Nonunion Contractors, 1971-1974

	Union		Nonunion	
Response	Number	Percent	Number	Percent
Yes	600	77.1	430	54.8
No	156	20.1	345	44.0
Not reported	22	2.8	9	1.1

Source: Industrial Research Unit Questionnaire.

of which are not available to the union employer faced with jurisdictional lines. He may "beat the bushes" for work which he would not actively solicit in busier times, perhaps even performing it at little or no profit simply to keep his work force occupied. He may construct, on speculation, apartments for rental or homes. He may simply give some workers a paid vacation. Open shop highway contractors and others devote considerable man-hours to machine rebuilding and preventive maintenance. Others utilize the slow months for intensive training activities, still others assign janitorial or any other duties available to "keep the men on." Several open shop contractors, interviewed by the Industrial Research Unit staff, emphasized that they purposely utilized summer help, particularly students, in order to minimize winter layoffs.

The dramatic drop in construction, especially housing and small commercial work in 1974-1975, has forced some open shop builders to lay off workers for the first time. What impact this will have on their future operations remains to be seen. Certainly, unemployment among union craftsmen has been substantial, and probably greater in many areas. Thus it remains true, even in recession, that open shop contractor responses to changing seasonal needs provide, in most cases, for a more stable work force for the employer and steadier employment for the worker.

SUMMARY

The open shop contractor recruits his work force through more informal channels than does his unionized counterpart. This gives him none of the advantages of a union hiring hall, but frees him from its significant disadvantages. Because of increasing needs for more effective recruiting tools, open shop contractor groups are developing centralized recruitment mechanisms suited to their needs, but these are still in an experimental stage and are relatively rare.

Open shop contractors have significant advantages in the deployment of manpower on the job. Unrestricted by union rules, they can pay employees according to skill and productivity while assigning them according to need. Free of worry of jurisdictional disputes, free to determine the skill content required, and free to determine the extent of job manning required, the open shop contractor can and indeed does, as a rule, utilize labor more efficiently. On the other hand, because of the absence of craft restrictions, skilled manpower can be retained on the payroll and used below skill levels when employment is down and it is desired to conserve such skills for the firm.

Finally, through greater use of supplementary summer help and a host of measures to contrive work in slow seasons, open shop contractors are both permitted and induced to maintain a more stable regular work force.

CHAPTER X

Manpower Training And Development

There are few industries which can function properly without ongoing efforts to generate trained manpower. The study of investment in human capital has itself become a specialty within the scholarly discipline of economics. Government, academe, the labor movement, and industry have all explicitly acknowledged the importance of manpower development in terms of individual fulfillment, industrial prosperity, and aggregate economic growth. The U.S. Department of Labor has put it this way:

> The greatest single investment that we as a people have is in our skills and know-how. It is imperative that we guard this investment carefully. Our future progress and strength as a nation depend upon a conscious concern with our manpower resources—their training and ultimate skills.[1]

The role of occupational training is especially critical in construction. Although all industries employ skilled workers,[2] construction employs exceptionally large numbers of them. In 1972, 69 percent of all manual workers in the industry were classified as skilled. Among other industries employing a substantial manual work force, the percentages were 38 for mining, 28 for manufacturing, and 39 for transportation and public utilities.[3] Construction employs about one-quarter of the skilled blue collar workers in the entire labor force.

---

[1] U.S. Department of Labor, Manpower Administration, *The National Apprenticeship Program,* 1968 ed. (Washington, D.C.: Government Printing Office, 1968), p. 1.

[2] The term "skilled" as used here relates roughly to the census classification "foremen, craftsmen, and kindred workers." Semiskilled and unskilled workers are officially designated as "operatives" and "laborers" respectively.

[3] Calculated from U.S. Bureau of Labor Statistics, *Handbook of Labor Statistics, 1973,* Bulletin 1790 (Washington, D.C.: Government Printing Office, 1973), p. 69.

These workers must be regularly replenished. Each year more than 2 percent of the work force dies or retires,[4] and an unknown but substantial number migrate to other industries. In addition, the industry grows: average annual employment has more than doubled since the end of World War II and, because of labor turnover, each new full-time job necessitates about 1.8 new workers. To the individual firm, as well as to the industry as a whole, training is thus a vital component of efficient labor market adjustment. As one open shop contractor put it metaphorically:

> Compare yourself as a construction manager to the coach of a successful basketball team, or any other kind of team in the world of sports, and you will realize for a coach to have a winner, he must have the "horses" in the slang of sports. A successful coach must first recruit his players and then coach them in the fundamentals and in his method of playing the game. And finally, he must put them all together as a team to become a winner. With good success in recruiting, coaching and teamwork, he will have a winner. The same is true in the construction industry. We must recruit our help, train our help and put all of the men together as a team in order to have a winner.[5]

Training for construction occupations takes place both within and outside the industry itself. Certain basic skills can be picked up in vocational or trade schools. Some workers have obtained training in branches of the military which perform their own construction work, or through various programs designed to prepare servicemen for civilian life. Others pick up trades on their own with the help of friends and relatives. Finally, some skilled building occupations can be learned through training or experience in other industries, such as farming, manufacturing, or shipbuilding. On the whole, however, the evidence strongly suggests "that the primary means of skill acquisition is training, formal and informal, within the industry itself." [6]

---

[4] Allan F. Salt, "Estimated Need for Skilled Workers," *Monthly Labor Review*, LXXXIX (April, 1966), p. 368.

[5] Associated General Contractors, "Excerpts from the AGC Regional Open Shop Conference, Atlanta, February 12, 1972," mimeo, p. 37.

[6] Howard G. Foster, "Nonapprentice Sources of Training in Construction," *Monthly Labor Review*, XCIII (February, 1970), p. 26.

INFORMAL TRAINING IN THE OPEN SHOP

There is no universally acknowledged distinction between formal and informal training. Indeed, learning forms may be viewed as ranging along a spectrum, from mere observation of the production process itself to highly structured programs involving both a set sequence of on-the-job experiences and rigorous off-the-job instruction. The point at which training becomes "formal" can be fixed in any number of ways: for example, the intent of the employer; the ordering of the trainee's assignments; the explicit role of the journeyman who is doing the training. Since these notions are difficult to deal with empirically, we shall regard here as "formal" only those approaches to training which include some form of supplemental instruction, either theoretical or manipulative or both, away from the work place.

By this definition, most training which occurs in construction, and in open shop construction particularly, is informal. Such training is, of course, purposeful, valuable, and effective. But few contractors who are asked about formal training (as we define it) deny that on-the-job learning is greatly facilitated by a grounding in the theory, terminology, and technology of the construction process—subjects which are most easily conveyed in a pedagogical setting. At the same time, related instruction can be expensive, so that our distinction between formal and informal training is also useful as an indicator of the employer's commitment to investing in his workers.

Even informal training, however, generally goes beyond mere observation by the trainee. Where employers report that all their training is "on-the-job," that may mean many things. Most commonly, it appears to mean that a new worker is assigned to work alongside a journeyman, performing first the simpler tasks associated with the particular job being performed and later graduating to more complex operations. The journeyman is expected to explain the job while doing it, and to give the trainee some practice under his direct supervision. The distinction between training and random learning is the role of the journeyman. If he is training, his work pace should be slowed; if he is simply being watched, it should not. Most contractors assert that their journeymen (or they themselves) actively engage in training, in that the trainee is not only expected to learn but also to be taught.

On-the-job training, if successful, performs a special service for the contractor in that it teaches the trainee precisely what he has to do to perform for the particular contractor, or particular type of construction work. On the other hand, such training may not prepare the trainee for jobs with other contractors. Since a strong tenet of open shop contractors is to hold their labor, whereas the union shop contractor depends upon the union hiring hall for labor supply, such on-the-job training is much more appropriate for the open shop.

Most informal training, on the other hand, does not appear to be sequential. In other words, there is no predefined ordering of job assignments which build upon each other. The trainee is assigned to a job that needs to be done at the time. If his prior experience is not sufficient to learn that job expeditiously, then he simply does not learn it expeditiously and the journeyman can use him only for less significant tasks. His role then becomes that of a helper rather than a trainee. Haber and Levinson draw the distinction as follows: "The principal difference between the helper and the apprentice is that the former is given no formal training, but concentrates full time on his semiskilled function." The result is "a more specialized labor force capable of doing an acceptable job in a limited area, but with virtually no competence in other important aspects of the trade."[7] Of course, many helpers do in time become craftsmen, and many apprentices never reach the first class journeyman class. The Haber and Levinson distinction is, however, suggestive of the basic difference in training concepts and aims.

Often, an employer can do quite well with the bulk of his work force specialized in very narrowly defined competences. There must, however, be some workers who have broad familiarity and expertise in the overall construction process. There must be someone who can read blueprints, lay out a job or sections of a job, perform the more delicate and exacting tasks associated with a trade, solve unforeseen problems as they arise, and generally supervise and orchestrate the work of others. In short, any project requires a complement of all-around journeymen:

> Training for craft occupations in construction is designed to produce a journeyman who is able not only to perform certain tasks under supervision but to supervise himself to a large degree. The

[7] William Haber and Harold M. Levinson, *Labor Relations and Productivity in the Building Trades* (Ann Arbor: Bureau of Industrial Relations, University of Michigan, 1956), pp. 98-99.

> journeyman is trained to perform much of the supervisory and planning functions that in other industries are the role of management. . . . The journeyman is expected to understand the fundamentals of his craft as well as how to perform specialized tasks; he may be asked to lay out work from blueprints and to supervise his own performance on the job.[8]

The worker who is trained informally on a "catch-as-catch-can" basis is less likely to attain this level of journeyman status—or at least he is not likely to attain it as quickly as one whose training is more systematic. The fundamentals of his craft are not easily or efficiently taught on the job; the supervising journeyman is not apt to interrupt the work to deliver a comprehensive lecture on blueprint reading or the composition and properties of cement. The contractor may be able to function with large numbers of semiskilled or narrowly trained specialists, but they cannot constitute his entire work force. The open shop employer, in particular, unfettered by union jurisdictional restrictions, may be able to subdivide the work so as to maximize the output of his specialists while minimizing his overall labor costs, but this practice puts a premium on the role of the exceptionally skilled and well-rounded craftsman who can coordinate and direct their work.

Conversely, the unionized contractor who must utilize all journeymen and no helpers must often require skilled personnel to perform unskilled or semiskilled work. Many such contractors frequently complain that they must pay the journeyman rate to persons with a wide spectrum of capabilities, including some that are far from all-around craftsmen. Thus the use of the on-the-job trained helper, or craftsman, of less than all-around competence by the open shop contractor, results from a work force organization responsive to practical job specifications. It is also a fundamental reason why open shop construction is more economical.

A significant advantage of on-the-job training in the open shop sector is that opportunity is afforded for intercraft mobility. Typically, employees with no experience are hired as laborers. If they show promise, and openings are available, they can win assignments for cement work and/or rough carpentry, or they may progress from one to the other. With craft union barriers absent, a capable person can change his line of work and im-

---

[8] Daniel Quinn Mills, *Industrial Relations and Manpower in Construction* (Cambridge: M.I.T. Press, 1972), pp. 183-184).

prove his income. Since open shop builders' wage rates depend on ability and performance, rather than on the particular craft involved, and since it is to the advantage of the open shop contractor that his employees have as many capabilities as possible, upward movement and line of work changes are encouraged.

Such movement is less likely to occur into the more specialized and difficult skills such as the electrical, mechanical, and plumbing trades for two principal reasons. For one thing, these trades are typically subcontracted. A general contractor's employees are thus not likely to have an opportunity to move into such crafts. And second, such crafts require greater technical and/or classroom training and thus are more difficult to enter by on-the-job instruction. Nevertheless, some mobility into these crafts has occurred, and cases were revealed by our field interviews in which skilled craftsmen (particularly plumbers and electrical helpers), were former laborers and cement finishers. To be sure, most were not yet journeymen, but their mobility had been considerable and probably would not have occurred in a union situation because their formal education and age excluded them from systematic apprentice programs. This type of mobility can be especially important for minorities who have been bypassed by the high educational, low age, and often discriminatory entrance requirements of union apprentice programs.

Despite the significance of on-the-job training, the critical part of the open shop journeyman is central to an understanding and appreciation of the formal training undertakings which have been increasingly expended by open shop contractors' associations. Nonunion employers have long engaged in structured training programs,[9] but the growth of open shop construction in recent years has been matched by a marked expansion of these efforts. Prior to this study, however, there has been no comprehensive inventory or assessment made of formal training in the open shop.

FORMAL TRAINING IN OPEN SHOP CONSTRUCTION—THE ASSOCIATION ROLE

The most common type of formal training in the construction industry is apprenticeship. Apprenticeship combines "a schedule of work processes in which an apprentice is to receive training and experience on the job" with "organized instruction designed

[9] Haber and Levinson, *op. cit.*, p. 98.

to provide the apprentice with knowledge in technical subjects related to his trade."[10] It also normally includes a wage progression throughout the indenture (usually calculated as a percentage of the journeyman's wage) and formal recognition upon completion of the program.

Apprentices may be indentured either to an individual employer or to a special multi-employer or union-employer organization. To gain certain benefits under public statutes (such as apprenticeship wage rates under prevailing wage laws or payments under the GI Bill) programs must be registered with the U.S. Bureau of Apprenticeship and Training (BAT) or with a state apprenticeship agency. Open shop employers have historically had difficulty in securing registration for their programs. The staffs of BAT and most state apprenticeship agencies have been drawn largely from union ranks,[11] and such agencies have traditionally considered union participation as a *sine qua non* of a plan's acceptance for registration.[12] The twin pressures resulting from the growth of the open shop and discrimination by unions and contractors against minorities led to a change in these policies during the Nixon administration. Prior to 1970, BAT would not register an apprentice program in an area where another was in existence if the new program's requirements were not as rigorous. Guidelines now in effect substitute national apprencticeship standards for the system of local standards previously applied.[13] Thus the ABC programs

[10] U.S. Department of Labor, *The National Apprenticeship Program, op. cit.*, p. 6.

[11] Writing in 1968, Professor Mangum summed it up this way for BAT: "The choice of apprentices, training methods, and costs of training were totally matters decided by local unions and employers. Its power bases were the Building Trades, Metal Trades, and Printing Trades, departments of the AFL-CIO, with a potent assist from the fact that the chairman of the Labor Department-HEW Appropriations Subcommittee was a former Building Trades man. The BAT Administrator was selected after consultation with the craft unions and most of the field staff were former union officials or journeymen." Garth L. Mangum, *MDTA: Foundation of Federal Manpower Policy* (Baltimore: The Johns Hopkins Press, 1968), pp. 45-46.

[12] In an interview published in ABC's journal, BAT's Director, Hugh Murphy, acknowledged that "the programs submitted by ABC have at times experienced inordinate difficulties in obtaining approval," but he believed that this is becoming "less the case, as more people have accepted that ABC is sponsoring and developing extremely fine apprenticeship programs. . . ." *The Contractor,* XX (June, 1974), p. 33.

[13] See the Court's opinion in *Clayton Dougherty et al.* v. *United States,* USDC S.D. Tex., CA No. 70-H-1096, July 22, 1974; summarized in *Construc-*

must still conform to the national standards, but they can vary from local ones where the definition of "more rigorous" might be regulations which extend training periods or set entrance requirements that limit the number of trainees.

Apprenticeship has traditionally been regarded by scholars as well as by administrators as a feature only of the unionized sector of construction, and the growth of training in the open shop is conspicuously unacknowledged in the literature. Although it is doubtless true that there are more union apprentices and union-contractor apprenticeship committees across the country than in nonunion construction, open shop training is growing, especially in areas where unions are relatively weak, but elsewhere as well. It is, therefore, significant that such an astute and knowledgeable observer as Mills could, as late as 1972, write about apprenticeship administration solely in terms of joint labor-management committees.[14]

There are other varieties of formal training besides apprenticeship. Preapprenticeship training is often used in connection with affirmative action programs to help minorities prepare themselves for entrance into apprenticeship itself. These programs are usually brief in duration—seldom exceeding six weeks—and concentrate upon improving literacy skills and providing exposure to the fundamentals of a trade. We shall again note them in Chapter XII when discussing minority representation in open shop construction. There are also programs for journeymen upgrading designed both to update the skills of the established craftsmen and to coach them in techniques for teaching these skills to on-the-job trainees. And there are management courses for supervisors and others, many developed by the AGC or other associations. All of these programs are much less widespread than apprentice training in both the union and open shop sectors.

Until recently, most formal training efforts—to the extent that there was any such training at all—were sponsored by individual employers for their own workers. Unlike the union contractor,

---

tion Labor Report, No. 981 (July 31, 1974), pp. A-1 to A-2. In this case, a local of the Sheet Metal Workers attempted to halt an ABC apprentice program because it followed national, not local, standards. Promulgation of such standards has been ruled the discretionary right of BAT director, provided that they are reasonable. (See also *General Electric Co.* v. *U.S. Department of Labor,* 268 F. Supp. 987 (D.S.C., 1967). Of course, new regulations could also be issued to harm open shop programs as well as to further them.

[14] Mills, *op. cit.,* pp. 186-189.

whose training is conducted under the administration of joint union-management apprenticeship committees (which are financed by contributions from all employers to an apprenticeship fund), the open shop contractor was usually obliged to underwrite his own program. Now, however, most contractors' associations with substantial open shop representation have organized formal training programs for their members. As these programs grow and are introduced into more and more areas, it may be expected that increasing numbers of contractors—both those who have provided training on their own and those who have not—will participate in association sponsored training activities. Because of their broad backing, multi-employer programs can offer training in a wider range of crafts and do it more efficiently.

Association training programs are presently found in the chapters of the Associated Builders and Contractors, the National Association of Home Builders, the Associated General Contractors, the Associated Independent Electrical Contractors of America, and by a consortium of associations in North and South Carolina, joined together as the Carolinas Construction Training Council under the leadership of the Carolinas AGC. Training by each of the organizations is examined in turn below; training efforts undertaken by individual contractors are discussed in the following section of this chapter.

Associated Builders and Contractors (ABC)

Perhaps the most extensive network of organized apprenticeship programs in the open shop sector has been developed by the Associated Builders and Contractors, which now employs a full-time training staff and encourages its chapters to do likewise. Most of these programs are of recent vintage. In many instances, according to various association spokesmen, individual chapters have had great difficulty getting their programs approved and registered by the U.S. Bureau of Apprenticeship and Training, or by state apprenticeship agencies, largely because of opposition from local building trades unions, and the already noted relationship of organized labor to these agencies. This opposition appears to have been substantially overcome, and in the past five years over 70 programs in more than twenty ABC chapters have been initiated. To date, the total number of programs in the eastern, southern, and midwestern states, where ABC chapters are located, is in excess of 100.

Table X-1 indicates the programs operating in various ABC chapters through 1974, as compiled by the director of training activities for the association. The most common trades which require training are carpenter, bricklayer, air conditioning mechanic, electrician, plumber, and sheet metal worker. In addition to the programs indicated in the table, there are scattered programs for asbestos worker, precast concrete specialist, lather, painter, and welder. Table X-1, moreover, understates the proliferation of training programs actually underway, apparently because of a lag in reporting from chapters to ABC headquarters. For example, our interviews with association executives in the field discovered nascent programs in eastern Michigan (Detroit area) and western Pennsylvania (Pittsburgh), as well as two programs in Central Ohio—heating and air conditioning mechanic and bricklayer—not cited in the summary provided to us by the ABC.

Programs are administered by local ABC chapters. Guidelines and specifications on the structure of the training process and the sequence of subjects to be covered tend to be fairly uniform across individual trades, conforming closely to the recommended standards published by the ABC national office. These standards, in turn, covering such matters as minimum admission requirements, amount and nature of related instruction, and overall duration of the program, are substantially identical to those used in union apprenticeship. These similarities, however, may reflect not so much an endorsement by the ABC of the traditional approach to apprenticeship, than a pragmatic acquiescence to the *de facto* requirements for program approval.

Some contractors interviewed, for example, regarded the conventional craft distinctions reflected in the programs as artificial and unrealistic. Their view was that programs should instead follow functional lines; in other words, they should combine skills associated with a particular phase of construction. A common illustration given was that of cement pouring. Open shop contractors maintain that there should be a single, integrated program encompassing the diverse skills required for this function, rather than separate programs for carpenters (who build forms), ironworkers (who place reinforcing rods), and cement finishers (who smooth the concrete).

Both BAT and the state agencies, however, are still thoroughly imbued with the traditional craft union approach, in terms both

TABLE X-1

Approved Apprenticeship Programs Conducted by the Associated Builders and Contractors, by Trade and Association Chapter, 1974

Trade	Chapter[a]																		
	1	2	3	4	5	6	7	8	9	10	11	12	13	14	15	16	17	18	19
Air conditioning mechanic	X	X		X		X	X	X	X			X	X	X	X	X	X		
Bricklayer					X	X	X				X	X				X		X	X
Carpenter	X	X	X	X	X	X	X	X		X	X	X	X	X	X	X	X	X	X
Cement mason					X							X						X	
Electrician	X	X	X	X	X	X	X	X	X			X	X	X		X	X	X	X
Heavy equipment operator		X										X							
Plumber/pipefitter	X	X	X	X	X	X	X	X	X	X	X	X	X	X		X	X	X	X
Sheet metal worker	X	X			X	X	X					X	X	X		X			X
Stonemason							X					X							

Source: Associated Builders and Contractors.

[a] **Key to chapters:**

1. Anne Arundel, Md.
2. Baltimore Metro.
3. Central Florida
4. Central Ohio
5. Central Pa.
6. Cumberland Valley
7. Delaware Valley
8. Florida Gold Coast
9. Florida Gulf Coast
10. Georgia
11. Kentuckiana
12. Keystone
13. Metro Washington
14. South Louisiana
15. South Texas
16. Tennessee
17. Texas
18. Western Michigan
19. Yankee

of staff and philosophy. They have been open to little experimentation, usually insisting that the open shop programs be modeled rather closely on the union ones. Most ABC apprenticeship groups, however, have apparently been able to work with BAT and state staffs without undue difficulty once their programs have been approved; provided, of course, that they adhere to the traditional concepts of apprenticeship both in terms of craft delineation and time required to complete apprenticeship courses.

Policy decisions for ABC programs are typically made by training committees for each chapter. In some cases, the committees are also responsible for day-to-day operations, but the preferable approach—and the one used by some of the larger and longer established programs—is to engage a full-time training coordinator. The coordinator has overall responsibility for such tasks as arranging related instruction classes, placing trainees when necessary, following up on apprentices who are lax in class attendance, and generally ensuring that individual contractors conform to the standards of training envisaged in the programs.

Our interviews with ABC executives and active members revealed that, in certain respects, their procedures differ significantly from most of those in the union sector.[15] In the first place, apprenticeship openings tend to be filled by workers referred directly by individual contractors. Applicants are sometimes actively sought from the community at large, especially where the chapter is engaged in concerted efforts to recruit minority workers. In most other cases, however, slots are filled with trainees who have already been employed by an ABC member and whom the contractor regards as a promising craftsman, or in some cases by members of the National Association of Home Builders, who cooperate with ABC chapters in a few areas. This process, in which enrollment follows hire rather than vice versa (as in the union sector), avoids what might be troublesome placement problems, but it also limits the pool from which successful apprentices might be drawn. As these programs expand, recruitment from the outside is likely to become a more important feature of the ABC plans if only because additional manpower can be procured only in this manner.

---

[15] For a brief description of procedures in unionized construction, see Howard G. Foster, "Apprenticeship in the Building Trades: A Sympathetic Assessment," *Labor Law Journal*, XXII (January, 1971), pp. 3-12.

A second, related feature is the method of financing the program. In the union sector, apprenticeship is financed through a uniform cents-per-hour assessment on all employers. ABC programs, by contrast, tend to be supported primarily by participating contractors (which helps explain, of course, why individual firms exercise great influence as to who is enrolled). Since the firm cannot be assured that the trainee will continue in its employ after the period of apprenticeship, there is a natural disincentive to invest substantial sums in training. One might predict that, as the programs grow, they will move toward an industry-wide funding arrangement which would reduce the marginal cost of training to the individual firm.

Given the newness of most ABC programs, it is not surprising that they have not yet begun to turn out large numbers of apprenticeship graduates. In 1973, only 185 workers in all trades finished their apprenticeship. Many programs have yet to graduate their first apprentice, and the graduations of others do not yet reflect the greatly expanding enrollments of recent years. Unfortunately, there are no data available on the dropout experience from ABC apprenticeship programs. In 1973, the ABC reported an enrollment of over 3,300 trainees, with electrical and plumbing programs accounting for nearly three-fourths of the total. And, as noted earlier, this figure does not include recently initiated programs in several chapters. The breakdown by chapter and trade is given in Table X-2.

The stress being put on training by ABC in recent years, combined with the growing needs of its members for skilled personnel, may still give rise to formal training that is innovative. Thus one training coordinator in planning to establish a welding training class to qualify carpenters to do welding, and to set up other programs which expand the capabilities of craftsmen to handle related work in other trades. Such programs cannot be registered in most states because of the rigid, union oriented regulations. Given the pressures on open shop contractors to find skilled personnel, to keep them employed, and to maintain their cost competitive advantages, it does seem likely that training innovations which disregard traditional craft barriers must be developed and/or expanded by open shop organizations.

Table X-2
Apprenticeship Enrollment and Graduations in ABC Programs, 1973, by Chapter and Trade, 1972-1973

Trade	Chapter [a]																			
	1	2	3	4	5	6	7	8	9	10	11	12	13	14	15	16	17	18	19	Total
Air conditioning mechanic		33				7	25	21				3	28	12		4	38			171
Asbestos worker												2								2
Bricklayer						11	1					11				12		12	11	58
Carpenter		71		39	9	22	54	25	59	6		80	46	13		40	12	33	9	518
Cement mason					4							3						1		8
Electrician		454	125	147	15	56	43	105	165			83	37	56		40	98	68	14	1,506
Heavy equipment operator		24										7								31
Plumber		359		73	9	17	30	69	84	47		44	45	10		25	44	33	17	906
Sheet metal worker		9			9	15	10			19		28	37	11		20			11	169
Total		950	125	259	46	128	163	220	308	72		261	193	102		141	192	147	62	3,369
Graduated 1973		54	0	1	8	8	16	0	2	28		44	3	0		5	0	16	0	185

Source: Associated Builders and Contractors.

[a] Key to chapters:

1. Anne Arundel, Md.
2. Baltimore Metro.
3. Central Florida
4. Central Ohio
5. Central Pa.
6. Cumberland Valley
7. Delaware Valley
8. Florida Gold Coast
9. Florida Gulf Coast
10. Georgia
11. Kentuckiana
12. Keystone
13. Metro Washington
14. South Louisiana
15. South Texas
16. Tennessee
17. Texas
18. Western Michigan
19. Yankee

Associated Independent Electrical Contractors of America (AIECA)[16]

This association, formed in 1956, had twenty-eight local chapters in June 1974, fifteen of which operate electrical apprenticeship programs. Like ABC, AIECA employs a full-time training staff and actively encourages its chapters to initiate and to expand apprenticeship programs. AIECA is concentrated in the South and Southwest where it was founded and is headquartered. All but two of its apprenticeship programs (Wichita and Central Arizona) are in the South, particularly Texas. Nationally promulgated apprenticeship standards serve as a guide to local chapters in developing programs which will be registered by state and federal apprenticeship agencies. These standards, which were approved by the Bureau of Apprenticeship and Training in 1972, do not appear to differ markedly from those used for union electricians. They cover such usual matters as minimum hours of on-the-job training and related instruction (2,000 and 144 per year, respectively), minimum qualifications for admission, wage schedules, affirmative action, subjects to be learned, and so forth.

Each program is administered by a local apprenticeship committee. By 1974, the local programs had a total of over 500 apprentices in training, with the first class (35 apprentices in Atlanta) scheduled to graduate in spring 1975. Over 300 of the association's 500 members had apprentices registered in a program. AIECA's director of training estimates that 15 to 20 percent of the trainees nationally fail to complete their programs, although he opines that most of the dropouts nevertheless remain in the electrical trade in some capacity.

Associated General Contractors (AGC)

As described in Chapter I, the AGC is preponderantly an organization of unionized contractors, but with a significant minority of open shops among its membership. Many chapters, however, are dominated by open shop employers, especially in the less industrialized states. Where a chapter is mostly union, its training efforts are likely to be limited to joint apprenticeship programs, but as noted below, exceptions are also found to this rule. Some of the predominantly open shop chapters have also

[16] Much of the information in this section was obtained from Mr. Jerry D. Parrish, Director of Training for AIECA. A letter to one of the authors, June 18, 1974, was especially helpful.

developed unilaterally administered training programs with local funding. The unique program in the Carolinas will be described below.

The only training in which the national office has taken a direct role is in connection with the Job Opportunities in the Business Sector (JOBS) program of the National Alliance of Businessmen (NAB).[17] As of July 1, 1974, this program became subject to sponsorship and funding by local manpower agencies under the Comprehensive Employment and Training Act of 1973 (CETA). Prior to this date, the program employed six to eight full-time coordinators throughout the country to promote training for the disadvantaged in construction trades. The training thus provided was of a short-term nature, furnishing what was, in effect, preapprenticeship instruction to trainees who might then enter a full-fledged apprenticeship program. At this writing, it is too early to say how many local sponsors will have continued or subscribed to participation in the program.

There is, unfortunately, no comprehensive information available on how many AGC chapters have initiated training efforts on their own, independent of joint union-management apprenticeship programs. Many have developed manuals to guide their members in training activities; others provide consulting assistance; and still others administer programs. A 1972 survey by the AGC's Manpower and Training Division elicited responses from 54 of the Association's 123 chapters. These chapters reported a total of 196 programs, mostly for carpenters, bricklayers, cement masons, operating engineers, and ironworkers. The survey did not reveal, however, how many of the programs were operated independently by open shop contractors.

Highway Programs. The Federal Aid Highway Act of August 23, 1968 (Public Law 90-495), exempted from Davis-Bacon provisions "employment pursuant to apprenticeship and skill training programs which have been certified by the secretary of transportation as promoting equal employment opportunity . . . ." On December 31, 1970 (sec. 110(b) of Public Law 91-605) it was amended to authorize the secretary of transportation, in cooperation with federal or state government agencies, or any other organization or person "to develop, conduct, and administer highway construction training, including skill im-

[17] The material on AGC training activities was obtained from unpublished material largely supplied by Mr. Irving F. de Milt, Director of AGC's Manpower and Training Division.

provement programs," and authorized $5 million per year for this purpose. Where employees are unionized, such training and affirmative action requirements have usually been met by formal apprentice training agreements, especially with the Operating Engineers, although this union and several of its locals have also sponsored other types of training under government contracts. The Federal Highway Administration has, however, encouraged and funded the job training programs which became operational in November, 1970. Since then, approximately 2,600 persons annually have received such training, of whom more than 50 percent were minorities.[18] FHA regulations require that trainees or apprentices, including a "suitable" proportion of minorities, be employed on each project which it funds.

A number of open shop AGC highway chapters have developed such training programs. The Georgia State program is utilized not only there but by open shop contractors throughout the country. The Texas highway chapter has special programs for various skills, and the Colorado chapter, which has only a minority of open shop contractors, nevertheless has developed a program for this segment of its membership.[19] The Carolinas chapter program is discussed below.

These highway training programs are basically designed to teach machine operating skills. Less comprehensive than apprenticeship, they nevertheless usually do include some related instruction, although they predominantly feature on-the-job training. Most of them are heavily concentrated toward minorities, which thus enable the contractors also to meet FHA's affirmative action requirements. Trainees, often laborers, are taught how to operate both trucks and earth-moving equipment, working from the more simple machines to the more complex. The period of training time varies, depending on the complexity of the machine, the capacity of the trainee, and the duration of the job. Since many highway contractors have difficulty attracting labor, these programs are often a virtual necessity to man some jobs. This conforms to the basic aim of the open shop contractors, which is to train permanent personnel who can operate a variety of machines.

A distinguishing feature of the open shop highway programs compared with union programs is the absence of the oiler classification. Open shop machine crews oil their own machines. Mi-

---

[18] Data supplied by Mr. K. L. Ziems, Federal Highway Administration.

[19] The remainder of this section is based on numerous field interviews.

norities have frequently found their way into highway work above the laborer classification by gaining employment as oilers. This is sometimes a step toward machine operator, sometimes a dead-end. As union training programs have become more formalized, the oilers have had increasing difficulty achieving upward movement. In the open shop, laborers move directly to the machine when upgraded, starting on smaller ones and progressing to the more complicated types.

Other AGC chapters besides the Carolinas and the highway ones are increasingly motivated to engage in training activities outside of the traditional union-management apprenticeship programs. More are likely to do so if the open shop movement within the AGC continues to grow. For example, in Vermont where unions have almost disappeared from the construction scene, the AGC chapter recently initiated unilateral programs in most of the basic trades, funded directly by participating contractors. The programs have been approved by the Vermont State Apprenticeship Council.

The foregoing account does not by any means include an account of organized training programs for open shop contractors sponsored by all AGC chapters. It does illustrate, however, the growing significance of the open shop movement within the AGC and the recognition of that fact both by AGC national and local officials, as evidenced by the increased services offered to this segment of the membership.

National Association of Home Builders (NAHB)

The various training efforts of the National Association of Home Builders are unique among open shop programs because they rely heavily upon federal financing. Between 1967 and 1973, the association invested over $4.3 million in its training programs, with an additional $1.3 million budgeted for 1974. Almost all of this money originated in grants from the U.S. Departments of Labor, and Health, Education, and Welfare under the Manpower Development and Training Act (MDTA).[20]

---

[20] NAHB's training department issues regular reports on its training activities. In addition, the authors have interviewed NAHB chapter executives throughout the country and the training department staff at NAHB headquarters several times. All were most helpful. See National Association of Homebuilders, Manpower Development and Training Department, *Report to the Executive and Finance Committee* (Washington, D.C.: The Association, January, 1974). See also Howard G. Foster, *Manpower in Homebuilding: A*

The most important of these programs is carpentry apprenticeship, initiated in 1967. The association, through its Manpower Development and Training Department, assists local home builders' associations in developing and implementing their individual programs. Funding is arranged through contracts between the NAHB and the local HBA's, and the national office provides technical help in obtaining approval from federal and state apprenticeship agencies. Through 1973, a total of forty-one programs had been established of which twenty were under current funding as of January 1, 1974.

Once a local program is established, it typically hires a full-time coordinator to oversee training activities. The contract provides funds for such expenses as the coordinator's salary, classroom instructors, books and materials. There are no direct expenses incurred either by the trainee or by the individual builder. Classroom instruction is provided either through local vocational schools or by the program directly.

The program progresses in two phases. There is, first, a six week preapprenticeship period, during which trainees are instructed in the rudiments of the carpentry trade. Subjects include, among others, mathematics for carpenters, construction materials, blueprint reading, carpenters' tools, and safety. Upon completion of this initial phase, trainees usually enter a full-blown apprenticeship program combining on-the-job training (through indenture with a local builder) and 144 hours per year of related instruction.

Between 1967 and 1973, the carpentry apprenticeship program enrolled a total of over 4,000 trainees, with an additional 800 projected for 1974. The NAHB asserts that most trainees complete the program, although there are no hard data on this proportion nor on the number who remain in the carpentry trade in the years following their graduation.

The association also sponsors a journeyman upgrading program, designed to prepare craftsmen for supervisory roles in construction. Conducted entirely within a classroom format, the program provides thirty-six hours of instruction in such areas as blueprint reading, job cost estimating, leadership and supervision, and new materials and technology. In 1972 and 1973, 729 carpenters had gone through the program, with another 225 pro-

---

Preliminary Analysis, Manpower and Human Resources Studies No. 3 (Philadelphia: Industrial Research, The Wharton School, University of Pennsylvania, 1974), pp. 90-93.

posed for 1974. There are as yet no data on the degree to which these trainees have actually assumed leadership and supervisory positions in residential construction.

Finally, the NAHB has, since 1970, conducted a preapprenticeship program in bricklaying for military servicemen. During the last six weeks of their duty, servicemen are given full-time instruction in such elements of the masonry trade as: use of tools, mathematics and blueprint reading, as well as some manipulative training on the post itself. These programs have been established at twenty military sites, of which fifteen were still in operation at the beginning of 1974. Unlike the carpentry program, however, trainees do not automatically proceed into a full-fledged apprenticeship program, and the NAHB acknowledges that placement, either with a builder or in an apprenticeship program administered by another agency, is a problem. Although the association tries to match trainees with employers in the area to which they return upon their discharge, there are no hard data on the extent to which these efforts have been successful.

Indianapolis. In Indianapolis, the NAHB program was directed particularly toward minority workers. The NAHB affiliate there, the Building Association of Greater Indianapolis, initiated a program after the union oriented Indianapolis Plan for Equal Employment declined to permit open shop firms to join. In Indianapolis, open shop firms were covered by government bid conditions which required affirmative action plans to obtain government work. In any case, they traditionally employed more minorities than did the union sector, and at the same time were anxious to recruit additional personnel. Most were in housing, low rise apartments and small commercial work and were members of BAGI.[21]

The first apprenticeship program which BAGI initiated was for carpenters, by far the largest individual craft in this sector, accounting for 35 to 40 percent of the workers, according to one contractor. The program began well and included minorities in each of the first few classes. Since most of the entrants quit the program after one year, it never progressed to third and fourth year training.

---

[21] This section is based upon an earlier Industrial Research Unit study, Richard L. Rowan and Lester Rubin, *Opening the Skilled Construction Trades to Blacks*, Labor Relations and Public Policy Series, No. 7 (Philadelphia: Industrial Research Unit, The Wharton School, University of Pennsylvania, 1972), pp. 162-163.

One of those asked to participate in the supervision of the program was Malone Zimmerman, a minority contractor who was active in seeking minorities for the industry. Zimmerman reorganized the program, altered the scheduled training, and built a classroom in his office. Since becoming involved with the carpentry program, Zimmerman has succeeded in establishing similar programs for plumbers, electricians, painters, and masons. While he admits that the nonunion sector is far from attaining the organization and proficiency of training that characterizes the union sector in construction, he feels that the gap is being closed.

One unusual aspect of the five nonunion training programs is that entrance requirements have been made as liberal as the Bureau of Apprenticeship and Training would allow. In the carpentry program, for instance, there is no subject matter or educational grade level requirement; only an ability to read and write is necessary. Zimmerman claims that BAT delayed approval for more than a year and a half; he believes that approval came only with a push by the National Association of Home Builders. The recently approved plumbing program which requires two years of high school, took nine months of negotiations before BAT approval was granted.

Denver. The Home Builders Association of Metropolitan Denver has a carpentry apprentice program registered with the Colorado apprenticeship agency and approved by BAT. In 1973, the program had seventeen registered apprentices and planned five to ten additional ones. The plan is very similar to the union carpentry program, as it was required to gain both state and federal approval. The Denver Association also has a preapprenticeship program—fifteen students twice a year—with emphasis on minorities, the disadvantaged and veterans, and a journeyman carpenter upgrading program. All these programs are operated by an apprentice program coordinator, follow NAHB procedures, and are funded by the U.S. Department of Labor through the NAHB.[22]

Denver is typical of the areas which make considerable use of the NAHB program. As in most other areas, the NAHB program is only one aspect of the training by builders. Some reimburse employees for taking adult education courses related to their trade. Most, however, rely primarily on OJT. Unskilled

---

[22] Based upon interviews in Denver, May 1973 and May 1974, especially with Mr. Larry Summers, Apprentice Program Coordinator, Home Builders of Metropolitan Denver, May 17, 1973.

persons are employed as laborers, learn on the job to become framing carpenters, and gradually move into more skilled carpentry work. They are likely to learn basic cement finishing work at the same time, and do that as required. Formal training affects only a small percentage of the homebuilding labor force in Denver, as elsewhere.

New Orleans. The Home Builders Association of Greater New Orleans does not subscribe to the NAHB program. Instead, it cooperates with ABC, and its members accept apprentices under the ABC plan and also take graduates of ABC plans. Although such interassociation cooperative efforts are not widespread, they may presage the potential for wide area programs, such as that instituted by the Carolinas Construction Training Council, described below.

Carolinas Construction Training Council

One of the most extensive training efforts initiated unilaterally is led by the Carolinas AGC, which covers all of North and South Carolina, and is comprised overwhelmingly of open shop contractors. In the late 1960's, the Carolinas AGC brought together five local training programs under the umbrella of a new organization called the Carolinas Construction Training Council (CCTC). Although the Carolinas AGC was instrumental in its formation, the CCTC is an independent unit with over 300 contractor members, less than one-half of whom are AGC members. The remaining participants belong to homebuilding and specialty contractor associations throughout the Carolinas. The CCTC was formed to initiate and coordinate a variety of training activities in both building and highway construction, and it was accomplished with the cooperation of numerous specialty contractor organizations. It began operations on January 1, 1969.[23]

The Council is administered by a twelve member board of trustees drawn from contractor members in the two states. Day-to-day operations are conducted by a five person office staff in Charlotte, North Carolina, and eleven field coordinators based in various locations in the two states. The coordinators assist member contractors in setting up and monitoring individual programs, taking major responsibility for such tasks as recruiting

---

[23] Information on the CCTC came from materials supplied by Mr. Tommy D. Caldwell, CCTC Administrator, and from our interviews at the Carolinas AGC headquarters, Charlotte, North Carolina, August 1973.

and transferring trainees, arranging for related instruction classes, and ensuring that the standards of apprenticeship and equal employment opportunity agencies are met. The coordinators are also responsible for keeping records on the activities of the various programs; as such they are the primary source of information on the progress of trainees.

The Council has two major sources of funds. The first is an assessment on members in the amount of two cents per man-hour worked in selected trades. In addition, the Council receives revenues under contracts with the National Association of Home Builders largely under that organization's carpentry apprenticeship program and with various federal agencies. The CCTC's dependence on federal funds has diminished in recent years, with member contributions now accounting for nearly two-thirds of its budget.

The CCTC presently administers two major kinds of training programs.[24] Its apprenticeship programs are designed primarily for building construction crafts and as of September, 1974, they enrolled over 1,000 apprentices in twelve trades. The Council also runs an on-the-job training program for highway construction under the sponsorship of the Carolinas Branch of the AGC. The OJT program, started in 1969 with funds from the Federal Highway Administration, has developed standards for fifty-eight separate trade classifications, but its enrollment generally runs at less than one-tenth of the apprenticeship programs. Each of these programs is discussed at greater length below.

The operations of the CCTC have, by all standards, grown markedly since the Council's inception, especially in its first three years. Table X-3 summarizes the pertinent data on the scope of CCTC training activity during its existence. Not revealed in the table is the growth of the Council's staff, expanding from five field coordinators at the outset to the present number of eleven. Unfortunately, as we shall see directly, this growth has not been translated into large numbers of fully trained and certified journeymen, although there is some reason to believe that the Council's contributions to manpower development are not fully reflected in the data on apprentice completions.

Apprenticeship Programs. CCTC apprenticeship programs are presently in operation for twelve crafts, with the bulk of the en-

[24] The Council also has small scale programs in journeyman upgrading and preapprenticeship for youthful offenders.

TABLE X-3
Selected Indices of Training Activity by the Carolinas Construction Training Council, 1969-1974

Indices	1969	1970	1971	1972	1973	1974
Member contractors	50	251	217	320	327	n.a.
Receipts [a]	86	176	201	260	284	n.a.
Expenditures [a]	82	n.a.	180	214	280	n.a.
Apprentices in training (January)	249	576	868	1,070	1,021	997
Completions	18	34	71	99	104	77 [b]

Source: Carolinas Construction Training Council.
[a] In thousands of dollars.
[b] Through September.

rollment in programs for bricklayer, carpenter, electrician, plumber, sheet metal worker, and heating mechanic. Like apprenticeship generally, the Council's programs include both OJT and related training components. Related instruction is usually carried out in cooperation with local trade and technical institutes. Instructors may be provided either by the school or by the Council itself. The CCTC also works with local high school vocational programs in recruiting apprentices: some 60 percent of all apprentices enroll directly from high school, some are given advanced standing because of their prior schoooling. Fifteen percent are recruited from the unskilled ranks of member contractors, with the rest coming from military service or "off the street."

Council spokesmen estimate that 25 percent of its apprentices are black, although representation in the various trades is uneven. The electrical and plumbing trades, as in much of construction generally, show the least minority penetration. The CCTC staff itself includes one black administrator at the central office and three black field coordinators. There are also a few black firms among the Council's membership.

The major problem plaguing the CCTC's apprenticeship programs is the attrition of trainees. During 1973, despite the addition of 1,016 new apprentices and only 104 completions, the number of apprentices in training actually fell. Although the Council's administrator referred in an interview to a 45 percent cancellation rate, the actual attrition seems from the Council's own figures to be considerably larger. In the first nine months of 1974, for example, CCTC apprenticeship programs had 614 accessions, 524 terminations, and only 77 completions. If we apply those 77 completions to the number of accessions during the first nine months of 1970, four years earlier, we find a staggering 86 percent attrition rate. Attrition in registered construction trades apprenticeship on the whole runs typically at about 50 percent.[25]

According to the 1973 *Annual Report of the Council,* the large number of cancellations is attributable to a number of factors, foremost among them the propensity for apprentices to join nonmember firms at higher wages or to be advanced to journeyman status prematurely, thus dulling their incentive to continue in the program. To the extent this is true, of course, apprenticeship contributes to the stock of skills even where trainees fail to complete the program. The CCTC administrator, moreover, stresses another factor that we noted in analyzing the ABC programs: the length of the programs as necessitated by federal apprenticeship standards which are, again, determined by requirements based on union negotiated standards. He points out that trainees either become impatient and drop out, or finish the program and become supervisors, in either case subverting the intent of developing journeymen. Similar to many open shop spokesmen, he sees much merit to moving in the direction of shorter, more specialized training programs, especially in the basic construction trades.

In short, the evidence on the CCTC apprenticeship programs seems to call for mixed reviews. The willingness of open shop contractors in the Carolinas to commit themselves to training is impressive enough, and the growth of the programs in most respects suggests that the commitment is not transitory. At the same time, at least as measured by results, CCTC apprenticeship seems yet to have contributed in a really major way to manpower development for open shops in the region served. With over 300 firms voluntarily contributing money for training purposes, however, and with the demonstrated ability to recruit 1,000 apprentices a year, the Council clearly has a base from which to address its attrition problem.

OJT Program. The CCTC's OJT program for highway contractors establishes training standards for fifty-eight occupational classifications used on highway construction projects. The

[25] *Manpower Report of the President* (Washington, D.C.: Government Printing Office, 1974), p. 370.

standards specify three kinds of employer obligations under the program: (1) a contribution to the CCTC based on total hours worked by all employees in classifications for which the contractor desires training; (2) specified numbers of hours to be spent at various components of the trade; and (3) minimum wage rates at progressive stages of the program. The duration of the program varies with the different classifications, ranging from 520 working hours for several of the trades to 2,080 hours for equipment mechanics.

Actual training is the responsibility of the contractor. CCTC coordinators assist in the recruiting and enrolling of trainees into the program. Contractors are expected to file weekly reports on each trainee with the Council, including information on hours worked within the training classification, an evaluation of the trainee's progress, and a statement of the wage rate paid. The contractor is also expected to assign a skilled journeyman or supervisor to oversee the training. Once the trainee is enrolled, the Council appears to have a minimal role in the training process, although coordinators are available to assist with any problems encountered by either employers or trainees.

The OJT program, however, performs a function beyond that of developing skills in that it is designed to meet the already noted training and affirmative action requirements of the Federal Highway Administration. There is an avowed goal of 65 to 70 percent minority enrollment, and coordinators maintain ties with recruiting sources in the minority community. Furthermore, enrollment in the approved CCTC program ensures that trainees may be classified under Federal Highway Administration and Davis-Bacon regulations, permitting a wage rate of something lower than the prevailing journeyman wage. CCTC personnel also advise participating employers on proper record-keeping procedures to assure Davis-Bacon compliance.

The rather loose control exercised by the Council over OJT activities raises the question whether the training purpose may be secondary to that of formally meeting federal stipulations. There is, for example, no explicit testing mechanism to ensure that trainees completing the program have in fact mastered the skills designed to be imparted. In a well-run apprenticeship program, there is, of course, staff monitoring of subjects taught through related instruction. In the present case, many of these subjects—such as safety, shop work, use and maintenance of tools and equipment, and in some cases even blueprint reading—

are expected to be taught on the job by the contractor himself, with little practical opportunity for oversight by program staff. To be sure, the conscientious contractor will comply with the standards, but it is the conscientious contractor who would probably do that even without a formal training program. Thus the major beneficiary of the program may well be the contractor interested less in training than in a convenient way to meet the obligations placed on him by the government. On the other hand, the CCTC program ensures that some training will occur, and at the same time encourages the open shop highway contractors to engage in training and to employ minorities. Otherwise, some contractors might neither train nor employ minorities.

Evaluation. Despite these criticisms, it must be noted that the CCTC and its member contractors are responding to a real need in the open shop construction sector. The Council's administrator himself acknowledges that the number of apprentices completing their programs is too small. He has under consideration a plan to speed the apprentice's progress by gearing his advancement to individual learning and testing standards rather than to rigid time periods. The OJT program must be viewed in light of the fact that training in highway construction has traditionally been less formal than in the building sector of the industry. Formal training by small open shop contractors generally is in a nascent period, and any shortcomings in these efforts are perhaps less important than the fact that the efforts are being made at all. Much of the labor force in highway work, especially where labor markets have been tight as in the Carolinas, is marginal and/or casual. Training is often difficult but necessary. Programs like that of CCTC provide the means to accomplish this need in addition to meeting federal requirements.

Association Training—Concluding Comment

The training programs discussed in this section are still largely in the formative stage and the number of trainees involved is not large. They are growing, however, and point up the fact that formal training in the construction industry is far from limited to joint apprenticeship programs. And, if open shop contractors continue to compete for larger construction projects, their dependence on formal training will grow, and the programs of their organizations will expand because of the obvious need. Meanwhile, individual open shop contractors have also been experimenting on their own with training. The next section discusses such training by the average contractor, the following section discusses training by the largest ones.

TRAINING BY ORDINARY SIZE INDIVIDUAL OPEN SHOP CONTRACTORS

Contractors may satisfy their need for skilled manpower in two ways. They may try to hire workers who have already been trained, or they may undertake to train their workers themselves. Our questionnaire to both union and open shop contractors sought to elicit information on both of these methods. One series of questions related to the prior training experience of workers, another dealt with training by contractors directly. Although employers may not always be aware of the backgrounds of their employees, their responses, nevertheless, shed some light on training patterns—as well as on intersector mobility—in construction.

The Industrial Research Unit Questionnaire

We asked contractors to indicate whether the workers whom they hired always, often, occasionally, or never had training in a variety of formats. These formats included vocational school, military service, several kinds of apprenticeship, or "on-the-job" training. The responses of open shop contractors suggest that their workers usually have not undergone formal training of any kind when they are hired. The most common form of training reported is "on-the-job," which, as we have seen, may mean little more than observation and working experience as an unskilled laborer. The responses to these questions are summarized in Table X-4.

In interpreting and analyzing Table X-4, we proceed on the assumption that a "no response" is likely to mean that the contractor was not accustomed to hiring workers with the particular training background in question, or at least that he was not aware of having hired workers with that experience. The most significant responses would seem to be "always" and "often," for these serve to designate the forms of training which make a significant contribution to the employer's inventory of skills.

It seems clear from Table X-4 that structured training processes are seldom found in the backgrounds of open shop workers. Although over two-thirds of our open shop respondents identified on-the-job experience as an important form of prior training, only about one-fifth of them so designated open shop apprentice-

TABLE X-4
Prior Training of Workers, Union and Open Shop Contractors, by Type of Training, 1974

Type of Training	Always		Often		Occasionally		Never		No Response	
	No.	Percent	No.	Percent	No.	Percent	No.	Percent	No.	Percent
Union [a]										
Vocational school	6	0.8	68	8.7	354	45.5	135	17.4	215	27.6
Military service	1	0.1	40	5.1	305	39.2	186	23.9	246	31.6
Union apprenticeship	149	19.2	355	45.6	171	22.0	47	6.0	56	7.2
Open shop apprenticeship	5	0.6	25	3.2	140	18.0	325	41.8	283	36.4
Other apprenticeship [b]	4	0.5	25	3.2	161	20.7	298	38.3	290	37.3
On-the-job	23	3.0	364	46.8	191	24.6	43	5.5	157	20.2
Open Shop [c]										
Vocational school	4	0.5	125	15.9	487	62.1	98	12.5	70	8.9
Military service	2	0.3	68	8.7	411	52.4	195	24.9	108	13.8
Union apprenticeship	1	0.1	34	4.3	210	26.8	405	51.7	134	17.1
Open shop apprenticeship	8	1.0	160	20.4	317	40.4	202	25.8	97	12.4
Other apprenticeship [b]	2	0.3	74	9.4	287	36.6	264	33.7	157	20.0
On-the-job	32	4.1	499	63.6	184	23.5	15	1.9	54	6.9

Source: Industrial Research Unit Questionnaire.
[a] N=778.
[b] Apprenticeship in an industry other than construction.
[c] N=784.

ship. Other forms of training were even less prevalent, although it is noteworthy that three of ten reported hiring workers, at least on occasion, who had been apprentices in the union sector. The finding that only 21 percent of the open shop contractors often or always hired workers with open shop apprenticeship training, while almost 66 percent of the union contractors often or always hired workers with union apprenticeship in their backgrounds, strongly suggests, perhaps not surprisingly, that formal training in the open shop sector is considerably less extensive than in union construction.

This point is corroborated by the respondents' own participation in training activities. Although more than 80 percent of the union contractors reported that they were participating in some local training program, only 42 percent of the open shop contractors claimed that any of their workers were enrolled in such a program. A total of 362 (46 percent) of the open shop contractors reported themselves to have any kind of off-the-job instruction for their workers. Of this group, 161 respondents provided instruction through their own facilities, 132 utilized local vocational schools, and 33 did both. The remaining 36 employers did not specify the nature of their training.

It must be acknowledged here, moreover, that the respondents to our questionnaire may not be representative of open shop contractors with respect to training activities.[26] Direct interviews by staff members of the Industrial Research Unit with open shop contractors and association executives revealed that in many areas the proportion of open shop employers who provide formal, off-the-job training is considerably lower than the 40 to 50 percent range suggested by the questionnaire responses. In the Philadelphia area, for example, our interview estimates suggested that only 5 to 10 percent of the open shop firms had set up their own formal training programs. In Baltimore, the estimate was 15 percent. These percentages do not necessarily reflect participation in association sponsored programs such as those of the ABC, but most association programs were reported to include only a small fraction of their respective groups' membership. And, in any event, there are many areas in which there are no local chapters of open shop associations. A large number of

[26] It will be recalled that the respondents tended to be larger than the average for all construction firms. Many of our sources were of the opinion that it is the large contractors who are more apt to engage in training.

contractors interviewed directly by the Industrial Research Unit staff revealed that their only form of training was on-the-job.

Examples of Individual Contractor Programs

This bare recital of statistics, however, does little to depict the character and substance of the training activities undertaken by individual open shop contractors. It may be useful at this point to describe in detail (on the basis of our field interviews), the approaches of some employers to ensure an adequate supply of skilled manpower. These illustrations are not necessarily representative of training generally, but they should serve to impart some flavor to what has heretofore been a rather general discussion of training forms.

General Contractor A specializes in water pollution control facilities. Based in New Hampshire, it operates throughout the Northeast. There are several approaches to training utilized. When a project is located within the jurisdiction of an ABC chapter, trainees may be enrolled in an ABC program on a selective basis, that is, enrolled only for those portions of the curriculum applicable to *A's* work. *A* also has a variety of carpentry programs with off-the-job components, some lasting only a few weeks and others four years. Some are highly specialized—for example, form building or blueprint reading. The company employs a full-time training director who fashions specific programs to meet immediate needs. The company president estimates that about 10 percent of his current workers (there are 400 in total) have undergone one or another of these programs.

General Contractor B operates exclusively in and around its New Hampshire base. Its training programs for carpenters had at the time of our interview 22 workers (total employment is 150). Classes met once a week for two hours, with instructors drawn from among the company's own supervisory staff. Instruction ran for 16 weeks and covered such subjects as blueprint reading and the care and use of tools. *B* also runs an informal program for equipment operators, during which workers are brought out to job sites during off hours and are taught the care and operation of heavy equipment used by the firm.

Electrical Contractor C employs 90 workers in Columbus, Ohio. At the time of our interview he was a participant in the local ABC apprenticeship program, but for some years before that he ran his own program. It met two nights a week for four years and proceeded to cover the electrical code book stage by stage. Instruction was led by the contractor himself or one of his journeymen and included both verbal pedagogy and manipulative practice. The program was selective, with no more than six trainees at one time.

Electrical Contractor D, with 25 employees in Detroit, had just joined the newly established ABC apprenticeship program. The classes met one or two days a week for four years and were paid entirely by the firm. The company owner believed that he was one of the few nonunion electrical contractors in the area who provided formal training for his employees.

Plumbing and Heating Contractor E, employing 95 workers in Columbus, had a rather skeletal program for plumbers and mechanics for a short time prior to joining the local ABC apprenticeship program. The firm ran its own school in the shop for four or five sessions according to a lesson plan developed by itself. Workers came on their own whenever they wanted to attend. Before that, all training was on-the-job.

General Contractor F is the largest in a central Texas city. This city was primarily union from World War II until the late 1960's. At that time, a series of jurisdictional disputes led to a determination by the city's largest contractors to go open shop. A series of strikes and decertification elections followed with the result that only the carpenters maintained a union contract, and this union's agreement was significantly modified to eliminate restrictive and costly practices.

One strike involved the bricklayers and this shut off a source of supply that could not be supplemented from the open market. The contractors therefore set up a special training institute, recruited twenty black laborers who previously had no skill training, paid them $2.00 per hour to learn, taught them to lay brick for eight hours per day over a six week period, then put them on the job. According to the town's largest contractor, "They may not be the best bricklayers in the world, but they can lay 500 to 850 bricks while the union guys were laying 400 to 500."

Electrical Contractor G is headquartered in San Antonio, Texas. He employs 38 persons permanently and his force goes up to 150 persons on occasion. This company does the electrical and sometimes also the mechanical work on water and power plants. For training they use a manual prepared by a Texas AGC chapter, augmented by correspondence courses. All superintendents and the three partners are journeymen electricians and they conduct training classes. The employees pay for correspondence courses by payroll deductions, but the money is refunded with interest if the course is completed. Moreover, job preference is given to those who complete courses. Since the company operates over a wide area of the Rocky Mountain and southwest regions, it is always looking for trainees who might make journeymen. It thus encourages this type of training at all locations.

Mechanical Contractor H is a large north Texas organization capable of handling jobs well over one million dollars. Its employee handbook states:

> You earn advancement by excelling at your present job. Performance, trainability, and length of service are all weighed whenever an advancement is considered. It is your primary responsibility to prepare yourself for promotion. One of your supervisor's primary responsibilities is to encourage, develop, and recommend his employees for promotion. Make sure you tell him of any special training you have had or are taking so that it may be entered in your personnel record.

The after hours education program includes a continuous effort to qualify personnel for journeymen and master mechanic ratings and to tutor them so that they can pass tests and obtain necessary licenses. Classes are held both after hours and in early mornings. The company has about twenty master mechanics although only one is required on each job. This, the company believes, is the key to continued expansion. Among the journeymen plumbers are several blacks; the company makes a special effort to obtain and train both blacks and Mexican-Americans. It also conducts extensive supervisory training programs in cooperation with a major university.

James T. Triplett, Inc., is a bridge construction contractor. With headquarters in Chester, South Carolina, the company operates throughout North and South Carolina. Instead of ceasing work during rainy periods, Triplett conceived the idea of conducting training activities inside large trucks. This led to the development of training courses and instructional matter which Triplett believes improved both supervision and employees and reduced turnover. As a result, Triplett decided to sell training as well as to do contracting.[27]

---

[27] This account is based upon interviews with the Triplett organization, Chester, South Carolina, December 1973, and in materials supplied concerning the Industrial Learning Corporation.

A unique feature of Triplett's training activities is that they are now conducted through an entirely separate company, Industrial Learning Corporation (ILC), which also contracts its services to other firms in various industries. Thus, the program embodies a philosophy of training, initially developed at Triplett, which is adaptable to jobs both within and without the construction industry.

Perhaps the key element of ILC's approach to training is its emphasis on the supervisor. Trainees, usually college graduates, are given intensive instruction for one week in the development of "learning packages." These packages consist of audio and visual materials which explain and illustrate the specific tasks to be performed in connection with a trade. The company estimates that once a trainee (called a "Course Communicator") has completed the one week orientation session, he will be equipped to produce a learning package for the jobs he will supervise in about three months. The program also includes instruction in the development of a test to determine the degree to which those utilizing the package can retain what is observed through the audio and visual components of the plan.

An interesting aspect of the program is the way in which it combines the processes of learning and teaching, a notion perhaps better established in the work of academe than in industrial training. Beginning teachers often discover that they learn much about the subjects which they will teach in the process of organizing the material before presenting it to the students. The learning package approach adopts this idea by teaching trainees to analyze jobs and to document their salient parts in ways which will facilitate their job of teaching others. The trainees are themselves ultimately responsible for building the packages specific to their domains, and this task necessitates their firm understanding of the job as a whole. Once the packages are developed, they may be used repeatedly until changes in the technology of the work indicate the need for updating. The end results, in theory at least, are a supervisor with a firm grasp of his function and a systematic tool for training those he will supervise.

Summary. These brief descriptions underscore the variety of training modes undertaken by various open shop contractors. They range from the highly informal, loose style of some, to the structured, well-developed programs of others which appear to resemble full-fledged apprenticeship programs in most important respects. As the experience of many contractors suggests, there is a broad middle ground. In open shop construction, training concepts embrace a wide range of experimentation activities and approaches.

EVALUATION—OPEN SHOP TRAINING GENERALLY

The picture drawn throughout much of this chapter thus far has, of necessity we think, projected somewhat of a dual image. It has had to steer a middle course between, on the one hand, depicting skill development in open shop construction as a totally haphazard, undirected process; and on the other hand a fully evolved institution rivaling the large, broadly organized apprenticeship programs administered by joint union-management committees. Training efforts in the open shop sector are, in fact, neither nonexistent nor stagnant. Their recent growth merits more attention than has been accorded them in the literature, but it must also be recognized that the open shop contractor who has committed himself to a large investment in formal training is still the exception rather than the rule. As we saw earlier, the open shop sector probably accounts for more than one-half of all construction in this country. Still, although we are unable to quantify precisely the total number of formally trained workers produced by open shop apprenticeship, it almost certainly does not approach the 25,000 or so graduated each year from union programs.

It could hardly be otherwise. The open shop sector has only recently begun to develop the cooperative training arrangements which employer organization facilitates. The NAHB carpentry program was initiated in 1967, and even now it is not clear that homebuilders are prepared to commit their resources to training rather than relying on public subsidies. The earliest ABC programs are little more than a decade old, and most of them are creations of the 1970's. Open shop contractors have only lately begun to assert their interests within the AGC; few chapters with substantial union and some open shop representation have attempted to design training programs specifically for the latter. It is perhaps noteworthy that although the national AGC does have an Open Shop Division, that division does not employ a staff member responsible specifically for training.

The benefits of formal training are widely recognized among open shop contractors. Few will argue that a skilled craftsman can be produced in a classroom, and asked to choose between six months of on-the-job training and six months of classroom instruction, most would opt for the latter. But formal training, as we have used the term, envisages not a choice but a combination. Just as some skills and knowledge are best imparted within the production process itself, others are better taught through planned, systematic guidance away from the rigors and demands of the job site. As most of the employers with whom we spoke acknowledged, the manipulative skills developed on the production line are more easily and more quickly inculcated in the trainee who has had some theoretical exposure to the fundamentals of his trade and to the materials, implements, and methods of construction generally.

All this is not to say that open shop workers will all one day flow from apprenticeship programs. It is now generally recognized that many union craftsmen learn their trades informally, despite that sector's much longer experience with widely organized apprenticeship programs. There will undoubtedly always be a place for the specialist who performs a simple, repetitive task which can be learned rather quickly by observation, as well as the journeyman who is less than an all-around craftsman but can do most jobs. As long as the building trades unions continue jealously to guard their jurisdictional lines, these specialists will play an even larger role in the nonunion work force. Nevertheless, as open shop contractors compete for an ever larger share of the traditional "union market;" as they challenge the union contractor for the larger jobs requiring sophisticated methods and coordination of complex activities; and as more union contractors opt for the open shop or "double-breasted" operations, the need for structured training forms will become increasingly apparent. Ten million dollar projects are not built entirely with specialists or all first class craftsmen.

In another sense, of course, the open shop contractor is even more dependent on training than his unionized counterpart. He does not have access to a pool of labor which can often be augmented by a telephone call from a business agent to outlying communities. Although open shops can and do cooperate by lending and trading workers, this process lacks the central brokerage agent which unions supply. Open shop "hiring halls" or referral agencies are still in their formative stage, even where they exist. For the open shop contractor, the most reliable source of skilled labor would seem to be a training program which can issue a steady flow of craftsmen. As we shall see in the next section, the largest open shop contractors recognize this.

It can be said with some confidence that investment in formal training by open shop contractors will in large measure be a function of their employer organizations. Except for the giants of the industry, these contractors are for the most part, even by the standards of the atomistic construction industry, small. The underwriting of a modern training program can be prohibitively expensive for the individual contractor, especially with the danger that the trained worker will leave to work elsewhere. By pooling his resources with others similarly situated, he can benefit from the economies of scale associated with most undertakings.

As seen in Chapter VII, employer organization in the open shop sector is growing, and with it a proliferation of new training activities. As the ABC adds new chapters, old chapters initiate apprenticeship programs. As open shop members gain influence and even predominance in some AGC chapters, such as the Carolinas and Vermont, training programs to benefit the open shop contractor are developed. As open shops gain footholds in other AGC chapters, such as New York, the process may be expected to accelerate. Smaller, more specialized associations like AIECA have also entered the training business, and more may follow.

The trend, of course, will not necessarily be linear. The unions may ultimately succeed in recapturing their lost markets and organizing the larger open shops. Since these firms have often been the backbone of open shop associations, and prime clients of their training programs, open shop apprenticeship might well wane. At this writing, however, we detect no signs of such a reversal.

In sum, then, the dominant form of manpower training and development in the nonunion sector is still the on-the-job variety. Most formal training programs sponsored by multi-employer organizations are quite recent; many have yet to issue their first graduates into the labor market. The open shop contractor who underwrites formal training on his own is rare, and even those efforts that are made are at times loose and skeletal. But it is nevertheless incorrect to regard construction apprenticeship as the exclusive province of the unions. Programs of comparable quality do exist in the open shop sector, and more are added yearly. As open shop contractors grow more aggressive and increasingly prone to penetrate the current union markets, their need for, and commitment to, more sophisticated and structured training forms will undoubtedly expand; and this expansion will probably take place in concert with a growth in their increasingly influential employer associations.

Moreover, as the open shop contractors grow in influence, their concepts of training may well have greater influence on national training policies. The narrow craft demarcations, length of time, and other rigidities of apprentice programs need serious reexamination. There is tremendous pressure to experiment based upon different work organizations and needs in the open shop sector. Such experimentation now largely lacks government sanction. But it is being done by the largest open shop contractors who can afford to supply their own training needs. This is the subject of the final section of this chapter.

TRAINING BY LARGE OPEN SHOP CONTRACTORS

The small size of most open shop contractors inhibits their developing elaborate training programs of their own. Broad scale training is usually feasible only through participation in a local multi-employer program sponsored by a contractors' association. The situation is different, however, in the case of the relatively few open shops whose volume places them among the largest construction firms in the country. Their manpower needs are so extensive as to warrant a heavy investment in training, including the establishment of a separate department within the organization devoted exclusively to manpower development. Their size, moreover, enables them to experiment with diverse training forms which are often geared to the needs of specific jobs.

In this section, we examine the training efforts of three of the largest open shop contractors: Brown & Root, Inc., of Houston, Texas; Daniel International Corporation of Greenville, South Carolina; and H. B. Zachry Company of San Antonio, Texas. Brown & Root and Daniel are two of the largest contractors—union or nonunion—in the nation, each with gross volumes of several billion dollars a year. Zachry's contracts in 1973 totaled over $214 million.

Brown & Root[28]

Founded in 1914, Brown & Root has grown to a multibillion dollar corporation employing over 40,000 persons throughout the world. The company constructs a variety of large industrial and heavy facilities, including power plants, petroleum refineries, chemical plants, smelters, and oil drilling platforms. It is organized into several corporate divisions reflecting the various activities of its employees and the different kinds of construction in which it is engaged. These divisions include Administration, Industrial/Civil, Allied Industries, Marine-Western Hemisphere, Petro-Chemical, and Power.

Brown & Root claims to be the first large open shop company to institute the modular system of training. All of its training activities are conducted under the general supervision and coordination of the Personnel Training and Development Department which was established in 1968, and which is divided into five divisional sections, each of them dealing specifically with the training needs of one of the company's divisions. Overall coordination of the department's training and development activities is the responsibility of its Administrative Section, which supports the other sections by the recruitment and preparation of instructors, arranging for classroom sites, the acquisition of training materials, and the maintenance of accounts and training records. The department's budget during the five years of its existence has averaged about $300,000 a year. In 1974, its staff totalled forty persons, up from eleven in 1972.

Formal craft training is administered and coordinated from the company's headquarters in Houston, with satellite operations at various locations in the United States and abroad where major projects are in progress. In 1974, the company conducted 167 classes for craftsmen in 46 subject areas. These subject areas can be combined in a variety of ways to enable employees to build a training path for one or more trades. Thus there are basic courses in blueprint reading, mathematics, and safety for beginning trainees. Trainees may pick up craft-specific courses to become carpenters, electricians, instrument fitters, millwrights, pipefitters, riggers, and welders.

---

[28] The discussion in this section is based largely on information contained in Annual Reports of Brown and Root's Personnel Training and Development Department and the company's Employee Training Handbook, plus interviews and information supplied by company personnel, July 1973 and November 1974.

All classes are designed to supplement the on-the-job activities of employees. They take place both during and after regularly scheduled work hours. For most craft training, the classes usually involve from 32 to 96 hours of classroom instruction, with a full curriculum comprising a sequence of several courses. For example, an entry-level carpenter could take the following required courses: Basic Blueprint Reading and Math Review (32 hours); Standard First Aid and Personal Safety (12 hours); Introduction to Carpentry (35 hours); Carpentry I (51 hours); Carpentry II (51 hours); and Welding Fundamentals (48 hours). The flexibility of this modular approach allows new employees and their supervisors to select from a variety of career paths and established craftsmen to broaden their capacities.

The growth of training activities at Brown & Root is reflected both in the increase of staff assigned to the Personnel Training and Development Department and in the dramatic rise in the number of workers trained—from 1,223 in 1972 to 3,140 in 1974. This expansion of training programs, however, also saw an increase in the proportion of workers who dropped out of classes—from 17 percent in 1972 to 31 percent in 1974. Over the years, about 17 percent of all Brown & Root's trainees have been members of minority groups; given the company's location, Mexican-Americans are the dominant minority.

Brown & Root's training differs from conventional construction industry apprenticeship in a number of respects. The modular approach itself stands in contrast to the more rigid sequences commonly found in other training forms, both in the union and open shop sector. The flexibility of modular training permits employees to develop their own career paths by selecting courses which are relevant to their own needs, and to build their training around specific job assignments which may contain elements of more than one trade. The modular approach also permits the development of new courses to meet the specific needs of particular field situations. In 1973-1974, for example, seven new courses were added to the Training Department's overall curriculum.

At the same time, there is considerably greater variety in the amount of classroom time associated with training for different career paths than is the case with more conventional apprenticeship. Most apprenticeship programs prescribe three or four years of training with 144 hours of classroom instruction each year. For every craft, Brown & Root's formal training is appreciably shorter. Thus, the five class for riggers could total 144 classroom and laboratory hours; carpenters could take 278 hours; pipefitters, 510 hours, and electricians, 554 hours. These are the maximum hours and are required only if an employee's supervisor believed that the employee desired or required the full menu of training in that particular craft area. It is, however, rare for an employee to take the full range of classes by craft area.

Perhaps a more important difference is that career and salary advancement at Brown & Root is based on performance rather than formal completion of a training program. The expectation is that training will lead to greater competence and productivity which will in turn result in faster promotion, but the correlation is not automatic. In most apprenticeship programs, trainees receive wage increases (usually expressed at a percentage of the journeyman's rate) at predetermined time intervals. At Brown & Root, these raises are based on individual evaluations of the trainee's actual skill progress by field supervisors.

Supervisory Development is yet another distinct feature of Brown & Root's training and development activities. Supervisory development courses can be combined by the individual supervisor in a variety of ways, allowing each supervisor to match his personal development to his particular needs. There are seminars specifically designed to develop supervisory skills including leadership, planning and scheduling, personnel procedures, computerized unit costing, warehousing, purchasing and inventory, and timekeeping and payroll. Supervisors may also take classes in a broad range of technical subjects which are designed for supervisors as well as for craftsmen in the various trades.

Formal training at Brown & Root is voluntary, and it is the employee himself who largely determines the career path he will follow. Through October 1974, a total of about 8,000 craftsmen and supervisors had completed classes; of these, approximately 90 percent are still active employees. Since Brown & Root currently employs some 40,000 persons, it is clear that on-the-job training still constitutes a significant avenue of skill acquisition for the company's craftsmen and supervisors. Recent trends, however, appear to indicate a greater emphasis on formal training, including supplementary classroom instruction, with a concomitant increase in the staff, activities, and expenditures of the Personnel Training and Development Department scheduled in 1975.

Daniel International Corporation [29]

Daniel's size rivals that of Brown & Root in terms both of volume and work force. In 1974 the company employed about 26,000 persons with an annual volume of some $1.7 billion. Its training activities, however, are even more extensive than Brown & Root's. Between October 1, 1973 and September 30, 1974, Daniel's programs trained 10,500 apprentices, journeymen, and supervisors, and the number is projected to grow to 12,000 for 1974-1975. Members of minority groups, largely black, constituted 21 percent of those trained in 1973-1974, with the proportion projected to grow to 25 percent for 1974-1975.

As with Brown & Root, formal training at Daniel has a relatively limited history. Prior to 1971, almost all training was on-the-job. Supplementary off-the-job instruction was sometimes provided by individual supervisors who took it upon themselves to establish programs for the specific projects which they were running, but there was no formal training coordinated on a company-wide basis. Since 1971, Daniel's program has advanced in various stages as new forms of training were progressively added, reaching its present form in early 1974. The company presently trains workers for all the construction trades except electricians. Most of its nonelectrical work is performed by Daniel's own employees, with little of it subcontracted.

Most training is conducted at the job site. Training needs are determined after alternate sources of recruitment are utilized. When the company prepares to begin work in an area where it has previously completed a project, it consults the records of the prior job and directly contacts workers whose past performance was satisfactory. Comprehensive records are kept on the three most recent jobs in an area, with all employees entered by craft, wage rate, skill level, and so forth. It also advertises locally for other skilled workers in the area. A third avenue of recruitment is transfers from the company's home base in South Carolina. Since wages there are comparatively low, the company has a core of workers who are willing to move long distances when job opportunities are available elsewhere. After as many skilled workers as possible are assembled, training programs are established to produce the remainder of those needed.

---

[29] Information on Daniel's training activities was obtained by interviews with various company personnel, Greenville, S.C., February 1974, and Philadelphia, September 1974, amplified by materials generously provided by these specialists.

Daniel's program, called Basic Employees Skills Training (BEST), has three components: preemployment training, on-the-job training, and after hours related instruction. The preemployment phase is made available predominantly for new hires with little or no prior experience at the trade, and entails a basic orientation to the methods and materials associated with the craft. Trainees attend sessions on a full-time basis for varying durations, during which they receive no remuneration. The length of this phase depends on the craft: insulating requires one week; carpentry two weeks; pipefitting four weeks; and welding eight weeks. (In the case of welding, this time is needed for the worker to obtain certification.) Thus, by the time the work and the formal training period starts, the worker has acquired an elemental familiarity with construction work generally and with the basic vocabulary, tools, and materials of his prospective trade in particular.

The preemployment phase of training is significant in at least three respects. First, it serves to screen out those workers whose interest in formal training is limited. About one-half of the workers entering preemployment training drop out during this phase of the program. Second, the substantive knowledge gained during preemployment training appears to facilitate the rest of the training process. Among trainees who enter a regular program from the preemployment phase, only about 10 percent drop out subsequently before finishing; among workers who bypass the preemployment phase, the dropout rate is over 20 percent. Third, specially designed preemployment training can provide a quick avenue to the generation of marginally trained workers who are nevertheless capable of some productive work right away. This training may serve to carry the company over a temporary labor shortage at a particular project. In one instance, at a major chemical plant project in North Carolina, Daniel trained 215 pipe insulators with two weeks of intensive preemployment instruction. This feat was accomplished by breaking down the relatively simple functions of the trade and using an unusually large ratio of trainees and helpers to journeymen. A large percentage of the trainees were black women.

Related instruction is usually arranged through the facilities of local technical education centers or high schools. The instructors, however, are invariably drawn from Daniel's own ranks. Classes are held either at the school or at the job site, depending on the distance between them. Trainees attend classes for about three hours a week on average (it varies by craft) and will normally complete the program in two years. Total class time in the program averages about 275 hours. The company attempts to coordinate a trainee's job assignment with the material that he is learning in the classroom at a given point in time.

Advancement within the program is organized around blocks of skills into which the requisites of each craft have been divided. As each block of skills is mastered, the trainee becomes eligible to move to a higher skill level with a commensurate increase in his wage. Records are kept on the length of time each trainee spends at specific functions of the trade. Information on the trainee's activities, both on-the-job and in related instruction, is prepared weekly at the project site and submitted to company headquarters.

Each project has an Evaluation Board, usually consisting of the craft superintendent, general foreman, foreman, project personnel supervisor, and project training coordinator. As trainees complete the time requirements of each skill level, the company transmits their names to the Evaluation Board, which meets monthly to consider whether a trainee should be advanced to a higher skill level and wage rate. A trainee is assumed to have met the requirements for a skill level within the indicated time frame unless his foreman is able to specify detailed reasons why he should not be advanced. It is possible for a trainee to advance ahead of the recommended time intervals if the individual's foreman can demonstrate his exceptional ability to the Evaluation Board. Promotion within the program is geared to meeting predetermined objective criteria. Thus, Daniel's program appears presently to place somewhat heavier emphasis on acquisition of craft-related subskills demonstrable to the Evaluation Board as a criterion for advancement than does Brown & Root's program, which leaves the question of promotion largely to the discretion and initiative of the supervisor. Daniel is presently in the process, however, of developing standardized tests to determine a trainee's advancement from one skill to level to another.

A somewhat innovative aspect of the Daniel training philosophy is a formal upgrading program whose aim is to upgrade selected hourly craftsmen to supervisory and management positions. Training courses have been established and are being taught in presupervisory training (future foreman), foreman and superintendent training.

Management training specialists visit Daniel construction sites on a periodic basis to conduct these seminars. This strategy upgrades management skills and also provides Daniel with a cadre of skilled supervisors and managers against future needs.

The concept of "skill levels" is somewhat analogous to the modular approach utilized by Brown & Root. It provides an element of flexibility which can facilitate the training process in at least two important ways. First, a new hire can be slotted into the program at a particular skill level, depending upon his prior training and experience. Since participation in the program is voluntary, new employees do not invariably enter training at all, In any event, however, they are evaluated by the company's hiring agent and placed at a pay scale commensurate with that of trainees who have reached an equivalent level of development. Second, an employee may enter training programs for various trades throughout his tenure on the project. For example, a worker may learn reinforcing iron work, and when that phase of the project is completed, he enters with some advance standing into a carpentry training program in order to continue working at the site.

A somewhat different element in Daniel's training efforts involves prisoners in South Carolina. The company now conducts three month training programs for inmates of maximum security prisons within the compounds. This training is roughly equivalent to the preemployment phase described earlier. Upon their release, trainees enter Daniel's regular BEST program. The company is also contemplating the development of an early release program, in which inmates are transferred to special compounds near the job site. Upon release, there would be efforts to relocate the worker to a project near his home, either in South Carolina or elsewhere. At present, these programs are too new and their scale too small to permit an evaluation of them.

H. B. Zachry Company [30]

This large general contractor, specializing in major heavy and industrial projects, conducts formal training programs for a variety of trades at its headquarters in San Antonio, Texas. In addition, when a project requires a rapid expansion of the work force in a short time, special programs are developed to meet the specific needs of that job. The company has programs for

---

[30] Information obtained through interviews with Mr. E. M. Hammond, Vice-President and Personnel Director, H. B. Zachry Company, Houston, Texas, July 1973, and San Antonio, Texas, November 1973, amplified by materials kindly supplied by Mr. Hammond.

all the crafts which it utilizes in its operations except sheet metal and ornamental iron work. The company also conducts courses in management for its foreman and superintendents, while voluntary courses in management are offered to journeyman.

The company employs a full-time staff member on each job requiring training to supervise and coordinate all the training programs, with overall responsibilities for recruiting and selecting trainees, placing them on particular jobs, arranging for related instruction, and monitoring the progress of trainees through the program. Overall responsibility and coordination is handled by the Personnel Department in the home office at San Antonio. On-the-job training is overseen by foremen or journeymen designated by the home office as Field Training Supervisors, who provide the basic orientation to company policies and safety regulations, ensure that the trainee is given experience at various facets of the trade, maintain weekly records of the trainee's progress, and determine whether the trainees are qualified to advance to successive stages of the program. Advancement is contingent upon successful completion of each phase of training without regard to actual time spent learning the tasks. Progressive wage rates are attached to the various phases, and trainees may be placed at any level depending on their previous training and experience. The number of trainees in the program at any one time is determined through an evaluation of the company's manpower needs for the particular jobs under contract.

The training programs have three components: classroom instruction, shop work and OJT. Classroom instruction is arranged through local educational institutions if adequate facilities are not found on the job site. It covers such subjects as the use of various tools and materials, blueprint reading, and basic construction mathematics. At the beginning of each phase of classroom work, the trainee is given a list of performance objectives, and the instruction is designed to prepare him to meet these objectives. When the trainee is able to pass a qualifying test for each phase, he moves on to the next phase. Shop work involves manipulative training under job-like conditions, where the trainee gains practice in the use of tools and equipment under conditions simulating actual job operations. On-the-job training is provided by the Field Training Supervisor. Trainees are assigned to observe and practice specific aspects of the trade and are moved to successive functions as their competency is developed to the satisfaction of the supervisor.

As noted earlier, special programs may be established at particular locations to meet immediate needs. One recent example involved a major chemical plant expansion in Texas. This program was designed to produce large numbers of semiskilled electricians, form setters (carpenters), pipefitters and welders, as well as to upgrade a number of electrician's helpers to "junior" journeymen status. The electrician's program was broken into three blocks or modules: high voltage electricity for four weeks; control and hookup for six weeks, and instrumentation for six weeks. As each module is completed, the trainees go into the field and work at that operation. They later may enter another module and ultimately progress to the three week upgrading program. The other programs varied in length from four to eight weeks.

The components of these programs also varied in relation to the needs of the trade being developed. Electricians and form setters spent two hours in class, two hours in the shop, and four hours on the job each day. The pipefitter's day was equally divided between classroom instruction and OJT, while welders spent most of their time in the shop. The electrician's upgrading program was predominantly OJT. These several programs were used to develop a total of 900 helpers in blocks of time not exceeding eight weeks. Once finished, the helpers were assigned to work closely with journeymen in the field.

CONCLUSION

Although training efforts by different contractors will vary, the general approaches outlined in the foregoing descriptions are probably not seriously unrepresentative of the activities undertaken by most large open shop contractors. It must be borne in mind that these firms face manpower problems different from those of other construction contractors. The large union contractor with projects scattered throughout different geographical regions will usually depend upon local unions to refer workers with the necessary skills. The small open shop, whose operations may be confined to a single labor market, will have well established contacts with area workers, and its modest needs can often be met by direct recruiting of trained workers in the open market. Furthermore, contractors with an attachment to a particular locality can pool their resources to develop ongoing multiemployer training programs which can survive the termination of a specific project.

For firms like Brown & Root, Daniel and Zachry, however, these options will not normally meet their needs. They do not have access, of course, to union hiring halls or apprenticeship, and their projects will typically require large pools of manpower exceeding the capacities of local open shop training programs (even where they exist). In general, they cannot rely exclusively on recruitment in the local market to fill all their requirements for skilled labor. They must, therefore, undertake to generate a pool of skills adaptive to their special needs. And since their work in a specific locality will often be of limited duration, their training forms must be designed to expedite the skill generation process.

The growth of open shop training by individual firms, as well as through contractors' associations, reflects a recognition that skilled manpower constitutes a major constraint to the ability of nonunion employers to compete in the big job construction market. In the past, even such giants as Daniel and Brown & Root relied heavily upon on-the-job training to supply their workers with the necessary skills. For reasons discussed earlier in this chapter, however, OJT can be a much more effective route to skill development when it is combined with supplementary classroom instruction which provides the basic grounding for a trade. The commitment of large companies to formal training devices suggests the recognition that OJT is easier and faster when there is a foundation in the theoretical understanding of construction work.

Still, the training approaches discussed above differ in significant respects from the more traditional forms of apprenticeship in the building trades. The hallmark here appears to be flexibility. Programs are designed to make maximum use of a trainee's skills even while he is progressing through the curriculum. Material tends to be organized in blocks, with each block developing a set of skills which can be put to immediate use at the work place. There is, furthermore, the idea that training need not be designed exclusively to develop all-around journeymen. It can, instead, be fashioned to turn out semiskilled employees who can work productively under the supervision of a journeyman. Indeed, open shop contractors are wont to stress the efficiency gained by utilizing work crews with fewer journeymen than those typical of a union project.

This approach to training also permits the short-term development of a large work force needed to complete a specific project expeditiously. The examples given above of Daniel in North Carolina and Zachry in Texas are cases in point. Such training allows the firm to minimize its investment while still generating sufficient skills to complete the job, a highly desirable feature for a company which will be leaving an area once the project is finished.

Another distinct characteristic of programs in the three large firms is the underscoring of individual advancement. In no case is it assumed that a trainee has mastered a particular block of skills simply because he has worked at it for a given time period. Formal testing and evaluation are built into the programs throughout their duration, not just at the end. Traditional apprenticeship tends to be more rigid, with specific time periods and wage rates for each chronological stage of the program. Open shop programs, at least in terms of their formal descriptions, tend more to emphasize the substance of learning rather than "time in rank."

These features of open shop training are at odds with some of the apprenticeship standards—including the overall duration required—promulgated by federal and state agencies for registration purposes. As a result, these programs tend not to be registered with an apprenticeship agency, and thus trainees cannot be used on work covered by the Davis-Bacon Act and other prevailing wage statutes. What is involved appears to be a fundamental conflict in philosophies between the one which sees formal training as appropriate only for the development of the most highly skilled journeymen, and the other which views training as adaptable in different forms to various kinds of needs, including the need for more narrowly trained helpers and semiskilled "craftsmen." The business success of companies like the three discussed above strongly suggests that the philosophical approach long adopted by the Bureau of Apprenticeship and Training could stand some review.

CHAPTER XI

Wages, Benefits, And Hours

Employee compensation in open shop construction is a very difficult subject to analyze, for there are no regular statistical series distinguishing the union and nonunion sectors. The most comprehensive wage and benefit data apply to union construction. These are published annually, and updated quarterly, by the U.S. Bureau of Labor Statistics and include extensive information on wages, hours, and benefits by craft and market area.[1] Figures broken down by industry division are published monthly, but they do not include any occupational detail nor do they separate the union and nonunion sectors. As a result, the only data on open shop construction are generated by sporadic special surveys, and these by their nature do not permit any longitudinal analysis.

The information necessary for an exhaustive study of open shop wages would be feasible only through the data collection facilities of the federal government.[2] Such a study would require a regular survey of compensation in representative areas, occupations, and industry divisions. In the absence of these series, we must here rely upon the intermittent government studies which have been done, the unofficial surveys which have been conducted from time to time by various contractors associations, and the data which we were able to generate through our own resources. The result will be a montage from scattered and sometimes disparate sources, but it will permit a few reasonably

[1] U.S. Bureau of Labor Statistics, *Union Wages and Hours: Building Trades*, (Washington, D.C.: Government Printing Office, published annually).

[2] The Bureau of Labor Statistics is currently compiling data from a pilot study of union and nonunion wages in selected cities. Results available at the time of this writing are reported below. It is not yet clear whether the BLS will update the data recurrently. If so, this would constitute a significant addition to our capacity to analyze comparative wage movements in construction.

confident conclusions to be drawn with respect to both wage levels and wage structures in open shop construction. The biggest gap, however, will be in regard to the behavior of wages over time; we shall be able to say little about the determinants of wage movements in the open shop, especially as they might relate to settlements in the unionized sector.

The various sources of information available on employee compensation suggest three firm conclusions, along with several plausible inferences which yet require further study. The three conclusions are:

1. *Average hourly wage rates in open shop construction are significantly lower than comparable union scales.* It is sometimes asserted that the nonunion contractor must pay at or near the union rate in order to recruit the labor he needs. The facts manifestly show otherwise.
2. *Wages in open shop construction are appreciably more dispersed than in the union sector.* Since most union workers are paid the negotiated wage, it is not surprising that there is more diversity of wages, both among and within employing units, for any given occupational group in the open shop sector. Somewhat less predictable perhaps is the observation that there also is a wider spread among occupations, especially between the skilled and unskilled.
3. *Supplementary employee benefits in the open shop are, on average, lower than those in the union sector and still lower than those in the labor force generally.* In other words, straight-time pay (or even gross pay) accounts for a larger proportion of total compensation in nonunion construction. This conclusion does not appear to have been significantly affected by the development of various benefit plans by open shop contractors associations, but such plans are still in their infancy.

Further hypotheses will be developed below. Before that, however, it will be useful to summarize the results of several recent federal studies which throw light on the level and structure of open shop wages and their relation to union scales. It will also be instructive to compare some of these findings to those of a comprehensive survey of construction wages conducted by the Bureau of Labor Statistics nearly four decades ago, for such a comparison may indicate whether the anatomy of wages in the industry has roots in the past.

THE BUREAU OF LABOR STATISTICS STUDY OF 1936

As noted in earlier chapters, this study covered over 13,000 projects by 5,450 contracts in 105 cities with populations of 10,000 or more.[3] These contractors employed about 186,000 workers. The study was limited to urban building construction and therefore cannot be held to represent conditions in rural areas or in other subdivisions of the industry.

Table XI-1 summarizes the major findings of the study. In the interest of space, only eleven of the thirty-one occupational groups covered are included in the table. In the aggregate, it appears that union wages were approximately half again as high as nonunion wages. Unfortunately, however, the detailed breakdowns do not reveal any systematic patterns of relationships across geographical areas. For example, the areas of greatest unionization (Middle Atlantic, Pacific, and East North Central) do not regularly show wider or narrower differentials than such relatively sparsely unionized areas as East South Central and West South Central. Nor are the data unambiguous when viewed across occupations. Relatively high differentials appear for such heavily organized crafts as electricians and cement finishers, as well as for trades with large nonunion components like painters, helpers, and laborers. On the whole, however, there is a slight tendency for the most tightly unionized occupations to depict lower union-nonunion differentials. This tendency becomes significantly sharper if electricians—who are the most unionized craft and have the highest differential—are excluded from the table. As we shall see, however, this relationship does not appear in the findings of later studies, which tend to reveal wider differentials where unions are strong.

LATER BUREAU OF LABOR STATISTICS STUDIES: 1965-1972

Since 1965, the Bureau of Labor Statistics has published five studies dealing specifically with construction wages which make some distinction between the union and open shop sectors. Three of the studies cover separately each of the three major divisions of the industry: general building contractors, heavy

[3] Edward P. Sanford, "Wage Rates and Hours of Labor in the Building Trades," *Monthly Labor Review*, XLV (August, 1937), pp. 281-300.

TABLE XI-1
Average Hourly Union and Nonunion Wages in Selected Occupations in the Building Trades, by Geographic Divisions, 1936

Occupation	United States			New England			Middle Atlantic			E. N. Central			W. N. Central		
	U[a]	NU[b]	Ratio	U	NU	Ratio	U	NU	Ratio	U	NU	Ratio	U	NU	Ratio
Bricklayers	$1.35	$0.97	.72	$1.25	$1.03	.82	$1.45	$0.94	.65	$1.34	$1.03	.77	$1.33	$1.02	.77
Carpenters	1.15	.81	.70	1.07	.80	.75	1.24	.85	.69	1.22	.80	.66	1.10	.77	.70
Cement finishers	1.22	.78	.64	1.25	.90	.72	1.30	.80	.62	1.21	.79	.65	1.18	.83	.70
Electricians	1.36	.86	.63	1.17	.90	.77	1.52	.89	.59	1.34	1.02	.76	1.26	.83	.66
Painters	1.09	.70	.64	1.00	.69	.69	1.14	.75	.66	1.25	.73	.58	1.11	.70	.63
Plumbers	1.28	.95	.74	1.21	.93	.77	1.36	.99	.73	1.31	1.00	.76	1.28	.92	.72
Sheet metal workers	1.20	.82	.68	1.25	.80	.64	1.30	1.01	.78	1.19	.82	.69	1.20	.85	.71
Structural-iron workers	1.40	1.11	.79	1.24	.76	.61	1.39	1.30	.94	1.35	1.09	.81	1.35	.88	.65
Hod carriers	.85	.58	.68	.76	.56	.74	.90	.60	.67	.80	.65	.81	.86	.56	.65
Helpers[c]	.78	.49	.68	.72	.51	.71	.80	.57	.71	.87	.52	.60	.75	.46	.61
Laborers	.63	.42	.67	.67	.49	.73	.57	.48	.84	.70	.49	.70	.74	.44	.59

TABLE XI-1 (continued)

Occupation	S. Atlantic			E. S. Central			W. S. Central			Mountain			Pacific		
	U	NU	Ratio	U	NU	Ratio	U	NU	Ratio	U	NU	Ratio	U	NU	Ratio
Bricklayers	$1.29	$0.95	.74	$1.21	$1.01	.83	$1.21	$0.89	.74	$1.32	$0.92	.70	$1.41	$0.93	.66
Carpenters	1.15	.76	.66	.90	.71	.79	.98	.75	.77	1.19	.80	.67	1.09	.92	.84
Cement finishers	1.24	.64	.52	1.01	.65	.64	1.01	.81	.80	1.17	.93	.79	1.16	1.01	.87
Electricians	1.36	.79	.58	1.04	.78	.75	1.12	.87	.78	1.21	.92	.76	1.24	.83	.67
Painters	1.05	.67	.64	.92	.65	.71	.96	.64	.67	1.16	.77	.66	.98	.80	.82
Plumbers	1.25	.87	.70	1.15	.93	.81	1.25	.99	.79	1.28	1.00	.78	1.21	1.05	.87
Sheet metal workers	1.25	.77	.62	.94	.77	.82	1.25	.83	.66	1.14	.71	.62	1.10	.80	.73
Structural-iron workers	1.57	.82	.52	1.12	.91	.81	1.01	.97	.96	1.22	1.01	.83	1.29	1.07	.83
Hod carriers	.60	.46	.77	.58	.43	.74	.55	.40	.73	.86	.61	.71	1.04	.61	.59
Helpers [c]	.59	.44	.75	.47	.41	.87	.46	.43	.93	.67	.51	.76	.70	.55	.79
Laborers	.56	.37	.66	.35	.34	.97	.36	.36	1.00	.51	.44	.86	.65	.57	.88

Source: Edward P. Sanford, "Wage Rates and Hours of Labor in the Building Trades," *Monthly Labor Review*, XLV (August, 1937), pp. 281-300.

[a] Union.
[b] Nonunion.
[c] Not elsewhere classified.

and highway contractors, and special trades contractors. The data were obtained directly from employers. The fourth study covered the entire work force, and construction is reported as one unit. The data there were obtained from workers through supplementary questions asked during the March 1971 current population survey. Finally, as noted earlier, there has recently been an extensive survey of construction wages covering certain selected cities. Each of these studies is discussed briefly below.

General Building Contractors (1965)[4]

This study was based on a sample of 409 companies employing about 69,000 workers. A distinction was drawn between employers with a majority of workers covered by bargaining agreements and those with none or a minority of workers covered by bargaining agreements.[5] Open shop workers were found to average less than 63 percent of the total compensation of union employees: $3.10 compared to $4.94. There is no breakdown, however, by craft or geographic region, nor is there an estimate of the relative annual earnings of the two groups.

The study provided further insights into the compensation picture of the open shop worker. Most of his remuneration took the form of wages: over 89 percent of total compensation was straight-time pay. The comparable figure for union workers was 84 percent. The most conspicuous difference was in the area of private welfare plans, particularly health insurance and pensions. Clearly, the benefit programs recently initiated by various open shop contractors' associations have responded to a real gap in the compensation practices of individual employers.

Finally, the study demonstrates that there is a considerable range of wage payments within the open shop sector. The nonunion employer at the 75th percentile offered a wage more than half again as great as his counterpart at the 25th percentile. In other words, the middle half of the open shop sample ranged from $2.15 an hour to $3.26. The comparable figures for the union sector were $3.90 to $5.06, or a difference of less than one-third. The numbers here suggest a considerably greater flexibility for open shop contractors in wage setting.

[4] U.S. Bureau of Labor Statistics, *Compensation in the Construction Industry*, Bulletin 1656 (Washington, D.C.: Government Printing Office, 1970), Appendix A.

[5] All information on union and nonunion differences is contained in a single table. See *ibid.*, Table A-3, pp. 85-86.

Heavy Construction Industry (1971)[6]

This study of the heavy and highway division paints much the same picture as the previous one, except that the spread between union and open shop compensation, and the difference in the proportions of supplementary benefits, are even larger. It is not clear, however, whether this represents an industry-wide change between 1965 and 1971 or an historical difference between the building and heavy/highway segments of the industry. Given the explosive settlements in union construction between 1969 and 1971, it is a plausible inference that the union-nonunion differential widened appreciably throughout the industry between the times of the two studies.

The heavy construction study covered 1,375 firms with a total payroll of about 159,000 manual workers. These numbers represented about 9 percent of all establishments and 22 percent of all workers in the industry division. A little more than one-half of all workers were employed in union establishments. The results are shown in Table XI-2. Open shop workers averaged only about 52 percent of average total compensation in the union sector, with nonunion highway and street contractors paying less than one-half of the comparable union rates. The differences are slightly less when only pay for work time is considered, since a larger proportion of compensation in the union sector takes the form of fringe benefits. For the division as a whole, work time pay is 82 percent in the union sector and nearly 88 percent among open shop firms.

As the authors of the study conclude, the compensation "gap results from a combination of factors including differences in skill and occupational mix of the work force, type of work, and geographic location, as well as the influence of unions on compensation levels."[7] They might have added the relative effects of intermittency of employment in the two sectors. Unfortunately, the study offers no clues as to the proportionate importance of these various factors.

---

[6] U.S. Bureau of Labor Statistics, *Employee Compensation and Payroll Hours, Heavy Construction Industry,* 1971, Report 428 (Washington, D.C.: Government Printing Office, 1974).

[7] *Ibid.,* p. 2.

TABLE XI-2
Construction Worker Compensation in Union and Nonunion Establishments, Heavy Construction, General Contractors, 1971

Compensation Item	Heavy Construction		Heavy Construction except Highway		Highway	
	Union	Non-union	Union	Non-union	Union	Non-union
Total	$8.06	$4.13	$8.17	$4.35	$7.92	$3.88
Pay for work time	6.61	3.62	6.73	3.80	6.49	3.41
Straight-time pay	6.30	3.42	6.44	3.62	6.15	3.19
Premium pay	.30	.20	.24	.17	.35	.23
Pay for leave time	.19	.05	.20	.06	.17	.04
Retirement	.62	.21	.62	.22	.63	.19
Life and health insurance	.52	.18	.54	.21	.49	.16
Unemployment benefits	.10	.05	.10	.05	.11	.05
Other	.02	.02	.02	.02	.02	.03

Source: U.S. Bureau of Labor Statistics, *Employee Compensation and Payroll Hours, Heavy Construction Industry, 1971*, Report 428 (Washington, D.C.: Government Printing Office, 1974), Tables 1.6, 2.11, and 2.12.
Note: Because of rounding, sums of individual items may not equal totals.

Special Trades Contractors (1969)[8]

This study was based on a sample of 41,000 workers in 823 establishments, or less than one percent of all firms and about 2.5 percent of all employees in the industry division. The report contains summary material on the specialty contractors as a whole, with separate detail on its three largest components: plumbing and heating, electrical, and masonry. The overall conclusions suggested by the findings are much the same as those of the previous studies, with open shop workers averaging 57 percent of the union rates. If, however, one looks at the three reports chronologically, there is an unmistakable trend toward a wider union-nonunion differential and a growing emphasis on fringe benefits in both sectors.

[8] U.S. Bureau of Labor Statistics, *Employee Compensation and Payroll Hours, Construction—Special Trade Contractors, 1969*, Report 413 (Washington, D.C.: Government Printing Office, 1972).

TABLE XI-3
Construction Worker Compensation by Bargaining Agreement Coverage, Construction—Special Trade Contractors, 1969

Compensation Item	Special Trades		Plumbing, Heating Air Conditioning		Electrical		Masonry	
	Union	Non-union	Union	Non-union	Union	Non-union	Union	Non-union
Total	$6.54	$3.71	$6.82	$3.62	$6.87	$3.51	$6.07	$4.28
Pay for work time	5.59	3.30	5.77	3.19	5.95	3.16	5.22	3.86
Straight-time pay	5.41	3.20	5.60	3.09	5.67	3.05	5.13	3.78
Premium pay	.18	.10	.17	.10	.28	.11	.09	.07
Pay for leave time	.12	.06	.14	.08	.16	.07	.06	.04
Retirement	.43	.16	.49	.16	.43	.16	.41	.18
Life and health insurance	.33	.13	.35	.13	.26	.08	.30	.13
Unemployment benefits	.06	.04	.06	.03	.05	.03	.07	.05
Other	.01	.03	.01	.02	.01	.01	.01	.01

Source: U.S. Bureau of Labor Statistics, *Employee Compensation and Payroll Hours, Construction—Special Trade Contractors, 1969,* Report 413 (Washington, D.C.: Government Printing Office, 1972), Tables 2, A-2, B-2, and C-2.

Note: Because of rounding, sums of individual items may not equal totals.

The results of the special trades study are given in Table XI-3. In the aggregate, open shop workers averaged less than 57 percent of the compensation of union employees. The table shows, however, a striking difference between plumbing and heating contractors and electrical contractors on the one hand, and masonry contractors on the other; open shop masons appear to fare much better in relation to their unionized counterparts. Although the difference may be in part attributable to sampling error (the sample included only 823 firms in all specialties), it may also reflect variations in the extent of union representation among the various specialties. Again, however, none of these relationships is controlled for employer size or location, so that the determinants of the wage structure cannot readily be discerned.

Table XI-3 also reveals the now familiar difference in the structure of total compensation, although here the spread between union and open shop firms is somewhat less than that found in the previous studies. Open shop establishments paid out 89 percent of total compensation in the form of pay for working time, compared to 85 percent in unionized companies.

Construction Industry (1970)[9]

This study reports on the employment and earnings profile of the United States labor force in 1970. Unfortunately, most of the earnings data are presented in terms of "year-round, full-time wage and salary workers," so that the relative effect of intermittency of employment in the union and nonunion sectors cannot be readily measured.[10] The data on year-round full-time workers, however, may be regarded as reasonably accurate reflections of wage rates.

Table XI-4 summarizes the pertinent results of the study. Again, union workers appear to earn about half again the average wage of open shop employees. The occupational and regional detail, not available in the establishment studies, offers further insight into the wage structure of the industry. Specifically, there is a marked difference in the union-nonunion ratio between skilled and unskilled workers and between the South and the rest of the nation. Since it is clear that laborers and the South both have lower levels of unionization in construction, it would appear that the presence of a sizable open shop component tends to hold down nonunion wages relative to union scales.

---

[9] U.S. Bureau of Labor Statistics, *Selected Earnings and Demographic Characteristics of Union Members, 1970,* Report 417 (Washington, D.C.: Government Printing Office, 1972).

[10] One exception is a table of median earnings by industry and region, which includes data on all workers. Such a statistic is problematical with reference to construction, however, because of the effect of summer workers who nevertheless work more hours in construction than any other industry and thus distort the averages. There is some evidence that these summer workers are more numerous in the open shop sector. See Howard G. Foster, *Manpower in Homebuilding: A Preliminary Study,* Manpower and Human Resources Studies, No. 3 (Philadelphia: Industrial Research Unit, The Wharton School, University of Pennsylvania, 1974). This would render the union-open shop comparison misleading. For the record, the figures show substantially higher differentials for all workers than for year-round full-time workers. See *ibid.,* Table 10. For more on this point, see Chapter IX, above.

TABLE XI-4
Median Earnings of Male Year-Round Full-Time Wage and Salary Workers In Construction by Occupation and Region, 1970

Industry, Occupation Region	Union	Nonunion	Ratio
Construction industry	$11,244	$7,619	.68
Occupation: carpenters [a]	10,274	6,897	.67
Other craftsmen [a]	11,223	7,826	.70
Laborers [a]	8,693	5,128	.59
Region: Northeast	11,226	9,185	.82
North Central	11,472	8,554	.75
South	10,089	6,346	.63
West	11,884	9,629	.81

Source: U.S. Bureau of Labor Statistics, *Selected Earnings and Demographic Characteristics of Union Members, 1970,* Report 417 (Washington, D.C.: Government Printing Office, 1972), Tables 6, 7, and 10.
[a] Includes construction workers employed outside the construction industry.

Finally, the study again demonstrates the greater dispersion of wages among open shops. Nearly 57 percent of male, year-round workers in open shops earned either less than $7,000 or more than $15,000 in 1970, while 43 percent earned between those amounts. By contrast, only 29 percent of the union workers were at the extreme of the distribution, while 71 percent earned between $7,000 and $15,000. Put another way, less than one-half of the nonunion workers fell within 30 percent of the median for that group, whereas the comparable proportion for union workers was about three-fifths.

Construction Industries (1971-1972)

In April and May 1971, the Bureau of Labor Statistics conducted a pilot study of wages and benefits in five labor market areas: Biloxi, Chicago, Des Moines, Houston, and Washington. Based on the experience of this pilot survey, the Bureau "launched its first occupational wage survey of union and nonunion construction, in September 1972, in 21 areas. The construction surveys resulting are now part of the BLS regular industry wage survey program."[11] Although the pilot was limited to employers in contract construction, the main study also included operative builders who erect buildings—mostly residential—for sale on their own account. The findings of this study currently contribute the most comprehensive and detailed governmental data yet published on comparative earnings in construction. Most of the major crafts are included, the most significant exclusion being painters (painters were included in the pilot survey).

Open shop firms, unfortunately, are underrepresented in the sample of firms surveyed, since a smaller proportion of smaller establishments than larger companies were included. As a result, the nonunion data base for some trades as a whole, and for other trades in several of the labor market areas, was not sufficiently large to meet BLS publication standards.[12] Thus, the study offers no comparative data for bricklayers, pipefitters, roofers, and structural-iron workers, and only a few for cement masons, electricians, plumbers, sheet metal workers, and equipment operators. Similarly, in heavily unionized areas like Chicago, San Francisco, Portland, and St. Louis, the BLS was unable to generate comparative wage rates for any of the trades surveyed. Despite the spottiness of the data, however, certain conclusions emerge, the thrust of which is largely consistent with the earlier studies described above. Average hourly earnings of workers covered by the survey are summarized in Table XI-5.

Table XI-5 depicts the familiar wage spread in different regions of the country, with the relatively low rates in the South as the most prominent feature. The table also reveals, however, a somewhat smaller range of union-nonunion differentials than those observed in earlier studies. It is especially interesting to compare these figures with those of the 1936 BLS survey (see Table XI-1); in both cases, where comparisons can be made, a union rate of about 1.5 times the nonunion rate appears to be the general norm. A further noteworthy observation is that the differential shows no systematic variation by level of skill of the trade. Laborers, for example, appear to

---

[11] U.S. Bureau of Labor Statistics, *Summary Tabulations, Earnings and Supplementary Benefits in the Construction Industries—A Pilot Study, April—May 1971* (Washington, D.C.: Government Printing Office, 1974), p. 1.

[12] In some cases, mainly in the South, the data base for union workers was too small for comparative analysis.

TABLE XI-5

Average hourly earnings of workers in construction industries, by selected occupations and areas, September 1972

Occupation and union status	Northeast					South					
	Boston	Buffalo	Hartford	New York [1]	Phila-delphia	Atlanta	Biloxi [2]	Dallas	Memphis	Miami	Wash-ington
JOURNEYMEN											
Bricklayers—total [3]	$8.13	$8.66	$8.56	$8.41	$8.41	$7.77	$5.23	$7.16	----------	$8.01	$7.87
Union	8.40	8.66	8.71	8.41	8.72	7.80	----------	7.38	----------	8.10	8.32
Carpenters—total	7.91	7.83	7.08	8.41	8.02	6.12	5.19	5.82	$5.72	7.77	6.49
Union	8.09	8.11	8.12	8.58	8.65	7.40	6.08	6.62	6.85	7.94	7.76
Nonunion	6.46	5.03	4.41	7.49	5.24	5.03	4.23	4.91	4.21	5.75	5.27
Cement masons—total	8.23	8.89	8.76	7.89	7.16	6.53	5.11	4.87	5.49	7.46	6.00
Union	8.63	9.04	8.76	8.09	7.52	6.95	6.02	6.50	6.57	7.71	7.52
Nonunion	----------	----------	----------	----------	5.37	3.61	4.29	4.41	4.88	5.58	5.18
Electricians—total	8.08	9.71	7.75	8.48	8.35	8.20	6.05	5.40	6.74	8.33	7.83
Union	8.58	9.71	8.72	8.49	9.30	8.67	6.37	7.40	6.83	8.50	8.72
Nonunion	5.07	----------	5.32	----------	5.86	----------	4.15	4.49	----------	7.00	5.64
Pipefitters—total [3]	9.01	9.30	8.31	8.07	8.69	7.57	----------	6.88	7.21	9.16	8.59
Union	9.01	9.30	8.79	8.07	8.98	7.76	----------	7.20	7.17	9.16	8.87
Plumbers—total	8.23	9.14	6.84	8.11	7.31	7.34	4.50	5.62	7.18	8.39	6.89
Union	9.35	9.20	8.65	8.43	8.98	----------	----------	----------	7.44	9.16	8.76
Nonunion	7.11	----------	5.52	5.40	5.36	----------	3.99	5.09	----------	6.23	5.36
Roofers—total	8.00	----------	8.01	7.46	----------	5.39	----------	4.21	----------	6.61	6.24
Union	8.00	----------	8.01	8.30	----------	5.65	----------	----------	----------	7.77	----------
Sheet-metal workers—total	7.85	8.50	8.70	9.81	9.16	4.61	5.88	6.06	6.87	8.67	6.73
Union	8.68	8.50	8.70	10.33	9.70	----------	----------	----------	7.22	9.20	8.05
Nonunion	----------	----------	----------	----------	5.68	3.91	----------	3.81	----------	----------	4.99
Structural-iron workers—total [3]	8.13	8.71	9.30	9.25	8.60	6.80	----------	----------	----------	8.25	8.28
EQUIPMENT OPERATORS											
Back-hoe operators—total	8.11	8.58	7.20	9.16	8.67	4.90	5.07	3.58	4.15	6.25	6.20
Union	8.71	8.59	8.01	9.14	9.37	7.03	----------	----------	6.08	7.22	6.91
Nonunion	----------	----------	6.60	9.54	----------	4.10	3.98	3.29	3.80	----------	5.75
Bulldozer operators—total	7.96	6.26	6.24	8.77	8.39	4.86	4.69	3.54	3.96	5.49	5.87
Union	8.16	8.53	6.83	8.98	8.39	----------	6.55	----------	5.79	6.03	7.01
Nonunion	----------	----------	5.62	----------	----------	3.85	3.71	3.54	3.46	4.11	4.93
Truckdrivers—total	6.08	7.36	5.06	6.61	5.41	3.06	2.58	2.76	3.11	3.39	4.05
Union	----------	7.19	5.61	6.61	5.59	----------	----------	----------	----------	----------	4.29
Nonunion	----------	----------	4.11	----------	4.04	2.97	2.34	2.76	2.76	3.21	3.68
HELPERS AND LABORERS											
Bricklayers' helper—total [3]	6.47	----------	6.25	7.42	6.17	----------	----------	4.04	----------	----------	4.37
Carpenters' helpers—total [3]	3.66	4.92	3.59	3.84	3.63	3.80	2.68	3.91	----------	4.21	4.02
Construction laborers—total	6.14	6.38	5.73	6.86	5.81	3.54	2.80	3.25	3.21	5.31	4.33
Union	6.36	6.43	6.39	7.04	6.11	4.49	3.92	4.64	3.97	5.74	5.66
Nonunion	5.04	----------	4.57	4.97	3.74	3.00	2.52	2.62	2.42	3.47	3.47
Electricians' helpers—total [3]	----------	----------	----------	----------	3.62	----------	2.77	2.87	----------	4.21	3.39
Plumbers' helpers—total [3]	3.24	----------	2.81	3.58	----------	----------	2.72	3.10	----------	3.23	4.44

See footnotes at end of table.

exhibit differentials of much the same magnitude as carpenters, electricians, and plumbers.

Union and open shop wages differ not only in respect to their levels, but also their relative dispersion. Union rates tend to be fixed at a single figure, with only minor variations around it. Even these variations, moreover, tend to represent differences among local unions within a metropolitan area, rather than among workers within a single employing unit. Nonunion rates, on the other hand, vary widely within a given area (and, as we shall see, even within the same employing unit). Since the data are too dispersed to present conveniently in tabular form, pertinent features of the relative wage structure are described below. For the sake of brevity, we shall confine the account to carpenters, although a perusal of the studies will quickly show the interested reader that the situation is much the same for the other trades:

TABLE XI-5 (continued)

Continued—Average hourly earnings of workers in construction industries by selected occupations and areas, September 1972

Occupation and union status	North Central						West			
	Chicago	Des Moines	Indianapolis	Kansas City	Minneapolis	St. Louis	Denver	Los Angeles[2]	Portland	San Francisco-Oakland
JOURNEYMEN										
Bricklayers—total[3]	$8.95	----	$7.87	$7.73	$7.61	$7.81	$8.21	$7.78	----	$8.50
Union	8.95	----	8.55	7.73	7.61	7.81	8.25	7.78	----	8.50
Carpenters—total	8.32	$6.18	7.69	8.00	7.12	7.79	6.29	6.76	$6.78	8.10
Union	8.32	7.01	8.17	8.00	7.13	7.79	6.57	6.76	6.78	8.10
Nonunion	----	----	5.77	----	----	----	4.81	----	----	----
Cement masons—total	8.88	6.80	6.82	8.14	7.66	7.24	6.43	6.16	6.81	7.18
Union	8.89	6.80	7.07	8.14	7.66	7.24	6.43	6.16	6.81	7.18
Nonunion	8.60	----	----	----	----	----	6.41	----	----	----
Electricians—total	8.98	7.47	7.97	7.81	7.99	7.85	7.64	9.09	7.50	8.03
Union	9.05	7.47	8.20	7.87	8.00	7.85	8.04	9.09	7.50	8.03
Nonunion	6.63	----	----	----	----	----	5.68	----	----	----
Pipefitters—total[3]	8.98	----	7.15	8.62	7.35	7.81	7.70	8.31	6.61	8.43
Union	8.98	----	7.90	8.62	7.35	7.81	7.70	8.31	6.61	8.43
Plumbers—total	8.69	7.05	5.80	8.71	7.34	8.18	7.50	8.19	6.61	8.29
Union	8.75	7.09	8.15	8.71	7.32	8.18	7.70	8.34	6.61	8.29
Nonunion	----	----	4.59	----	----	----	----	7.35	----	----
Roofers—total	8.62	----	----	----	----	----	----	7.02	----	7.92
Union	8.62	----	----	----	----	----	----	7.09	----	7.92
Sheet-metal workers—total	8.54	7.50	6.10	8.70	7.78	7.95	8.17	8.80	6.83	8.11
Union	8.54	7.50	7.93	8.70	7.78	7.95	8.17	8.80	6.83	8.11
Nonunion	----	----	5.14	----	----	----	----	----	----	----
Structural-iron workers—total[3]	9.30	6.98	8.25	8.50	----	8.05	7.25	8.58	7.31	8.57
EQUIPMENT OPERATORS										
Back-hoe operators—total	8.68	5.91	7.01	8.50	7.57	7.86	5.64	7.87	6.86	8.59
Union	8.68	6.28	7.48	8.50	7.57	8.08	5.73	7.87	----	8.59
Nonunion	----	----	----	----	----	----	5.50	----	----	----
Bulldozer operators—total	8.52	5.94	7.29	8.48	7.38	8.06	5.56	7.89	----	8.27
Union	8.52	6.13	7.57	8.48	7.38	8.06	5.59	7.89	----	8.27
Nonunion	----	----	----	----	----	----	----	----	----	----
Truckdrivers—total	5.98	5.10	4.94	7.07	6.53	6.67	4.65	6.34	6.18	6.89
Union	6.01	5.10	4.95	7.07	6.56	6.67	4.93	6.34	----	6.89
Nonunion	----	----	----	----	----	----	----	----	----	----
HELPERS AND LABORERS										
Bricklayers' helpers—total[3]	----	----	----	5.93	6.05	7.23	4.74	6.00	----	----
Carpenters' helpers—total[3]	----	----	----	----	----	----	4.19	----	----	----
Construction laborers—total	6.21	5.12	4.82	6.24	5.91	6.88	4.23	5.50	5.01	5.47
Union	6.22	5.73	5.51	6.23	5.93	6.89	4.36	5.50	5.10	5.47
Nonunion	5.85	3.27	3.74	----	5.46	----	3.41	----	----	----
Electricians' helpers—total[3]	----	----	----	----	----	----	3.31	----	----	----
Plumbers' helpers—total[3]	----	4.94	----	5.78	----	7.32	3.71	----	----	----

[1] The survey reference month was October 1972.

[2] Shortened terms for Biloxi-Gulport and Pascagoula area and combined SMSA's of Los Angeles–Long Beach and Anaheim–Santa Ana–Garden Grove area.

[3] Insufficient published data to warrant separate presentation of union and/or nonunion rates.

NOTE: Dashes indicate no data reported or data that do not meet publication criteria. Average hourly earnings exclude premium pay for overtime and hazardous work and for work on weekends, holidays, and late shifts. Zone rates (usually based on distance between local union headquarters and the construction site) are included in straight-time rates for purposes of this survey.

The survey covered establishments employing 8 workers or more and engaged primarily in construction, i.e., building construction by general contractors; construction other than building by general contractors; construction by selected special trades contractors; and construction by operative builders, those building for sale on their own account. (Industry Groups 15, 16, part of 17, and 656 as defined in the 1967 edition of the Standard Industrial Classification Manual, prepared by the U.S. Office of Management and Budget.) Specifically excluded were special trades contractors primarily engaged in painting, paper hanging, and decorating; plastering and lathing; terrazzo, tile, marble, and mosaic work; floor laying; water well drilling; ornamental iron work; glass and glazing work; and special trades contractors not classified separately in the Manual.

All areas studied except Biloxi were Standard Metropolitan Statistical Areas, as defined by the Office of Management and Budget through November 1971.

Source: Reproduced from Martin E. Personick, "Union and Nonunion Pay Patterns in Construction," *Monthly Labor Review*, XCVII (August, 1974), pp. 72-73.

1. *Biloxi, Miss.* Of 96 union carpenters, 81 earned between $6.00 and $6.20. Of 88 nonunion carpenters, 33 earned less than $3.60 and 15 more than $6.00.
2. *Memphis.* All 695 union carpenters surveyed were at $6.85. Of 522 nonunion carpenters, 130 were below $3.80 and 75 above $5.00.
3. *Dallas.* All 465 union carpenters were at $7.38. Nonunion carpenters (543), in commercial construction, ranged from $4.00 to over $6.60. Most of the 736 nonunion residential carpenters ranged from $4.00 to $5.60.

4. *Miami.* Virtually all the 2,083 union carpenters made between $7.80 and $8.00. Of 176 nonunion carpenters, 51 made less than $5.20 and 52 more than $6.00.

5. *Atlanta.* All 443 union carpenters were at $7.80. The 721 nonunion commercial carpenters ranged from $4.00 to $7.80. The nonunion residential carpenters ranged from $3.00 to $6.20.

6. *New York (including Long Island).* The 8,700 union carpenters ranged from $7.80 to $9.00, with only small variations by type of construction. The 600 nonunion residential carpenters (low rise) ranged from $4.00 to $8.00. An additional 908 nonunion carpenters earned between $8.60 and $9.00.

7. *Denver.* Virtually all 3,612 union carpenters were between $6.40 and $6.60. The 694 nonunion carpenters (mostly residential) ranged from $3.00 to over $7.20.

8. *Boston.* Most of the 2,156 union carpenters ranged between $7.40 and $8.80. Of the 267 nonunion carpenters (almost all residential), 116 earned under $5.60 and the rest earned $7.00 or more.

9. *Hartford, Conn.* Virtually all the 813 union carpenters were at $8.12. Most of the 317 nonunion carpenters ranged from $3.40 to $5.80.

10. *Buffalo.* The 573 commercial and highway union carpenters earned between $8.00 and $8.60. The 56 nonunion carpenters (all residential) ranged from $4.40 to $5.60.

11. *Philadelphia.* Most of the 3,501 union carpenters (commercial and highway) earned between $8.40 and $9.20. The 140 nonunion commercial carpenters were between $4.20 and $5.20. Nonunion residential carpenters, however, ranged all the way from $2.70 to $8.80, with representation throughout the spectrum.

12. *Washington, D.C.* Virtually all the 2,774 union carpenters earned $7.76. Most of the 2,889 nonunion carpenters (mostly residential) were thoroughly dispersed throughout a range between $4.00 and $6.80.

13. *Des Moines.* Most of the 201 union carpenters made $7.00. The 93 nonunion carpenters ranged from $3.40 to $5.20, with most of them between $4.20 and $4.80.

14. *Indianapolis.* The 823 union commercial carpenters earned between $8.00 and $8.40, with the 124 highway carpenters somewhat lower. Most of the 231 nonunion carpenters (mostly residential) were between $5.20 and $6.20, with about one-half of them between $6.00 and $6.20.

This recital of figures should be sufficient to illustrate the central point here: wage rates in open shop construction exhibit a much stronger tendency toward dispersion than do those in the union sector. Nor is the difference attributable to variations in subdivisions of the industry. Nonunion workers in commercial construction—although usually higher paid on average than those in residential buildings—still show a tendency to cover a wide range of wage rates in marked contrast to their union counterparts. This range, moreover, reflects more than variations in the willingness or ability of different contractors to pay; as we shall demonstrate below, individual contractors often pay their workers differing wages according to their experience and/or productivity, a point which was made in Chapter X, above, and which materially enhances the flexibility of open shop contractors to deploy labor. This in turn gives open shop contractors a further, and significant, opportunity to enhance the already substantial wage-cost differential in their favor.

Summary

As we observed earlier, the data provided by various government studies over a 36 year period are too spotty and lacking in comparability to permit confident conclusions as to the behavior of open shop wage rates over time. It can be said, of course, that nonunion wages have historically been significantly lower—as well as more dispersed—than union scales, but the movement of this differential is difficult to trace. Any further statement must necessarily be speculative. Taking the several sets of findings at face value, however, there does emerge a plausible chronological description of the effects of labor market forces on nonunion wages.

The 1936 BLS survey suggested a union-nonunion ratio of about 1.5, or an average nonunion rate of about 67 percent of union scales. Successive surveys of contractors between 1965 and 1971 found progressively lower proportions: 63 percent for general building contractors in 1965; 57 for special trades contractors in 1969; and 52 percent for heavy and highway contractors in 1971. The data given in the September 1972 survey of 21 areas are fragmentary and, moreover, cannot be weighed appropriately, but a simple average of 71 trades and areas where comparisons are made shows a proportion of 68 percent. If we presume—an admittedly chancy presumption—that these percentages are representative in their direction, even if not in their magnitude, the events of the late 1960's and early 1970's may fall into place.

By 1966 or 1967, there began to appear harbingers of the explosive wage settlements which were to culminate in the imposition of controls in March 1971. During this period, it is plausible to assume that nonunion wage increases lagged behind those in the union sector, since any labor market adjustments to these abrupt union wage increases would take some time to appear. This line of reasoning is consistent with the growing union-nonunion differentials observed in the three BLS surveys between 1965 and 1971. At the same time, it is noteworthy that it was during this period that the attention of union contractors, newspaper reporters, and even some union leaders began to be focused on the growth of open shop construction. Thus, by September 1972, two factors were operating to reduce the wage differential. Wage controls in construction served to stem the rise in union wages, while the growth of open shop construction served to increase the demand for nonunion labor. Together, these factors should have militated somewhat toward a convergence of union and nonunion wages. Thus, if market forces have functioned at all in recent years, they would have acted on the union-nonunion differential in a way congruent with the admittedly piecemeal findings of these federal surveys.

INDUSTRIAL RESEARCH UNIT SURVEY

The Industrial Research Unit's survey both of union and open shop contractors solicited wage information in a somewhat different way from the various government studies discussed thus far. The principal point of departure stemmed from the already noted hypothesis that nonunion contractors, in particular, often pay differing wages to employees in the same trade. Accordingly, the questionnaire asked respondents to report both the highest and lowest wage rates paid to employees in several occupational categories. One important purpose of this approach was to determine the nature of wage structures within employing units as well as among them. At the same time, the data may be used to compare the overall results of this survey with the magnitudes found in the more comprehensive federal studies.

Table XI-6 shows the median wage rates reported by union and nonunion respondents in the three trades—carpenter, equipment operator, and laborer—most commonly employed by firms in our sample. The differences between union and nonunion rates appear to be on the same general order of magnitude as those found in previous studies. As before, it is difficult to discern a clear pattern of variations among geographic areas or trades, although the skilled-unskilled differential is an appreciably higher percentage among the open shops. Still, the union-nonunion differentials are not systematically higher (or lower) in the skilled trades or in the more heavily unionized regions of the country. Both union and nonunion wages, however, are highest in the northeastern and east central states, and lowest in the southern and mountain states.

But the unique contribution of our wage survey probably lies in its ability to provide insights into the differing internal wage structures of union and open shop contractors. Table XI-7 presents the median wages reported by respondents for both their highest paid and lowest paid workers in eight trades. Since the high and low figures relate to the same group of employers, they are not seriously affected by differences prevailing between industry divisions (for example, residential and commercial construction) or between geographical areas. For the higher paid workers, median wages in the union sector average about 54 percent higher than the nonunion sector for the eight trades. Among lower paid workers, however, the union sector is nearly double the open shop average.

The results of the Industrial Research Questionnaire survey also permit a comparison of the relative dispersion of wage rates among firms in a region. As we saw earlier, previous studies have found substantially more dispersion among nonunion firms, and our findings do nothing to disturb that conclusion. An appropriate measure of relative wage dispersion, where two distributions have widely differing means, is the coefficient of variation, which is derived simply by dividing the standard deviation by the mean.[13] Coefficients of variations are shown in

---

[13] See Frederick E. Croxton *et al.*, *Applied General Statistics*, third ed. (Englewood Cliffs, N.J.: Prentice-Hall, 1967), p. 199.

TABLE XI-6

Median Wage Rates Reported by Contractors in Three Trades, by Region and Union Status, 1974

Trades	New England	Middle Atlantic	E. N. Central	W. N. Central	South Atlantic	E. S. Central	W. S. Central	Mountain	Pacific
Union Firms									
Carpenter-high	$9.00	$8.94	$9.03	$8.05	$8.08	$7.75	$7.28	$8.26	$7.77
Carpenter-low	8.75	8.60	8.63	7.50	7.75	7.38	6.70	7.31	7.50
Eq. op.[a]-high	8.76	10.06	9.20	8.38	7.76	7.50	6.94	7.32	8.86
Eq. op.-low	8.67	8.57	8.31	7.59	6.76	6.00	6.25	7.12	8.01
Laborer-high	7.00	7.18	7.08	6.46	5.59	5.64	4.90	5.71	6.33
Laborer-low	6.60	6.73	6.65	5.96	4.80	5.00	4.25	5.53	6.00
Nonunion Firms									
Carpenter-high	5.94	6.29	5.91	4.98	5.15	5.75	5.79	5.76	*
Carpenter-low	4.66	4.81	4.68	3.83	4.10	3.75	3.95	5.00	*
Eq. op.-high	5.76	5.82	5.90	5.21	4.83	5.35	4.85	6.08	*
Eq. op.-low	4.82	4.55	4.91	3.86	3.59	4.21	3.46	5.75	*
Laborer-high	4.59	4.44	4.93	3.60	3.59	3.47	3.44	3.95	*
Laborer-low	3.34	3.38	3.36	2.64	2.68	2.62	2.55	2.85	*

Source: Industrial Research Unit Questionnaire.

* Responses too few to permit calculation of median.

[a] Equipment operator.

TABLE XI-7
Median Wages of Highest Paid and Lowest Paid Workers, by Union Status and Trade, 1974

Trade	Union			Nonunion		
	Number Reporting	High	Low	Number Reporting	High	Low
Bricklayer	221	$8.75	$8.45	174	$6.53	$5.21
Carpenter	405	8.36	7.87	398	5.74	4.37
Electrician	165	9.51	9.07	151	6.10	4.38
Equipment operator	397	8.79	7.86	342	5.25	3.94
Laborer	519	6.54	5.97	518	3.99	2.83
Painter	99	7.63	7.18	98	4.87	3.71
Plumber	155	9.38	9.10	109	6.28	4.80
Sheet metal worker	108	8.94	8.75	92	5.64	3.85

Source: Industrial Research Unit Questionnaire.

Table XI-8, broken down by region, trade, and union status. It is apparent that dispersion is appreciably greater in the open shop sector. Not only are the nonunion coefficients for every trade higher on a national basis, but with only a handful of exceptions they are also higher within regions.

Perhaps the most revealing feature in Table XI-7, however, is the range between the highest and lowest paid workers among open shop contractors. In almost all cases the difference in medians among union employers is minimal, reflecting the single wage paid under union contracts. Even the small differences shown are probably attributable to some respondents including apprentices and/or foremen in their reporting. (The relatively large difference for equipment operators is doubtless a reflection of the various wages paid to operators of different machines under most union agreements). Among nonunion contractors, on the other hand, the differences in the high-low medians range from $1.16 for painters to $1.82 for electricians.

The greater variability in the internal wage structures of open shops was also revealed in a separate Industrial Research Unit questionnaire dealing with the Davis-Bacon Act. Contractors were asked whether they had a practice of paying different wage rates within a given craft in their employ. Of 566 union re-

TABLE XI-8

Coefficients of Variation in Wage Rates Reported by Respondents to the Industrial Research Unit Questionnaire, by Region, Trade, and Union Status

Trade	New England	Middle Atlantic	E. N. Central	W. N. Central	South Atlantic	E. S. Central	W. S. Central	Mountain	Pacific	United States
Union										
Bricklayer-high	.12	.20	.11	.09	.11	.20	.10	.10	.19	.16
Bricklayer-low	.22	.28	.12	.16	.23	.35	.19	.24	.26	.23
Carpenter-high	.15	.12	.12	.15	.22	.27	.11	.22	.13	.17
Carpenter-low	.25	.22	.16	.21	.28	.33	.23	.22	.16	.23
Eq. op.[a]-high	.27	.15	.14	.21	.20	.25	.18	.23	.09	.19
Eq. op.-low	.37	.20	.19	.26	.30	.38	.28	.18	.17	.24
Electrician-high	.06	.19	.14	.08	.33	*	.11	.16	.07	.15
Electrician-low	.32	.21	.27	.21	.42	*	.30	.28	.16	.24
Laborer-high	.17	.21	.17	.24	.27	.27	.15	.16	.19	.23
Laborer-low	.30	.25	.22	.34	.35	.31	.25	.26	.18	.29
Painter-high	*	.22	.19	.15	*	.27	.15	.14	.36	.22
Painter-low	*	.24	.25	.18	*	.23	.21	.25	.36	.26
Plumber-high	.04	.12	.11	.05	.18	.08	.10	.09	.09	.11
Plumber-low	.24	.14	.11	.13	.32	.17	.22	.20	.18	.18
Sh met wkr[b]-high	*	.19	.10	.09	.15	.10	.08	*	.11	.14
Sh met wkr-low	*	.27	.10	.13	.29	.18	.25	*	.24	.24
Steamfitter-high	.30	.08	.10	.04	.16	.07	.11	*	.09	.12
Steamfitter-low	.36	.21	.11	.12	.24	.16	.20	*	.20	.19

Nonunion										
Bricklayer-high	.19	.22	.33	.18	.28	.37	.23	*	*	.27
Bricklayer-low	.27	.26	.40	.26	.34	.39	.24	*	*	.32
Carpenter-high	.23	.23	.24	.20	.26	.37	.28	.25	*	.26
Carpenter-low	.24	.28	.30	.25	.29	.38	.30	.26	*	.30
Eq. op.-high	.34	.33	.25	.25	.26	.28	.23	.17	*	.30
Eq. op.-low	.35	.32	.26	.29	.32	.26	.28	.21	*	.33
Electrician-high	.15	.30	.21	*	.17	.26	.20	*	*	.23
Electrician-low	.26	.37	.36	*	.28	.32	.28	*	*	.32
Laborer-high	.30	.27	.20	.29	.27	.28	.24	.33	*	.29
Laborer-low	.28	.29	.29	.29	.26	.31	.20	.30	*	.31
Painter-high	.22	.20	.17	*	.37	.22	.42	*	*	.29
Painter-low	.24	.26	.32	*	.37	.27	.47	*	*	.34
Plumber-high	.26	.29	.27	*	.27	.26	.33	*	*	.29
Plumber-low	.33	.30	.31	*	.30	.29	.33	*	*	.31
Sh met wkr-high	.20	.39	.22	*	.23	*	.25	*	*	.26
Sh met wkr-low	.11	.43	.39	*	.43	*	.33	*	*	.37
Steamfitter-high	.23	.39	.22	*	.22	.14	.10	*	*	.26
Steamfitter-low	.32	.41	.28	*	.27	.28	.20	*	*	.31

Source: Derived from Industrial Research Unit Questionnaire data.
* Coefficients not shown where number of respondents is fewer than six.
[a] Equipment operator.
[b] Sheet metal worker.

spondents, 431 (76.1 percent) answered in the negative, but 548 of 707 open shop (77.5 percent) responded affirmatively.[14]

To some extent, the ranges depicted in Table XI-7 may be misleading. Wages paid by nonunion contractors will differ not only according to worker competence, but also as a function of training and experience. Low paid "carpenters" may, in fact, be helpers or trainees whose wages will rise steadily as they gain practice at their trade. The union rates in Table XI-6, however, appear to reflect journeyman wages, as they are largely consistent with the average rates reflected by the BLS. Unfortunately, in the absence of uniformly accepted occupational definitions, it is impossible to state with precision how much of a rate range stems from differences in competence and how much from differences in extent of training or experience.

Some light on this question, however, was shed by our direct interviews with open shop contractors. A wage hierarchy of the following description appears to be typical. Suppose a contractor employs a number of carpenters. There will be a more or less fixed rate for journeymen carpenters who can perform the various tasks which the employer routinely demands of them, such as building forms or framing a house. There will also be an entry level rate for new hires with minimal experience. Depending on the contractor, these new hires may be called helpers, trainees, apprentices, laborers, or even carpenters. As these workers learn to perform more and more tasks, their wages will be increased accordingly; in some cases the faster they learn, the faster the wage progression. This should be distinguished from the union sector, where advances are strictly a function of time on the job. The carpenter's wage, however, does not necessarily reach its limit when he is recognized—formally or informally—as a "journeyman" by his employer. The open shop contractors will often pay a premium to his key workers, both in recognition of their value to him and to guard against their being attracted away. These key workers may assume important supervisory or training roles, or they may simply be especially productive.

Illustrations of this kind of wage hierarchy are provided in the following case examples. One plumbing contractor in Ohio

---

[14] This questionnaire was sent to every other contractor on the various association lists. Thus, one-half the contractors received the open shop questionnaires, one-half the Davis-Bacon one. Results of this questionnaire are on file in the Industrial Research Unit Library.

paid a starting rate of $2.75, which went to $5.75 upon the worker's obtaining a license, one designation of "journeymanship". Plumbers then moved gradually to a top journeyman's rate of $7.00, with two key men who served as project supervisors earning $8.00. A general contractor in Massachusetts paid his laborers from $4.00 to $6.00 and his carpenters from $6.60 to $7.80, with the carpenter foreman earning $8.53. Finally, a brick cleaning contractor in Michigan had a starting rate of $5.00, gradually advancing to a journeyman's rate of $10.00, with workers he considered "self-starters" earning $12.00. In all these cases, then, the contractor has a substantial range of "journeyman" rates, geared in large measure to the worker's individual capacity. In several instances, we found, the rate for the very top people equaled or exceeded the prevailing union scale, although the average wage was invariably well below it.

PREVAILING WAGE LAWS [15]

Any analysis of the wage advantage enjoyed by open shop contractors cannot be complete without reference to the application of prevailing wage laws to public construction projects. The earliest and best known of the federal statutes, the Davis-Bacon Act, is only one of scores of federal laws which employ the prevailing wage principle.[16] In addition, most states have their own laws covering construction work supported, in whole or in part, by state funds, some of them predating the enactment of Davis-Bacon in 1931.[17] As a consequence, there are few public works on which wage rates can be freely set by the contractor.

The ostensible purpose of prevailing wage laws is to render the impact of public construction "neutral" with respect to local wage standards. Much of the legislative debate on the Davis-Bacon Act focused on the "itinerant" [18] contractor who was able

---

[15] For a comprehensive review of the history and administration of prevailing wage laws, see Armand J. Thieblot, Jr., *The Davis-Bacon Act,* Labor Relations and Public Policy Series, Report No. 10 (Philadelphia: Industrial Research Unit, The Wharton School, University of Pennsylvania, 1975).

[16] For a list of these statutes, see *ibid.*, Appendix C.

[17] *Ibid.*, Appendix D.

[18] ". . . the word "itinerant" is a pejorative one. There seems to be no reason why local contractors should be protected against competition any more than local manufactures, local storekeepers or local professors are." *Ibid.*, note 1, pp. 1-2.

to undermine local standards by importing cheaper labor from distant parts, a practice facilitated by the depressed economic conditions of the time. By requiring that workers be paid according to locally prevailing wages, the Act sought to preclude federal construction projects from contributing to downward pressure on wage rates arising out of "unfair" competition. Although there is no explicit intention to exert an upward pressure on wages either, there appears to be a general consensus among students of the Act that this has in fact been the result.

Federal prevailing wage laws are administered by the Employment Standards Administration of the U.S. Department of Labor. The Davis-Bacon Act covers contracts for federally owned facilities valued at $2,000 or more, and it requires that such contracts

> contain a provision stating the minimum wages to be paid various classes of laborers and mechanics which shall be based upon the wages that will be determined by the Secretary of Labor to be prevailing for the corresponding classes of laborers and mechanics employed on projects of a character similar to the contract work in the city, town, village, or other civil subdivision of the state in which the work is to be performed. . . .[19]

A 1964 amendment to the Act redefined "wages" to include the costs of such supplemental benefits as pensions, medical insurance, and holiday or vacation plans. When a planned project nears the bidding stage, the contracting federal agency must secure a prevailing wage determination from the Department of Labor. These determinations are published in the *Federal Register* and, unless amended or challenged, apply to all similar projects in the area. Because of the administrative burden involved in making actual wage surveys, area determinations may cover a wide territory, including urban, suburban, and rural localities, and sometimes encompassing an entire state.

Since the statute provides little guidance as to the definition of a "prevailing wage," the Secretary of Labor has wide discretion in making his determinations. At present, the operative standard used by the Labor Department is known as "the 30 percent rule," whereby the prevailing wage rate is held to be that paid to the largest number of workers in the area so long as that number constitutes at least 30 percent of the work

---

[19] The Davis-Bacon Act (Public—No. 403—74th Congress—S.3303).

force. If no single wage rate is paid to 30 percent of all workers, then the average rate in the area is used. Since 1964, the Department has provided an appeals mechanism, vested in a three member Wage Appeals Board, to consider objections to the determinations fixed by the Employment Standards Administration. In these instances, the appellant bears the burden of showing that the original determinations were in error. Since such an appeal will normally necessitate a private survey of local wages, thus requiring considerable investigatory resources, it is not surprising that the case load of the Wage Appeals Board has not been large,[20] especially since the protestor has no guarantee of winning a contract even if he wins his case.

There are at least four aspects of the statutory language and Labor Department administrative policies which have, in the views both of many contractors and of most academic observers, served in practice to distort the original intent of Davis-Bacon. In many cases the result has been merely to expand the standards established by collective bargaining agreements to cover the entire industry or area. In others it has been to promulgate arbitrary wage rates which relate neither to any logical concept of "prevailing" wages nor to collectively bargained standards. Perhaps the most telling irony is that a law initially directed at "itinerant" contractors may have had its greatest adverse impact on indigenous open shops with strong ties to the locality in question.

Prevailing Wages. It seems clear that the natural effect of the 30 percent rule is to give disproportionate weight to collectively bargained wage rates. As we have seen, the wages paid by open shop contractors tend to fall along a broad spectrum both within and among employing units. The union rate, on the other hand, is typically a single figure. To take the most extreme example, a locality which is exactly 30 percent unionized may have 70 percent of its workers in a given craft earning a wide range of wage rates all below the union rate; yet the "prevailing" rate would be fixed at the union scale. In theory, of course, the rule can act to fix wages well below, as well as above, the union scale,[21] but in practice this outcome

---

[20] It currently averages about fifteen cases a year. *Op. cit.*, p. 41.

[21] See, for example, U.S. Comptroller General, *Report to the Congress: Need for Improved Administration of the Davis-Bacon Act Noted Over a*

is unlikely, especially in light of the relatively small number of determinations which are made by actual wage surveys.[22]

Definition of Locality. The determination of the relevant geographic area to which the prevailing wage is applied can have a decisive impact on the setting of that figure. Although the Act makes explicit reference to "city, town, or village," the Department of Labor has frequently made liberal use of the catchall phrase "other civil subdivision of the state."

> In certain instances the Department has gone beyond the county in which the project was located, and even beyond the adjacent counties or to another state, with the result that rates from areas having different labor conditions have been applied. This procedure has permitted the application of rates from noncontiguous counties and the use of union rates in nonunionized areas.[23]

Nearly two-thirds of the determinations studied by Gujurati were imported from other counties or applied statewide.[24] Although some of these cases undoubtedly involved projects in remote areas where the very concept of a prevailing wage is ambiguous, it is difficult to see the justification for importing standards set in distant metropolitan communities. If a wage is set lower than that necessary to attract sufficient numbers of workers, then the market will provide the adjustment. But if the wage is fixed at the union scale many miles away, it may well be substantially higher than is necessary to man the job. In any event, there is no apparent need to protect locally established standards since there are none.

Worker Classification. As a general rule, the Department of Labor recognizes only three classifications of workers: journeymen, laborers, and certified apprentices. An exception may apply where open shop contractors predominate, in which event a separate determination for the "helper" category may be made. Otherwise, nonunion contractors may face the Hobson's choice of paying journeyman's wages to their helpers or not using them on the job at all. Surveys by the General Accounting

---

Decade of General Accounting Office Reviews, B-146842 (Washington, D.C.: General Accounting Office, 1971), pp. 22-23.

22 In a major study of the Davis-Bacon Act, D. Gujurati found that over 80 percent of a sample of Department of Labor determinations were pegged at the union scale, and only 8 of 372 determinations were based on actual wage surveys. D. Gujurati, "The Economics of the Davis-Bacon Act," *Journal of Business*, XL (July, 1967), pp. 303-316.

23 U.S. Comptroller General, *op. cit.*, p. 16.

24 Gujurati, *op. cit.*, p. 309.

Office, moreover, have revealed other instances of the Department of Labor using inapplicable classifications to fix prevailing wages.[25] In one case, the rate for ornamental ironworkers was applied to workers erecting chain link fence; in another, a carpenter rate was applied to insulation installers. In both instances, the determined rate was substantially higher than that actually earned by private sector workers in the classifications in question. Thus, the General Accounting Office concluded, "our reviews have shown that failure to identify each class of worker and to determine its local pay scale often has resulted in the application of higher rates than that actually prevailed in the locality." [26]

Identification of "Similar" Projects. The Davis-Bacon Act mandates that prevailing wages be determined according to wage rates paid "on projects of a character similar to the contract work," but the application of the term "similar" is left to the discretion of the Department of Labor. Perhaps the most controversial of the Department of Labor's decisions in this regard have involved public housing projects, where prevailing wage determinations were based on commercial building scales rather than those in the largely nonunion home building sector. After coming under severe criticism from the General Accounting Office on this issue,[27] the Labor Department in 1972 agreed to have the Department of Housing and Urban Development conduct its own wage surveys on federally funded housing construction.[28] In other instances involving heavy or highway construction, determinations have at some times been based on substantially dissimilar projects. On other occasions, the definition of a similar project has been drawn so narrowly that it was necessary to import wage standards from very distant regions. In many cases, of course, it must be acknowledged that the task of specifying a similar project in the immediate locality is not an easy one. In these instances, however, it might well be questioned whether the very notion of a "prevailing" wage is particularly meaningful.

There appears to be little doubt that the effect of the Davis-Bacon Act and other prevailing wage laws has been to inflate

---

[25] U.S. Comptroller General, *op. cit.*, pp. 14-15.

[26] *Ibid.*, p. 15.

[27] *Ibid.*, pp. 16-17.

[28] Thieblot, *op. cit.*, p. 61.

the cost of public construction, not in the least measure by requiring open shop contractors to bear wage rates higher than what they would otherwise have to pay. One study has placed this excessive cost at 6.5 percent, which amounted to an extra $567 million borne by taxpayers in 1970.[29] This study assumed a union-nonunion wage differential of 33 percent and a putative demand shift of 22.5 percent to the nonunion sector if Davis-Bacon were repealed. The first assumption, based on our earlier analysis of wage differentials, appears conservative; the second assumption is speculative, although it seems reasonable to presume that Davis-Bacon repeal could shift some work to open shops. At the same time, the model takes no account of the possibility of a general downward pressure on union wage rates resulting from repeal.

It should not be inferred that the effects of prevailing wage laws on the operations of open shop contractors are unvaryingly negative. Despite the substantial reduction or elimination of the wage advantage they would otherwise enjoy, many nonunion firms have been eminently successful in competing for public contracts. Because of their greater flexibility in deploying manpower; their freedom from costly disputes; and their being unfettered by such requirements as showup pay, guaranteed work week, and strict overtime hours; some open shops experience significantly lower labor costs even while paying collectively bargained wages and supplemental benefits. Many of our field interviews with highway and public works contractors discerned precisely this situation.

Prevailing wage standards, moreover, largely remove one nagging problem often faced by nonunion firms: the recruitment of labor. Employers paying wages rates upwards of ten dollars an hour are not obliged to beat the bushes for help; those we interviewed talked rather of long waiting lists of applicants.

On the other hand, open shops may face a peculiar employee relations problem not encountered by their unionized counterparts. Where the firm performs work in both the public and private sectors, it may find itself paying grossly disparate wage rates on different projects. Some contractors expressed dismay at the difficulty of maintaining morale and satisfaction among workers who knew that other employees were making several

---

[29] John P. Gould, *Davis-Bacon Act: The Economics of Prevailing Wage Laws*, Special Analysis No. 15 (Washington, D.C.: American Enterprise Institute, 1971).

dollars more an hour because they were employed on a prevailing wage job. Although some contractors reported a conscious effort to rotate opportunities on the higher paying projects, this was not a uniform practice. Another alternative, of course, is to pay the higher scale on all work, but not surprisingly, few employers were wont to surrender willingly their competitive wage advantage where they were not so obliged.

On balance, it is not entirely clear as to the extent which prevailing wage laws have impacted in the direction of blunting open shop construction. Although highway and heavy construction in many states remains substantially penetrated by nonunion road builders as was pointed out in Chapter VI, the unions have used the Davis-Bacon Act both to organize large segments of these types of construction—the sectors of the industry most affected by this Act—and to maintain their hold therein during the recent upsurge of the open shop in other sectors. Municipal sewer workers and water treatment facilities have also been targets of open shop competitors. The large wage differential in private commercial work, where open shops have far from completely displaced unionized contractors, itself attests to the fact that wages are not the only terrain on which union and nonunion firms compete. A disappearance of prevailing wage laws would not magically oust union contractors from the public construction scene, although it would put them on the defensive in a number of areas where the open shop has nearby strength—for example, the Southwest other than Texas, western Pennsylvania, eastern Ohio, and parts of Iowa and Missouri. In areas where unions are strong in private work, they would in all probability maintain their strength in public construction even without Davis-Bacon. Where they are weak in private work and in large segments of the highway sector, however, prevailing wage laws undoubtedly give them leverage that they would otherwise be unable to exert.

WAGE SUPPLEMENTS

The union-nonunion wage differential does not fully reflect differences in total compensation received by the two groups of workers. The Bureau of Labor Statistics studies of employee compensation, results of which are summarized in Table XI-9, show clearly that open shop workers obtain an apparently larger proportion of their remuneration in direct wage payments, with

TABLE XI-9
Construction Worker Compensation, by Union Status and Type of Expenditure, 1965-1971

Expenditure	Union	Non-union	Union	Non-union	Union	Non-union
Total	100.0	100.0	100.0	100.0	100.0	100.0
Pay for work time	86.7	90.7	85.4	88.8	82.0	87.7
Straight-time	84.4	89.4	82.6	86.2	78.2	82.8
Premium pay	2.3	1.3	2.8	2.6	3.7	4.8
Pay for leave time	1.0	.7	1.8	1.5	2.3	1.1
Vacations	.1	.3	.1	.9	.3	.6
Holidays	.2	.2	.1	.6	.4	.4
Payment to funds	.7	.2	1.6	*	1.6	*
Retirement programs	4.4	3.2	6.6	4.4	7.7	5.0
Social security	2.4	2.8	3.3	4.0	3.2	4.1
Private plans	2.0	.4	3.3	.4	4.6	.9
Life/health Benefit programs	5.3	3.1	5.0	3.5	6.4	4.4
Life/health insurance	2.3	.6	2.8	.8	3.7	1.0
Sick leave	*	*	*	.1	*	.1
Workmen's compensation	3.0	2.5	2.1	2.6	2.6	3.3
Unemployment Benefit programs	2.1	2.0	1.0	1.0	1.3	1.2
Unemployment insurance	2.1	2.0	.9	1.0	1.3	1.1
Severance pay	*	*	*	*	*	*
Supplemental unemployment benefit funds	*	*	*	0	*	*
Nonproduction bonuses	.5	.2	.2	.7	.3	.5

Source: U.S. Bureau of Labor Statistics, *Compensation in the Construction Industry,* Bulletin 1656, Table A-3; *Employee Compensation and Payroll Hours, Heavy Construction Industry, 1971,* Report 428, Table 1.6; *Employee Compensation and Payroll Hours, Construction —Special Trade Contractors, 1969,* Report 413, Table 2, (Washington, D.C.: Government Printing Office, 1970, 1974, and 1972 respectively).

Note: Because of rounding, sums of individual items may not equal totals.

* Less than 0.05 percent.

a considerably lower proportion (from 3.4 to 5.7 percentage points lower) in supplemental benefits. Even these differences are somewhat understated, for the supplements include legally required expenditures for social security, unemployment insurance, and workmen's compensation. The data below (from Table XI-9) summarize the percentages of employer expenditures for voluntary, private benefits in each of the industry divisions:

General Building		Special Trades		Heavy/Highway	
Union	Nonunion	Union	Nonunion	Union	Nonunion
5.8	1.9	8.1	3.5	10.9	3.6

Perhaps the most striking differences in Table XI-9 are in regard to provisions for health insurance and pensions. A perusal of any recent Bureau of Labor Statistics report on construction wages in cities of 100,000 or more reveals employer contributions to trust funds covering these benefits as almost universal.[30] Although these benefits are increasingly common among nonunion firms, they are far from universal. In 1965, according to the Bureau of Labor Statistics study of general building contractors, only 28 percent of the nonunion workers were employed in establishments with any practice of granting health insurance, and only 12 percent enjoyed pension benefits. The comparable percentages for union workers were 90 and 78, respectively.[31] Unfortunately, comparable data were not published in the later Bureau of Labor Statistics surveys.

Open Shop Benefit Plans

Vacations and holidays, virtually unknown in the industry a decade ago, are becoming increasingly common both in the union and open shop sectors. Nonunion workers are typically given time off directly by their employers, whereas union members in some trades and areas can tap trust funds supported for the purpose by employer contributions. There are, finally, some relatively minor benefits which nonunion workers tend to receive more commonly than union workers. The Industrial Research Unit questionnaire found, for example, that 42 percent

---

[30] The most recent is U.S. Bureau of Labor Statistics, *Union Wages and Hours: Building Trades, July 1, 1972,* Bulletin 1807 (Washington, D.C.: Government Printing Office, 1974), pp. 19-73. The survey covers 68 cities.

[31] Bureau of Labor Statistics, Bulletin 1656, *op. cit.*, p. 86.

of the open shop respondents had bonuses or profit sharing arrangements for all or most of their employees, and 25 percent gave paid sick leave. The comparable figures for union firms were 15 percent in both cases.

The propensity for open shop contractors to provide supplementary benefits may increase somewhat with the development and dissemination of multi-employer plans by associations like the Associated Builders and Contractors. The ABC currently offers to its members participation in medical and disability insurance and a retirement plan. As of March 1, 1975, ABC had 1,192 firms, 15,336 employees, and including employees and dependents, 35,000 individuals covered by its health and welfare package, and had paid out more than $7,300,000 in claims. The ABC plan is portable among Association members so that an employee may carry it with him if he transfers from one participating member company to another. The ABC pension plan has grown more slowly and is still in the formative stage.[32]

In addition to the ABC, the Associated General Contractors and the Associated Independent Electrical Contractors of America have organized various fringe benefit programs to which members may subscribe. AIECA's plans provide various types of employee insurance, including life, accident and dismemberment, medical and hospitalization, and dental coverage. Its group insurance plans, by the end of 1974, had been adopted by over 230 firms, or about one-half of the regular membership, covering some 2,000 employees.[33]

The AGC national program was initiated in 1973 to service primarily its open shop members. Many AGC members, however, participate in plans promulgated earlier by individual chapters, some of which are being merged into the national program. Benefits of the program include a full complement of life, disability, and hospitalization insurance. The plan, like the ABC's, is fully portable. By the end of 1974, the plan had recruited about 100 participating members covering some 1,800 employees, one-half of them hourly. In addition, it was scheduled to have substantially greater coverage as the large chapter programs in the Carolinas was folded into the national plan in early 1975. Another sizable program in Texas was

[32] Information supplied by ABC.

[33] Information supplied by AIECA.

contemplating merger. The Texas group had over 1,500 salaried and 1,000 hourly employees enrolled as of December 31, 1974.[34]

Despite these advances, it is apparent that a majority of open shop contractors are not participating in group benefit plans. Many larger open shop contractors do, of course, have programs of their own, but several sources—including those identified in Table XI-9, the five area Bureau of Labor Statistics pilot survey of construction wages in 1971, and the Industrial Research Unit questionnaire—show that there are still a considerable number of open shop employees without any health or pension benefits. Multiple-employer programs, with their broader scope and administrative convenience, are beginning to attract some of these contractors in greater numbers, but they still have a substantial way to go.

HOURLY PRACTICES AND RESTRAINTS

There are some significant differences between union and open shop contractor practices regarding workday and workweek practices. The 1972-1973 U.S. Bureau of Labor Statistics survey of overtime provisions in construction labor agreements found that 442 of the 769 agreements, or 57 percent, paid penalty overtime daily after eight hours, or in some cases, after seven hours. In addition, about an equal percentage paid overtime when the employee worked outside of his regularly scheduled hours. Open shop contractors generally do neither, paying such overtime rates only after forty hours per week as required by the Fair Labor Standards Act. The only usual exceptions were when open shop contractors were required to conform to prevailing wage laws. Moreover, a significant number of construction agreements—229 of 769, or 29 percent—required such overtime pay at double time, whereas the open shop sector practice is to maintain the legally required time-and-one-half standard.[35]

All the 769 construction contractors surveyed by the Bureau of Labor Statistics for 1972-1973 required the payment of penalty overtime rates for Saturdays and Sundays as such; open shop

---

[34] Data from administrators of the various plans.

[35] Data on union practices are from U.S. Bureau of Labor Statistics, *Characteristics of Construction Agreements*, Bulletin 1819, *op. cit.*, Part VI, VII and IX. Open shop practices are based upon our field notes and questionnaire.

contractors pay such overtime, again, only for weekly hours in excess of forty hours. Moreover, 508 of the 769 agreements, or 66 percent, required double time on Saturday and 712, or 92 percent, double time on Sunday.

The right of union contractors to change hours or work schedules was forbidden, limited, or penalized by penalty overtime provisions in almost all contracts examined; open shop contractors can be flexible in such matters. The differential situation existed also for shift work, which, of course, is not common practice in construction.

Nearly all construction agreements required from one to eight hours reporting pay if the worker reports and there is no work unless he has been notified beforehand. Open shop contractors do not have this practice, but instead strive to keep the work force working whenever possible. Thus, when the weather is inclement, union workers are laid off without pay but open shop contractors keep working if at all possible. A number of the larger open shop contractors, including Daniel International and on some jobs, H. B. Zachry, have adopted a ten hour day, Monday-Thursday schedule. If weather makes work impossible, Friday or Saturday, if necessary, is scheduled in place of the bad weather period. Other open shop contractors use Saturday or even Sunday to make up the lost time. Contractual restraints and penalty overtime provisions preclude such flexibility for union shop contractors.

To make up for their lower rates and to push jobs to a fast conclusion—a significant saving in itself on interest rates, cash flow, etc.—open shop contractors often offer their work force significant overtime opportunities. Large users, at one time, pushed their contractors to work overtime also, but have found that this was counter-productive. In recent years, therefore, the Business Roundtable, the organization of large construction users, has encouraged its members to permit overtime only on a spot basis and to avoid scheduled overtime. The Roundtable has published a study which concluded that:

> Placing field construction operations of a project on a *scheduled* overtime basis is disruptive to the economy of the affected area, magnifies any apparent labor shortage, reduces labor productivity, and creates excessive inflation of construction labor cost with no material benefit in schedule.[36]

---

[36] "Effect of Scheduled Overtime on Construction Projects", in *Coming to Grips with Some Major Problems in the Construction Industry,* a Business

It found that work fatigue and holding back on production to ensure overtime, offset productivity gains from the extra hours; that overtime was often scheduled to attract labor, but induced a whole area to adopt an overtime schedule, thus not reducing job hopping nor increasing the supply of manpower, and that such scheduled overtime increased the demands of unions for higher rates. Consequently, the main impact was inflationary, rather than faster job completions. Even prior to the publication of this study, the efforts of the Roundtable had significantly reduced scheduled overtime on major industrial projects.

The net effect of these differences in hourly premiums and policies add up to significant cost advantages for the open shop contractors. The employee of that contractor, in turn, who accepts these smaller premiums or lack of premiums, is paid on rainy days, or works a schedule that permits forty hours pay regardless of bad weather.

CONCLUSION

The foregoing account of compensation in open shop construction provides several insights into the nature of the competitive threat posed by nonunion contractors to the building trades unions. A primary element, of course, is the very differential in average wages between the two sectors. Although, as we have seen, the precise magnitude of this differential is difficult to pinpoint, an estimate of 50 percent is reasonably consistent with the available evidence. Thus, if labor is assumed to be 24 percent of the total cost of a project, then, other things equal, the open shop contractor's total cost of production will be 8 percent lower as a result of the wage difference alone.

The wage differential itself appears to have two elements. First, even the top workers in open shop construction are very often paid less than the union scale. The situation appears to prevail less in strongly unionized areas like New York, Chicago, and Detroit, where data from the twenty-one area Bureau of Labor Statistics survey and our own inquiries suggest that some nonunion workers at the top of their range command the equivalent of union wages. In many other localities, however, as the Bureau of Labor Statistics data discussed above reveal, the

---

Roundtable Report (New York: The Roundtable, 1974), p. 1. Italics in original.

highest nonunion rates fall considerably short of negotiated wages. Among the open shop respondents to the Industrial Research Unit questionnaire, only 47 percent reported that any of their workers earned at or above union rates, and 31 percent reported that more than one-fourth of their employees reached that level. It should be remembered, moreover, that our sample overrepresents the larger, and presumably higher paying contractors; and it includes contractors operating under prevailing wage laws.

Second, there tends to be an appreciably broad range of wages paid to journeymen of differing levels of skill and experience. The union contractor is usually bound to pay all workers who fall under a given trade classification the same wage. The open shop firm, on the other hand, can and often does, especially in private sector work, pay different rates even within trades. The result is a wage distinction between the fully qualified craftsman and the narrowly trained specialist, one which the union employer cannot make. Thus, even in those areas and firms where top nonunion craftsmen are paid the equivalent of the union scale in order to retain them, average wages in the open shop will still be lower than in the union shop.

The wage differential alone does not account for the total difference in worker compensation between the two sectors. Studies have consistently shown that open shop workers receive a greater proportion of total employment expenditures "in the envelope" than do their organized counterparts. This factor, of course, adds to the labor cost advantage enjoyed by open shop firms, as does the absence of daily premium requirements, call-in pay, and other additions to compensation. None of this, moreover, takes account of possible differences in worker productivity or job components to which, according to many open shop spokesmen, are attributable the most significant labor cost advantage for their contractors.

For the analyst, however, the absence of systematic longitudinal data on open shops constitutes the major impediment to a broader understanding of wage determination in construction. It would be especially instructive to ascertain the behavior of nonunion wages during the past half decade, when it appears that open shop contractors made significant inroads into previously union markets. It would also be edifying to examine the behavior of union and nonunion wages in different parts of the country, in order to determine how the extent of open shop activity affects the wage differential. Unfortunately, these kinds of questions will have to await the accumulation of detailed data from government wage surveys for the construction industry.

For the present, it can only be posited that nonunion wages are essentially responsive to market factors, at least more so than union wages which have tended, in many areas, to rise dramatically in the face of widespread unemployment and growing open shop competition. The dispersion of wage rates, both among and within employing units, suggests a rough correspondence between wage and marginal product. The tendency for differentials to be relatively narrow in tightly organized localities, and wider where open shop activity is more substantial, again intimates an accommodation of nonunion wages to the dictates of labor supply. Thus, an important determinant of the union-nonunion differential is the extent to which the building trades are able to raise their members' wages above market determined levels. The size of the prevailing differential suggests that this ability is considerable, and the behavior of the differential in the future will depend in large measure on the effectiveness of the response of the building trades unions to open shop competition.

CHAPTER XII

Minority Employment

The construction industry has always been a key source of employment for minorities, particularly Negroes. This is especially true in the South, where the black craftsman has played a key role since slavery days. On the other hand, the construction industry has also featured some of the most invidious discrimination against minorities found anywhere. Black craftsmen from the South have been denied work and/or union membership in the North, and training was closed to blacks, North and South, in many areas prior to recent years.

Within this context, the relative utilization of minorities by union and open shop contractors, like most other aspects of open shop activity, has not heretofore been explored in depth, and indeed will apparently remain so until the Industrial Research Unit completes a volume in its Studies of Negro Employment on that subject.[1] In this chapter, we set forth our tentative findings made in conjunction with our research on the other aspects of open shop construction.

NEGRO EMPLOYMENT IN CONSTRUCTION SINCE 1890

Table XII-1 shows the number and proportion of Negroes in the construction industry generally and in six crafts (or seven, if, as in that table, plasterers and cement finishers are counted as two crafts) in the United States, and in the ten states of the old Confederacy, 1890-1940. Some very clear trends

[1] Studies of Negro Employment now cover seven sets of industries: Volume I, "Basic Industries" (automobiles, aerospace, steel, rubber, petroleum, and chemicals); Volume II, "Finance" (banking and insurance); Volume III, "Public Utilities" (electric, gas, and telephone); Volume IV, "Southern Industry" (paper, lumber, tobacco, coal, and textiles); Volume V, "Land and Air Transport" (railroads, air transport, trucking, urban transit); Volume VI, "Retail Trade" (department stores, drugstores, and supermarkets); and Volume VII, "Maritime" (shipbuilding, longshore, and offshore maritime).

TABLE XII-1

Total Workers, Number and Proportion of Negroes in Selected Occupations of the Building Trades in the United States and the South,[a] 1890-1940

	1890			1900			1910		
	All Workers	Negroes	Percent Negro	All Workers	Negroes	Percent Negro	All Workers	Negroes	Percent Negro
Carpenters									
U.S.	611,482	22,318	3.6	602,741	22,435	3.7	682,490	29,039	4.3
South	70,327	18,017	25.6	78,728	17,241	22.5	104,606	24,624	23.2
Painters									
U.S.	219,912	4,386	2.0	277,990	5,934	2.1	273,441	8,035	2.9
South	13,105	2,911	22.2	17,763	3,821	21.5	22,212	5,628	25.3
Bricklayers									
U.S.	158,518	9,647	6.1	161,048	14,457	9.0	160,151	12,014	7.5
South	14,628	6,857	47.0	14,855	7,933	53.4	16,125	8,817	54.7
Plasterers and cement finishers									
U.S.	39,002	4,006	10.3	35,706	3,754	10.5	47,682	6,175	13.0
South	2,408	1,261	52.5	2,964	1,841	62.1	3,329	2,213	66.5
Plumbers									
U.S.	56,607	616	1.1	97,884	1,197	1.2	119,596	1,990	1.7
South	n.a.	n.a.	n.a.	4,375	781	17.9	8,822	1,368	15.5
Electricians									
U.S.	n.a.	n.a.	n.a.	n.a.	n.a.	n.a.	47,024	293	0.6
South	n.a.	n.a.	n.a.	n.a.	n.a.	n.a.	8,056	250	2.9
Total Seven Crafts									
U.S.	n.a.	n.a.	n.a.	n.a.	n.a.	n.a.	1,330,384	57,546	4.3
South	n.a.	n.a.	n.a.	n.a.	n.a.	n.a.	163,150	42,900	26.3

TABLE XII-1 (continued)

	1920			1930			1940 [c]		
	All Workers	Negroes	Percent Negro	All Workers	Negroes	Percent Negro	All Workers	Negroes	Percent Negro
Carpenters									
U.S.	887,379	34,217	3.9	929,426	32,413	3.5	690,526	25,427	3.9
South	125,913	25,774	20.5	125,714	20,699	16.5	129,779	17,785	13.7
Painters									
U.S.	248,497	8,026	3.2	430,105	15,677	3.6	439,472	16,841	3.8
South	23,067	5,228	22.6	40,184	6,830	17.0	52,194	7,578	14.5
Bricklayers [b]									
U.S.	131,264	10,606	8.1	170,903	11,701	6.9	135,013	8,159	6.0
South	13,634	7,317	53.6	17,386	7,716	44.4	19,228	6,050	31.5
Plasterers and cement finishers									
U.S.	45,876	7,079	15.4	85,480	13,465	15.8	68,750	10,431	15.2
South	4,105	2,619	63.8	10,325	6,317	61.2	10,515	5,729	54.5
Plumbers									
U.S.	206,718	3,516	1.7	237,814	4,729	2.0	198,477	4,299	2.2
South	15,287	2,002	13.1	20,340	2,445	12.0	22,210	2,461	11.1
Electricians									
U.S.	212,964	1,342	0.6	280,317	1,913	0.7	217,075	1,555	0.7
South	15,393	393	2.6	23,659	391	1.7	29,119	443	1.5

Total Seven Crafts									
U.S.	1,732,698	64,786	3.7	2,134,045	79,898	3.7	1,749,312	66,712	3.8
South	197,399	43,333	22.0	237,608	44,398	18.7	263,045	40,046	15.2

Reproduced from Herbert R. Northrup, *Organized Labor and the Negro* (New York: Kraus Reprint Company, 1971) pp. 18-19.

Source: U.S. Census of Occupations, 1890-1940.

[a] Includes states of Alabama, Arkansas, Florida, Georgia, Louisiana, Mississippi, North Carolina, South Carolina, Tennessee, and Virginia.

[b] Includes stone cutters in 1940.

[c] Includes totals of "employed" and "experienced workers seeking work" groups, which are roughly comparable to "gainful worker" definition of previous enumerations.

emerge from these data. First is the high concentration of black craftsmen in the South, where as late as 1940, more than three-quarters of our black population dwelled. Second is the steady erosion of the Negro position in nearly all these crafts (plasterers and cement finishers are the exceptions) over the fifty year period in the South without gains in the country as a whole; and third is the wide discrepancy between black representation in the older crafts (carpentry, painting, and the "trowel" trades of bricklaying, plastering, and cement finishing) on the one hand, and the newer crafts of electrical and plumbing work on the other. This differentiation between the old and new is even more stark if one understands that the bulk of black plumbers in the South were sewer workers, while the newer work with metal connections for water and gas became overwhelmingly a white job.[2]

The role of unions in these developments was substantial. Race is a convenient tool to enhance job monopoly. Craft consciousness and race consciousness went hand in hand. Whereas in the South Negroes were admitted to unions on a nondiscriminatory basis, as in the trowel trades, or given "separate but equal" local unions as in the carpenters or painters, these black members found themselves unwelcome and were denied work when they traveled to border or northern states. The electrical and plumbers unions excluded Negroes on a national scale by tacit consent, as did the bridge, structural and ornamental iron workers. The sheet metal workers, still one of the most discriminatory unions in the country, offered Negroes membership in "auxiliary unions" which were under the supervision of white locals, or excluded them altogether, and discriminated against them invidiously.

A key role in the electrical and plumbing trades in eliminating the competition of blacks, North and South, was also played by licensing agencies. Unions are usually represented on these agencies, and blacks found it very difficult, if not impossible, to pass tests and to receive certification in these trades. If they did they found that inspectors, often card carrying unionists, found their work unsatisfactory and refused to pass or to certify it.

---

[2] Discussion of the period 1890-1940 is based upon Herbert R. Northrup, *Organized Labor and the Negro* (New York: Kraus Reprint Co., 1971), Chapters I and II.

Even though unions were weak in the South, their role was significant. There, as elsewhere, they were represented on licensing boards and as inspectors. The construction union members derived from the white working class who had historically been in competition with blacks and whose hatred of blacks has been legendary. Having the vote, which Negroes did not, they were a force beyond their size.

The discrimination was, however, community-wide. Black, segregated vocational schools did not teach the trades that the students needed to compete. Contractors did not train them and they were denied admission to apprentice programs. In short, they lost ground between 1890 and 1940 in the older crafts and never developed strength in the newer ones. And important for this study is the fact, except in the trowel trades, and to a much lesser extent in carpentry and painting, those Negroes that did succeed in breaching the barriers outside of the trowel trades, were likely to have done so in the nonunion sector, particularly residential and small commercial construction. Moreover, it was to this source of labor that the aspiring open shop builder in the South turned and depended upon both because it was low cost and because of the mutual antagonisms between the craft unions on one side and the black workers and open shop builders on the other.

The Great Depression to 1964

The antagonisms between craft unions and blacks became more severe during the great depression of the 1930's. Recognizing the need to aid Negroes out of work, special programs were inaugurated by the Roosevelt Administration to obtain a share of public works and relief employment for black construction workers. Quotas were established and pressure applied to contractors and unions to effectuate this program. The result was some improvement in black employment, and some increase in black union membership. In many areas, however, blacks did not receive their share of work in various crafts, and when they did, they were given work permits for sizable fees and not admitted to the unions.[3]

---

[3] *Ibid.*, Chapter II; Robert C. Weaver, *Negro Labor, A National Problem* (New York: Harcourt, Brace and Company, 1946); and Mark W. Kruman, "Quotas for Blacks: The Public Works Administration and the Black Construction Worker," *Labor History*, XVI (Winter 1975), pp. 37-51.

The relief construction of the 1930's was followed by the great defense and war construction of World War II years. Union strength was greatly enhanced. Again the federal government moved to aid black workers and again, it had limited success. The same period saw major migrations of Negroes from the South to the northern, midwestern, and western urban areas. Black construction workers, except for laborers, found again that discrimination by unions was often more severe in the North than in the South. Moreover, northern union contractors were not accustomed to employing black craftsmen and usually made no effort to do so.

Table XII-2 shows the number and proportion of blacks in the construction industry and in the same six crafts listed in Table XII-1 for the United States and for the ten southern states, 1950-1970. This table also includes data for construction laborers. The data therein indicate rather clearly that the decline in the proportion of black craftsmen in the South has been arrested since 1940, and some small gains have been made both in the country as a whole and in the South. Nevertheless, the stabilization for the South has been close to the 1940 figure, the lowest proportion for blacks for the fifty years prior thereto, and the gains in the electrical and plumbing trades remain very modest. Moreover, black representation in the crafts, except for the trowel trades, continues to be substantially below their labor force ratio, both for the country as a whole and in the South. In contrast, their share of the construction laborer category remains disproportionately high.[4]

During the post-World War II period until the passage of the Civil Rights Act of 1964, the construction union racial policies were attacked by a number of northern civil rights groups and state fair employment agencies; but although there was much agitation, change appears to have been slight. Negro membership in electrical, plumbing, and sheet metal worker unions remain minimal throughout the country and their share of the unionized work outside of the trowel trades, small.[5] Meanwhile, however, residential construction became increasingly open shop, the open shop firms began their growth in com-

[4] It is not known why the black share of laborers in the South declined in 1970 from 1960.

[5] For the period of the 1950's, see Ray Marshall, *The Negro and Organized Labor* (New York: John Wiley & Sons, Inc., 1965), especially Chapters 5, 6, and 8.

TABLE XII-2

Total Employed Males, Number and Proportion of Negroes in Selected Occupations of the Building Trades, in the United States and the South,[a] 1950-1970

Occupation and Area	1950			1960			1970		
	All Workers	Negroes	Percent Negro	All Workers	Negroes	Percent Negro	All Workers	Negroes	Percent Negro
Carpenters									
U.S.	907,728	34,582	3.8	816,195	35,830	4.4	831,363	43,530	5.2
South	195,564	22,565	11.5	187,150	22,513	12.0	195,327	24,726	12.7
Painters, glaziers, paperhangers									
U.S.	409,947	21,953	5.4	386,463	26,289	6.8	323,175	29,065	9.0
South	70,536	10,229	14.5	77,736	11,020	14.2	73,052	11,818	16.2
Masons, tile setters, stone cutters									
U.S.	172,876	18,003	10.4	191,169	21,738	11.4	191,432	29,083	15.2
South	33,055	11,256	34.1	42,503	13,385	31.5	50,315	17,589	35.0
Plasterers and cement finishers									
U.S.	89,112	17,227	19.3	86,678	18,772	21.7	92,950	25,457	27.4
South	16,327	9,167	56.1	17,592	9,801	55.7	21,833	13,197	60.4
Plumbers and pipefitters									
U.S.	275,892	8,290	3.0	303,541	10,120	3.3	377,769	17,371	4.6
South	40,383	4,409	10.9	48,600	5,157	10.6	69,358	7,488	10.8

TABLE XII-2 (continued)

Electricians									
U.S.	307,013	3,236	1.1	334,732	4,978	1.5	459,843	13,408	2.9
South	44,066	887	2.0	54,233	1,148	2.1	88,704	3,085	3.5
Total Six Crafts									
U.S.	2,162,568	103,291	4.8	2,118,778	117,727	5.6	2,276,532	157,914	6.9
South	399,931	58,513	14.6	427,814	63,024	14.7	498,589	77,903	15.6
Laborers									
U.S.	649,341	164,357	25.3	608,541	157,724	25.9	589,906	130,903	22.2
South	131,197	69,843	53.2	133,420	73,393	55.0	148,784	67,103	45.1

Source: *U.S. Census of Population*:
1950: Vol. II, *Characteristics of the Population*, United States Summary, Table 128, State Volumes, Table 77.
1960: Vol. I, *Characteristics of the Population*, United States Summary, Table 205, State Volumes, Table 122.
1970: PC(1)-D, *Detailed Characteristics*, United States Summary, Table 225, State Volumes, Table 173.

[a] Includes states of Alabama, Arkansas, Florida, Georgia, Louisiana, Mississippi, North Carolina, South Carolina, Tennessee, Virginia.

mercial work, and the black craftsmen increasingly found work in these sectors of the industry.[6]

The Period Since 1964

Since the passage of the Civil Rights Act of 1964, the federal government has attempted to expand black participation in skilled construction jobs by a variety of approaches: encouragement and support of apprenticeship and training; enforced and voluntary plans to expand employment in various cities; contractual provisions to accomplish the same goal; and litigation to end discriminatory practices. The results have broken down barriers, opened up training and apprenticeship, and scored a number of local successes.[7] Overall, however, change has been slow, as the data in Table XII-2 indicate.

A feature of the governmental programs to expand black employment is that many have been applied to union construction only. This is particularly the case with so-called apprentice outreach programs whose function is to get minorities into union-contractor joint apprentice programs, and to the voluntary and enforced city plans, where again work on union jobs and entry into the union is the goal. Yet if the analyses in this study are correct, the open shop sectors of the industry are the ones which are expanding the most rapidly.

A fundamental problem which minorities in the unionized sector face is the very structure of union organization. Union craft lines institutionalized the status quo, making it difficult for a laborer to gain experience in other crafts. Unlike the open shop, where a worker may progress from laborer to helper and thus pick up craft knowledge, this opportunity in union shop construction has been seriously diminished, by the elimination of the helper and by separate unions for laborers and each of the crafts. Since minorities are disproportionately concentrated in the laborer

---

[6] These comments derive from numerous interviews throughout the country, as well as thirty years observation of these trends by the senior author.

[7] For analyses of these various programs, see Stephen A. Schneider, "Apprenticeship Outreach Program," in Charles R. Perry, *et al.*, *The Impact of Government Manpower Programs*, Manpower and Human Resources Studies, No. 4 (Philadelphia: Industrial Research Unit, The Wharton School, University of Pennsylvania, 1975), Chapter 10; and Richard L. Rowan and Lester Rubin, *Opening the Skilled Construction Trades to Blacks: A Study of the Washington and Philadelphia Plans for Minority Employment*, Labor Relations and Public Policy Series, Report No. 7 (Philadelphia: Industrial Research Unit, The Wharton School, University of Pennsylvania, 1972).

classification, craft union lines act as a barrier to hold them down and to prevent their advancement. The absence of such barriers in open shop is a major advantage for minorities.

Numerous court cases involving union and union shop contractor discrimination attest to difficulties which minorities have had in gaining entrance to, or fair employment under, union rules, regulations, and policies.[8] Relief has usually resulted to some degree, but fundamentally, until the organization structure is changed, and especially given the craft consciousness and the desire to limit the labor market which derives directly from that consciousness, the problem is likely to remain, and blacks and minorities are likely to continue to remain underrepresented especially in the electrical, plumbing, and mechanical trades.

RELATIVE MINORITY EMPLOYMENT— OPEN AND UNION SHOP

It was a common although not universal view among persons contacted in our field surveys that the open shop contractors employ a larger portion of minorities in skilled work than do their unionized counterparts. There are, however, no definitive data on this subject. One reason, of course, is that open shop contractors are concentrated in the South where the tradition of black craftsmen in trowel and other trades remains strong, and where slightly more than one-half of the black population and a sizable proportion of the Spanish-surnamed population dwells. Another cause is undoubtedly that minorities, having experienced discrimination from the construction unions, have tended to seek work where those unions cannot influence employment decisions.

As we noted in Chapter II, however, there are also contrary factors. The most significant is that the prevalence of open shop construction varies inversely with the distance of central cities, and central cities are where the bulk of blacks live, North and South. Consequently, we found that this often reduces the potential for minority employment, particularly in residential construction.

---

[8] The cases may be found in any legal service, e.g., the *CCH Reports* or the Bureau of National Affairs, Inc., *Fair Employment Reports*.

The 1970 Bureau of Labor Statistics Study

In 1970 the U.S. Bureau of Labor Statistics made a study of the demographic characteristics of union members.[9] It found that the extent of organization among black workers exceeded that for whites in most industries, and blacks had a higher labor union participation rate than whites in nearly every industry within each region. Construction was, however, an exception. About 9 percent of union construction workers in the sample were black, but blacks represented 10 percent of the industry's total wage and salary employment. In the South, where the highest percentage of blacks are found in the industry, 23.2 percent of the whites were union members, but only 17.4 percent of the blacks. For construction craftsmen, the relative membership was even more disparate—56.2 percent for whites, 36.8 percent for blacks. Even for laborers, blacks' union participation rates trailed, 30.2 percent to 29 percent.[10]

This lower black union participation rate could, of course, mean many things. It does, however, seem to indicate that blacks either are, or feel themselves, less welcome in construction unions than in other unions; and therefore, they are more likely to seek employment with open shop firms. There may, of course, be other possible interpretations, but logically this one seems to comport with most of the information which we have been able to obtain.

Industrial Research Unit Questionnaire

In our questionnaire, we asked contractors whether they estimated the level of minority employment in open shops to be greater, less, or the same as that in unionized ones. Table XII-3 summarizes the replies. Of the unionized contractors answering, 25.7 percent felt that the open shops had a higher level, 24 percent felt the level was the same in both, and only 9.7 percent believed that union shop contractors had a higher level.

The open shop contractors were more emphatic, with 42.3 percent believing the level of minority employment higher in

[9] U.S. Bureau of Labor Statistics, *Selected Earnings and Demographic Characteristics of Union Members, 1970,* Report 417 (Washington, D.C.: Government Printing Office, 1972).

[10] *Ibid.,* pp. 3, 5, and Table 1, p. 6, and Table 8, p. 21. It should be noted, however, that these occupational designations are not limited to construction workers in the contract construction industry.

TABLE XII-3
Percent Distribution of Respondents' Estimates of Level of Minority Employment in Open Shop Construction Compared to Union Construction by Region and Union Status, 1974

	Union				Nonunion			
Region	Total	Greater	Less	Same	Total	Greater	Less	Same
Not reported	89	25.8	13.5	33.7	83	53.0	6.0	21.7
New England	27	29.6	11.1	40.7	63	42.9	4.8	30.2
Middle Atlantic	125	31.2	16.8	28.8	134	52.2	10.4	31.3
E.N. Central	147	27.9	14.3	28.6	75	49.3	4.0	36.0
W.N. Central	60	18.3	11.7	41.7	45	44.4	6.7	33.3
S. Atlantic	68	47.1	10.3	23.5	220	55.0	5.9	25.5
E.S. Central	32	31.3	9.4	43.8	45	51.1	2.2	28.9
W.S. Central	45	57.8	4.4	26.7	92	71.7	2.2	17.4
Mountain	52	38.5	9.6	32.7	21	57.1	4.8	19.0
Pacific	133	35.3	12.0	27.8	6	50.0	0.0	50.0
Total	778	25.7	9.7	24.0	784	42.3	4.5	21.3

Source: Industrial Research Unit Questionnaire.

their sector, 21.3 percent stating it was about the same as the union shops, and a bare 4.5 percent believing that the level was higher in the union shops.

Then we asked the contractor respondents to indicate along a sliding scale the percentage of their black and Spanish-surnamed employment. The results, set forth in Tables XII-4 and XII-5, are very interesting. A larger percentage of open shop than union shop contractors had no black employees, but in the higher proportions, the open shop contractors definitely had the higher proportions of minorities. In the southern states, union contractors reported a somewhat higher level of blacks, and in general, the figures, which include laborers, do not support the perceptions reported by the same respondents, or those garnered in our personal interviews.

The picture in regard to Spanish-surnamed Americans, as set forth in Table XII-5, is also mixed. In the highly union Pacific region, the union contractors lead in the employment of this minority, but in the West South Central area, which is almost

TABLE XII-4
Percent Distribution of Black Workers
In Current Work Force by Region and Union Status, 1974

Region	Total	0	1-5	6-10	11-25	26-50	51-97	98-100
Union								
Not reported	89	24.7	20.2	9.0	11.5	24.2	2.2	0
New England	27	40.7	25.9	11.1	14.8	0	3.7	0
Middle Atlantic	125	31.2	28.0	14.4	12.8	5.6	3.2	0
E.N. Central	147	32.7	21.8	17.0	19.7	4.1	2.0	0
W.N. Central	60	33.3	35.0	11.7	10.0	3.3	0	0
S. Atlantic	68	16.2	16.2	10.3	20.6	25.0	7.4	0
E.S. Central	32	9.4	28.1	15.6	18.8	9.4	9.4	0
W.S. Central	45	13.3	13.3	22.2	24.4	20.0	2.2	0
Mountain	52	48.1	30.8	7.7	3.8	3.8	0	0
Pacific	133	46.6	23.3	12.8	9.0	0.8	0	0
Total	778	24.7	18.6	10.4	11.3	6.2	1.9	0
Nonunion								
Not reported	83	31.3	18.1	7.2	13.3	14.5	13.3	0
New England	63	71.4	12.7	6.3	1.6	3.2	1.6	0
Middle Atlantic	134	57.5	12.7	9.0	6.0	6.7	1.5	0.7
E.N. Central	75	68.0	8.0	8.0	9.3	1.3	2.7	0
W.N. Central	45	44.4	26.7	13.3	6.7	0	0	0
S. Atlantic	220	21.4	11.8	12.3	22.3	19.1	8.2	0
E.S. Central	45	17.8	24.4	17.8	11.1	24.4	2.2	0
W.S. Central	92	30.4	16.3	12.0	15.2	18.5	5.4	0
Mountain	21	76.2	19.0	0	0	4.8	0	0
Pacific	6	50.0	16.7	16.7	0	0	0	0
Total	784	32.1	11.5	8.1	9.8	9.5	4.0	1.0

Source: Industrial Research Unit Questionnaire.

as open shop as the Pacific region is union shop, the open shop companies are by far larger employers of minorities.

The vagaries and shortcomings of our sampling may well account for these discrepancies between contractor perceptions and employment reports. Their perceptions, which take account of the employment policies of contractors not responding to our questionnaire, may well be more representative of the industry

TABLE XII-5
Percent Distribution of Spanish-Surnamed Workers In Current Work Force by Region and Union Status, 1974

Region	Total	0	1-5	6-10	11-25	26-50	51-97	98-100
Union								
Not reported	89	59.6	18.0	1.1	5.6	3.4	0	0
New England	27	74.1	14.8	3.7	3.7	0	0	0
Middle Atlantic	125	76.0	16.0	0.8	0.8	1.6	0	0
E.N. Central	147	72.1	17.7	3.4	1.4	1.4	1.4	0
W.N. Central	60	63.3	28.3	0	1.7	0	0	0
S. Atlantic	68	73.5	8.8	5.9	4.4	2.9	0	0
E.S. Central	32	90.6	0	0	0	0	0	0
W.S. Central	45	51.1	13.3	11.1	4.4	11.1	4.4	0
Mountain	52	34.6	19.2	7.7	17.3	15.4	0	0
Pacific	113	39.8	11.3	15.8	18.8	5.3	1.5	0
Total	778	48.5	12.0	4.2	4.9	2.9	.6	0
Nonunion								
Not reported	83	69.9	13.3	4.8	3.6	3.6	2.4	0
New England	63	79.4	11.1	4.8	1.6	0	0	0
Middle Atlantic	134	82.8	6.7	2.2	1.5	0	0.7	0
E.N. Central	75	84.0	8.0	5.3	0	0	0	0
W.N. Central	45	62.2	20.0	6.7	2.2	0	0	0
S. Atlantic	220	75.9	11.4	2.3	2.7	0.5	0.9	1.4
E.S. Central	45	91.1	6.7	0	0	0	0	0
W.S. Central	92	41.3	8.7	10.9	12.0	13.0	12.0	0
Mountain	21	57.1	19.0	9.5	4.8	9.5	0	0
Pacific	6	33.3	33.3	16.7	0	0	0	0
Total	784	57.0	8.4	3.5	2.5	1.8	1.6	.3

Source: Industrial Research Unit Questionnaire.

generally. The lack of skilled-unskilled breakdown, the over-representation of large concerns, and the greater likelihood that union firms have government contracts requiring higher minority obligations, may well skew our questionnaire results. Moreover, since union firms outside of the South are concentrated in the cities, and open shop firms outside of these areas, this fact is likely, as noted, to affect the availability of minorities. Finally, the representation of minorities in construction varies with different types of construction work. For example, the data discussed below show a very high representation of minorities in highway work. Nevertheless, regardless of reason, it must be stated that our questionnaire does not yield a definitive answer on relative minority employment in open shop and union shop construction.

A final question elicited answers in regard to participation of contractors in programs resigned to upgrade minority workers. Table XII-6 shows the responses by union status and region. It should come as no surprise to see that a larger portion of union firms are participating than are open shop firms. In Chapter X we noted that more union than open shop firms are likely to be involved in formal training programs than are open shop firms. Such programs usually carry stipulations (not necessarily practiced) that require special efforts for minorities. Second, construction unions have negotiated numerous contracts with the Department of Labor for contracts to train minorities. Third, Department of of Labor "voluntary" plans to increase minority participation in skilled trades are confined in practice to the unionized sector. Open shop firms are excluded,[11] and the Department goes to great lengths to ensure that exclusion,[12] or to decline to certify a plan if the unions will not participate.[13] Finally, it should be noted that our questionnaire was not sent to members of the National Association of Home Builders, the bulk of whom are nonunion, and therefore did not encompass the participants in NAHB plans which strongly stress minority upgrading.

Table XII-6 shows that open shop contractor participation in minority upgrading plans is greater where open shop associations

[11] For the vain attempts of the open shop builders in Indianapolis to come under that plan, and their willingness to more than meet that plan's obligations, see Rowan and Rubin, *op. cit.*, pp. 162-164. As a matter of fact this situation is typical. If plan administrators place a minority with an open shop firm, the plan generally receives no credit for a placement!

[12] In Charlotte, North Carolina, for example, there are only four major union builders. All the rest are open shop, and as a matter of fact, the union shop builders have "double-breasted" open shop companies that usually do their work in the Carolinas. Yet the Department of Labor signed a plan agreement with these four builders, refused to include others, and when the Carolinas AGC sought a more representative plan, it was denied.

[13] In Dallas, the local AGC chapter drew up a plan with union and minority community representatives, but it was never effectuated because some unions would not sign the agreement and therefore the Department of Labor would not approve it.

TABLE XII-6
Percent Distribution of Participation in Local Programs to Upgrade Minority Workers by Region and Union Status 1974

Region	Union		Nonunion	
	Yes	No	Yes	No
Not reported	64.0	32.6	27.7	60.2
New England	55.6	44.4	30.2	66.7
Middle Atlantic	67.2	29.6	33.6	58.2
E.N. Central	63.3	31.3	36.0	58.7
W.N. Central	61.7	33.3	51.1	35.6
S. Atlantic	57.4	41.2	40.5	53.2
E.S. Central	71.9	21.9	31.1	62.2
W.S. Central	46.7	48.9	52.2	42.4
Mountain	82.7	72.2	38.1	57.1
Pacific	15.4	23.3	50.0	50.0
Total	65.3	30.8	38.1	54.7

Source: Industrial Research Unit Questionnaire.

are strongest, as in the southern regions or the West North Central area. As we noted in Chapter X, the ABC and the open shop chapters of the AGC clearly stress minority recruitment in their training activities. They realize the significance of the minorities for their present and future labor supply, and emphasize this to their members. It was also clear from our interviews that the largest open shop contractors are also very cognizant of this fact. Many of these contractors are southern-based and have depended upon black and/or Spanish-surnamed minorities as a key labor element both for skilled and unskilled work since the inception of their companies. It is, therefore, likely that open shop contractor participation in training minorities will continue to expand.

THE HIGHWAY SECTOR

The highway sector of the industry, as we noted in Chapter VI, has several unique features including a less skilled labor force, different craft requirements, and a greater dependence upon federal funding. Since highway builders are also major users of minority labor, and since further, a unique availability of data exists, we devote a special section of this chapter to minority employment in this sector.

The Census Data

Table XII-7 shows that 7.3 percent of the excavating, grading, and road machine operators in the United States, and 17.6 percent of those in the ten former Confederate states are black. Moreover, almost another 4 percent in the United States, 17.2 percent in Texas and 14.4 percent in California are of Spanish heritage (essentially Mexican-Americans). Of course, not all such equipment operators work in the highway sector. Most do, however, and given the fact that the laborers on highway construction, as well as many of the carpenters and other employees, are heavily minorities, the significance of this type of work for blacks and Spanish-surnamed Americans is clear. Likewise it is apparent that blacks have a far greater share of machine operator work in the South, where it is overwhelmingly open shop, than in other parts of the country, much of which is unionized.

The Texas and California census data are also of interest. In Texas, 8.7 percent of the roadbuilding machine operators are black and 17.2 percent are of Spanish heritage; in California the percentages are 3.1 Negro and 14.4 are of Spanish heritage. In Texas, machine operators of both races are commonly used by the overwhelmingly open shop highway contractors. In California, the Operating Engineers union has until recently been very inhospitable to blacks, but the utilization of the Spanish-surnamed minority in this highly unionized state is obviously high.

The Federal Highway Administration Data

The Federal Highway Administration periodically collects detailed data on employment by region, occupation, and minorities on all highway projects for which federal funds are allocated. These data for July 31, 1974, are shown in Table XII-8.

Overall, 21 percent of the 141,923 employees on these projects were minorities, of whom one-half were laborers. Minorities were underrepresented as officials or managers (4 percent), supervisors (5 percent), but held 11 percent of the foremen jobs (probably working foremen, and including laborer straw bosses), and

TABLE XII-7

Total Employed Male Excavating, Grading and Road Machine Operators, Construction Industry, by Race, United States, Ten Southern States, Texas and California, 1970

Region	All Workers	Negroes	Percent Negro	Persons of Spanish Heritage	Percent Persons of Spanish Heritage
United States	306,353	22,516	7.3	11,873	3.9
South [a]	74,934	13,189	17.6	497	0.7
Texas	22,708	1,978	8.7	3,909	17.2
California	25,140	769	3.1	3,610	14.4

Source: U.S. Census of Population, 1970. PC(1)D, *Detailed Characteristics,* United States Summary, Table 225, State Volumes, Table 173.

[a] Includes Alabama, Arkansas, Florida, Georgia, Louisiana, Mississippi, North Carolina, South Carolina, Tennessee and Virginia.

9 percent of the clerical jobs. Their share of blue collar jobs included 15 percent of the equipment operators, 8 percent of the (equipment) mechanics, 52 percent of the cement finishers, and a surprising 14 percent of the electricians and 31 percent of the plumbers and pipefitters, a substantially higher proportion than found in commercial or industrial construction. A majority of trainees (54 percent) and 38 percent of the apprentices were minorities.

The regional breakdowns, which we utilized in Chapter VI to provide clues to the extent of open shop penetration, also provide estimates of comparative union and open shop minority utilization. The key job is equipment operator. The highest percentage of minorities in this category, 35 percent, is found in Region 6, dominated by the open shop Texas area. Next is Region 9, 23 percent, which includes the highly unionized state of California and Nevada, followed closely by Region 4, 22 percent, the almost completely open shop area of the Southeast. All other areas are 10 percent or under in minority participation for this classification.

As we shall see below, Local 3 of the Operating Engineers, which dominates the California-Nevada area, is under a court consent decree to open up jobs to minorities. It appears from these data that the decree is having its affect. In general, however, the open shop areas, which of course include a high percentage of blacks and Mexican-Americans, clearly lead in minority utilization for equipment operators.

In the craft jobs, Region 4, the Southeast, and Region 6, the Southwest, have a decided edge in nearly every category for minority utilization, with again Region 9 their only close competitor. Both the Southwest and California areas benefit in this regard from the training received by Mexican immigrants in their homeland. In the Southeast, and in the states of Texas, Louisiana, and Oklahoma, the black minority has a craft tradition, but much of the training must be done by contractors.

It is thus apparent from these data that minorities play a major role in highway construction. Although the proportion of minorities in the highly unionized Region 9 ranks near the top, it is clear that the largely open shop areas of the South lead the country in this regard. Region 3, New England and Middle Atlantic, ranks fourth, and it is also heavily open shop in New England, central Pennsylvania, central New York, and much of Maryland, Virginia, and West Virginia. We thus conclude that in minority utilization in the highway sector, the open shop sector probably has the clear lead.

The Policies of the Operating Engineers

The key union in the highway sector is the Operating Engineers International Union. Its policies on racial employment were inhospitable to minority employment for many years, and today vary considerably, depending upon the local union involved. Thus Professor Mangum reported in 1964:

> The question of a color bar in the membership requirement of the operating engineers' union arose only at one convention. The issue was debated in 1910 when a southern local advocated a 'white only' clause. The color bar was rejected on pragmatic grounds. The union was then essentially a stationary engineer's organization with no control of the labor supply. The Negro engineers could not be excluded from employment. Therefore it was considered preferable to include them in order to control them. Negro members of stationary locals are not uncommon today, but they are rare in hoisting and portable locals. The matter has remained in local hands, and there is no doubt that considerable discrimination exists. Until racial discrimination became a widespread issue in the nation and in the labor movement, the international union developed no policy in the matter. As the issue has grown hotter, international officers have begun to warn local unions of possible

TABLE XII-8

STATISTICAL SUMMARY OF EMPLOYMENT DATA FOR ALL FEDERAL-AID HIGHWAY PROJECTS

Compiled as of July 31, 1974 (Includes Minority Breakdown)

REGION	NUMBER OF PROJECTS	TOTAL DOLLAR VALUE OF PROJECTS	OFFICIALS (MANAGERS)			SUPERVISORS			FOREMEN			CLERICAL			EQUIPMENT OPERATORS			MECHANICS			DRIVERS TRUCK			IRON WORKERS & WELDERS			CARPENTERS			CEMENT MASONS (FINISHERS)		
			Total Employees	Minorities	Percent	Total Employees	Minorities	Percent	Total Employees	Minorities	Percent	Total Employment	Minorities	Percent	Total Employment	Minorities	Percent	Total Employment	Minorities	Percent	Total Employment	Minorities	Percent	Total Employment	Minorities	Percent	Total Employment	Minorities	Percent	Total Employment	Minorities	Percent
1	325	1,157,881,761	139	7	5	436	16	4	302	83	27	247	22	9	2650	118	4	433	21	5	1728	90	5	591	63	11	1025	87	8	221	37	17
3	837	1,998,940,718	235	7	3	724	14	2	1807	113	6	355	20	6	1469	452	10	530	16	3	2284	564	25	437	71	16	1786	203	11	732	308	42
4	804	1,901,493,212	214	3	1	771	25	3	1905	204	11	281	12	4	6163	1341	22	630	71	11	2260	694	31	409	143	35	1647	446	27	993	767	77
5	1064	2,018,499,729	286	9	3	862	23	3	1975	111	6	365	23	6	8773	712	8	493	22	4	4013	423	11	864	87	10	1787	154	9	890	251	28
6	588	1,257,020,752	187	7	4	546	60	11	1213	263	2	268	37	14	4184	1447	35	430	92	21	1618	717	44	355	232	65	1170	583	50	779	618	79
7	410	414,665,396	107	2	2	340	10	3	577	20	3	95	4	4	2288	108	5	265	8	3	1055	72	7	288	43	15	510	53	10	226	56	25
8	492	1,207,482,492	117	1	1	349	18	5	594	34	6	139	7	5	3010	206	7	517	31	6	1993	109	5	63	3	5	355	49	14	162	34	21
9	242	954,288,634	245	26	11	257	30	12	915	241	26	259	63	24	2106	477	23	230	42	18	1057	197	19	383	162	42	782	219	28	265	175	66
10	246	472,797,915	84	7	8	173	10	6	328	23	7	138	10	7	1969	141	7	236	15	6	1114	72	6	179	28	16	293	16	5	106	36	34
TOTAL	5008	11,383,070,609	1614	69	4	4458	206	5	9616	1092	11	2147	198	9	32,612	5002	15	3764	318	8	17,122	2938	17	3569	832	23	9355	1810	19	4374	2282	52

REGION	ELECTRICIANS			PIPE-FITTERS PLUMBERS			PAINTERS			LABORERS SEMI-SKILLED			LABORERS UNSKILLED			APPRENTICES			ON-THE-JOB TRAINEES			TOTAL NUMBER OF EMPLOYEES	TOTAL NUMBER OF MINORITIES	PERCENT OF MINORITIES TO TOTAL NUMBER OF EMPLOYEES	TOTAL NUMBER OF MINORITY SEMI-SKILLED AND UNSKILLED LABORERS	PERCENT OF MINORITY SEMI-SKILLED & UNSKILLED LABORERS TO TOTAL NUMBER OF EMPLOYEES	PERCENT OF MINORITY SEMI-SKILLED & UNSKILLED LABORERS TO TOTAL NUMBER OF MINORITIES
	Total Employment	Minorities	Percent	Total Employment	Minorities	Percent	Total Employment	Minorities	Percent	Total Employment	Minorities	Percent	Total Employment	Minorities	Percent	Total Employment	Minorities	Percent	Total Employment	Minorities	Percent						
1	174	22	13	9	1	11	98	17	17	2821	591	21	2025	228	11	155	55	35	341	182	53	13,395	1,403	10	819	6	58
3	261	53	20	41	5	12	137	23	17	1938	845	44	4594	1234	27	207	39	19	482	241	50	18,019	3,928	21	2079	12	53
4	123	16	13	82	53	65	87	11	13	2890	1227	42	6303	2654	42	71	15	21	596	320	54	25,425	7,667	31	3881		51
5	267	27	10	30	6	20	81	10	12	3381	808	24	6414	1349	21	662	230	35	544	353	65	31,687	4,015	13	2157	7	54
6	63	9	14	27	20	74	28	12	43	2600	1547	60	4018	2466	61	46	22	48	331	191	58	17,863	8,110	45	4013	22	49
7	86	3	3	23	1	4	39	5	13	1059	155	15	1479	178	12	69	35	51	256	116	45	8,762	718	8	333	4	46
8	45	2	4	8	1	13	5	0	0	1040	187	18	1893	286	15	133	41	31	149	85	57	10,572	968	9	473	4	49
9	148	43	29	24	11	49	23	3	13	1475	877	59	924	545	59	461	251	54	10	5	50	9,564	3,111	33	1422	15	46
10	175	12	7	97	9	9	11	0	0	801	88	11	690	93	13	127	37	29	115	43	37	6,636	560	8	181	3	32
TOTAL	1342	187	14	341	107	31	509	81	16	18005	6325	35	28,340	9033	32	1931	725	38	2824	1536	54	141,923	30,480	21	15,358	11	50

Source: Office of Civil Rights/Federal Highway Administration.

TABLE XII-8 (continued)

a. Regions as defined by the Federal Highway Administration as follows (there is no Region 2):
1. Connecticut, Maine, Massachusetts, New Hampshire, New Jersey, New York, Rhode Island, and Vermont.
3. Delaware, District of Columbia, Maryland, Pennsylvania, Virginia, and West Virginia.
4. Alabama, Florida, Georgia, Kentucky, Mississippi, North Carolina, South Carolina, and Tennessee.
5. Illinois, Indiana, Michigan, Minnesota, Ohio, and Wisconsin.
6. Arkansas, Louisiana, New Mexico, Oklahoma, and Texas.
7. Iowa, Kansas, Missouri, and Nebraska.
8. Colorado, Montana, North Dakota, South Dakota, Utah, and Wyoming.
9. Arizona, California, and Nevada.
10. Alaska, Idaho, Oregon, and Washington.

> problems from external sources in the future if discrimination is not ended. Beyond this, the international has taken no action.[14]

Since 1964, a number of Operating Engineers local unions, under national leadership, have encouraged minority membership through training programs and through contracts for training with the U.S. Department of Labor. This has resulted in opening up previously closed ranks in a number of areas, such as Pittsburgh,[15] Chicago,[16] and several other locations. On the other hand, it has been necessary for the government or for individuals to file suits to end discriminatory admission and work practices in California, Oregon, Philadelphia, Ohio, and Kentucky and other areas. In Philadelphia, the commonwealth of Pennsylvania obtained an injunction to prevent Local 542 and some of its members and agents from "pursuing a course of conduct designed to intimidate, harass and preclude" blacks from pursuing a law suit against that local.[17] In California, the U.S. Department of Justice obtained a consent decree which ended the practice of confining blacks and Mexican-Americans to the less desirable jobs, refusing to give them credit for past experience, and denying them apprenticeship opportunities.[18] On February 5, 1975, Local 18 of the Operating Engineers and the Ohio Operating Engineers Apprenticeship Fund agreed not to exclude persons from the Fund's apprenticeship training program because of race or color; to admit at least 90 of 154 prior applicants; to give black trainees who previously applied for apprenticeship, the opportunity to transfer into the apprenticeship program without any loss in rate of pay or credit for prior training experience; and after 90 black prior applicants are admitted,

---

[14] Garth L. Mangum, *The Operating Engineers: The Economic History of a Trade Union*, Wertheim Publications in Industrial Relations (Cambridge: Harvard University Press, 1964), pp. 232-233.

[15] See Irwin Dubinsky, *Reform in Trade Union Discrimination in the Construction Industry: Operation Dig and Its Legacy* (New York: Praeger Publishers, 1973).

[16] Preliminary research by the Industrial Research Unit on the "Chicago Plan" indicates that the Operating Engineers local there is one of the few in that city which attempted seriously to meet its obligations.

[17] *Commonwealth of Pennsylvania et al.* v. *Local Union No. 542, International Union of Operating Engineers, et al.*, U.S.D.C., E.D.Pa., Civil Action No. 71-2698, August 4, 1972.

[18] *United States* v. *Operating Engineers Local 3 et al.*, Civil No. C-71-1277 RFP, Permanent Injunction in Partial Resolution of Lawsuit, February 8, 1973.

to select an additional 600 minorities among the next 1,200 applicants admitted. The decree, which stays into effect until its provisions are filled, covers apprenticeship selection in all but three counties in Ohio and in five Kentucky counties as well.[19]

A fundamental complaint against Operating Engineer policy and training programs is that too often minorities end up as oilers and serve in that capacity as a deadend job, or are confined to the smaller, and lower wage rated machine jobs. In open shop construction, the equipment operators usually oil their own machines, but upward movement is sometimes also difficult for minorities. On the other hand, the absence of craft jurisdictional lines in the open shop sector smooths the way for the laborer to be upgraded to equipment operator or truck driver, to cross over between the latter two jobs and to progress from the smaller equipment to the larger. Unquestionably, in highway construction, as in other sectors of the industry, the rigidity of craft jurisdictional lines act as barriers to advancement. Since blacks and other minorities are overly concentrated in the laborer classification, the result is to retard minority improvement.

CONCLUSION

In the absence of definitive data, it is not possible to state categorically that open shop construction is more hospitable to minorities than is the union shop. Most observers, however, including union shop contractors answering our questionnaire, believe this to be the case, and most data point in this direction, although the responses to our questionnaire in regard to the respondent's own situation did not bear this out. The historic attitudes and policies of the craft unions, the barriers which craft organization sets up against upward movement, the large number of civil rights cases involving the construction unions and the lack of major success of many programs attempting to expand minority employment in construction, all point to a greater problem in the union shop sector.

At the same time it should be noted that underutilization of minorities in the electrical, plumbing, and mechanical areas exists also in the open shop sector. Years of discrimination and lack of training have taken their toll. There are also open shop contractors who do not practice equal opportunity, and some who do

---

[19] *Daily Labor Report*, No. 76 (April 18, 1975), p. A-15.

have been forced to improve nonetheless even when they attempt to do so. Thus, Brown & Root, which has a domestic labor force more than one-fourth minority, signed a consent decree brought against it by the EEOC and five of its employees in which the company set higher goals for blacks, Spanish-surnamed Americans, and women in craft jobs, supervision, administrative, engineering, and professional staff positions; established special communication and referral measures to notify qualified women and minorities of company job opportunities; and created a fund to give additional training to minorities and women. The decree which covers five counties in Texas will be in effect until 1980.[20]

It does appear, nevertheless, that the open shop sector is both more hospitable as a whole to minority employment and, being without craft restrictions and union rigidities, more capable of dealing with the problem.

[20] *Ibid.*

PART FOUR

Summary And Conclusion

CHAPTER XIII

Concluding Remarks

It is difficult to summarize the findings of a study of so vast a subject as open shop construction. We have been examining a huge number of individualistic businesses each of which operates distinctively in many ways. Moreover, as we have stressed throughout this study, the information and data available are fragmentary at best. Nevertheless, at least some findings have been made which can be summarized here, and then some tentative conclusions can be drawn therefrom.

EXTENT OF OPEN SHOP

It is, first of all, very clear that open shop construction has made substantial gains in recent years. The residential construction sector's homebuilding segment had already become 80 to 90 percent nonunion before the recent surge of open shop gains began. Apartments, town houses, and other multiple dwellings are much more unionized with the degree of unionization varying with building height (over three stories) and location in relation to center city. Open shop builders may control as much as 50 percent of this work, including more of the low rise and less of the high rise.

Commercial construction is more difficult to estimate because of its greater diversity, but certainly it is in this sector that the open shop builders have made their greatest gains during the last ten years, and also have the greatest potential for future gains. Again, the smaller the building and the farther from center city, the greater is the open shop penetration. But experience in small jobs permits a builder to attempt a bigger one, and one success leads to another up the ladder. The inflation of wages, benefits and other costs—land, interest, etc.—have accelerated the search for more economical alternatives. The open shop builder has provided one to which more and more users have turned. The result has been larger and larger facilities built by the open shop group. It is likely that the commercial sector is at the lowest ebb of unionization since World War II, but probably remains 55 to 65 percent union.

The industrial sector remains the key source of union strength. Only a few open shop builders—Brown & Root, Daniel International, J. Ray McDermott, and H. B. Zachry—can challenge the members of the National Constructors Association on the largest projects, although several other open shop contractors could well attain such capability during the next several years. The large open shop contractors have been obtaining all the business which they can handle during recent years and have been compelled to forego bidding on jobs where they were invited to do so. In some areas, such as Houston, this has enabled the unionized National Constructors Association members to increase their share of business.

Our data showed that open shop builders have increased their share of the large industrial jobs during the last several years, but 75 percent or more of such work is probably unionized. If the open shop builders continue to grow, however, they may well win a larger share of such business.

Highway and heavy construction is more unionized than residential, less than commercial, but not changing as fast as commercial although the open shop constructors have made some gains here too. The Davis-Bacon Act and other prevailing wage legislation seems to be the principal reasons for this relative stability.

Locational and regional factors have played a key role in the expansion of the open shop sector. The union strength is greatest in the center cities and weakens as one moves to suburbia and then to exurbia and the rural areas. The older cities particularly have been losing population and business activity to their neighbors and this in turn has provided work for open shop builders at the expense of the city directed unionized ones.

Regionally, the South, despite its union enclaves, remains the open shop heartland. This is where the largest open shop builders grew and prospered; and here the bulk of the largest open shop builders are headquartered.

Conversely, the Middle Atlantic, the midwestern states and the Pacific region are the most highly unionized, with New England, the Great Plains and Rocky Mountain areas remaining considerably less unionized. Of key importance is that the open shop segment is concentrated in many of the areas which are growing industrially at the fastest pace. It has also its greatest strength in the less unionized areas of the country, an undoubtedly key factor.

Overall, it appears likely that the open shop builders are in the majority and probably control 50 to 60 percent of the total work. Of course, this varies with the current construction mix, but there seems little doubt that open shop construction is the larger segment by a clear, and we believe, growing margin.

LABOR MARKET FACTORS

Open shop contractors hire, deploy, train, and compensate labor differently than do their unionized counterparts. Emphasis in the open shop sector is much more on job stability, diversity in job assignments, informal training, and annual earnings rather than hourly wages. Open shop contractors gain by not having to concentrate their hiring through union hiring halls, but suffer because of the lack of centralized employment sources. As a result, a number of open shop groups are commencing to establish employment referral systems.

Deployment flexibility provides open shop contractors with a major advantage over their unionized competitors. Employees are utilized out of craft concentration, unnecessary personnel are not employed, and skilled personnel are not utilized for unskilled and semiskilled work, all at major cost savings. These productivity impact factors were repeatedly stressed in our interviews as to why the open shop sector had registered major gains in recent years.

Most training in the open shop sector is the informal, on-the-job type. The large open shop contractors have developed interesting training programs with emphasis on upward movement with accomplishment rather than time, and the open shop associations have developed traditional apprentice programs. These are growing but remain a minor segment of open shop training. If the open shop sector is to expand, it obviously must increase its formal training or the skilled manpower needed will simply not be available.

Although some open shop craftsmen receive hourly wages equal to, or even in excess of, the union rate, most open shop construction workers are paid less per hour. Open shop employers pay a range of rates depending upon the individual's service and competence; construction unions require a single rate for a classification, and the union rate is usually above the open shop one for the same classification. Pay for time not worked is significant in the unionized sector, and generally absent in the open shop one. Fringe benefits are much more prevalent in the unionized sector than in the open shop one where they are actually just beginning to develop. The open shop claims that by flexible working hours, work during inclement weather, and steady employment, its employees approximate or even exceed the annual earnings of unionized ones, and this could well be true in some, but certainly not all cases. Certainly, on the basis of all the data that we have been able to gather, open shop wages are lower and benefits less common and generous than are unionized ones. Moreover, in recent years, the evidence indicates that the wage rate spread between the two sectors has grown and that this has been a key factor in the expansion of the open shop sector during this period.

Hours of work also differ between the open and unionized sectors. Open shop builders pay smaller and fewer overtime premiums, use varied workweeks and weekends to make up for inclement weather delays, and freely alter daily starting and closing times to expedite work and to reduce costs. Such flexibility is often made prohibitively expensive by union rules.

There is no definite analysis of the extent of minority employment in the various construction industry sectors, nor is there decisive evidence that the open shop builders employ a larger percentage of minorities than do the unionized ones. Such information and data which we have been able to gather do, for the most part, point in this direction. The long record of discriminatory treatment of minorities by many construction unions and the natural community of interest between minorities and open shop builders to provide jobs for the former and a labor force at less cost to the latter, also point in this direction. In addition, minorities are concentrated in many areas where the open shop contractors are the strongest, especially the South and Southwest. Discrimination is certainly not absent in the open shop sector, but the factors already noted seem to have made it more hospitable to minority employment.

THE FUTURE OF OPEN SHOP CONSTRUCTION

The expansion of open shop construction in recent years is, in effect, the result of the operation of market forces. The inflation of labor costs, including wages, fringes and work rule inhibitions on productivity, undoubtedly has provided the basis for open shop expansion and for user interest in finding less costly alternatives to unionized construction. Open shop builders were prepared to take advantage of their opportunities by years of development in suburban, exurban, and rural areas, and in the South and other regions where the construction unions are weak. The economic forces during the late 1960's and early 1970's proved strong enough to overcome institutional and government restraints, such as past relationships of builders and users, political support of unionism and union-favoring prevailing wage laws. The interesting question is whether these trends will continue and the expansion of open shop construction proceed at the same or a greater pace.

In Chapter VIII, we examined how the construction unions responded to open shop competition by economic means, by use of the legal weapons of conflict, and by violence. We noted that the economic response varied, but that it by no means met the competitive threat in many areas. In May 1975, unemployment in construction rose to an all time recorded high of 21.8 percent, as compared with a general unemployment rate of 9.2 percent. Meanwhile, unions continued overall to push up wages of construction workers to an average of $7.12 per hour and $259.88 per week, while 832,000 construction workers remained out of work.[1] With the rate of unemployment apparently cresting, concessions by unions to meet open shop competition are likely to become even less prevalent. It does not, therefore, seem likely that the expansion of open shop construction will be halted by union economic concessions.

We also do not believe that union violence will stop the expansion of open shop construction although it is quite clear that such violence and the lack of even-handed police protection in many areas inhibit users from utilizing open shop builders and the latter from attempting to operate. Moreover, violence in a particular area often has the immediate effect of frightening prospective users from offering opportunities to open shop builders to compete. Nevertheless, the open shop contractors now

[1] *Engineering News-Record* (May 8, 1975), p. 3.

have an organization, the Associated Builders and Contractors, and are sufficiently strong in the Associated General Contractors, to have launched a strong counterattack against violence. It appears that, as a result, law enforcement agencies have been compelled to act and to make violence much less productive.

The greatest threat to the continued expansion of open shop construction lies in the possibility of a new set of rules governing the weapons of conflict which would permit the construction unions the right to use secondary boycotts to drive open shop constructors and nonunion employees off jobs. The recent decision of the U.S. Supreme Court making unions liable for antitrust violations if they attempt to force contractors to subcontract only to union firms, should aid open shop expansion. But this could change if the Congress enacts so-called common situs picketing, legislation long advocated by the construction unions. As summarized by the Associated General Contractors:

> In the next several months, general contractors, both open shop and those operating with union agreements, will again be faced with a serious challenge to their very existence. Organized labor has once again . . . [backed] legislation to legalize secondary boycotts in the construction industry. Secondary boycotts are strikes and picketing to force a cessation of business relationships between a firm with whom a union has a dispute and other firms who are not involved in the dispute. If successful, one construction union could cause a total work stoppage on the entire Alaska pipeline from Valdez to the North Slope because of an isolated labor dispute anywhere on the project.
>
> Pending legislation would abolish the existing rule that a construction union, while free to strike and picket the firm in dispute, must not willfully picket or pressure any other firm on the site who is neutral in the particular dispute. The change would enable any of the building trades unions having a dispute with one of several firms on the site to picket indiscriminately and shut down the total project.
>
> Unions with a bona-fide dispute can presently strike the primary employer involved, subject to the rules of fair picketing. Innocent employers and employees are thus afforded reasonable protection.[2]

In Chapter VIII, we briefly noted that the National Labor Relations Board and the courts have so construed the Taft-Hartley Act so as to permit considerably more latitude in picketing and boycotting than many believe was intended by the Act's framers. Senate Bill No. 1479 and House Bill No. 5900 in the

---

[2] "Common Situs—More Trouble for a Troubled Industry." An addendum to the May 8th [(1975)] AGC Newsletter.

1975 Congress would abolish effective restrictions on picketing and boycotting open shop contractors and make it impossible for them to operate in many areas. The impact on open shop growth would be immediate and profound, and possibly eliminate many, if not all "double-breasted" operations as well.

Many other imponderables exist, including the character of prevailing wage law administration, government support of construction activity, and the state of the economy. Assuming, however, a continuation of present policies, and a reasonably strong economy, it seems likely that open shop construction will continue to expand unless inhibited by the already noted possible change in the Taft-Hartley Act's secondary boycott restrictions. The reason seems clear: open shop construction is an economically viable alternative that in a growing number of situations can compete successfully against its unionized rival. If open shop construction is further restricted by legislation that grants more power to the already powerful construction unions, then it would seem to follow that construction wages and costs will rise still more simply because a competitive restraint has been removed.

Finally, it should be emphasized that much of the future for open shop contractors lies with themselves and their organizations. They must develop the managerial and financial capability to manage larger and larger jobs; they must develop new mechanisms for recruiting labor; they must train much more so that they have a skilled work force available; they must develop wage and benefit programs that meet their growing status and maintain their labor forces; and although they probably lead the unionized sector in minority employment, they must realize the opportunity for a labor source that minorities portend and expend more effort in affirmative action training and development to achieve this opportunity. In sum, much of their future is in the hands of the open shop builders themselves.

APPENDICES

Appendix A

THE CONSTRUCTION INDUSTRY[1]

Construction, one of the most complex and important industries in the United States, may be briefly defined as a composite of interrelated production activities involving the erection and maintenance of physical structures such as residential, commercial, and industrial buildings, highways, and earthworks. The construction production process is vastly different from that of most manufacturing concerns in that it involves the fabrication and assembly of unique, custom designed productions at a special location. In 1974, new construction was valued at $135.4 billion, or about ten percent of the gross national product. Construction maintenance expenditures accounts for an additional 4 percent of GNP. Contract construction—that performed by contractors for the use of others—represents about 70 percent of all building work, with most of the rest (called "force account" construction) undertaken by nonconstruction enterprises for their own purposes.

Contract construction employed an average of 4.0 million workers during 1974, or about 5 percent of total average annual employment. The averages are misleading, however, because of the industry's extraordinary high turnover rate. Thus in 1972, the latest year for which such data are available, 5.3 million workers had their longest job in the industry. Construction is the only goods producing industry whose share of total employment has not declined markedly in the past quarter century. About one-half of the work force is comprised of skilled tradesmen; over three-quarters of it is made up of production workers generally. Some 15 percent of all the skilled blue collar workers in the country are employed in construction.

IMPORTANCE OF LOCAL MARKETS

Most construction work is performed at the site where the finished product will be situated, a site usually selected by the

[1] This Appendix draws heavily from Armand J. Thieblot, Jr., *The Davis-Bacon Act*, Labor Relations and Public Policy Series, No. 10, (Philadelphia: Industrial Research Unit, the Wharton School, University of Pennsylvania, 1975), pp. 181-202.

purchaser rather than the producer. There are some instances of off-site prefabrication of components, such as window assemblies, climate control systems, or elevators, and in a few cases there has been experimentation with modular factory production of entire sections of a building. On the whole, however, very little construction activity is undertaken in advance at a location different from the actual construction site. The typical construction firm has no inventory of finished products ready for immediate sale. The major exception to this rule is the residential builder who erects large housing tracts on speculation.

Most contractors perform the majority of their business within their home state. In 1967, 88 percent of the total receipts received by construction firms were generated from contracts within the home state of the contractor. With the single exception of heavy (nonhighway) construction activity, in no sector of the construction industry were home state receipts less than 89 percent of the total sector receipts. Even the heavy construction sector received the majority (62 percent) of its receipts from home state projects. Somewhat surprisingly, the highway construction sector also does the preponderance of its work in the home state of its contractors—in 1967, 91 percent of the highway sector receipts came from home state projects.[2]

Besides the preponderance of onsite erection, the local nature of the construction industry is also attributable to several other significant factors. As we shall see, most construction firms are relatively small. This means that they do not have sufficient resources to undertake projects far away from their home base of operations. In addition, the importance of close business or political relationships in obtaining public contracts prevents many construction firms from working far away from home. In many areas of the United States, local and state political conditions dictate that contractors must have a certain "rapport" with influential public officials in order to obtain public construction contracts. It is difficult for a contractor in one state or other political subdivision to establish this type of relationship in another state or similar political subdivision, thus limiting his operation to his home state.

The local character of both labor markets and product markets in construction should not be overdrawn. There are, of course, major contractors whose work carries them across the country

[2] Daniel Quinn Mills, *Industrial Relations and Manpower in Construction* (Cambridge: MIT Press, 1972), p. 8.

and, indeed, throughout the world, just as there are peripatetic construction workers who follow large scale construction jobs wherever they may lead. Even in these instances, however, the conditions of employment are usually determined by local standards, in both the union and nonunion sectors of the industry. Given the immobility of the construction product, and the relatively few workers who are prepared to lead a nomadic life, it could hardly be otherwise.

Most construction projects are built according to precise specifications for several reasons. Each building site is unique, and varying topography and land use criteria preclude building standardization. An urban setting often requires the construction of a high rise building, while a rural setting will allow the construction of a low rise one. Because buildings and other structures are designed to fulfill the precise needs of the customer, no two buildings are exactly alike. The specifications of a library are very different from those of an office building. Differences in building codes are also reflected in design differences. The design of a building in California must be more concerned with the possibility of an earthquake than the design of a building in New York. Terrain considerations make it impossible for any two dams, bridges, or highways to be constructed in exactly the same manner. The absence of product standardization has important implications for the construction industry.

Use of Construction Machinery

To be economically feasible, a machine must be useful on many projects, or else it must be able to replace a large number of workers. As a general rule, except in earthmoving, machinery has not yet become sophisticated enough to achieve a level of performance warranting widespread use in the industry. In the instances where useful equipment has been perfected, contractors have often found it cheaper to rent than to purchase. In other instances, contractors have found it more desirable to use labor rather than to attempt to use new equipment.

Capital requirements do, however, vary greatly with the size of the contractor and with the type of construction work performed. Firms that specialize in heavy construction activity are more likely to invest in labor-saving equipment than firms specializing in building construction. Heavy construction contractors usually perform most of the work on a project themselves instead of subcontracting it. This characteristic makes it more attractive financially for them to purchase and use their own equipment. In contrast, building contractors often rent the necessary equipment for a particular project or will subcontract out a large proportion of the work to lessen the need for capital investment.[3] As a general rule, equipment investment climbs in proportion to the firm size, but in 1973, diversified contractors whose incomes ranged from $25 to $49 million had a median investment of $85,000 for each million in contracts, whereas diversified contractors with incomes of $50 to $99 million had a median investment of $42,000 for each million in contracts. These investment figures are greatly exceeded by the highway/heavy sector, which averages $420,000 in equipment investment for each million in contracts.[4]

Subcontracting

As noted above, the lack of construction standardization has led to the widespread use of specialty contractors and subcontractors. Many primary contractors subcontract large phases of work on most of their large projects. Electrical and plumbing work are most often subcontracted out because the specialty contractor is able to do the work more efficiently than the general contractor and has access to the necessary skilled labor.

Contractual and subcontractual relationships are often very complex in the construction industry. The general contractor subcontracts the parts of the job that he does not desire to undertake or is technically unable to perform himself. Subcontracting, therefore, acts to lower the general contractor's capital requirements and allows him more flexibility. Without subcontracting, small contractors would be seriously limited in the type and size of projects they could pursue and would be dominated more often by larger firms which could afford required capital outlays. In some instances, the subcontractor may also subcontract certain aspects of a project. The *1967 Census of Construction Industries* showed that 44 percent of gross construction receipts were received by subcontractors. Census data also show that general contractors subcontracted 63 percent of their total receipts and that specialty contractors subcontracted 15 percent.[5]

---

[3] Peter J. Cassimatis, *Economics of the Construction Industry*, Studies in Business Economics, No. 111 (New York: National Industrial Conference Board, 1969), p. 23.

[4] "The ENR 400," *Engineering News-Record* (April 11, 1974), p. 49.

[5] U.S. Bureau of the Census, *1967 Census of Construction Industries*, Vol. 1 (Washington, D.C.: Government Printing Office, 1971), Table 1B-3.

The relationship between contractors and subcontractors is not of a uniform character. In some cases, subcontractors are barely distinguishable from employees, in that their "business" is limited to a single contractor. The contractor may have, in fact, been the subcontractor's employer at one time. These subcontractors are usually individuals or groups of individuals with no employees of their own, and they are often compensated by the "piece" (per brick laid, per foot of drywall installed, etc.) rather than by the job. On the other hand, the subcontractor may be a well established business firm which provides services (and often materials) to a variety of contractors. These establishments will employ a work force of their own and in some cases may undertake work directly at the behest of the purchaser. The more informal (and ephemeral) subcontractor of the first type described above is more often found in residential or other small scale building.[6]

Table A-1 shows the employment patterns between general, highway/heavy, and specialty contractors. During the 1967-1972 period, the proportion of construction workers employed by general building contractors fell slightly from 31 percent in 1967 to 29.2 percent in 1972. During the same period, special trades employment rose from 47.9 percent of all construction employment to 49.5 percent, while highway/heavy construction employment rose slightly from 21.1 to 21.3 percent. This trend suggests that the construction industry may be becoming more specialized.

The Factor Mix

Since construction products exhibit such prodigious variety, it is not surprising that there are large variations among different kinds of projects in the relative importance of labor costs. In general, labor accounts for an appreciably higher proportion of total cost in building construction than in heavy and highway construction. The difference, of course, is largely counterbalanced by the much greater cost of equipment and machinery in nonbuilding work.

Variations in factor mix, however, are not limited to those occasioned by types of product. Different technologies may be

---

[6] For more on this point, see Howard G. Foster, *Manpower in Homebuilding: A Preliminary Analysis*, Manpower and Human Resources Studies, No. 3 (Philadelphia: Industrial Research Unit, the Wharton School, University of Pennsylvania, 1974), pp. 31-36.

TABLE A-1
The Construction Industry
Number of Construction Workers on Contract Construction Payrolls By Type of Contractor
(In thousands)

Period	All Contract Construction	General Building Construction		All Heavy Construction		All Special Trade Construction	
		Number	Percent	Number	Percent	Number	Percent
1967	2,708	840.5	31.0	570.0	21.1	1,297.6	47.9
1968	2,768	847.5	30.6	583.0	21.1	1,337.6	48.3
1969	2,896	898.7	31.0	600.3	20.7	1,397.1	48.3
1970	2,820	847.8	30.1	607.2	21.5	1,365.2	48.4
1971	2,832	833.2	29.4	606.6	21.4	1,391.8	49.2
1972	2,908	849.9	29.2	620.1	21.3	1,437.8	49.5
1973	3,011	880.1	29.2	636.5	21.2	1,494.1	49.6

Source: *Construction Review,* February/March 1974, p. 56.
Note: Adjusted to March 1971 benchmarks.

found within product classifications in response to variations in relative factor costs. In the South for example, labor costs tend to be significantly lower than elsewhere in the nation, and furthermore the skilled-unskilled wage differentials tend to be higher. As a consequence, construction in the South is relatively labor intensive, with greater use of unskilled labor than is found elsewhere. This latter point is illustrated in Table IX-3. The relative absence of unionism in the South, as discussed at length in Chapter VII, is doubtless a key element in these variations.

INSTABILITY IN CONSTRUCTION

Bidding

Bidding for construction work has often been seen as a stimulus to competition in the industry. Most firms bid on a relatively large number of projects to ensure that they will be able to secure enough work to stay in business. If the number of projects bid on can be roughly equated with the level of competition, then it is generally agreed that competition varies inversely with the business cycle.[7] When the business

[7] Cassimatis, *op. cit.*, pp. 39, 40.

cycle is near its peak, competition is usually less intensive as firms tend to bid on fewer jobs than when the cycle is on the downturn. During a boom, firms usually have adequate amounts of work to remain solvent and, in fact, may be unable to undertake any additional projects. In contrast, during an economic slowdown, the level of competition usually becomes much more intense because each firm must bid on a greater number of projects if it is to secure enough work to remain solvent. During such periods, large firms have a tendency to bid in areas usually dominated by smaller firms. On the other hand, during a boom it is usually impossible for smaller firms to reciprocate by bidding on large projects because such projects are beyond the capabilities of most small firms.[8]

In some cases, however, the existence of bidding can reduce, rather than enhance, the level of competition. One reason is the widespread use of "prequalification of bidders." This practice rates each contractor through a comprehensive analysis of his assets, experience, credit rating, and past performance on other projects. Consequently, as the scope of a project increases in size and complexity, new or small construction firms find it more difficult to qualify to enter bids. New firms face an additional barrier to entry because they are often unable to underbid the more experienced, established firms.

Economic Instability

Wide fluctuations exist in the total number of job opportunities available from month-to-month and from year-to-year. This variability fosters economic instability, another characteristic of the industry. Table A-2 shows how the month-to-month employment in the construction industry varied during the years 1968 through 1973. As logically expected, construction employment is higher during the warmer months of the year, and usually peaks during July and August. The seasonal employment variations reflect the fact that much construction work is done outdoors, and therefore, weather is a significant factor. Seasonal variations also reflect the traditional patterns of bid letting and other institutional practices that act to inhibit winter work, such as penalty pay provisions that cover employees who fail to receive a minimum number of hours of work each week.

---

[8] *Ibid.*, p. 40.

TABLE A-2.
The Construction Industry
1968-1973 Average Monthly Employment Variations, by Type of Contractor
(In thousands)

Month	All Contract Construction	General Building Contractors	All Heavy Construction	All Special Trade Contractors
January	2,478	764.0	437.9	1,276.5
February	2,478	762.8	444.1	1,271.1
March	2,574	786.7	479.0	1,308.6
April	2,742	822.4	557.4	1,362.6
May	2,864	840.8	634.8	1,388.5
June	3,035	893.0	696.8	1,444.7
July	3,109	921.0	717.9	1,469.8
August	3,159	936.7	727.2	1,495.3
September	3,114	917.5	714.0	1,482.6
October	3,100	918.3	700.3	1,481.6
November	3,000	898.5	644.9	1,456.2
December	2,816	852.6	553.2	1,409.7

Source: *Construction Review*, February/March 1974, p. 56.

Note: Adjusted to March 1971 benchmarks.

Such provisions encourage contractors to suspend work for longer periods than would otherwise be necessary.[9]

In addition to seasonal fluctuations in the number of employees, the average weekly hours of employment also vary considerably. Table A-3 gives the average weekly hours of employment per worker for the same categories as Table A-2. Not surprisingly, employment fluctuates most in the heavy construction sector and least in the special trades sector. In the case of highway construction, monthly employment more than doubled each year between January and July or August. In 1973, highway construction employment rose 132.8 percent between January and August.[10]

The instability problem is compounded by the short duration of most construction projects. The widespread use of subcontracting means that the practitioners of many crafts are employed only during certain (often brief) phases of a project. The uncertainties of bidding create difficulties for contractors in planning their work to ensure steady employment. As a result of these employment fluctuations, only a small number of employees are considered permanently associated with a particular contractor. Nonunionized firms apparently feel the effects of this situation more intensely. Nonunion firms do not have access to a union hiring hall and therefore have a greater incentive to retain employees over slack periods in preference to hiring new ones later.

Not only is the construction industry beset with seasonal instability, but it also suffers from cyclical instability in which general market downturns and tight credit conditions have a magnified effect on it. During such periods, businesses have little incentive to construct new facilities, and individual persons are typically less able to buy new houses, thereby causing a serious decline in construction demand. During the economic slowdown of 1970, the total number of construction firms declined by 3 percent, and the following year, construction employment fell by almost 2 percent. Neither employment nor number of firms surpassed the 1969 level until 1972.[11] In 1974, under continued

[9] U.S. Department of Labor, *Seasonality and Manpower in Construction*, Bureau of Labor Statistics, Bulletin No. 1642 (Washington, D.C.: Government Printing Office, 1970), p. 4.

[10] U.S. Department of Commerce, *Construction Review* 20, No. 2 (February/March, 1974), p. 56.

[11] Calculated from data in Tables A-4 and A-5.

TABLE A-3.
The Construction Industry
1968-1973 Average Variations in Weekly Hours of Employment
By Type of Contractor

Month	All Contract Construction	General Building Contractors	All Heavy Construction	All Special Trade Contractors
January	35.6	34.8	38.0	35.4
February	36.0	35.4	38.6	35.4
March	36.8	36.1	39.8	36.2
April	37.2	36.1	40.4	36.5
May	37.5	36.4	40.7	36.8
June	38.2	36.6	42.3	37.1
July	38.4	36.8	42.8	37.1
August	38.6	37.0	43.1	37.3
September	37.8	36.3	41.9	36.9
October	38.1	36.7	41.8	37.2
November	36.6	35.6	39.4	36.0
December	36.7	35.8	39.1	36.4

Source: *Construction Review*, February/March 1974, p. 60.

Note: Adjusted to March 1971 benchmarks.

conditions of tight money, economic stagnation, and inflation, construction demand fell precipitately. Construction unemployment in some specific markets in the summer of 1974 was reported to exceed 30 percent of the available work force.

Employer-Employee Relationships

Because of these continuous fluctuations in employment, there is a relatively weak employer-employee attachment in the industry, particularly in the unionized sectors. Many workers drift from job to job and employer to employer. When a contractor needs a large work force with diverse skills to build a large and complex project, workers may be drawn from a wide area surrounding the work site, especially if the site is a remote one. Such instances may be the first and last time that a particular employee will work for a particular contractor. Large contractors who secure projects throughout the country have often never previously worked in the area where they are beginning a new project. Once there, they usually try to hire as many local people as possible, finish the project, and then leave, perhaps never to return to the area to perform another job there.

Some workers do, however, become permanently attached to a particular contractor. Many contractors keep a nucleus of key employees on the payroll throughout the year. Such a crew usually consists of supervisory personnel and workers who have unusual skills or who have demonstrated a particular expertise that the contractor desires. These employees can be used to work on various projects during the "slow" season when few workers are needed. When the amount of work begins to increase rapidly during the warmer months of the year, or when a large project comes along, these same employees can provide an excellent base from which the contractor can quickly and effectively develop a larger work force.

In the unionized sector, the workers are more closely attached to the craft unions, which act as referral agencies, rather than to the employer. Nonunion contractors are more likely to have a permanent relationship with their employees. This permanent relationship fosters employment stability and is the primary feature by which the nonunion contractor attracts workers. In order to be able to provide full-time employment, the open shop contractor may require his employees to work in several different crafts or trades. This multiple assignment of jobs often gives the open shop contractor added flexibility and increased productivity over his union counterpart.

CONSTRUCTION FIRM CHARACTERISTICS

As stated previously, the majority of construction firms tend to be small and to operate primarily in their home states. Table A-4 shows the distribution of construction firms in terms of employment from 1947 to 1972; almost 70 percent of all construction firms employed 7 people or less in 1972. This proportion has fallen slightly over the past 25 years. The proportion of firms employing 3 or fewer persons grew during the 1950's and early 1960's, but appears to be on the decline now. The proportion of firms employing between 4 and 7 workers fell through the mid-1960's, but is now increasing. The medium-sized firms (8-99 employees) appear to be increasing in proportion, although the largest firms (250 employees or more) have fallen slightly in terms of employment.

Table A-5 shows the distribution of employment in terms of firm size. More workers are employed by the medium-sized firms than by the small or very large firms. Although, as stated previously, almost 70 percent of all construction firms employed seven people or fewer in 1972, these same firms employed only 18.5 percent of all construction workers.

Since the overwhelming majority of construction firms are small, it is not surprising that most of them are sole proprietorships (78.3 percent in 1970). The structure of the industry, however, appears to be shifting from partnerships and sole proprietorships to corporate firms. Data contained in Table A-6 show that the proportion of corporate firms has grown steadily over the past few years, as the proportion of proprietorships and partnerships has declined.

Although corporations are greatly outnumbered by sole proprietorships and partnerships, they perform a much larger dollar volume of work. Corporations receive over three-fourths of the industry's total receipts, although they comprise only about 16 percent of all firms (see Table A-7). These data indicate that the construction industry is becoming somewhat more concentrated. Although most of the firms are small and are either sole proprietorships or partnerships, the industry is becoming increasingly dominated by a relatively small number of corpor-

TABLE A-4.
The Construction Industry
Comparison of Contract Construction Firms
By Size of Employment, 1947-1971

Year	Number of Businesses Reporting (In Thousands)	Classes of Firms, by Number of Employees (In Percent)							
		1-3	4-7	8-19	20-49	50-99	100-249	250-499	500+
1947	181	51.5	23.8	15.8	6.0	1.8	1.0		0.09
1951	248	53.1	23.6	14.6	5.8	1.8	0.9	0.2	0.08
1953	263	55.6	22.4	13.6	5.5	1.8	0.8	0.2	0.07
1956	295	56.2	20.9	14.6	5.7	1.8	0.7	0.1	0.04
1959	302	57.0	20.3	14.6	5.6	1.7	0.7	0.1	0.04
1962	296	57.9	20.0	14.0	5.6	1.6	0.7	0.1	0.04
1964	313	56.6	20.2	14.6	5.9	1.7	0.7	0.1	0.04
1966	323	54.0	20.8	15.6	6.4	2.0	0.9	0.2	0.06
1968	310	51.7	21.4	16.6	7.0	2.2	1.0	0.2	0.06
1969	308	51.0	21.3	16.8	7.4	2.2	1.0	0.2	0.06
1970	299	51.0	21.0	16.7	7.6	2.3	1.1	0.2	0.07
1971	296	50.4	21.4	17.2	7.5	2.2	1.0	0.2	0.07
1972	312	47.8	22.5	18.1	8.1	2.2	1.0	0.2	0.06

Source: Calculated from data contained in U.S. Census Bureau, "County Business Patterns," annual issues for years listed in the table.

Note: Percents may not add to 100.0 because of rounding.

TABLE A-5.
The Construction Industry
Distribution of Contract Construction Employees
By Size of Firm, 1968-1972

Year	Total Number of Employees	Firm Size by Number of Employees							
		1-3	4-7	8-19	20-49	50-99	100-249	250-499	500+
1968	3,115,958	8.9	11.0	19.6	20.7	14.7	13.8	6.0	5.3
1969	3,189,325	8.6	10.7	19.3	21.6	14.7	13.9	6.0	5.2
1970	3,197,382	8.2	10.1	18.6	21.6	14.5	14.5	6.4	6.1
1971	3,133,884	8.2	10.5	19.3	21.6	14.3	13.6	6.5	6.0
1972	3,398,188	7.8	10.7	19.9	22.7	14.0	13.3	—[a]	—[a]

Source: Calculated from data contained in U.S. Census Bureau's "County Business Patterns," annual issues for years listed.

[a] Figures withheld to avoid disclosure of operations of individual reporting units.

TABLE A-6.
The Construction Industry
Comparison of Type of Firm Ownership in the Contract Construction Industry
1963-1970

Year	Total Number of Firms	Proportion of Corporations %	Proportion of Sole Proprietorships %	Proportion of Partnerships %
1963	848,487	11.4	81.5	7.1
1964	856,765	12.1	81.2	6.7
1965	876,392	12.9	80.4	6.7
1966	858,330	13.1	80.4	6.5
1967	855,982	14.4	79.5	6.1
1968	838,988	15.0	79.1	5.9
1969	900,832	14.2	80.2	5.6
1970	874,549	15.9	78.3	5.8

Source: U.S., Internal Revenue Service, *Statistics of Income, Business Income Tax Returns*, annual issues, 1963-1970.

TABLE A-7.
The Construction Industry
Comparison of Contract Construction Industry Receipts By Type of Firm Ownership, 1966-1970

Year	Total Receipts (In Thousands)	Proportion Going To Corporations %	Proportion Going To Sole Proprietorships %	Proportion Going To Partnerships %
1966	90,058,788	70.0	21.3	8.7
1967	93,300,082	72.9	19.7	7.4
1968	99,072,137	72.9	19.5	7.6
1969	112,795,547	74.4	19.0	6.6
1970	116,647,196	76.3	17.2	6.5

Source: U.S., Internal Revenue Service, *Statistics of Income, Business Income Tax Returns*, annual issues 1966-1970.

ations. Most of the very large firms operate on a union basis, although two of the largest, Brown & Root, Inc., and Daniel International Corporation, are predominantly open shop.

Rate of Entry

Since most of the firms in construction are fairly small and require little initial capital investment, there has been an historical tendency for a high rate of entry into the industry. The rate of entry is considerably higher than in most other industries. The rate of failure, however, is so great that during the past few years the overall number of firms has changed very little. Data contained in Table A-4 show that the overall number of firms has remained fairly stable from 1968 to 1972 and that there were actually fewer firms in 1972 than in 1964, reflecting, in fact, the adverse economic conditions of the early 1970's.

LABOR FORCE CHARACTERISTICS

As previously noted, the construction industry provides employment for over 5 percent of the total labor force and approximately 15 percent of all skilled blue collar workers. The construction labor force comprises over two dozen crafts and many more specialties. A list of the most predominant crafts includes:

Laborers
Bricklayers
Equipment operators
Electricians
Roofers
Sheet metal workers
Carpenters
Cement finishers
Iron workers
Plumbers
Boilermakers
Lathers
Painters
Operating engineers
Truck drivers

The number of crafts employed on a given project will be dictated by the nature of the project and by whether the contractor operates union or open shop. The pattern of craft use can vary from area to area and from sector to sector. General building contractors usually hire the basic trades (laborers, cement finishers, and carpenters); the subcontractors hire various specialty journeymen. The widest use of the trades is by nonresidential building contractors. Heavy and highway contractors generally use only carpenters, cement finishers, laborers, truck drivers, and operating engineers. Because of varying labor requirements, each trade has a different employment opportunity in each sector of the industry.

Economic instability and the lack of job security in the construction industry has led to a significant role of the union in labor market practices. Three of the most important of these activities involve the recruitment of workers, manpower training and development, and wage determination, all discussed in Part Three, but expanded in several details here.

The Hiring Hall

The union hiring hall is often instrumental in the employment process of the industry.

> A union hiring hall is a union-administered job-referral system whose referrals enjoy advantages over all other job applicants. . . . What is essential to all hiring halls as defined here is employer agreement or acquiescence in according job preference; it is both historically inaccurate and analytically useless to call union referral services "hiring halls" where there is no job preference.[12]

Prior to the passage of the Taft-Hartley Act in 1947, there were few cases where employers were required to utilize union facilities when seeking new workers. Control over hiring was exerted, not through the use of a hiring hall, but through the use of the closed shop, which was enforced by union stewards and business agents at the job site.

After the enactment of the Taft-Hartley Act, which outlawed the closed shop, the unions began adopting formal hiring hall arrangements. In some instances, these arrangements were, in effect, closed shops. In other instances, these were an elaborate set of rules establishing preferences in union referrals, based on the employee's years of experience, previous employment, and other demonstrated qualifications. There are presently few data to show how these arrangements work in actual practice. As Philip Ross concludes,

> It is difficult to classify these exclusive hiring halls because the imposition of formal procedures upon a wide variety of local practices has produced situations where the formal hiring procedure exists next to a shadow system of job allocation which may or may not correspond to the written rules. . . . On the surface, all hiring halls conform to the legal requirement forbidding discrimination

[12] Philip Ross, "Origin of the Hiring Hall in Construction," *Industrial Relations*, XI (October, 1972), p. 366.

> against nonmembers, however, any conflict between hiring hall rules and the attainment of union goals is inevitably resolved in favor of the latter.[13]

The Department of Labor recently undertook a survey of the formal hiring procedures specified in 291 contracts covering 1,000 workers or more. Of these 291 contracts, 45 percent provided for "exclusive" work referrals, requiring the employer to use the union hiring hall as his only source of workers; 33 percent allowed the employer to hire workers from other sources; and the remaining had no referral provision at all. Exclusive referral agreements were found to be most common among electricians, operating engineers, and plumbers, and least common among bricklayers, carpenters, ironworkers, painters, and teamsters.[14]

Even exclusive hiring hall arrangements frequently allow the employer a certain degree of discretion in hiring workers. He is sometimes free to rehire workers whom he has hired in the past to specify a need for a worker with special qualifications, and to reject unsuitable applicants. The open shop contractor, on the other hand, hires his employees in the open market, although open shop contractors in a few localities are beginning to develop their own forms of employment exchanges.

Apprenticeship Training[15]

Most formal training in the construction industry is accomplished through apprenticeship programs. Apprenticeship usually combines on-the-job training with classroom instruction. Most apprenticeship programs in the building trades conform to standards set by the U.S. Bureau of Apprenticeship and Training, in which the construction unions have a strong voice. These standards include the teaching of a series of manipulative skills according to a set schedule, in-school related instruction designed to supplement training on the job with some theoretical foundations of the trade, a progressively increasing wage schedule, supervision by qualified journeymen, periodic evaluation of the

[13] *Ibid.*, pp. 378, 379.

[14] U.S. Department of Labor, Labor-Management Services Administration, *Exclusive Union Work Referral Systems in the Building Trades* (Washington, D.C.: U.S. Government Printing Office, 1970), p. 25.

[15] Some of the discussion in this section is based on Howard G. Foster, "Apprenticeship Training in the Building Trades: A Sympathetic Assessment," *Labor Law Journal*, XXII (January, 1971), pp. 3-12.

apprentice's performance and a union-management committee to ensure that each apprentice receives the proper training.

Apprenticeship training programs involving unions are funded by a small assessment from each employer for every man-hour of labor employed, whether or not the employer uses apprentices. To be admitted to a training program, an applicant must meet certain requirements. Besides minimal age and educational requirements, the applicant must pass a job aptitude test. The applicants are then ranked and placed on a list. After the program is filled, those left over remain on the list as alternates to be called in the event that someone declines to accept placement in the program. Rarely do the number of openings exceed the number of qualified applicants, a condition often resulting in a long waiting list of people unable to gain entrance into any apprenticeship training program.

Apprenticeship programs have drawn substantial criticism in recent years. Many people feel that entrance requirements are highly discriminatory. Minorities are often unable to meet certain educational admission requirements. Some trades, such as electricians, require that applicants be able to pass certain mathematics requirements which the poorly educated cannot fulfill. Many contractors complain that the standards set by the Bureau of Apprenticeship and Training (BAT) are unrealistic, with the apprenticeship taking three to five years to complete. These contractors feel that this is a much longer period than is necessary. The apprentice may be required to learn a number of skills which he will never use as a journeyman. The rigid standards set down by the BAT have stifled attempts by some open shop contractors to institute innovative training programs which would address much of the current criticism aimed at the present programs. As noted in Chapter X, nonunion contractor associations have experienced great difficulty in securing Bureau of Apprenticeship and Training approval for their training programs, although the number of approvals has been increasing in the past years. Unfortunately, to gain approval, these open shop programs must adhere to the patterns long established in the union sector. Experimentation is thus discouraged, as we have noted in Chapter X.

Wage Negotiations

Wage rates in construction are substantially higher than those in other industries. Until recently, moreover, the wage differential between construction and the rest of the labor force had been steadily widening. The explosive settlements negotiated by the building trades in the late 1960's and early 1970's tended somewhat to obscure the fact that wages in the industry had been rising faster than those elsewhere for many years.[16] Table A-8 traces the patterns in various industries throughout the post-World War II period. Although the wages in Table A-8 include both the union and nonunion sectors, there is little doubt that negotiated settlements, rather than purely market forces, were instrumental in producing the wage structure illustrated therein. Table A-9 shows the differences in recent years among the three main segments of construction.

An additional effect of collective bargaining in construction, as in many other industries, has been to alter the structure of compensation in the direction of greater emphasis on supplementary benefits. In the fourth quarter of 1974, for example, employer contributions to benefit trust funds amounted to 14.8 percent of total compensation.[17] As we saw in Chapter XI, unionized contractors appear to devote a greater proportion of compensation to supplementary benefits than do open shops.

Most observers agree that much of the success of the building trades over the years in raising their wage rates disproportionately lies largely in an imbalance of bargaining power in the industry. The balkanization of the collective bargaining structure among myriad crafts and localities, along with the small size and heterogeneity on the employers' side, makes for great difficulty in their resisting the unions' demands. Indeed, it is likely that a major factor in the relative restraint exhibited by the building trades in recent years is that the constraints of the market have been pushed beyond their limit, a limit in no small measure attributable to the growing role of the open shop contractor in the industry.

---

[16] For a discussion of these differentials, see Howard G. Foster, "Wages in Construction: Examining the Evidence," *Industrial Relations*, XI (October, 1972), pp. 336-349.

[17] U.S. Department of Labor, News Release No. 75-124, March 6, 1975, p. 1. This percentage was only 11.5 in 1970 and 7.1 in 1965.

TABLE A-8
Weekly Earnings of Production Workers in the United States, by Industry Group, 1947-1974

Year	All Private		Contract Construction		Mining		Manufacturing	
	Earnings	Percent Change	Earnings	Percent Change	Earnings	Percent Change	Earnings	Percent Change
1947	45.58		58.87		59.94		49.17	
1950	53.13	16.6	69.68	18.4	67.16	12.0	58.32	18.6
1955	67.72	27.5	90.90	30.5	89.54	33.3	75.70	29.8
1960	80.67	19.1	113.04	24.4	105.44	17.8	89.72	18.5
1965	95.06	17.8	138.38	22.4	123.52	17.1	107.53	19.9
1970	119.46	25.7	195.45	41.2	164.40	33.1	133.73	24.4
1974	154.45	29.3	249.44	27.6	220.48	34.1	176.00	31.6
1947-1974		238.9		323.7		267.8		257.9

Year	Transportation and Utilities		Trade		Finance, Insurance and Real Estate		Services	
	Earnings	Percent Change	Earnings	Percent Change	Earnings	Percent Change	Earnings	Percent Change
1947			38.07		43.21			
1950			44.55	17.0	50.52	16.9		
1955			55.16	23.8	63.92	26.5		
1960			66.01	19.7	75.14	17.6		
1965	125.14		76.53	15.9	88.91	18.3	73.60	
1970	155.93	24.6	95.66	25.0	113.34	27.5	96.66	31.3
1974	218.16	39.9	118.67	24.1	140.21	23.7	127.16	31.6
1947-1974				211.7		224.5		

Source: *Monthly Labor Review*, XCVIII, No. 5 (May, 1975), Table 14.

TABLE A-9.
The Construction Industry
Average Weekly and Hourly Earnings in the Contractor Construction Industry
By Type of Contractor
1967-1973

Period	All Contract Construction	General Building Contractors	All Heavy Construction	All Special Trade Contractors
	Average Weekly Earnings			
1967	154.95	145.64	154.13	161.25
1968	164.93	153.79	167.68	170.09
1969	181.54	169.82	185.64	187.59
1970	195.98	184.40	196.39	202.94
1971	212.24	197.64	209.92	221.68
1972	224.22	209.07	217.88	235.95
1973	240.68	222.84	229.54	255.83
	Average Hourly Earnings			
1967	4.11	3.99	3.75	4.37
1968	4.41	4.26	4.07	4.66
1969	4.79	4.64	4.42	5.07
1970	5.24	5.08	4.79	5.56
1971	5.69	5.49	5.12	6.09
1972	6.06	5.84	5.42	6.50
1973	6.47	6.19	5.71	6.99

Source: *Construction Review*, February/March 1974, pp. 58, 59.
Note: Adjusted to March 1971 benchmarks.

Appendix B

UNIVERSITY of PENNSYLVANIA
PHILADELPHIA 19174

The Wharton School

INDUSTRIAL RESEARCH UNIT
VANCE HALL — THIRD FLOOR
3733 SPRUCE STREET
HERBERT R. NORTHRUP, *Director*

OPEN SHOP CONSTRUCTION QUESTIONNAIRE

This questionnaire, prepared by the Industrial Research Unit of the University of Pennsylvania, concerns open shop construction. It is being sent to several thousand firms representing a cross-section of the construction industry. Whether you operate union or open shop, whether you are in favor of or opposed to unions or to open shop construction, your response is essential to the accuracy of this survey. The Associated General Contractors and the Associated Builders and Contractors are cooperating in this study.

The questionnaire is in three parts. The first asks questions about your company, the second asks about the area in which you operate, and the third about your labor market activities. We are interested in your views whether you work open or closed shop.

It should not take you more than thirty minutes to complete the survey. When completed, please staple it so the return address is on the outside, and mail. Postage is prepaid.

If you would like a statistical compilation of the finished survey, check here ____ and we shall send you one. These statistics will become part of a major study of all aspects of open shop construction. If you prefer to remain anonymous, you can still get a copy of the survey results by sending a separate letter.

We shall greatly appreciate it if you return your completed questionnaire within two weeks or as soon as possible.

Thank you.

Herbert R. Northrup

SECTION ONE
YOUR FIRM

1. What is the name and address of your firm?

____

____

____

____

(Omit this question if anonymity is desired)

SECTION ONE -- YOUR FIRM

2. Are you primarily a general contractor _____ or a subcontractor _____?

3. If you are a subcontractor, what kind of work do you specialize in? (e.g., flooring, electrical, concrete, etc.) ____________________.

4. What was the approximate volume of your business in 1973 (or last fiscal year)? $____________________.

5. Approximately what proportion of your work last year was in each of the following industry divisions?

Residential (single family and low rise)	______%
Residential (high rise)	______%
Commercial (stores, offices, etc.)	______%
Industrial (factories, power plants, etc.)	______%
Highway (streets, roads, interstates, etc.)	______%
Heavy (bridges, dams, sewers, etc.)	______%
Other (please specify)____________________	______%
TOTAL	100 %

6. Which of the following trades do you normally have on your payroll <u>excluding</u> subcontractors? (Please check all appropriate spaces.)

____bricklayer	____electrician	____plumber
____carpenter	____ironworker (structural)	____painter
____cement mason	____ironworker (rod)	____sheet metal worker
____equipment operator	____laborer	____steamfitter

7. Approximately what has been the average seasonal <u>high</u> number of <u>non-supervisory</u> workers on your payroll over the past three years? ____________ The seasonal low? ____________

8. Is the firm signatory to any union agreements, either individually or through a contractors association? ____ Yes ____ No

9. If "yes," which union(s)? ____________________ ____________________

10. Do you operate on a double-breasted basis? ____ Yes ____ No

11. If you are a <u>general contractor</u>, please list below the four trades you subcontract most frequently and indicate by a check (✓) how often you use <u>nonunion</u> subs.

	Always	Often	Occasionally	Never
a.____________				
b.____________				
c.____________				
d.____________				

12. If the answers to all of the above were "never," are there any trades for which you use nonunion subs at least occasionally? What are they?

_______________ _______________

13. If you are a <u>subcontractor</u>, please check below how frequently you do work for unionized and open shop general contractors, respectively:

	Always	Often	Occasionally	Never
For union contractors				
For open shop				

SECTION TWO -- YOUR AREA

1. The table below refers to the amount of construction performed on an <u>open shop</u> basis in your geographic area. Please try to estimate wherever you can the percentage of open shop work in each type of construction indicated. Please insert a check (√) where appropriate:

	Percent Open Shop					
<u>Type of Construction</u>	0-20	21-40	41-60	61-80	81-100	Don't Know
Residential (single and low rise)						
Residential (high rise)						
Commercial (offices, etc)						
Industrial (factories, power plants, etc.)						
Highway (streets, etc.)						
Heavy (bridges, etc.)						
All construction (average)						

2. Are any of the percentages you indicated in the previous question different from what you would have said a few years ago? ___ Yes ___ No

3. If "yes," would you please indicate by an (X) in the above table the percentages that would have been appropriate then. (Example: if single-family residential is 81-100% open shop now and was 61-80% open shop a few years ago, please put a check (√) in the 81-100 column and an (X) in the 61-80 column.)

4. Regardless of the general level of open shop construction, are there any specialty areas (e.g., masonry, electrical, heating, etc.) which are significantly more tightly unionized than others? ___ Yes ___ No

5. If "yes," which ones? _______________ _______________

6. Have you ever directly experienced violence to person or property in connection with a labor dispute? ___ Yes ___ No

SECTION THREE -- LABOR MARKET ACTIVITIES

1. In the table below, please place checks (✓) to show how often you use each of the indicated methods in seeking to hire new workers:

Method	Frequency Used			
	Always	Often	Occasionally	Never
Ask current employees to recommend someone				
Ask other employers to recommend someone				
Contact workers you have employed in the past				
Use union hiring hall				
Run a newspaper ad				
Contact workers who have approached you for a job in the past				
Use the state employment service				
Contact local vocational schools				
Hire "off the street"				

2. If you are an open shop employer, about what proportion of your workers were once (or are currently) union members? ________%

3. In the table below, please place checks (✓) to show how often the workers you hire come to you with prior training from each of the sources indicated:

Source of Training	Frequency			
	Always	Often	Occasionally	Never
Vocational school				
Military (Corps of Engineers, CB's, etc.)				
Union apprenticeship				
Open shop apprenticeship				
Apprenticeships in other industries (farming, manufacturing, etc.)				
On the job with prior employer				
Other: ________				

4. Do you participate in any local training programs administered by an employer's association <u>or</u> by a union-management apprenticeship committee? ___ Yes ___ No

5. If "yes," how many of your employees are enrolled? ________

6. Do you provide any of your workers with <u>off the job</u> training or instruction on your own? ____ Yes ____ No

7. If "yes," please indicate the following:
   a. Number of employees receiving such training now ______________
   b. Number who have already received such training ______________
   c. Is instruction given by your own people ______________
      or through a vocational school ______________?
   d. How long does training usually last (in weeks)? ______________
   e. How long are the classes (hours per week)? ______________

8. Please use this space to describe any training efforts you have undertaken which are not suggested in questions 4 through 7.

____

____

____

9. Do you typically put on supplementary summer help (college students, etc.) ____ Yes ____ No

10. If "yes," about how many did you employ in summer of 1973? ______________

11. Have you had to lay off any workers in the past three years because of <u>seasonal</u> slowdowns? ____ Yes ____ No

12. If "yes," about how many were laid off in winter 1973-74? ______________

13. Do you participate in any local programs to upgrade the employment opportunities of minority workers? ____ Yes ____ No

14. If "yes," who runs this program? ______________

15. About what proportion of your current workforce is black? __________% Spanish speaking? __________% Indian? __________%

16. In your estimation, is the level of minority employment in open shop construction greater than ________, less than ________, or about the same as ________ that in union construction? (Please check.)

17. In the table below, please indicate the range of wage rates your workers receive: ($ per hour)

	Wage Rates		
Trade	Low	High	Foreman
Bricklayer			
Carpenter			
Equipment Operator			
Electrician			
Laborer			
Painter			
Plumber			
Sheet Metal Worker			
Steamfitter			

18. If you are an open shop employer, please estimate the percentage of your workers whose hourly wage is as high as or higher than the union scale. ________________%

19. In the table below, please show by a check (✓) the approximate number of your workers who receive each of the fringe benefits indicated:

Benefit	Number of Workers Receiving			
	All	Most	Few	None
Health insurance				
Life insurance				
Paid vacation				
Paid holidays				
Paid sick leave				
Bonus or profit-sharing				
Other:________________				

20. If you are an open shop employer, do you participate in any funded benefit plans such as those administered by an employers' association? ____ Yes ____ No

21. If "yes," who administers the fund? ________________________

FIRST CLASS
PERMIT No. 898
Philadelphia, Pa.

BUSINESS REPLY MAIL
No postage stamp necessary if mailed in the United States

Postage will be paid by

UNIVERSITY of PENNSYLVANIA
THE WHARTON SCHOOL
INDUSTRIAL RESEARCH UNIT
VANCE HALL CS
PHILADELPHIA, PA. 19174

Appendix C

NONUNION CONSTRUCTION STUDY

INTERVIEW SCHEDULE

These questions are designed for direct face-to-face administration to nonunion contractors and (particularly) spokesmen for nonunion contractors associations. They are purposely broad and open-ended to allow for maximum probing.

A. *Extent and Pattern of Nonunion Construction Activity*

1. What proportion of the work in your area is performed by nonunion contractors?
2. To what extent does the amount of nonunion work vary by industrial sector (industrial, commercial, heavy, and highway, residential, etc.)?
3. To what extent does it vary by size of contractor?
4. To what extent does it vary by functional specialty?
5. Has there ever been a history of more extensive union penetration in those fields which presently have a large nonunion component?
6. If so, what caused the unions to lose strength in those fields?
7. To what extent are nonunion contractors in your area represented by employer associations? (Get details on which *kinds* of contractors are represented by which associations.)
8. What labor relations functions, if any, do these associations perform? (e.g., gathering and disseminating wage information, sponsoring training, acting as intermediary in job-man matching, etc.)
9. To what extent do contractors operate on *both* a union and nonunion basis? In which fields?

10. To what extent do nonunion contractors operate with unionized subcontractors? In which fields are the subcontractors most likely to be unionized?

11. To what extent have union contractors gone nonunion in recent years? In any particular fields?

12. To what extent do nonunion workers migrate to the union sector? To what extent do union workers migrate to the nonunion sector. What are the reasons, if any, for these movements? Are they more prevalent for some trades than others?

B. *Labor Market Practices (Other than training)*

1. To what extent do each of the following provide a source of trained or partially trained workers for nonunion contractors:

   a) Vocational Schools

   b) Military

   c) Union construction

   d) Other industries (farming, manufacturing, etc.)

   e) Other (probe)

2. How might these sources vary with different trades?

3. What procedures or agencies are used by nonunion contractors to find the workers they need? Do they vary by trade? By size of contractor?

4. To what extent are craftsmen used to perform functions outside their primary craft (e.g., a carpenter laying brick)?

5. In your experience, what trades are most closely related so that an individual worker is likely to be able to perform in more than one?

6. About what proportion of nonunion craftsmen start out as laborers or helpers on construction jobs and work their way up? Is this process more prevalent in some trades than others?

7. During the summer months, about what proportion of nonunion workers are part-time (e.g., students)? Does this vary by trade?

8. How extensive is the practice of using students on a part-time basis while school is in session? Does this vary by trade?

9. If a contractor is unable to find the workers he needs, what adjustments is he most likely to make?

10. What is the normal seasonal ratio of employment from peak to trough? How does this vary by functional area?

11. For how many weeks might a regular employee of a nonunion contractor expect to be laid off during the slow season in a "normal" year? How does this vary by functional area?

12. Does the process of allocating and dividing work among employees (especially skilled vs. unskilled) differ during slow and busy periods? If so, how so? Does the practice vary by trade?

13. About what proportion of the nonunion work force would you characterize as "highly skilled"? To what extent does this proportion change with the tightness of the labor market? Could you try to describe the mechanics of this change, if any.

C. *Training and Upgrading*

1. Are there any industry-wide training programs, sponsored either locally or by a national organization, in your area?

2. If so, please describe the program. (Probe—information on nature of program, trades covered, administration, admission criteria, number of trainees, funding, post-training experience, etc.)

3. Do any individual contractors have their own programs? If so, describe.

4. Are there any formal arrangements between contractors (singly or as a group) and local vocational schools or institutes? If so, describe.

5. Apart from formal programs, what *specific* practices do contractors have to generate skilled workers? (If response is "OJT", try to learn what OJT entails—i.e., does

it include anything *outside* the normal production process?) Do these practices differ by type of contractor?

6. In your experience, are workers with formal training likely to reach a given skill level slower, faster, or in about the same time as one trained on the job? If there is a difference (either way), to what do you attribute this difference?

7. Do the training backgrounds of key people (e.g., foremen, supervisors, or contractors) tend to differ from those of rank and file craftsmen? Do these differences vary by trade?

8. Does the rate of which workers are upgraded internally vary with the pace of work at the time? Is the experience different for different trades?

9. Do you have (or know of) a *formal* upgrading mechanism? In other words, does a worker who moves up receive any explicit recognition that his status has changed?

10. Are the training practices of the large contractors different from the smaller ones?

D. *Minorities*

1. About what proportion of the nonunion construction work force in your area is black? Hispanic? Other minority?

2. Would this proportion vary by trade? If so, how?

3. In your estimation, is the level of minority participation greater than, less than, or about the same as that in the unionized sector?

4. If there is a difference, to what is it attributable?

5. Is there, in your area, any local program designed to increase minority participation in construction generally or nonunion construction in particular?

6. If so, do you have an opinion on how the program has worked? If it has worked well, why and by what standard? If not, why not?

7. Do you feel that minority participation in your industry should be increased? If not, why not? If so, what in your judgment are the factors—and their relative importance—which have kept minority participation low up to now?
8. To your knowledge, are there any (or many) minority *contractors* in your area? If so, do they tend to be concentrated in any particular trades?
9. Do minority contractors face any special problems not typically experienced by white contractors?
10. Do you feel there should be any action taken by government or the industry to encourage minorities to become contractors? If not, why not? If so, what form might this action take?

E. *Employee Compensation*

1. Could you estimate the *range* of wage rates paid in your area to each of the following trades:

   a. carpenter
   b. bricklayer
   c. electrician
   d. equipment operator
   e. cement finisher
   f. plumber/pipefitter
   g. sheet metal worker
   h. roofer
   i. ironworker (rod)
   j. ironworker (structural)
   k. painter
   l. plasterer
   m. tile setter
   n. laborer

2. Are there any multi-employer benefit plans in your area? In which trades or among which kinds of contractors?
3. Could you estimate the prevalence and level of each of the following benefits in nonunion construction in your area:

   a. health insurance
   b. life insurance
   c. pension
   d. paid vacation
   e. paid holidays
   f. Christmas bonus
   g. profit-sharing
   h. severance pay
   i. SUB pay
   j. sick leave
   k. other (specify)

4. Do these benefits vary by trade or type of contractor?
5. Is overtime paid, and at what level, for:
   a) over 8 hrs/day?
   b) weekends?
   c) over 40 hrs/wk?
6. How prevalent is the "helper" classification with a pay scale between that of journeyman and laborer? Does it differ by trade?
7. About what proportion of the work performed by nonunion contractors is subject to Davis-Bacon type regulations?
8. What is the impact of Davis-Bacon type regulations on the pay scales *and* pay structure of the industry?
9. About what proportion of hourly-paid nonunion workers earn at or above the union rate in their respective trades? Would this proportion vary by trade?
10. To the extent that nonunion wages are, on average, lower than those in the union sector, what in your judgment allows this differential to be maintained?

DAVIS-BACON QUESTIONS

1. Have you ever bid on a job where prevailing wages (according to the Davis-Bacon) applied?
2. If so, were you successful? If not was the DB requirement significant?
3. Were wage rates representative of the area rates?
4. How much could your bid have been reduced if the DB wages didn't have to be paid?
5. Have you any comments on how the DB Act effects:
   1) the cost structure of your bid,
   2) work force morale
   3) other?

6. 1) Unions, when they are a part of a "hometown plan", have the affirmative action requirement of the DB Act fulfilled. How do open shop firms comply with these requirements?
   2) Have DB requirements caused minority hiring problems?
   3) Have you had difficulty in reporting your compliance with DB requirements?

SUBCONTRACTING QUESTIONS

1. Do open shop employers in your area ever pay their employees by some form of piece work? If so, what type of employer is most likely to do so? How common is the practice?
2. Are there many subcontractors who do most or all of their work with a single contractor? If so, what type of subcontractor is most likely to do so?
3. Do contractors ever set up their own employees to be subcontractors? If so, what kinds of subcontractors are most likely to be so established? Why do contractors do this?
4. Does the general contractor typically supply materials for any of his subs? If so, which ones?
5. What kinds of work is the general contractor most likely to do with his own employees, and what kinds is he most likely to contract out?
6. *Note to interviewer*: If answers to previous questions seem to reflect a certain pattern of relationships with one group of subs (e.g., those doing basic structural work) and a different pattern with another group (e.g., those doing electromechanical or finishing work), try to find out *why* these patterns exist.

Index

Racial Policies of American Industry Series

1. *The Negro in the Automobile Industry,* by Herbert R. Northrup. 1968. $2.50
2. *The Negro in the Aerospace Industry,* by Herbert R. Northrup. 1968. $2.50
3. *The Negro in the Steel Industry,* by Richard L. Rowan. 1968. $3.50
4. *The Negro in the Hotel Industry,* by Edward C. Koziara and Karen S. Koziara. 1968. $2.50
5. *The Negro in the Petroleum Industry,* by Carl B. King and Howard W. Risher, Jr. 1969. $3.50
6. *The Negro in the Rubber Tire Industry,* by Herbert R. Northrup and Alan B. Batchelder. 1969. $3.50
7. *The Negro in the Chemical Industry,* by William Howard Quay, Jr. 1969. $3.50
8. *The Negro in the Paper Industry,* by Herbert R. Northrup. 1969. $8.50
9. *The Negro in the Banking Industry,* by Armand J. Thieblot, Jr. 1970. $5.95
10. *The Negro in the Public Utility Industries,* by Bernard E. Anderson. 1970. $5.95
11. *The Negro in the Insurance Industry,* by Linda P. Fletcher. 1970. $5.95
12. *The Negro in the Meat Industry,* by Walter A. Fogel. 1970. $4.50
13. *The Negro in the Tobacco Industry,* by Herbert R. Northrup. 1970. $4.50
14. *The Negro in the Bituminous Coal Mining Industry,* by Darold T. Barnum. 1970. $4.50
15. *The Negro in the Trucking Industry,* by Richard D. Leone. 1970. $4.50
16. *The Negro in the Railroad Industry,* by Howard W. Risher, Jr. 1971. $5.95
17. *The Negro in the Shipbuilding Industry,* by Lester Rubin. 1970. $5.95
18. *The Negro in the Urban Transit Industry,* by Philip W. Jeffress. 1970. $4.50
19. *The Negro in the Lumber Industry,* by John C. Howard. 1970. $4.50
20. *The Negro in the Textile Industry,* by Richard L. Rowan. 1970. $5.95
21. *The Negro in the Drug Manufacturing Industry,* by F. Marion Fletcher. 1970. $5.95
22. *The Negro in the Department Store Industry,* by Charles R. Perry. 1971. $5.95
23. *The Negro in the Air Transport Industry,* by Herbert R. Northrup *et al.* 1971. $5.95
24. *The Negro in the Drugstore Industry,* by F. Marion Fletcher. 1971. $5.95
25. *The Negro in the Supermarket Industry,* by Gordon F. Bloom and F. Marion Fletcher. 1972. $5.95
26. *The Negro in the Farm Equipment and Construction Machinery Industry,* by Robert Ozanne. 1972. $5.95
27. *The Negro in the Electrical Manufacturing Industry,* by Theodore V. Purcell and Daniel P. Mulvey. 1971. $5.95
28. *The Negro in the Furniture Industry,* by William E. Fulmer. 1973. $5.95
29. *The Negro in the Longshore Industry,* by Lester Rubin and William S. Swift. 1974. $5.95
30. *The Negro in the Offshore Maritime Industry,* by William S. Swift. 1974. $5.95
31. *The Negro in the Apparel Industry,* by Elaine Gale Wrong. 1974. $5.95